International Migration and Human Rights

International Migration and Human Rights

The Global Repercussions of U.S. Policy

EDITED BY SAMUEL MARTÍNEZ

Global, Area, and International Archive
University of California Press

BERKELEY   LOS ANGELES   LONDON

The Global, Area, and International Archive (GAIA) is an initiative of International and Area Studies, University of California, Berkeley, in partnership with the University of California Press, the California Digital Library, and international research programs across the UC system. GAIA volumes, which are published in both print and open-access digital editions, represent the best traditions of regional studies, reconfigured through fresh global, transnational, and thematic perspectives.

University of California Press, one of the most distinguished university presses in the United States, enriches lives around the world by advancing scholarship in the humanities, social sciences, and natural sciences. Its activities are supported by the UC Press Foundation and by philanthropic contributions from individuals and institutions. For more information, visit www.ucpress.edu.

University of California Press
Berkeley and Los Angeles, California

University of California Press, Ltd.
London, England

Library of Congress Cataloging-in-Publication Data

    International migration and human rights : the global repercussions of U.S. policy / edited by Samuel Martínez.
      p.   cm. (Global, area, and international archive)
    Includes bibliographical references and index.
    ISBN: 978-0-520-25821-1 (pbk. : alk. paper)
    1. Emigration and immigration—Government policy.
2. Immigrants—Civil rights.   3. United States—Emigration and immigration—Government policy.   4. Immigrants—Civil rights—United States.   5. United States—Foreign relations—1989– .   I. Martínez, Samuel, 1959– .

JV6038.I616   2009
325.73—dc22   2009023255

© Manufactured in the United States of America

18 17 16 15 14 13 12 11 10 09
10 9 8 7 6 5 4 3 2 1

The paper used in this publication meets the minimum requirements of ANSI/NISO z39.48–1992 (R 1997) *(Permanence of Paper).*

*In memory of Richard Rust, Nelson Enríquez,
Daniel Zarrow, Joseph Danticat, and the
uncounted thousands more who have fallen
victim to immigration restrictionism*

Contents

Acknowledgments

This book grows out of a project, sponsored by the Committee for Human Rights of the American Anthropological Association (AAA), to track the effects that the U.S. government's response to the events of September 11, 2001, was having on immigrant communities in the United States as well as on would-be, bona fide U.S. visa applicants and asylum seekers in other countries. At the time of the project's inception it seemed natural to activate the anthropological community's vast accumulated expertise, contacts, and geographical breadth of knowledge on international migration matters in the service of immigrant communities at risk. A first effort to formulate an anthropological response to this particular aspect of the post-9/11 situation took the shape of a double panel at the 2003 American Anthropological Association Annual Meeting. The dialogue between anthropologists and practicing migrant-rights advocates was one highlight of that session, pointing toward the need for a multifaceted approach. Equally striking was the call from more than one panelist to consider post-9/11 policies not in isolation but in a much broader policy context, going far beyond U.S. borders and immigration policy per se. Based on field research in countries near to and far from the United States, these panelists described pressures to emigrate and seek refuge eventuating from the effects of U.S.-backed policies on free-market reform, regional economic integration, official U.S. government human rights and antitrafficking initiatives, and the U.S. government's overwhelming recourse to military might (at the expense of diplomatic, legal, and other channels of "soft power") in response to the security challenges emanating from Islamism and the illicit drug trade. The unexpected message from the anthropologists at that panel, then, was to pay close attention to the personal and local microcosms of international migration, but then to theorize local migrant rights crises in terms of large-scale forces and trends. At this scale, the United States remains the preeminent influence on the global policy environment. Thus, even those panelists at the 2003 meeting who could not in the end contribute a paper to this book (Linda Green, Mary Meg McCarthy, Ev Meade, Alison Werner, and our panel's discussant, Josh DeWind) made a lasting contribution to molding this volume's distinctive approach.

The book also evolved as immigration reform emerged from the shadows of 9/11 to become once more a major topic of national debate, though this time talk about immigration was tangled up as never before with concerns about national security. That return of public discourse to consideration of immigration's economic and cultural impacts has made this book's message if anything more timely. The present impasse between immigration liberals and restrictionists points to the simultaneous need for a broader frame and sharper terms. The essays in this volume urge us to think beyond U.S. borders and beyond the bounds of immigration policy, narrowly construed, in order to encompass the effects (intended and unintended) of many kinds of U.S. policies on the conditions under which migrants leave their homes and cross international borders. Linking immigration trends to larger developments in the U.S. and global economies is perhaps the dimension that has been most sorely lacking in the immigration debate. This book is intended to be a modest step toward articulating a politically progressive position in the current U.S. immigration debate, distinct from (but not dismissive of) the restrictionist and liberal positions that dominate the current discourse.

A book of this scale and diversity can be achieved only through the help of many people. This project would never have gotten off the ground without the support and encouragement of fellow members of the AAA's Committee for Human Rights. The contributors (especially those who have been involved in the book since its inception) have shown patience, tact, and indeed true mercy to me through repeated lengthy delays and rounds of revision. The Committee's graduate fellow Lorraine Chaudhry-Campbell provided valuable bibliographic assistance early in the process. Editorial assistance on selected chapters by Elizabeth A. Badger and Jennifer E. Telesca is gratefully acknowledged. Heartfelt thanks go to those next of kin who kindly gave me permission to dedicate this volume to the memory of Richard Rust, Nelson Enríquez, Daniel Zarrow, and Joseph Danticat. Thanks are due also to Daniel Zwerdling and Jim Hanks for facilitating contact with family members. Early discussions with Jim Lance, of Kumarian Press, were instrumental in defining the book's particular niche within migration studies and international political economy. No one could ask for a better editor than Nathan MacBrien, editor of the University of California's Global, Area, and International Archive. On this project, I, as much as anyone else on any other book, needed someone like Nathan on my side: smart, patient, persistent, a good listener, who knows when and how to provide guidance. Lastly but certainly not least, the contributors and I are deeply grateful to the anonymous reviewers of the manuscript. While any remaining errors of omission or fact are our responsibility alone, their generous praise and tough comments brought many improvements to the book. I am sure I speak not just for myself among the book's contributors, finally, in noting that forbearance and moral support have been gratefully received from our nearest and dearest (in my case, Monica, Saskia, and Nico): may your lights keep on shining bright!

Introduction

Samuel Martínez

Of the important human-generated processes that now link people across the planet, international migration is perhaps the most dramatically visible in its scale and its political and cultural effects. According to Migrants Rights International, "one out of every 35 persons worldwide is an international migrant. According to UN estimates, some 175 million people are now living permanently or temporarily outside their country of origin. This vast number includes migrant workers and their families, refugees, and permanent immigrants."[1] It has been something of an upstream battle for international migration to reach these levels; in response to political controversies generated by large-scale immigration, country after country has made increasingly muscular efforts to contain immigration. The liberal democracies of Western Europe and North America promoted labor migration in the immediate aftermath of the Second World War but their leaders grew anxious about immigration as rates of economic growth slowed after the first major recession of the postwar period, 1973–74. At that time, many were surprised to find for the first time that immigrants did not go home as the jobs they had come for disappeared (Cornelius, Martin, and Hollifield 1994: 4). In all of the industrialized democracies, governments have since attempted to restrict immigration—typically by tightening border policing and heightening bureaucratic obstacles to immigration and asylum—but these efforts have largely failed: contrary to the goals of national immigration policy, *more* immigrants entered. The growing gap between policy intentions and actual outcomes has only intensified public pressure to adopt even more restrictive policies (ibid.: 3).

As a result, during an era of growing global commitment to free markets and individual liberties, controls on the free movement of labor remain "the most compelling exception to liberalism in the operation of the world economy" (Bhagwati 1984: 680, cited in Andreas 2001: 107). It may, in principle, be contradictory to find the free movement of money, goods, and ideas appealing but the free movement of people appalling; yet it is no accident that public concerns about immigration in the major migrant-receiving countries have reached a peak just as financial and consumer markets across the world have reached unprecedented levels of integration. Based on a careful review of studies conducted in major migration systems worldwide, Douglas Massey (Chapter 1 in this volume) concludes that greater numbers of people are now crossing international borders precisely because market forces now reach billions more people today than in the decades prior to the fall of Soviet-style socialism. The economic and social transformations being wrought by liberalizing markets is the ferment pushing people to cross international borders in search of greater attainments and freedoms. The contradiction between "restrictionism"—politics and policies aimed at reducing officially authorized immigration and bringing unauthorized immigration to a halt—and global economic integration may also be observed, in microcosmic form, at ports of entry, the places where "unwanted" goods and people are to be stopped, and desired commerce and immigrants permitted to enter. In chapter 2, Josiah Heyman finds that interdiction efforts at ports of entry on the U.S.-Mexico border collide frontally with the economic imperative of permitting rapid and massive passage of goods and people across international frontiers. As market forces expand their reach ever further geographically and deeper into the lives of people who previously stood on the margins of the global economy, the "push" side of migration's "push-pull" dynamic seems to have become uncontrollable. According to Massey (Chapter 1), "Governments can do little about the penetration of markets into developing regions of the world, or about the progressive incorporation of peripheral areas into global trade."

Yet even if we accept that states can do little to *slow* either globalization or the migration stimuli that come with it, the world's most powerful states (together with international financial and trade regulating institutions) may still be significantly influencing the political and economic circumstances under which people decide to leave their home places and then cross international borders. While the contributors to the present book accept that restrictionism is futile and even counterproductive, whether seen from the vantage point of business, government, or migrants, they also seek through their essays to go beyond that insight. Recent studies of government policy's effects on migration have been concerned mainly with measuring and explaining immigration's rates, types, avenues and selectivity, as well as evaluating the possibility of controlling these dimensions. [2] The contributors to this book seek, by contrast, to uncover the political and economic circumstances of migrants' departure from home, explore the means by which people cross international borders, and ponder the possibility of an international migration order that is more respectful of human rights. We focus, in a word, not on the incidence so much as the *conditions* of international migration. Even if the leading states can do little to stanch the flow of international migrants, they can and do participate in shaping the conditions under which migration takes place, through economic, trade, security, immigration, and global governance policies that influence whether or not immigrants can exercise real choice, cross borders safely, and win respect for their human rights even as they travel far from home.

An aim broadly shared by the contributors to this book is highlighting the threats to migrants' rights and safety that flow from U.S. policies relating to immigration control, international trade, drug-trafficking suppression, and national security. Recent studies of United States efforts to restrict unauthorized passage across its border with Mexico have concluded that the main direct effect of border policing has not been to stop unauthorized entry but to divert the migrants to more isolated crossing points (Andreas 2001; Reyes, Johnson, and Van Swearingen 2002), making the migrants more dependent on guides to traverse the rugged wilderness through which they must now pass, and driving up the monetary cost of unauthorized entry.[3] These developments have eventuated in sharp increases in migrant mortality, human smuggling, and even debt servitude (when immigrants are obligated to work for migration brokers or others to whom their debts may be sold).[4] The essays in this book suggest that the human rights crisis unfolding on the U.S.-Mexican border is but the tip of an expanding iceberg of infringements of migrants' rights and freedoms worldwide. Beginning with levels of poverty and dearth of economic alternatives so severe as to leave many millions little choice but to emigrate, and continuing with border controls and internal police practices that drive more migrants into smugglers' hands and make the migrants bear all the human costs of immigration restrictions, there are troubling signs that in the global scheme of human mobility those people whose knowledge and skills have no significant market value effectively possess few or no rights (Ong 2006: ch.9).

A second way that this book stands apart from earlier policy analyses is that its contributors reach beyond consideration of immigration policy per se to encompass also the repercussions of the U.S. global leadership in *several* fields. Particular attention is given here also to the effects on migrants of U.S.-led strategic and humanitarian military intervention, human rights promotion, and effective control over the policies of institutions of international finance and trade regulation (e.g., World Bank/International Monetary Fund, World Trade Organization). Much of this book seeks to turn around the terms of the immigration debate, by drawing attention to the effects that U.S. economic, military and diplomatic power, joined with the difficult-to-control forces of the global economy, are having in creating dire political and economic conditions in countries near and far. The "rising wave" of global undocumented migration, human smuggling and trafficking has neither welled up by itself nor emerged out of forces completely beyond the reach of U.S. policy. Rather, millions of people have been put on the move by the seismic shocks set off in country after country by U.S.-supported economic "adjustments," by official American tolerance for other states' use of heavy-handed security measures, and by U.S. deployments of military force, whether directly, as in Iraq, or by proxy, as in Colombia's antinarcotics war. Many of the book's contributors are in agreement that the U.S. dialogue on immigration is out of touch with the considerable amount of actual leverage that the United States can exert, through its leadership in international relations, on the economic and political circumstances under which migrants leave home and their legal status as they cross borders, even in places far from U.S. territory.

In brief, we seek to bring the state back into scholarly theorizing and analysis of international migration. We do so *not* in order to blame the United States for all and sundry wrongs in far-flung nations, but to unveil connections between immigration and a range of political and economic issues and processes, connections which must be brought into consideration in any effort to craft a truly *comprehensive* immigration reform. Such reform hinges on policymakers broadening their vision of what issues are immigration-related, to bring into consideration a range of domestic and international policy arenas not currently gaining mention in the U.S. immigration debate even though these impinge on immigrants' safety, dignity, and freedoms.

A corollary of our efforts to broaden the thematic scope of analysis is a wider geographical reach than in most prior surveys of U.S. immigration policy. Through case studies done among people of several countries, several of this book's authors contribute to the broad aim of documenting the far reach and severity of U.S. policy's repercussions on migrant and asylum rights around the world. In this way, the book adds a neglected international dimension to other, primarily U.S.-focused, studies concerning U.S. violations of migrant rights. The book reaches beyond U.S.

borders, recent events, and legal analysis by following the global effects of U.S. policy, tracing the historical antecedents and development of today's heightened official security concerns surrounding international migration, and describing the human costs felt among migrant communities.

Lastly, this book's contributors also seek to take discussion beyond the level of whole states and national populations at which much of the scholarly debate about immigration policy has been couched, to try to capture the realities of international migration as these are perceived by the individuals involved. Rather than presenting country studies based on census data or other national-level statistics, the contributors to this book focus either on particular histories of policy debate or assess policy outcomes through a fine-grained ethnographic approach. Regardless of whether it concerns migrants and displaced people, detainees, border guards, local law enforcement officials, anti-immigration vigilantes, advocates for migrant rights, or members of host communities, our starting premise is that people's perceptions, priorities, and dilemmas matter. This concern with trying to remain true to migrants' and other actors' perspectives is reflected in the project's origins in an initiative of the Committee for Human Rights of the American Anthropological Association to study the human effects on migrants of post-9/11 security measures. Even as the project grew to include analyses by legal scholars and sociologists, it has remained characteristically anthropological in its conception of migration as a social process, in its attentiveness to individual voices and stories, and in its concern with the far-reaching human consequences of the actions of the powerful.

In the remainder of this introductory chapter, I aim to situate U.S. immigration policy in the dual context of history and the emerging global political economic circumstances that have pushed the United States to admit more immigrants even as the nation has experienced a new upsurge of fear regarding threats from outside its borders.

U.S. IMMIGRATION POLICY: HISTORICAL AND HUMAN RIGHTS PERSPECTIVES

In spite of its reputation as a land of opportunity for immigrants, the U.S. record during the late 19th and 20th centuries can be characterized equally as one of fear and resentment toward immigrants, in both popular sentiment and the law (chapter 3, by J. C. Salyer, presents many details regarding the history of discriminatory immigration legislation and policing in the United States). In 1965, Congress inaugurated a short-lived era of more equitable and human rights–centered immigration legislation, by replacing national origins quotas with a system of preferences, giving highest priority (74 percent) to family reunification (Reimers 1998: 26). Another politically progressive milestone was congressional passage of the Refugee Act of 1980, which eliminated political and geographical criteria (according to which "refugees" had to come from either communist countries or countries in the Middle East), replacing these with a politically and geographically neutral adjudication standard, to be applied equally to all applicants regardless of country of origin (U.S. Citizenship and Immigration Services 2005).

In the 1980s and 1990s, immigration legislation took a punitive turn, even as rates of immigration and U.S. dependence on immigrant labor grew to levels unprecedented since the highpoint of European immigration in the 1900s and 1910s. The Immigration Reform and Control Act of 1986 (IRCA) offered amnesty to almost three million long-time unauthorized U.S. residents. At the same time, IRCA included provisions to fine employers for hiring aliens without legal work authorization. Without providing effective means for employers to verify if their prospective employees' identity and residency documents were genuine, the law "turned out to be a rather generous amnesty without teeth for employers' sanctions" (Reimers 1998: 27). Unauthorized immigration only grew in the years after IRCA's passage, and, in a bow to economic realism, Congress in 1990 raised the ceiling for employment-related legal immigration to 140,000 annually and permitted larger numbers of temporary worker (H) visas (Daniels 2004: 238). Over the same period, anti-immigrant agitation swelled. A symbolic victory for restricting immigration was won in 1994, with the decisive passage by California voters of Proposition 187, which severely restricted immigrants' access to public services. Even though nearly all of the provisions of "Prop 187" were soon struck down as unconstitutional, the idea of punishing immigrants by restricting their eligibility for government services caught on, and the country's general mood toward immigration soured.

Three pieces of federal legislation, adopted in the months before the 1996 presidential election, reflect the charged political atmosphere surrounding immigration policy in the wake of Prop 187. Immediately after the bombing of the federal building in Oklahoma City of 19 April 1995, acting under the mistaken assumption that the attack was carried out by foreign nationals, Congress expanded mechanisms to bar certain aliens from the United States, narrowed asylum provisions, and approved measures to expedite the deportation of criminal aliens (Doyle 1996). Later in 1996, the Personal Responsibility and Work Opportunity Reconciliation

---

OFFICIAL 1994 CALIFORNIA VOTER INFORMATION:
PROPOSITION 187, "ILLEGAL ALIENS"

Makes illegal aliens ineligible for public social services, public health care services (unless emergency under federal law), and public school education at elementary, secondary, and post-secondary levels.

Requires various state and local agencies to report persons who are suspected illegal aliens to the California Attorney General and the Immigration and Naturalization Service. Mandates California Attorney General to transmit reports to the Immigration and Naturalization Service and maintain records of such reports.

Makes it a felony to manufacture, sell, or use false citizenship or residence documents.

SOURCE: Daniels 2004, p.243.

Act stripped legal alien residents of entitlement to a wide range of government public assistance (Daniels 2004: 246–47). Congress and the courts would later rescind some of the more extreme provisions. Even so, the timing of the bill's enactment, only weeks before the 1996 election, amplified the Act's public resonance as a symbol of Congress' aim to go beyond "tough" and get downright *mean* with immigrants.

One piece of legislation, enacted in 1996, would inflict lasting harm on migrant rights: the Illegal Immigration Reform and Immigrant Responsibility Act (IIRIRA). This law introduced a range of new restrictions. It limited rights of unauthorized entrants and asylum seekers to appeal decisions made by immigration and asylum hearing officers and immigration judges, mandated new penalties and bars on legal entry for deportees, increased border enforcement personnel, and authorized the construction of barriers along the Mexican border. Besides the expedited procedures for the removal of inadmissible aliens arriving at ports of entry, two other provisions of IIRIRA have caused lasting concern among migrant rights advocates: IIRIRA mandated the detention of asylum applicants while under removal proceedings as well as the detention and deportation of criminal aliens following upon completion of their prison sentences. Between 1994 and 1999, the number of unauthorized entrants under INS detention, while waiting decisions regarding removal or deportation, jumped from 5,500 to 16,400 (Meissner 1999). The number of detainees rapidly exceeded the capacity of the immigrant detention facilities, forcing immigration authorities to place *asylum* seekers, who were not guilty of any crime, into penitentiaries alongside convicted criminals. Human Rights Watch (1998) found even children, charged with no crime, held for months while undergoing removal proceedings in prisonlike conditions with juveniles accused of murder, rape, and drug trafficking. A National Public Radio news investigation (Zwerdling 2005) revealed a number of instances in which prison wardens and medical staff seemed to show deliberate indifference to medical emergencies, ending in the deaths of immigrant detainees. Cheryl Little, an immigrant advocate interviewed in Florida, reported that the detainees' most commonly voiced complaint is that "repeated requests for medical care are simply ignored." In one death investigated by NPR, inmates' pleas to their guards to help a Jamaican detainee suffering a heart attack were answered only with ugly epithets and the application of physical force to shoo away detainees from the dying man's side.

Human rights concerns were also raised about an uncounted number of cases in which aliens have been deported for being convicted of committing nonviolent crimes and who seemingly should have qualified for clemency on the basis of having legally resident spouses, children, and other dependents. Some have been deported after conviction for relatively minor crimes, like jumping subway turnstiles, other misdemeanors and nonviolent drug offenses. Investigations in Haiti, the Dominican Republic, and El Salvador reveal that the deportees are ostracized in their countries of origin as "thugs" and are commonly recruited as foot soldiers by violent street gangs or targeted for murder at the hands of the police (Brotherton 2003; DeCesare 1998a and 1998b). Some have been deported even though they entered the United States at such a young age that they have no first-hand knowledge of life in their home countries, feel culturally alienated there, and may even lack the language skills to get by on their own.

COMPETING PERSPECTIVES ON MIGRANT RIGHTS

The experts on migration who have contributed essays to this book are in agreement: the U.S. record on migrant and refugee rights was already deteriorating in the years prior to 2001 and has subsequently worsened further. Sadly, it is necessary today to remind legislators, opinion-shapers, and the public that migrants, too, have rights, even if they enter the United States without legal authorization: being an "illegal alien" does not make you an "illegal person."

As Susan Akram and Kevin Johnson observe in chapter 4, "In important ways, contemporary immigration law ignores a constitutional revolution

WHAT'S IN A NAME? "ILLEGAL ALIEN" VERSUS "UNDOCUMENTED IMMIGRANT"

The dividing line between immigration restrictionists and advocates of migrant rights is perhaps nowhere more clear than in the words each side uses to designate immigrants who lack official authorization to reside in the United States. In the eyes of restrictionists, these people are "illegal," plain and simple: according to the Web site of Adversity.net For Victims of Reverse Discrimination, "An 'illegal alien' is a foreigner who (1) does not owe allegiance to our country; and (2) who has violated our laws and customs in establishing residence in our country. He or she is therefore a criminal under applicable U.S. laws." (see http://www.adversity.net/Terms_Definitions/TERMS/Illegal-Undocumented.htm). By contrast, the National Association of Hispanic Journalists (NAHJ) calls for stopping the use of "illegals" as a noun, and curbing the phrase "illegal alien." To them, the growing media trend to use the word "illegals" as a noun, shorthand for "illegal aliens" is "offensive and dehumanizing because it criminalizes the person rather than the actual act of illegally entering or residing in the United States" (http://www.nahj.org/nahjnews/articles/2006/March/immigrationcoverage.shtml). NAHJ recommends that journalists instead use the terms "undocumented worker" or "undocumented immigrant."

Even the NAHJ statement implies that being out of status is a criminal act, when in fact it is a violation of civil immigration laws (I thank J.C. Salyer for bringing this distinction to my attention). The second problem with the term "illegal alien," therefore, is that it falsely equates that status of being in the United States without legal authorization with being "a criminal." Along these lines, Leo Chavez (1992: 11-12) points out that the term "illegal alien" is imprecise because it is literally prejudicial: legality or illegality are matters for judges to decide in legal proceedings; some immigrants without papers, were they to get a legal hearing, would be judged to have grounds on which to be permitted to stay, and others not; absent such a legal proceeding we should pick a less judgmental term to talk about out-of-status immigrants. Kevin R. Johnson (1996: 277) amplifies upon this principle: "Many nuances of immigration law make it extremely difficult to distinguish between an 'illegal' and a 'legal' alien. For example, a person living without documents in this country for a number of years may be eligible for relief from deportation and to become a lawful permanent resident. He or she may have children born in this country, who are citizens, as well as a job and community ties here. It is difficult to contend that this person is an illegal alien indistinguishable from a person who entered without inspection yesterday."

Recent scholarship questioning the epistemological and historical foundations of the term "illegal immigrant" add to these assertions that illegal is a prejudicial and demeaning descriptor. Jonathan Xavier Inda (2006) delves into the public discourse built around the notion of immigrant illegality and finds abundant evidence that the adjective "illegal" crystallizes an unsavory set of perceptions around the out-of-status immigrant: law breaker, menace, invader, potential welfare-dependent, simultaneously inassimilable into the mainstream yet also the agent of the "browning of America" and polluter of established custom, civility and ethical standards. Nicholas De Genova (2002) adds that what is really being referenced through the term "illegal immigrant" is not the migrants' mode of entry so much as the path of exit desired or held open for them, via presumptive excludability and deportability. Illegality, when analyzed historically as the latest in a succession of official paradigms of alienage, provides for almost automatic recourse to be made to deportation, as a means for dealing with unruly or surplus immigrant labor, but does so in a manner that is clothed with the seeming impartiality of the law rather than the racial discrimination nakedly visible, for example, in the Chinese Exclusion Law of 1882 or the Great Depression era mass deportations of Mexicans and Mexican-Americans.

While the contributors to this volume use a range of terms—including *undocumented immigrants/workers, unauthorized entrants,* and *out-of-status* or *irregular immigrants*—we are united in seeing a need on the whole to reject the term *illegal alien/immigrant.* In keeping with the "note on methods and terminology" of a recent Urban Institute fact sheet (Passel, Capps, and Fix 2004: 2), legal residents are understood to be, specifically, (1) legal permanent residents, i.e., "green-card" holders, (2) refugees and asylees, or (3) legal temporary residents, including students, high-tech workers, agricultural workers, and other temporary visa holders. "Undocumented immigrants" are those who fall into none of these legal categories, the greater part of whom either entered the country without official authorization or entered with valid visas but overstayed their visas' expiration or otherwise violated the terms of their admission.

that embraced the norm of nondiscrimination against racial minorities, symbolized by *Brown v Board of Education,* over the latter half of the twentieth century." Instead of expanding legal protections for people vulnerable to abuses of official power, recent U.S. legislation on immigration has narrowed the rights of out-of-status aliens and asylum seekers and sought to confine them within a parallel immigration judicial system, which does not publish its findings, permit extensive outside scrutiny, or allow for appeal to other courts of law.

In this connection, a gap may be perceived between an important segment of scholarship on the problem of immigration control and the experiences of migrants and their lawyers in struggling against deportation and indefinite detention. Whereas specialists in migration studies see broad and expanding rights for unauthorized immigrants in the world's liberal democracies, legal scholars and immigrants' advocates perceive a significant hardening of laws and legal judgments. The leading migration scholars Wayne Cornelius, Philip Martin, and James Hollifield (1994: 9), for example, sustain, in apparent contrast with Akram and Johnson, that "[t]he gradual extension of rights to ethnic minorities and foreigners over a period of several decades, from the 1960s through the 1980s, is one of the most salient aspects of political development in the advanced industrial democracies."[5] Several leading students of immigration policy agree that one reason why liberal democracies have difficulty containing "unwanted immigration" is that these states face pressure to respect legal safeguards for migrant rights and nondiscrimination.[6] Certain newly industrializing countries, such as Kuwait and Singapore, are exceptions that prove the rule: these states are exceptionally efficient in excluding unwanted immigrants in large part because they accord few if any rights protections to migrant workers (Massey, this volume). Though it may be far from these authors' intentions, many readers will infer that if only liberal democracies were a bit less punctilious about respecting the rights of aliens, then immigration could be controlled in more economically rational and bureaucratically efficient ways.

These observations raise questions of both principle and fact. Regarding principles, it may be asked whether we should we judge U.S. compliance with migrant rights by the standard of Kuwait or Singapore, or follow these states' example by stripping immigrants of certain rights of legal representation and appeal. Massey is emphatic that the answer to both these questions is "no": in the section of his chapter devoted to policy recommendations he makes a cogent case that the foundation of any effective and enlightened reform of U.S. immigration policy must be the expansion of all workers' rights and the creation of safe and legal venues for needed immigrants to enter the United States. If the point is that liberal democracies should find it unacceptable to institute heavy-handed and intrusive surveillance and policing—targeted specifically at people whose appearance, line of work, or other identity markers makes them suspect as possible "illegals"— then I think most U.S. citizens would agree that that kind of "profiling" is not consistent with American ideals. Or, as Nancy Naples' chapter in this volume points out, most would come around to this conclusion once they realized that low-tolerance policing, ostensibly aimed at immigrants, has a funny way of entrapping them and their children in its net.

WHAT RIGHTS DO MIGRANTS HAVE?

The International Convention on the Protection of the Rights of All Migrant Workers and their Families was ratified by the UN General Assembly in 1990 and entered into force in 2003. While reaffirming and complementing existing human rights instruments, this convention has forged new standards and placed human rights in the specific context of migrant rights. The Convention protects all migrant workers and members of their families, irrespective of their legal status. Nevertheless, the rights granted to documented and undocumented workers are not identical. (The complete text of the Convention is available at http://www .unhchr.ch/html/menu3/b/m_mwctoc.htm). Below is a brief list of the rights to which all migrant workers are entitled, regardless of the legal status of their residence in the host country.

Basic freedoms:

- Right to freedom of movement to and from their countries of origin (article 8);
- Right to life (article 9);
- Right to freedom from torture or cruel, inhuman or degrading treatment or punishment (article 10);
- Right to freedom from slavery, servitude or forced compulsory labor (article 11);
- Right to freedom of thought, expression, conscience and religion (articles 12 & 13);
- Right to privacy (article 14);
- Right to property (article 15);

Due process:

- Right to a fair and public hearing with all the guarantees of a due process (articles 16-20);
- Right to be provided with necessary legal assistance, interpreters and information in an understood language (article 16);
- Right to liberty and security and freedom from arbitrary arrest or detention (article 16);
- Right to be presumed innocent until proved guilty (article 19);
- Prohibition to be subject to measures of collective expulsion (article 22);
- Right to have recourse to diplomatic or consular assistance and protection (article 23);
- Right to recognition everywhere as a person before the law (article 24);

- Right to equality with nationals before the courts and tribunals (article 18);

Employment:

- Right of equal treatment with nationals in respect to remuneration and other conditions of work such as overtime, holidays, etc. (article 25);
- Right to join freely any trade union (article 26);
- Right to enjoy the same treatment as nationals regarding social security benefits in so far as they fulfill the legislation requirements (articles 27);
- Right to emergency medical care (article 28);

Family and children of migrant workers:

- Right to a name, registration of birth and nationality (article 29);
- Right of access to education (article 30);

Cultural and economic rights:

- Right to preserve a cultural identity (article 31);
- Right to transfer earnings and savings upon the termination of their stay in the State of employment (article 32);

Information:

- Right to information by the State of origin, State of employment, or the State of transit of their rights arising from the present Convention, the conditions of their admission, and their rights and obligations in those States (article 33)

SOURCE: Migrants Rights International, "Basic Rights Provided by the Migrant Workers Convention" (http://www.migrantwatch.org/1990 unmrc/1990_un_mrc.html).

Yet it now seems less certain than before 9/11 that noncitizens are in fact protected from heavy-handed and intrusive surveillance, policing and profiling. Here, questions of fact must be raised about the assertion that the world's liberal democracies find their hands tied by rights safeguards when it comes to dealing with immigrants. Is it empirically verifiable to lay the fault for liberal democracies' difficulty in controlling immigration unequivocally at the door of migrant rights? Just about any experienced and competent immigration lawyer can relate stories of nightmare cases in which immigrants have been unjustly deported, often after having been detained for months or years and being shifted repeatedly from prison to prison, all the time permitted extremely limited communication with counsel, and at times suffering the abuse of guards or cellmates. Taking the experiences of immigrants and their advocates into account, there seems to be room to debate whether in practice U.S. immigration policy may be accurately characterized as friendly to migrant rights.

To this it may be added that recent legal opinions in the United States, for example, place *citizens'* rights above immigrants' rights in the reasons why courts have struck down highly intrusive government programs of internal enforcement of immigration law. In October 2007, for example, a Federal judge placed on indefinite hold a Department of Homeland Security (DHS) rule that would have required employers to fire any workers whose employee identity information does not match the Social Security Administration's records (Preston 2007). If allowed to take effect, the judge found, this rule would have led to the firing of many thousands of legally authorized workers (so laden with errors are the Social Security records), bringing "irreparable harm to innocent workers and employers." It is clear from this wording that it is the rights of citizens and legally authorized immigrants that matter; any protections that accrue to the undocumented are immaterial, even if possibly unavoidable.[7]

Even considering such equal protection spillover benefits for irregular immigrants, uncertainty also surrounds the question, Are the authorities constrained by law from making use of all the controls they would be technically capable of applying against unauthorized immigration? It may be illuminating in this context to consider the distinction drawn by the legal scholar Linda Bosniak (2007: 86) between "immigration questions" and "alienage questions." According to her, whereas immigration is a federal policy domain, alienage policy "is a composite of rules and standards set by both state and federal law across a wide variety of regulatory domains"; and whereas "the government's exclusionary power in the sphere of immigration is exceptionally unconstrained," in alienage law, "the balance of power between the government and immigrant is more complex." Alienage policy extends certain protections even to the undocumented largely as a means of avoiding pathologies that would flow from excluding irregular immigrants from schooling, health care, and protection of the law. The distinction between the two legal domains is useful precisely because in practice it is *blurry;* as Bosniak (2007: 87) writes, "The lives of undocumented immigrants are at times governed by liberal individual rights norms, at times by exclusionary border norms, and very often by both at once." The controversy about whether local law enforc-ers should be empowered to enforce immigration law (a decision whose effects in one Iowa town are described by Naples' chapter in this book) is clearly a question defined at the frontier between immigration and alien-age policy. The "interior enforcement strategy" unveiled by the DHS in 2006 seeks to push the envelope in favor of prioritizing immigration law over state and local determination of alienage policy, by building stronger worksite inspection and compliance mechanisms and instituting a train-ing program for local police to enforce immigration law as stipulated by Section 287(g) of the Immigration and Nationality Act.[8] Whether a person should be permitted to enter and stay is a distinct question from how that person should be treated once they are in but the public debate generally elides the two, obscuring rather than illuminating a centrally important tension. Federal policymakers see the distinction clearly and have set the goal of pushing the boundary between immigration and alienage policy to the federal government's advantage.

A second question of fact relates to the DHS' seeming slowness to pursue worksite enforcement through raids and other intrusive methods (as opposed to delegating employers to determine the legality of their potential employees, at pain of legal sanction), though that hesitancy, too, may be disappearing. Does this restraint respond primarily to DHS qualms about infringing migrant and minority rights or from their fears of contradicting the interests of businesses whose profits batten on the employment of cheap, unregulated labor? In other words, the second point of fact to be questioned about liberal democracies' seeming difficulty in ridding themselves of "unwanted immigrants" is whether irregular immi-grants are uniformly or unambiguously *unwanted.* Consider that IRCA, the legislation that in 1986 tightened internal controls, heightened border enforcement and provided for employer sanctions, was accompanied by a massive initiative to legalize the status of long-term out-of-status resi-dent aliens. These two, seemingly contradictory moves—of authorizing increased restrictions and punishments while also according legal resi-dency and work permits to millions who may have contravened the very same rules—are again the cornerstone of proposals for "comprehensive" immigration reform considered by Congress as late as 2008 (and subse-quently set aside in the wake of the presidential election season and global financial crisis). To the degree that the undocumented immigrant is in fact "unwanted," she or he is paradoxically also regarded as economically indispensable by many in Washington's halls of power.

Taking a human rights perspective on international migration also raises questions about why one category of people—unauthorized immigrants—have been singled out to bear the entire brunt of official surveillance and punishments, when clearly many U.S. citizens are involved in facilitating unauthorized immigration and hence equally responsible for any wrongs or ills that may flow from it. In the larger public debate on immigration, it is often said that undocumented immigrants are unfairly exploiting weaknesses in U.S. enforcement of immigration laws; little is heard about how U.S. employers are unfairly exploiting immigrants who lack legal work authorization. Even as promoting "individual responsibility" has become a Washington catchword, employers have as a group escaped *their* responsibility for rights abuses committed against undocumented workers. According to Human Rights Watch (2000a), many migrant children, both documented and undocumented, labor on U.S. farms, working long days, suffering injuries and exposure to pesticides, and often earning less than minimum wage. Labor rights and workplace safety infringements increase just as the jobs are captured by undocumented immigrants, in a pattern that extends also to nonagricultural labor. "Many foreign migrant workers in the United States work in industries with low wages and long hours, few benefits, and unsafe and unhealthy working conditions. The efforts of undocumented workers to exercise their right to unionize are easily thwarted by managers who threaten to retaliate by reporting them to the INS. The fear of deportation also discourages these workers from filing unfair labor practice charges" (Human Rights Watch 2001; see also 2000b).

The historical and human rights perspectives introduced in the preceding paragraphs underscore the need to amplify the scope of U.S. immigration debates, to take into consideration the gap that has opened between official immigration policy, on the one hand, and ever more globally integrated structures of trade, production, and governance, on the other. Granted, many of the problems and concerns articulated in this book are part of a much broader global pattern and are not reducible to U.S. policy. Yet it is to be hoped that this book will bring even many a skeptical reader to ask whether the United States is doing enough, intelligently and compassionately enough, to address the ultimate causes of the global swell of human smuggling, trafficking, and state and employer infringements of migrants' rights. Is the United States doing what it can to support peaceful, rights-respectful, and "roots-up" solutions to the world's major economic and political upheavals? Or are U.S. policies sooner amplifying those crises and then trying to contain the spillover through ineffective and even counterproductive law enforcement and military responses? Can U.S. legislators find the breadth of vision and political will to seek immigration reform that is truly "comprehensive" in seeking betterment for citizen and immigrant workers alike? Or will the immigration debate remain mired in liberal versus restrictionist rhetorical exchanges in which both sides tacitly assume that gain to immigrants must bring loss to those U.S. citizens who compete with immigrants for jobs? In varied ways, this book's contributors seek to make the case that there are more policy options available to U.S. leaders than just either throwing open the gates to immigration or building more walls against it.

THE ORGANIZATION OF THIS BOOK

The essays in this book are divided among four sections, each section developing a different angle on the repercussions of U.S. policy for the rights of migrants at different points in history and in various parts of the world.

In his essay in Part I, "The Political Economy of International Migration," Douglas Massey points out that today's increasingly aggressive official restrictions on borders and immigration stand in contradiction with the progressive freeing up of international trade in all areas, bringing unnecessarily high costs to the U.S. government and creating highly negative effects for migrants. While skeptical of the ability of states to stanch immigration flows, he provides realistic recommendations for policies that might permit liberal democratic regimes to manage immigration with greater efficiency and respect for human rights. Of particular interest to scholars of international migration, Massey's concluding comments anticipate what kinds of new research might still be needed to guide nations toward more effective and enlightened immigration policies.

In the chapter 2, Josiah Heyman brings a wide range of sources, including firsthand observation of ports of entry and interviews with border inspectors, to bear on the question of whether U.S. borders can be successfully secured against outside threats via new computer databases and sensing technologies. As U.S. pursuit of global trade integration expands international commerce, it also effectively stimulates emigration from countries being opened to U.S. goods. Consequently, the challenge to port inspectors, of simultaneously facilitating authorized entry and egress and interdicting unauthorized goods and people, will increase greatly, probably exceeding the capability of either advanced technology or human monitoring.

The official U.S. response to the 9/11 attacks followed a disturbing historical pattern, in which the freedoms of noncitizens, a minority group with no vote, have been sacrificed at moments of national emergency in the interest of preserving citizens' security. Part II, "Historical Perspectives," includes three essays that trace the pre-9/11 roots of the post-9/11 upsurge in anti-immigrant sentiment. The Red Scare and Palmer Raids of the 1910s and 1920s and the Japanese internment during the Second World War, J. C. Salyer points out, were precipitated by national security crises but did not materialize suddenly. These anti-immigrant backlashes were prefigured by years of news reportage and political oratory raising fears that these immigrant groups posed a threat to essential American values. A similar kind of racial labeling has gone on around Mexican immigration. "If there has been one constant in both pre- and post-9/11 public discourse on national security," asserts Leo Chavez in chapter 4, "it has been the alleged threat to the nation posed by Mexican immigration and the growing number of Americans of Mexican descent in the United States." Based upon a study of more than thirty years of feature stories on immigration published in leading U.S. news magazines, Chavez charts the escalation of rhetorically-driven fear regarding Mexican immigration. As Susan M. Akram and Kevin R. Johnson describe in chapter 5, elite discourse, media vilification, and selective government persecution of Middle Eastern and South Asian Muslims before 9/11 in like manner prepared the ground for the sweeping state security response to be unleashed after that day.

The chapters of Part III, "Policing the Borders of the Security State," examine first the application of internal immigration controls within the United States and then turn to the U.S.-Mexico border, to report on the low-intensity conflict on unauthorized immigration being waged by U.S. authorities.

Christopher Dole's chapter shifts the focus to the highly personal level of the post-9/11 experiences of Arab and Muslim men in the United States. He brings forward the testimony of men for whom the U.S. government's responses to 9/11 brought back memories of psychologically traumatic repression they had suffered before, in Jordan, Syria, Lebanon, and Morocco, eliciting fears that they thought they had escaped by migrating to the United States. Whatever security gains have accrued to the majority population, a prevalent experience of Middle Easterners and South Asians in the United States, post-9/11, has been the renewal of long-dormant feelings of *insecurity*.

Nancy Naples draws on long-term ethnographic study of two small Iowa towns, in which large numbers of Mexican and Mexican-American migrants have found work in meatpacking and other food processing plants, to explore the ways that citizenship is policed within the borders of the United States. She finds that the social regulation of citizenship, through policing by federal, local and nonstate agents, makes itself felt immediately by citizens as well as noncitizens as a source of increased risk rather than enhanced security. In reaction to INS raids and stepped up surveillance and harassment by local police, which swept up U.S. citizens and legal resident aliens as well as undocumented workers, long-term residents of the communities studied by Naples have surprisingly taken steps toward greater inclusion of recent immigrants within the boundaries of community membership.

Tricia Gabany-Guerrero's chapter takes up where corporate media treatments of immigration control efforts typically leave off, at the point of apprehension, which (perhaps not coincidentally) is the last point at which the unauthorized entrant can be portrayed unambiguously as a villain. Excessive violence and other types of mistreatment committed by the Border Patrol during the apprehension of unauthorized entrants constitute only the tip of an iceberg of injustice experienced by irregular immigrants. Other serious injustices revealed by deportation narratives told by repatriated Mexicans include (1) recently heightened restrictions on due process and appeal in detention, processing, and deportation; (2) abuses committed against detainees as a result of their confinement as criminals in prisons; (3) the separation of children from parents during detention and processing and as a result of deportation; and (4) vulnerability to abuse, once in the United States, stemming from being unable to claim the legal protections available to those who have residency and work permits. Add economic constraints to these flagrant rights abuses— the increasingly hopeless economic prospects for small farmers in the Mexican countryside and the constriction of viable income-producing alternatives to one option, trying to emigrate to the north—and one has a recipe for unfreedom, epitomized by crimes of debt bondage and other forms of modern slavery perpetrated in the United States against irregular immigrants in agriculture, domestic labor, and sex work. The U.S. government indirectly abets these crimes and a range of lesser infringements of liberty not only through policies that make it practically necessary for irregular immigrants to incur huge debts and surrender their freedom to smugglers but by tacitly playing the part of "enforcer" of labor discipline: in an untold number of cases employers rid themselves of less-than-perfectly compliant undocumented laborers by calling in ICE. In focusing on deportation and its consequences, therefore, Gabany-Guerrero not only evokes the human cost of U.S. immigration policy but also examines a meeting point for many of the contradictions of U.S. immigration policy.

Part IV, "Beyond U.S. Borders," examines how U.S. foreign policy, in the areas of national security, free-market reform, and suppression of illicit drug production and trafficking, uproots legions of new migrants and refugees and channels them across international borders under circumstances that are illegal, unsafe, and potentially unfree.

In chapter 9, Alexia Bloch contends that U.S. initiatives to stem the international migration of women as sex workers should not settle for simplistic, moralistic assertions of victimage. According to Bloch, an effective and humane policy toward trafficking must take account of the experiences of a broad range of the women who enter into these flows, including those who are informed and willing as well as those who are duped or coerced. In also bringing into consideration the social and economic constraints under which women "decide" to leave Russia for sex work abroad, her study reveals conditions that have been worsened appreciably by the application of structural adjustment policies favored by major international financial institutions.

The repercussions of one of the principal agendas of the George W. Bush administration, the "Global War on Terror," have also been felt through less direct channels overseas. Julia Hess points out how antiterrorist policies implemented after 9/11 have had effects not only on migrants already in the United States but also on people who are as far away as the margins of the Chinese state. Chinese policy toward the Uighurs, a predominantly Muslim ethnic group in China's northwest province known as the Xinjiang Uygur Autonomous Region (XUAR), became increasingly repressive after 9/11, when, in an echo of the U.S.-led war on terror, the Chinese state mounted an international campaign to label all Uighur separatists "terror groups." The human rights situation of Uighurs in China has deteriorated, marked by increasing repression, including arrests, repatriation of Uighurs in neighboring countries to China, detention, torture, and execution. Hess also draws attention to the "transnational" dimensions of the struggle for Uighur rights, as Uighurs increasingly seek asylum abroad and Uighur expatriates in the U.S. join with human rights monitors to generate publicity and mobilize sympathy for their cause.

Long before 9/11, the United States pursued policies that created insecurity in states deemed to contain threats to its citizens. According to María Teresa Restrepo-Ruiz, the flight of tens of thousands of Colombians to neighboring countries and the internal displacement of millions more are traceable to counterinsurgent violence and antinarcotics operations made worse by U.S. support for the Colombian military. Though this support has exacted an enormous cost—not only billions of dollars in direct assistance but also in the deaths and uprooting of so many Colombians—it is again doubtful in this case whether the United States has come closer to achieving its stated national security policy goal, of stopping illicit drug trafficking.

The roles of nongovernmental humanitarian organizations in the complex politics of international refugee crises are examined in the final chapter of Part IV, "Challenging U.S. Silence: International NGOs and the Iraqi Refugee Crisis," by Kathryn Libal and Scott Harding. Their chapter draws links between U.S. militarism/unilateralism, the consequent creation of a refugee crisis, and the dilemmas this situation has posed for the international community. From this chapter it emerges once more that public debate concerning post-9/11 U.S. actions suffers from historical amnesia. The U.S. invasion of Iraq in 2003 is but the latest and most muscular of a lengthy series of Washington interventions in Iraq's affairs, including long-term support for the despotic government of Saddam Hussein, all of which has in the main worsened the potential for civil conflict in post-Hussein Iraq and heightened Iraqi suspicion of and resistance to U.S. policy aims. Unresolved internal sectarian/ethnic schisms and the United States' low level of political legitimacy in Iraq have contributed to amplifying the outflow of refugees that could have been predicted to result from any war into a millions-strong exodus with few other parallels in recent world history. Left to the international humanitarian organizations is the daunting task of picking up the pieces for the United States, by drawing international attention and directly administering to the refugees' urgent needs.

In her afterword, Carole Nagengast first takes up the issue of international migration's relationship with the restructuring of the international division of labor. Under the pressure of IMF/World Bank restructuring, free market reforms, and regional economic integration—processes intensified under the North American Free Trade Agreement—semisubsistence agriculture has declined as a basis for survival and, as a consequence of this, unauthorized immigration to the United States from Mexico has risen sharply. Over the same period of time, jobs in the United States that once provided steady middle-class incomes with benefits have disappeared through outsourcing or have been downgraded as a result of reductions in benefits, lax enforcement of workplace and labor regulations, and anti-union state and corporate policies. As real incomes for the lower segments of the U.S. work force have declined, employers have also cut costs and solved labor recruitment problems by turning increasingly to immigrant workers. Nagengast thus brings the book's analyses full circle, by bringing into consideration the effects of U.S.-promoted international economic restructuring and regional integration on both migrant sending and receiving countries. Economic growth bought at the price of increasing inequality among rich and poor in both countries is at the base of both the push and the pull of unauthorized immigration today. Simultaneously, fear of noncitizens has been stoked by restrictionist rhetoric, likening immigration to a foreign invasion, as well as by the horror of 9/11 and the subsequent "Global War on Terror." Against this background, Nagengast warns that the United States' liberal tradition of individual freedoms may not be enough to protect foreigners from "the depredations of an oppressive state." Rejecting militarized responses to both terrorism and unauthorized immigration, Nagengast suggests that there is a growing need for us, citizens and immigrants alike, to be vigilant and active, and she accordingly concludes by pointing out ten ways in which we can seek to protect migrant rights.

PART I

The Political Economy
of International Migration

1. The Political Economy of Migration in an Era of Globalization

Douglas S. Massey

At the dawn of the twenty-first century all industrially developed nations in the world have become countries of immigration, whether or not they choose to recognize it. As a result, policies that govern the number, characteristics, and terms under which foreigners enter a country have become salient policy and political issues worldwide. Traditional immigrant-receiving nations (e.g., the United States, Canada, and Australia) have long histories of legislation to address issues surrounding immigration, settlement, and integration. Newer countries of immigration (e.g., Germany, Austria, and France) are still searching for appropriate legal, administrative, and political mechanisms to control and regulate mass immigration. The very newest nations of immigration (e.g., Italy, Spain, and Ireland) have been forced to build a body of law and civil procedure virtually from scratch. Certain newly industrialized countries (NICs) of East and Southeast Asia and the Middle East (e.g., Kuwait, Saudi Arabia, and Singapore) have avoided an "immigration policy" altogether, preferring rather to import foreigners strictly as workers and not recognizing any rights for them as residents or citizens.

Whatever a country's specific history, it is clear that the formulation of policies to regulate the entry, residence, and departure of foreigners will loom large in this century. The need for enlightened, well-reasoned, and efficacious policies to govern immigration has never been greater. Since enlightened policy begins with an objective understanding of the social and economic forces responsible for the phenomenon under consideration, I begin this chapter by outlining a general theoretical explanation for contemporary immigration derived from a recent review of the world research literature. I then consider the role of the state in shaping immigrant flows and describe the sorts of policy actions that are likely to be attempted in the coming decades. After outlining the likely consequences of these actions, I suggest a more efficacious approach to immigration policy that might be followed by liberal democratic regimes seeking to manage immigration humanely in an era of expanding trade and globalization. I conclude with an assessment of the research that is still needed to guide nations toward more effective and enlightened immigration policies.

WHY IMMIGRATION HAPPENS

Most policymakers and citizens in developed countries think they know why foreigners seek to enter their nations. Standards of living are low in developing countries and high in the developed world, and by migrating between the two poor migrants can expect to realize a net gain in their material well-being. In economic terms, migrants in the developing world are thought to make a cost-benefit calculation that weighs the projected costs of moving against the expected returns, both monetary and otherwise, from living and working in a developed country. Since this balance is large and positive for most inhabitants of the Third World, according to this reasoning they rationally choose to emigrate, thus accounting for high rates of population movement between developing and developed nations.

Unfortunately, reality is more complicated than this scenario suggests. A decade ago my colleagues and I (Massey et al. 1998) undertook a comprehensive review of theories purporting to account for international migration. We evaluated each theory against research conducted in the world's various international migration systems to discern the degree of support for its propositions. Based on this review we proposed a synthetic theoretical explanation for the emergence and persistence of international migration in the contemporary world. We focused on six bodies of theory: *neoclassical economics* (Todaro 1976), the *new economics of labor migration* (Stark 1991), *segmented labor market theory* (Piore 1979), *world systems theory* (Sassen 1988), *social capital theory* (Massey, Goldring, and Durand 1994), and the theory of *cumulative causation* (Massey 1990). Based on the empirical review of the degree of support for propositions derived from each theory, we then developed a synthetic theoretical explanation for the emergence and persistence of international migration at the dawn of the twenty-first century.

We concluded that international migration originates in the social, economic, and political transformations that accompany the expansion of capitalist markets into nonmarket or premarket societies (as hypothesized under world systems theory). In the context of a globalizing economy, the entry of markets and capital-intensive production methods into peripheral nonmarket or premarket economies disrupts existing social and economic arrangements and brings about the widespread displacement of people from customary livelihoods, creating a mobile population of wage laborers who actively search for new ways of achieving economic sustenance. Studies consistently show that international migrants do not come from poor, isolated places that are disconnected from world markets, but from regions and nations that are undergoing rapid change as a result of their incorporation into global trade, information, and production networks. In the short run, international migration does not stem from a lack of economic development, but from development itself.

One means by which people displaced from traditional livelihoods seek to assure their economic well-being is by selling their services on emerging national and international labor markets (neoclassical economics). Because wages are generally higher in urban than in rural areas, much of this process of labor commodification is expressed in the form of rural-to-urban migration. This movement occurs even when the probability of obtaining an urban job is low, because when multiplied by high urban wages, the low employment probabilities still yield expected incomes above those prevailing in rural areas, where wages and employment are both low. According to the neoclassical model, if the difference between incomes expected in urban and rural sectors exceeds the costs of movement between them, as is typical, people migrate to cities to reap higher lifetime earnings.

Wages are even higher, of course, in developed countries overseas, and the larger size of these international wage differentials inevitably prompts some people displaced in the course of economic development to offer their services on international labor markets by moving abroad for work. In developing countries, labor markets—both rural and urban—are volatile, characterized by wide oscillations and structural limitations that render them unable to absorb streams of workers being displaced from precapitalist or noncapitalist sectors. Since national insurance markets are rudimentary and government unemployment insurance programs are limited or nonexistent, households cannot adequately protect themselves from risks to well-being stemming from their under- or unemployment. Thus, the lack of access to unemployment insurance creates an incentive for families to self-insure by sending one or more members overseas for work. By allocating members to different labor markets in multiple geographic regions—rural, urban, and foreign—a household can diversify its labor portfolio and reduce risks to income, as long as conditions in the various labor markets are weakly or negatively correlated.

Household members who remain behind to participate in the ongoing structural transformation of agriculture, meanwhile, lack access to insurance markets for crops and futures. As households shift from subsistence to commercial farming, they are forced to adopt new production methods that make use of untested technologies, unfamiliar crops, and untried inputs. As they plunge into the unknown world of production for the market rather than self-consumption, the lack of insurance or futures markets leaves agrarian households vulnerable to economic disaster should these new methods fail, providing yet another incentive for them to self-insure against risk through international migration. Should crops fail or commodity prices fall precipitously, households with at least one worker employed overseas will not be left without a means of subsistence.

Developing countries also lack well-developed markets for capital and consumer credit. Families seeking to engage in new forms of agriculture or looking to establish new business enterprises need capital to purchase inputs and begin production. The shift to a market economy also creates new consumer demands for expensive items such as housing, automobiles, electronics, and appliances. The financing of both production and consumption requires rather large amounts of cash, but the weak and poorly developed banking industries characteristic of most developing nations cannot meet the demands for loans and credit, giving households one final motivation for international labor migration. By sending a family member temporarily abroad for work, a household can accumulate savings and overcome failures in capital and consumer credit markets by self-financing production or consumption.

Thus, whereas the rational actor posited by neoclassical economics takes advantage of a temporary geographic disequilibrium in labor markets to move abroad *permanently* to achieve higher lifetime earnings, the rational actor assumed by the new economics of labor migration seeks to cope with failures in insurance, futures, capital, and credit markets *at home* by moving abroad *temporarily* to repatriate earnings in the form of regular remittances or lump-sum transfers. In this way migrant-sending households control risk by diversifying sources of income, and they self-finance production or consumption by acquiring alternate sources of capital.

Direct empirical contrasts between neoclassical economics and the new economics of labor migration are scarce and confined largely to the North American literature, but wherever they have been done, propositions associated with the new economics have proven to be more powerful in explaining the migration behavior of individuals and households. Indeed, wage differentials often do not produce international movement (witness the lack of movement between south and north within the European Union), and migration often ceases before wage differentials have disappeared (witness the case of Puerto Rico and the United States), outcomes that are difficult (though not impossible) to explain under neoclassical assumptions but which are readily accommodated under the new economics of labor migration. In addition, the massive flows of remittances catalogued around the world (and the uses to which they are put) are anomalous under neoclassical theory but specifically predicted by the new economics.

In sum, a preponderance of evidence from around the world suggests that wage differentials, the favored explanatory factor of neoclassical economics, account for some of the historical and temporal variation in international migration, but that failures in capital, credit, futures, and insurance markets—key factors hypothesized by the new economics of labor migration—create more powerful motivations for movement. In theoretical terms, wage differentials are neither necessary nor sufficient for international migration to occur. Even with equal wages across labor markets, people may have an incentive to migrate if other markets are inefficient or poorly developed. Large-scale international movement is rarely observed in the absence of a wage gap, but the existence of a wage differential still does not guarantee international movement, nor does its absence preclude it.

Whereas the theory of the new economics of labor migration seems to explain well why migrants move between certain countries and not between others, segmented labor market theory and world systems analysis seem to account better for why demand for immigrant labor arises in host societies. While the early phases of economic development in poor nations may create a mobile population seeking to earn more money, self-insure against risk, or self-finance production or consumption, postindustrial patterns of economic growth in wealthy nations yield a bifurcation of labor markets. Whereas jobs in the primary sector provide steady work and high pay for native workers, those in the secondary sector offer low pay, little stability, and few opportunities for advancement, repelling natives and generating a structural demand for immigrant workers (as theorized by segmented labor market theory). The process of labor market bifurcation is most acute in certain *global cities*, where a concentration of managerial, administrative, and technical expertise leads to a concentration of wealth and a strong ancillary demand for low-wage services (world systems theory). Unable to attract native workers, employers turn to immigrants and often initiate immigrant flows directly through formal recruitment (segmented labor market theory).

Although instrumental in initiating immigration, recruitment becomes less important over time: the same processes of economic globalization that create mobile populations in developing regions, and which generate a demand for their services in global cities, also create links of transportation, communication, as well as politics and culture, to make the international movement of people cheaper, quicker, and easier (world systems theory). Immigration is also promoted by foreign policies and military actions that core developed nations undertake to maintain international security, protect foreign investments, and guarantee access to raw materials, foreign entanglements that create links and obligations which generate ancillary flows of refugees, asylum seekers, and military dependents.

Eventually labor recruitment becomes superfluous, for once begun, immigration displays a strong tendency to continue through the growth and elaboration of migrant networks (social capital theory). The concentration of immigrants in certain destination areas creates a "family and friends" effect that channels immigrants to the same places and facilitates their arrival and incorporation. If enough migrants arrive under the right conditions, an enclave economy may form, which further augments the demand for immigrant workers (segmented labor market theory).

The spread of migratory behavior within sending communities sets off ancillary structural changes, shifting distributions of income and land and modifying local cultures in ways that promote additional international movement. Over time, the process of network expansion itself becomes self-perpetuating because each act of migration creates social infrastructure capable of promoting additional movement (the theory of cumulative causation). As receiving countries implement restrictive policies to counter rising tides of immigrants, they create a lucrative niche into which enterprising agents, contractors, and other middlemen move to create migration-supporting institutions that also serve to connect areas of labor supply and demand, providing migrants with another resource capable of supporting and sustaining international movement (social capital theory).

During the initial phases of emigration from any sending country, the effects of capitalist expansion, market failure, social networks, and cumulative causation dominate in explaining the flows, but as the level of out-migration reaches high levels and the costs and risks of international movement drop, movement is increasingly determined by international wage differentials (neoclassical economics) and labor demand (segmented labor market theory). As economic growth in sending regions occurs, international wage gaps gradually diminish and well-functioning markets for capital, credit, insurance, and futures come into existence, progressively lowering the incentives for emigration. If these trends continue, the country ultimately becomes integrated into the international economy as a developed, capitalist society, whereupon it undergoes a migration transition: net out-migration progressively ceases and the nation itself becomes a net importer of labor. Historically, this *migratory transition* took about eight or nine decades in European nations (Hatton and Williamson 1998); but recent evidence from East Asian nations such as Taiwan and Korea suggests that it may now be compressed into as little as three or four decades (Massey, Durand, and Malone 2002). What determines the length of the transition is how long it takes a nation to build a capitalist economy with well-functioning markets, not just for labor but for capital, credit, and insurance as well as goods and services.

THE ROLE OF THE STATE

Although the foregoing theoretical account fits reasonably well when applied to explicate patterns and processes of international migration throughout the world, considerable variation between nations stems from the fact that governments attempt to intervene in transnational flows to influence the numbers and characteristics of immigrants. Immigration policy is the outcome of a political process through which competing interests interact within bureaucratic, legislative, judicial, and public arenas to influence the flow of immigrants. Shughart, Tollison, and Kimenyi (1986) identify three key interest groups in the political competition to formulate immigration policy: workers, capitalists, and landowners. Workers want high wages and struggle politically to limit the supply of labor, pressuring politicians to pass more restrictive laws and to more strictly enforce them. Capitalists favor expanding the labor supply to reduce wages and keep labor markets flexible. They pressure politicians to pass more expansive legislation and relax the enforcement of restrictions. Capitalists are joined by landowners in this effort, as the latter favor immigration as a means of increasing rents. Foreman-Peck (1992) argues that labor must also be differentiated along skill lines. Because immigrants take mostly unskilled jobs, it is *unskilled* native workers who lose the most when immigration expands, whereas owners of complementary factors of production (skills as well as capital and land) can be expected to gain through immigration.

Building on these efforts, Timmer and Williamson (1998) developed a comprehensive theoretical model of policy determination and tested it using time series data on immigration policies in five countries between 1860 and 1929. Their analysis revealed that shifts in immigration policy had little to do with the political environment, the relative number or quality of immigrants, or with most macroeconomic circumstances. Rather, the strongest and most consistent influence on immigration policy came from the *relative* wages of unskilled workers. As the earnings of unskilled workers declined relative to average income, countries tended to adopt more restrictive immigration policies. Less restriction was associated with periods of ideological commitment to free trade, although the effect was not as strong or consistent as that associated with relative wages.

Whereas Timmer and Williamson focused exclusively on national policies in the industrial era before 1930, Meyers (2002) analyzed U.S. policies in both the industrial and postindustrial periods. He hypothesized that the restrictiveness of immigration policies was determined by six basic factors. First was the economy, with downturns generating greater pressures for restriction. Second was the volume of immigration, with relatively high levels yielding greater pressures for restriction. Third was social conformity, which he measured by an index that coded limitations on freedom of expression. He argued that broader shifts toward social conformity were associated with a reaction against immigrants as aliens, and, hence, restrictive immigration policies. For his fourth factor, foreign relations, Meyers created a dummy variable to indicate years corresponding to the failure of anticommunist movements overseas and to peak years of the Cold War conflict. He hypothesized that Cold War tensions would be associated with relatively expansive immigration policies. Fifth, he argued that industrial unrest, measured by the frequency of strikes, would yield moves toward restriction. Finally, Meyers entertained the possibility that the political party in power might make a difference.

From 1890 through 1989, Meyers found that restrictiveness was unrelated to the frequency of strikes or to the party in power, but as strongly and positively related to the unemployment rate, the volume of immigration, and the degree of social conformity. It was also strongly and negatively related to Cold War tensions. When he divided the sample into industrial and postindustrial periods, moreover, he found very different patterns in the two epochs. Before 1945, immigration policy was tied principally to unemployment, the volume of immigration, and social conformity. Afterward unemployment fell substantially in significance and policy came to be dominated by foreign policy considerations, social conformity, and, again, the volume of immigration. The relative frequency of strikes had no effect on policymaking, nor did which party was in power (Democrats or Republicans).

After reviewing this and other evidence, I came to three basic conclusions about the determinants of immigration policy in receiving societies (Massey 1999). First, even though doubt remains about precisely *which* economic conditions are most relevant, it is clear that a country's *macro-economic health* plays an important role in shaping its immigration policy. Periods of economic distress are associated with moves toward restriction, whereas economic booms are associated with expansive policies. Second, immigration policy is sensitive to the *volume* of international flows, with higher rates of immigration generally leading to restrictive policies, even though in the long run such shifts may be mitigated as a growing stock of immigrants exerts its influence within specific legislative districts (an effect obviously limited to representative democracies that enfranchise immigrants). Third, immigration policy is associated with *broader ideological currents* in society, tending toward restriction during periods of social conformity and toward expansion during periods of support for open trade and also during periods of intense geopolitical conflict along ideological lines, such as the Cold War.

These conclusions suggest that in the current century developed countries will increasingly move to restrict in-migration from the developing world. The past two decades have witnessed a rising volume of immigration, increasing inequality, and, outside of North America, persistent unemployment, precisely the conditions that prior work has shown to be associated with the implementation of harsher immigration restrictions. At the same time, the end of the Cold War has eliminated a major foreign relations motivation for developed countries to accept international migrants from poor countries. Only the continued hegemony of free trade ideology would seem to augur for more open immigration policies; but on balance recent economic and political trends suggest a more restrictive immigration policy regime in the next century. Although passport controls have been eliminated among states within the European Union, and while most OECD countries do not require visas for short term travel among themselves, since the late 1980s all have moved forcefully to impede the entry of migrants from developing countries.

THE EFFICACY OF RESTRICTION

The foregoing review suggests a postmodern paradox in the early twenty-first century: while the global economy unleashes powerful forces that produce larger and more diverse flows of migrants from developing to developed countries, it simultaneously creates conditions within developed countries that promote the implementation of restrictive immigration policies by increasing the share of foreign-born residents, raising levels of inequality, and increasing economic insecurity. The central question for analysts seeking to understand the future of immigration is which set of forces will prevail: those promoting the restriction of international migration, or those promoting its expansion.

During the period from 1945 to 1975, immigration policies in receiving countries reflected the prevailing political and economic conditions and were relatively expansive. Rapid economic growth, falling inequality, and relatively low rates of international population movement kept immigration largely off the public agenda, and in most developed countries policy was formulated through a client politics of negotiation between bureaucrats and special interests. Immigration policy took the form of decisions made about temporary labor migration and the admission of political refugees. Since 1975, however, as the volume of immigration has risen, the presence of immigrants has become more permanent, economic growth has slowed, and wage inequality has increased, policymaking has progressively shifted from the bureaucratic to the public arena, and from client to electoral politics.

The politicization of immigration policy has created difficult dilemmas for political parties and politicians, because the interests favoring and opposing immigration do not fall neatly along party lines. On one side are special interests such as employers, ethnic lobbies, and humanitarian and libertarian groups that favor immigration; on the other side are nativist politicians, environmentalists, the general public, and unions who oppose it—both sides operating against a backdrop of globalization that encourages international movement. Given these alignments, Cornelius, Martin, and Hollifield (1994) noted the emergence of two common policy trends throughout the developed world: a convergence in the policy instruments chosen for immigration control and a widening gap between the goals served by these instruments and actual immigration outcomes.

In recent years, despite increasingly restrictive policies, virtually all developed countries have come to accept a large (though varying) number of "unwanted" immigrants (Joppke 1998). Even though most countries have enacted formal policies to prevent the entry and settlement of immigrants, liberal democratic states have found their abilities to enforce these restrictions constrained by several factors. First is the global economy itself, which lies beyond the reach of individual national governments but which generates structural transformations and unleashes socioeconomic forces that tend to promote large-scale international population movements (Sassen 1996, 1998). Second is the internal constitutional order of liberal democracies, reinforced by the emergence of a universal human rights regime that protects the rights of immigrants and makes it difficult for political elites to address the racial or ethnic concerns of citizens (Hollifield 1992; Cornelius, Martin, and Hollifield 1994; Freeman 1992, 1994, 1995, 1998; Jacobson 1997).

Although rights-based policies have taken different forms in different countries, the net effect has been similar in liberal democracies: increased civil rights for immigrants, an outcome that significantly undermines the capacity of states to control immigration. As Cornelius, Martin, and Hollifield (1994: 10) note, "it is the confluence of *markets* and *rights* that explains much of the contemporary difficulty of immigration control in Europe and the United States" (emphasis in original). In many countries, universal human rights are reinforced by moral obligations that stem from specific histories of colonialism, guest worker recruitment, or Cold War politics (Joppke 1998).

A third constraint on the restriction of immigration is the existence in most representative democracies of an independent judiciary that is shielded from the political pressures to which elected politicians must respond. Immigrants and their advocates turn to the courts to combat restrictive policies implemented by the legislative and executive branches. According to Joppke (1998b), the rise of a liberal doctrine of human rights is not sufficient to protect the rights of immigrants and thwart governmental efforts at restriction. There must also be a means of guaranteeing those rights within a specific national polity, and this typically requires a written constitution and a strong, independent judiciary.

Faced with mounting public pressure to control immigration, but with the root causes of international migration lying largely beyond their reach in the forces of the global economy, and with formal policies of restriction under increasing moral and judicial challenge, politicians in many developed countries have turned increasingly to *symbolic* policy instruments to create an *appearance* of control (Calavita 1992; Cornelius, Martin, and Hollifield 1994; Andreas 1998a). Repressive policies such as vigorous border enforcement, the bureaucratic harassment of aliens, and the restriction of immigrants' access to social services may or may not be effective, but they all serve an important political purpose: they are visible, concrete, and generally popular with citizen voters (Espenshade and Calhoun 1993; Espenshade and Hempstead 1996). Forceful restrictive actions enable otherwise encumbered public officials to appear decisive, tough, and engaged in combating the rising tide of immigration.

Little research has been done outside North America to evaluate the

TABLE 1.1. Conceptual Classification of Factors Affecting State Capacity to Implement Restrictive Immigration Policies

Relationship to state capacity	Strength of bureaucracy _positive_	Demand for entry _negative_	Strength of constitutional protections _negative_	Independence of judiciary _negative_	Tradition of immigration _negative_	Continuum of state capacity
Kuwait	high	moderate	low	low	low	high
Singapore	high	moderate	moderate	moderate	low	↑
Britain	high	moderate	low	moderate	low	
Switzerland	high	moderate	high	high	low	
Germany	high	high	high	high	low	
France	high	high	high	high	moderate	
Argentina	low	high	moderate	moderate	high	
Spain	low	moderate	high	high	low	
Canada	high	high	high	high	high	
United States	moderate	high	high	high	high	low

efficacy of such policies, although it is clear that, despite growing restrictions, undocumented migration is on the rise worldwide (see Massey et al. 1998). The efficacy of restriction, however, is likely to vary substantially from country to country depending on five basic factors: the relative power and autonomy of the state bureaucracy; the relative number of people seeking to immigrate; the degree to which political rights of citizens and noncitizens are constitutionally guaranteed; the relative independence of the judiciary; and the existence and strength of an indigenous tradition of immigration. The interplay of these five factors produces a continuum of state capacity to implement restrictive immigration policies, as illustrated in Table 1.1.

At one extreme are centralized authoritarian governments that lack an independent judiciary and a well-established regime of constitutional protections, and that have no tradition of immigration, as in the oil-exporting countries of the Persian Gulf. Saudi Arabia and Kuwait, for example, are homogeneous Islamic societies led by hereditary monarchs who preside over centralized, nondemocratic states. Officials in the Gulf States are thus in a strong position to enforce restrictive immigration policies, and laws and regulations governing migration within the region are consequently much harsher than those prevailing in Europe or North America (Dib 1988; Sell 1988). None of the Gulf States recognizes the right to asylum, allows residence without a job, recognizes a right of family reunification, guarantees legal access to housing, social benefits, or medical care, or grants migrants any right of appeal with respect to decisions about their status; all permit deportation at any time by administrative decree (Dib 1988). Although migrants may be incorporated into the economic organization of the Gulf States, they are explicitly excluded from their social and political structures (Weiner 1982).

Next on the continuum of state capacity to restrict immigration are democratic states in Western Europe and East Asia with strong, centralized bureaucracies, but with moderate demand for entry and little native tradition of immigration. Political elites in these countries can expect to meet with some success in restricting immigration, but, as described above, immigrants nonetheless have important resources—moral, political, and legal—to forestall state actions and evade legal restrictions on entry and settlement. Next on the scale of state capacity are the nations of Southern Europe and South Asia, which likewise lack strong traditions of immigration but which also lack strong centralized bureaucracies capable of imposing their will efficiently throughout society. Immigrants to Spain, Italy, Greece, Thailand, or Malaysia thus have considerably more leeway to overcome barriers, and the states have less capacity to enforce restrictive immigration policies and bureaucratic procedures.

Finally, at the opposite end of the spectrum from the Gulf States are countries that lack a highly centralized state and that have strong traditions of individual liberty and long-standing cultures of immigration. Such countries as Canada and Australia have well-developed social and political infrastructures to support immigrants, protect their rights, and advance their interests. The most extreme case in this category is obviously the United States, which faces an intense demand for immigrant entry and has a deeply ingrained commitment to individual rights, a long-standing history of resistance to central authority, a strong written constitution protecting individual rights, and an independent and powerful judiciary. In the United States immigration is not simply a historical fact, it is part of the national myth, and the very idea of a national personal identification system is anathema.

The imposition of restrictive policies in the United States does not appear to have been effective in limiting either documented or undocumented migration. Despite successive amendments to the Immigration and Nationality Act intended to make it more difficult for migrants from developing countries to enter the United States legally, the volume of legal immigration has continued to grow, rising from an average of 330,000 per year during the 1960s, to 450,000 per year during the 1970s, 734,000 per year during the 1980s, and finally exceeding 1 million per year during the 1990s (U.S. Immigration and Naturalization Service 1997).

Since 1986, the United States also has embarked increasingly on a repressive policy toward undocumented migrants, criminalizing the hiring of unauthorized workers, denying legal as well as illegal migrants access to selected social benefits, increasing inspections at work sites, and expanding the personnel and resources devoted to border enforcement (Heyman 1995; Dunn 1996). Yet a comprehensive analysis by Massey, Durand, and Malone (2002) indicates that these measures have not deterred undocumented migrants from leaving for the United States, discouraged former undocumented migrants from making return trips, prevented illegal migrants from crossing the border, encouraged settled migrants to return home, or prevented employers from hiring unauthorized workers.

A NEW APPROACH TO IMMIGRATION POLICY

Few of the causal processes underlying mass immigration are easily controllable using the policy levers normally available to public officials. Governments can do little about the penetration of markets into developing regions of the world, or about the progressive incorporation of peripheral areas into global trade, information, and production networks anchored in world cities. Likewise, reducing a demand for unskilled labor that stems from the structural segmentation of the labor market would require a wholesale re-engineering of society that most political leaders find daunting, and state policies cannot prevent social networks and other transnational structures from arising to support international migration. Trade agreements such as NAFTA generally set in motion structural changes in sending regions that promote international movement while creating new links of transportation and communication and new social connections that make migration between trading nations easier.

To date, state efforts at immigration control have conceptualized international movement mainly as a cost-benefit decision. By patrolling the border, punishing employers who hire unauthorized workers, barring immigrants from social programs, and limiting the rights of the foreign born to housing, health care, schooling, and employment, officials seek to drive up the costs and lower the benefits of international migration, in hopes of reducing the incentives for entry. Such repressive policies, however, do not address the broader structural causes of international migration, and they focus on income maximization to the exclusion of other motives for international movement such as risk diversification and capital acquisition.

The failure of states to recognize the complex, multicausal nature of contemporary international migration yields the worst of all possible worlds: continuing immigration combined with lower wages, poorer working conditions, increased crime, more disease, and greater social marginalization. Repressive policies seeking to regulate immigration by influencing the costs and benefits of immigration are likely to fail. As long as the world's powerful economies are incorporated within global networks, they will tend to receive international migrants. In both theoretical and practical terms it has proved difficult to lower barriers to the movement of capital, information, and goods while at the same time raising barriers to the movement of workers, as immigration is simply the labor component of globalizing factor markets.

Rather that trying to stop international migration through repressive means, a more enlightened approach might be to *recognize immigration as a natural outgrowth* of a developing country's insertion into the global economy and then work to *maximize* its desirable features while working to *minimize* its negative consequences. While skilled and educated workers would be welcomed whatever their country of origin, repressive enforcement actions against unskilled and undocumented immigrants would be reserved for those from nations otherwise unconnected to the receiving country by virtue of trade or investment relations. For immigrants coming from nations otherwise connected via well-established flows of capital, information, goods, and culture, policymakers would work to achieve outcomes that serve the interests of the receiving society rather than simply trying to suppress the flow. These would include policies to promote shorter stays, limit settlement, and encourage return migration; to protect internal wages and labor standards; and to encourage economic development in sending regions.

Rather than trying to suppress a natural flow and inviting counterproductive outcomes, an alternative is to accept immigration as inevitable and to design programs to enhance immigrants' connections to the sending society and to maximize their propensity for return migration. These goals could be accomplished in a variety of ways. One is to make temporary work visas freely available, so that migrants can reasonably expect to migrate again should their economic circumstances warrant, thus lowering the incentives to stay on in the receiving country for fear of not being able to return. A portion of immigrants' wages might be held back and only paid to a foreign bank account upon return to the sending country. Several Asian nations, notably South Korea and the Philippines, have successfully harnessed immigrant earnings in this fashion. Interest rates might be subsidized in foreign accounts to provide a return above the market, thus luring back migrants and their money. Finally, since migrants are often motivated by lack of access to insurance and capital, destination countries might enter into cooperative agreements with sending nations to establish public programs and private businesses to meet these needs.

With state resources freed up from unproductive attempts to suppress immigration, receiving countries could increase internal inspections of work sites in sectors that employing large concentrations of immigrants, not to round up and deport illegal aliens but to assure employers' compliance with minimum wage laws, social insurance legislation, occupational safety and health regulations, tax codes, and mandated fair labor standards. This enforcement strategy has two advantages for the receiving society: it lowers the demand for immigrant workers by preventing employers from using them to avoid expensive labor regulations, and it prevents the formation of an underground, clandestine economy that puts downward pressure on the economic and social well-being of natives and immigrants alike.

Finally, since much international migration is brought about by the displacement of people from traditional livelihoods and an absence of well-developed markets for insurance, capital, and consumer credit, an indispensable part of any enlightened immigration policy should be the creation of binational programs to enhance markets and promote economic growth and development in sending regions. Some of the initiatives already proposed to encourage return migration simultaneously achieve these goals: namely, the creation of social insurance programs and development banks accessible to former migrants. Funds for these enterprises might be raised through a special tax levied on migrant workers and their employers. Developed nations might also work more broadly to finance development programs and promote balanced economic growth within the nation as a whole.

FUTURE RESEARCH NEEDS

The globalization of capital and labor markets and the internationalization of production pose strong challenges to the very concept of the nation-state and the idea of national sovereignty itself, requiring people to move beyond nineteenth-century conceptions of territory and citizenship and to expand them to embrace the transnational spaces that are currently being formed around the world through massive immigration. These changes are especially daunting because they will occur at a time when the forces of globalization are also producing downward pressure on wages and incomes in developed nations. Because immigrants and immigration policies will necessarily be discussed in a very heated and politicized environment, social scientists have special responsibilities to policymakers and the public.

First, they must establish the basic facts about immigrants and immigration. Among the three fundamental fields of demography—fertility, mortality, and migration—the latter remains the least well-developed methodologically. Unlike birth or death, mobility is more of a social than a biological event. The definition of a move requires fixing a line and agreeing that it has been crossed; but *where* that line is drawn geographically and administratively is very much a social and political construction. Although international migration, by definition, involves crossing a national boundary, the simple act of boundary-crossing does not necessarily mean that immigration has occurred, for it depends on who is doing the crossing and what their intentions are.

Consider, for example, two men of the same age from the same town in Poland who cross the border into Germany. Both speak Polish exclusively and neither has ever before been abroad; yet if one person has a grandparent born in Germany, he will be classified by state authorities as a returning German while the other will be considered a foreigner and possibly an immigrant. He is only "possibly" an immigrant, because it also depends on the purpose of the border-crossing. If it is to visit relatives for a short time and return, the state classifies him as a tourist. If his purpose is to reunite with a German bride and settle in Germany, he will be a legal immigrant. If he tells authorities he is just visiting but then violates his tourist visa by taking a construction job in Berlin, he will be considered by the state to be an undocumented, illegal, or unauthorized migrant. The conceptual problems multiply when one considers that intentions may change over time: the "returning" German may discover he dislikes Germany and goes home; the sincere tourist may encounter an unexpected job opportunity and decide to stay; or the undocumented migrant may marry a German woman and legalize to appear suddenly as an "immigrant."

Obviously, where and how a state's politicians and bureaucrats choose to draw geographic, political, and administrative boundaries determines the number of immigrants and their characteristics. Although demographers have developed objective criteria to define international migrants (see Zlotnik 1987), no country has adopted them and wide variations exist between countries in the way that migration statistics are tallied and reported. Under these circumstances, the responsibility of researchers is threefold: first, to pressure national statistical offices and census bureaus to adopt scientific standards for collecting and tabulating data on international migration; second, to disentangle the government statistics that *are* reported to reveal the objective numbers and characteristics of international migrants as well as their patterns and processes of assimilation; and third, to go beyond official statistics to develop independent and more detailed sources of data on international population movements.

In addition to establishing the facts about immigration, researchers should test the various theoretical explanations comparatively across nations and migratory systems to determine which theoretical explanations prevail under what circumstances and why. Although we concluded (in Massey et al. 1998) that alternative theoretical explanations were mostly complementary rather than competing, we were not able to state with any precision which theories were most important empirically in accounting for variations in the number, rate, and characteristics of immigrants over time and whether and why different theories may account more or less well for immigration patterns in different times and places. Relatively little research has been done to compare the strength of effects hypothesized under various theories, and what little has been done is confined to the North American system, and within that system, mainly to the case of Mexico-U.S. migration. More research needs to be done on immigration in different countries and systems, and more of it needs to compare alternative hypotheses directly within the same statistical analysis.

Finally, researchers not only have an obligation to establish the fundamental facts of international migration and to explain them theoretically, they must also communicate their findings to state officials and the public in ways that are simple and nontechnical yet accurate and intuitively sensible. International migration and the interethnic relations it produces will be among the most important and potentially divisive topics of public debate in the next century, but all too often social scientists confine their writing to professional journals and their speaking to scholarly conferences. As a result, public discussions of immigrants and immigration policy have been dominated by myths, misinformation, and, at times, outright lies that are grounded in ideology rather than scientific understanding. It is the responsibility of social scientists not only to generate knowledge about immigration, but to make sure that it finds its way into the public arena where it can accurately inform debate, and hopefully, yield more enlightened and efficacious policies to regulate the entry and integration of immigrants.

The advent of worldwide international migration in the late twentieth century offers many formidable challenges to scholars and policymakers. Perhaps the most profound of all will be faced by citizens in migrant-receiving countries, who will have to move beyond the state of denial that so often has characterized their immigration policies to date. They must develop an approach that recognizes the inevitability of labor flows within a globalized economy characterized by well-established regional networks of trade, production, investment, and communications. Attempts to suppress population flows that are a natural consequence of a nation's insertion into these economic networks will not be successful, but they will present grave threats to individual rights, civil liberties, and human dignity.

These are formidable challenges indeed, but they will have to be met, for international migration will surely continue. Barring an international catastrophe of unprecedented proportions, immigration will most likely expand and grow, for none of the causal forces responsible for immigration show any sign of moderating. The market economy is expanding to ever farther reaches of the globe, labor markets in developed countries are growing more segmented, transnational migration and trade networks are expanding, and the power of the nation state is faltering in the face of this transnational onslaught. The twenty-first century is shaping up to be one of globalism, and international migration undoubtedly will figure prominently within it.

2. Ports of Entry in the "Homeland Security" Era

Inequality of Mobility and the Securitization of Transnational Flows

Josiah McC. Heyman

Ports of entry are those places, such as airports, sea ports, and land border crossings, where people, goods, and conveyances are inspected for legal admission into a nation. Although uninspected entry away from ports garners the most attention (e.g., jumping a fence or wading across a river) and is what people often associate with the word "borders," the volume of people and commodities that patiently wait to cross through ports is several hundred times greater. According to conventional thought about national security and law enforcement, ports of entry are crucial places in the effort to keep dangerous things and unauthorized people out of the territory of the nation, and thus to protect its people. Ports thus offer sites for anthropologists and other social and behavioral researchers to examine the practice and limitations of such conventional assumptions.

The killings on 9/11 and sense of terror in the United States that followed gave considerable impetus to the "securitization" of the border, a development that was already well under way. Securitization takes major public issues from the ordinary world of political debate and shifts them to a framework of fundamental threats to the continued existence of the very government and people themselves. In other words, securitization treats issues such as immigration or drug trafficking as if they were equivalent to mass terrorism or nuclear war (Wæver 1995; Buzan, Wæver, and de Wilde 1998). The word *securitization* is not a simple noun (like *security*) but a process word that draws attention to the ways in which issues are raised to the highest perceived level of threat and response; it indicates that issues are not just handled in a strictly objective fashion (Huysmans 1995). As a concept, then, securitization points out how terrorist violence against domestic civilians has been merged with narcotics smuggling and undocumented migration in border policy.

Securitization strengthens the central government (Wæver 1995), adding to its manpower, technologies of detection and force, and its impunity from public scrutiny and control; when we securitize a place or issue, we put it on a war footing. This has been happening at the U.S.-Mexico border over the last two decades. Timothy Dunn (1996) meticulously documented the militarization of the border during the 1980s and 1990s, largely due to drug interdiction efforts, and this trend has strengthened with the fear of terrorists and weapons of mass destruction entering from outside the nation. Concentration of police effort and media attention to perilous borders distracts public debate and policy initiatives away from the U.S. interior and the rest of the world, even though migration, drug use and production, and transnational violence come from and go to places well beyond the boundary region itself and involve domestic as much as international causes. Borders powerfully symbolize threats, since they enclose the imagined national community and distinguish the inside from the outside, that which belongs from that which doesn't (Douglas 1966: 114–28, as exemplified in Chavez's chapter in this volume). Such cultural processes account for the disproportionate emphasis (in law enforcement terms) on border control over other kinds of prevention and control in U.S. policy (Heyman 1999a, Nevins 2001). Since the securitization of boundaries is not just a simple and objective policy (which is not to say that it is never justified), it is important to observe exactly how it is taking place at the border and what this tells us about the workings of government power and consequences for human rights in this crucial era.

This chapter covers the process of securitization in ways generally applicable to all types of ports, but it focuses especially on U.S. ports of entry at the Mexican border, my research concentration. Its time frame is the period since 9/11, and the particular concern is with the emergence of new security practices and ideas in this period, which falls into the most recent phase of the growth of integrated cross-border production and trade under the North American Free Trade Agreement (NAFTA). This is also the period after two large federal police agencies at ports, Customs and Immigration and Naturalization (INS), plus some smaller agencies, were merged into the Bureau of Customs and Border Protection (BCBP) within the Department of Homeland Security. I have observed Mexican border ports for several decades during research and residence in this region, and conducted systematic fieldwork on U.S. ports during 1991–1992 as part of an ethnography of INS officers and U.S. state power (see Heyman 1995, 1998, 2000, 2001, 2002). Since 2003 I have been part of a collaborative project to model the everyday border crossing system, with an eye to predicting and reducing harm from human and naturally caused disasters at ports (from earthquakes to hazardous chemical spills to acts of terrorism). I have also been part of a public policy initiative, the Border and Immigration Task Force, that has consulted a wide range of social sectors and developed human-rights-oriented policy recommendations, including for ports of entry. Thus, I have a baseline for tracing continuities and changes in ports and their relations to wider border society.

THE CONTEXT OF PORT OPERATIONS
AND THE NEED FOR ETHNOGRAPHY

Ports exemplify Massey's point (in chapter 1) about the close relationship of migration and globalization, and the political contradictions that follow between the forces of openness and restriction. This contradiction is particularly acute at ports, which simultaneously facilitate the movement of legal trade, tourism, and migration, and interdict the movement of restricted or prohibited people and goods. Speed in checking people, vehicles, and cargo ("inspections") is essential; border traffic simulations suggest that even short delays in inspecting and moving traffic through land ports rapidly result in long wait-times and urban disruption on both sides of the boundary. A tight policy at ports might result in a few more arrests, but it would tie up traffic interminably and cause howls of protest. A loose operation would reduce delays, but would weaken the port's screening function.

This is not merely a technical problem of working out the best balance, for there is a powerful but contradictory political scenario surrounding port operations. On the one side are those who want rapid movement through ports, which implies reduced or selective inspections: these include industrial and commercial shippers, border city retailers (who seek shoppers from the other nation), and transportation operators (especially international airlines at airports). Legal and illegal employers of border-crossing workers (such as maids at the U.S.-Mexico border) also quietly promote lax border enforcement.

On the other side, there are substantial budgetary and status rewards inside the government bureaucracy for being aggressive in certain operations, such as detecting large drug shipments. Recent developments have heightened the political pressures on port management and promoted the search for new systems of detection and documentation. NAFTA, for example, caused a doubling of U.S.-Canada commercial traffic and tripling of U.S.-Mexico commercial traffic (Hufbauer and Vega-Cánovas 2003: 130), and thus strengthened the constituencies for fast border crossing. Since

9/11, however, concerns about terrorism have greatly strengthened the political impetus for slow, careful border inspections. Indeed, a number of policy advocates and scholars (Andreas and Biersteker 2003, Flynn 2002, Meyers 2003) argue that ports are central to the emerging system of police and intelligence-controlled globalization.

To make things even more challenging for ports, it is by no means obvious who is violating a law or regulation. Unlike people in open desert who are clearly trying to avoid the law, at ports the vast majority of crossers are completely legitimate. In this context, inspections involve interesting rules of thumb for asking questions and pulling aside people. Such rules of thumb, and their extension into formal risk prediction, intelligence use, and detection technology, are essential in the balancing act of ports. They allow a certain degree of efficiency and also create a degree of social bias in deciding that some entrants are trustworthy insiders, not worth even minimal efforts at physical scrutiny and questioning (average inspection times I have collected for low-scrutiny vehicular entrants are twenty-two seconds), while others are singled out for minutes, sometimes hours of questioning. Classifying, labeling, and decision-making (see Heyman 2001, 2004) are thus fundamental to the functioning of ports. Identifying and analyzing such processes are among the greatest strengths of ethnography. Furthermore, hidden within seemingly small rules of thumb are the major issues of public policy and social power at borders (Heyman 1995): who is acknowledged, who is stigmatized, and indeed who is the target of securitization.

THE INSPECTION PROCESS

Ports of entry, whether land, sea, or air, have two main stages of inspection, primary and secondary. There are other functions, such as detention and interrogation, that occur after these stages, and pre-inspection in the country of origin adds further complexity (Alvarez 2001).

Primary is the first encounter of the entering person or vehicle with the inspector. The key decision at this stage is whether to allow the entrant to proceed without further checking or divert the entrant to secondary for additional inspection. Primary inspection involves a tremendously complex set of information gathering and evaluations, compressed into a very short period of time. Primary inspection is the main bottleneck in the flow of traffic through ports, and is thus highly politicized inside and outside the Department of Homeland Security. In thirty-three seconds (the observed average length of noncommercial vehicular primary inspection at the Santa

Fe bridge, El Paso, Texas), the inspecting officer examines and enters document and license plate numbers, checks chemical and radioactivity detec-
tors, reads intelligence from a computer terminal, visually surveys the
vehicle for hidden compartments, ascertains the citizenship and immigration status of the driver and passengers, listens to the entrants' declarations
and stories about their destination and purpose of travel, and "reads" their
body language and tone of voice for lies and anxiety.

The possible legal grounds for referral to secondary inspection are
many, including goods, weapons, immigration, alcohol and drugs, and
prohibited agricultural goods. If there are serious questions, the inspector directs entrants into secondary inspection, but the challenge is often
whether something slightly "off" about the entrant is sufficient grounds
for making this judgment. People sometimes complain to port management, Congressional representatives, or consulates when they are sent to
secondary inspection, both because of the time delay and the implication
of possible wrongdoing, so there is a political cost to taking this step.

Secondary inspection allows for more extended physical inspection
(including application of technology), documentary or database checks,
and questioning. Even in secondary inspection, time is constrained, since
it requires multiple officers and working space for examining cargos and
vehicles. To take a long (but common and relevant) example, it can take a
team of four officers up to three hours to thoroughly inspect a single tractor-
trailer container truck. At secondary inspection, evidence may be gathered
for seizure of goods and vehicles, exclusion of people from the country, and
the approval or removal of travel documents. Judgments about people and
goods are particularly crucial at this stage.

Such judgments come from four main mixtures of evidence and infer-
ential reasoning on the part of inspectors (see longer discussions in Heyman 2001, 2004). First, there is the behavior of the entrant that may betray
nerves and also may demonstrate either confidence (or defiance) or humility
(or respect). This is a real but non-obvious source of evidence and involves
considerable social-psychological stereotyping and interpretation. Second,
there are social cues, connected to ideas about kinds of people and why
they cross borders. These include ideas about nationalities or apparent races
(e.g., a Mexican person might be suspected of commuting to work without
authorization, a Saudi might be a focus of national security questioning,
and a white U.S. national treated lightly) and about social class (e.g., a person with credit cards is treated in general as a legitimate tourist versus
one without, who is treated as a potential undocumented worker). Third,
inspectors listen to the "stories" given by entrants and construct their own

hypothetical narratives, which may support or diverge from these narratives of origin, destination, purpose, and so on, in ways that enable the government officer to decide what formal legal classifications and actions to apply and how. (Obviously, the stories are filled with the sorts of social and behavioral observations and inferences listed just above.) Finally, documents are crucial in coming to decisions about admission or refusal, prosecution or nonprosecution, but documents often are not simple and do not "speak" for themselves. A perfectly correct border crossing card or tourist visa may be seen as evidence of illegal labor or terrorist intent through an interpretation of the surrounding context. It is through such complex patterns of evidence, reasoning, and judgment that securitization enters the border crossing scene.

Airport inspections of 9/11 hijackers offer an example of the micropolitics of security judgments. INS Inspector Jose E. Melendez-Perez (without accent marks in the original) turned away Mohamed al Kahtani, the putative twentieth 9/11 hijacker, at the Orlando, Florida, International Airport. Melendez-Perez did this in secondary because al Kahtani (who had a tourist visa) had a one-way ticket, did not know who would meet him, had little idea about where he was going in the United States, and because of his strong, assertive demeanor (the inspector was concerned that he was trained as a "hit man"). It is worth noting that the documents carried by al Kahtani seemed legitimate (though incompletely filled out) and the computer databases signaled no problems. Rather, as Melendez-Perez testified, the entrant's story "did not seem plausible," so the inspector created a counter-interpretation (entrant as "hit man"). (The interpretative work of inspection is also demonstrated in Melendez-Perez's comments on his feel for the situation, what inspectors often call a sixth sense: "when the subject looked at me, I felt a bone chilling cold effect. The bottom line is, 'He gave me the creeps.' You just had to be present to understand what I am trying to explain" [National Commission on Terrorist Attacks upon the United States 2004a].)

This interpretation was also politically sensitive. Melendez-Perez presented the case for returning al Kahtani on the next plane to his supervisor, who called the Assistant Area Port Director (an upper manager) at home, who then grilled Melendez-Perez on the phone, but ultimately did support him. Although in this case the would-be entrant was turned away, the inspector testified that in general there were palpable pressures in the organization not to deny entrance to Saudis (National Commission on Terrorist Attacks upon the United States 2004a). The cases of the nineteen hijackers who did gain entrance to the U.S. are complicated (see National

Commission on Terrorist Attacks upon the United States 2004b) but some involve similar entrants with stories and documents that did successfully pass through U.S. consulates overseas and/or ports of entry. Of course, inspectors' approaches to young men from Saudi Arabia and other Islamic nations have changed since 9/11, from permissive to restrictive. Either way, interviewing an entrant at the port of entry involves the inspector in a complex interpretation, subject to political influences.

THE TURN TOWARD TECHNOLOGY IN INSPECTIONS

The United States relied and continues to rely heavily on direct personal inspection of entrants by consular officials (for visas) and inspectors (at ports of entry). This approach has come under criticism and has undergone modification, especially in the post-9/11 period. There is concern about its being unsystematic and incompletely effective, especially against sophisticated threats. There is also concern that substantial direct inspections of all entering people and conveyances will create enormous delays, which is particularly troublesome in a period of increasing cross-border commerce and travel (Flynn 2000, 2002, 2003). In other words, the basic dilemma of ports—to be both enforcer and facilitator—again comes into play. The responses to these concerns include expansion of detection technology, intelligence, identification and documentation, profiling and risk labeling, and pre-inspection/certification systems that geographically extend control systems beyond international boundaries.

In 2001, the United States and Canada created a "smart border" agreement, and a similar (but not identical) agreement with Mexico followed in early 2002. These agreements include preclearance of shippers and vehicles, sharing of intelligence, and compatible immigration databases, among other components (Meyers 2003, Andreas 2003, Clarkson 2003). A "smart" border implies in its language a more secure border, a more effective border. It suggests the application of advanced detection technologies and sophisticated intelligence, documentation, and surveillance and tracking methods (Ackelson 2003a). The term "smart border" sounds impressive, but we should not assume that this image matches reality. Many technologies are speculative, have limited implementation, or provide information that is only part of the total inspections decision-making process (Ackleson 2003a, 2003b). In addition—and here is an important strength of the ethnographic approach, as Martínez emphasizes in the introduction to this volume—we need to assess the effects of new security systems on people, as individuals and members of particular social groups.

Watch lists have long been used to identify and interdict border crossers but had significant limitations in the past, including difficulty of access—in some cases still being on paper—and the failure to merge the intelligence agencies' lists with the list of the Immigration Service at ports (National Commission on Terrorist Attacks upon the United States 2004c). The trend toward the securitization of border crossings has had two broad effects in this field. The first is the application of network-accessible computer databases and unification of various databases. This means that ports will be on the lookout (in a much more comprehensive way) for people highlighted by the key intelligence agencies of the U.S. state, including the CIA, DIA, FBI, and DEA. (Not all agencies share their watch lists, however.) It is also the case that inspectors will have access to a wider variety of information about entrants, such as multiple entries and exits, via various specific ports, visa and passport records, and even (through linkage to other databases) domestic and international criminal records, arrests as well as convictions.

Also, the sophistication of documentation is improving. Physical passports and visas are becoming more difficult to alter or counterfeit. For example, paper border crossing cards (short term, distance visiting and shopping visas issued to many Mexicans at the southern border) have been converted into "laser visas," with more secure features and a computer readable data strip. Such data strips have the capacity to be encoded with significant amounts of information, including so-called biometric identifiers, such as computer-readable fingerprints. However, implementation and usage of formal systems of document inspection (including database look-ups) is highly inconsistent at land border ports of entry (U.S. Government Accountability Office 2007). For example, cards are often looked at by inspectors but not swiped or otherwise registered.

Even if all documents were to be automated (e.g., by swipe card readers for laser visas), the human element of interpretation, and thus the social frameworks imposed by inspectors, could not be eliminated entirely. For example, a crosser may carry a "laser visa," an apparently automated entrance document described just above, but a border inspector at her discretion may detain and question the entrant on the suspicion of either residing or working off the books in the United States, and even return her to Mexico stripped of the document, based entirely on the sorts of fuzzy but powerful judgments discussed earlier in this chapter, without regard to the formalized system of entry control. The Homeland Security "entry-exit" program, which requires nonimmigrant visitors to the United States to register electronically upon entry and exit, has only been applied at entry and has been abandoned for exit at land borders because it is "unimplementable" under

policies that favor outbound transnational flows. Even reliable documentation does not solve the inspectors' decision about whether or not to question
the border crosser's purpose in entering the nation, and what they might
be carrying. Finally, intelligence itself is humanly created and imperfect. It
will inevitably miss potentially dangerous individuals and target innocent
individuals for investigation, along patterns reflecting the social prejudices
of the data collecting and evaluating officers.

The need to trade off the detection of the unlawful against clearing traffic rapidly favors simple rules of thumb for deciding on whom to devote
further time in reviewing documents and reading records, watch lists, and
other intelligence on databases (it is worth mentioning that standards of
search and seizure, such as reasonable suspicion and probable cause, do not
apply at ports). No amount of automation matters when inspectors make
a snap decision to bypass a computerized record check and admit someone
to the country rapidly to maintain the flow of traffic. Racial, class, gender,
and other social profiling is important in these sorts of snap investigatory
decisions, as observed by and attested to me by many inspectors at U.S.-
Mexico border ports in my 1992 research. People who appear to be clean
cut white (or "Anglo") Americans are given less scrutiny than Mexican-
appearing people, of any nationality, and scruffier or poorer males of all
backgrounds. These easy, if prejudicial and imprecise, devices sort out business commuters and tourists from possible out-of-status (illegal) workers
or drug users and carriers. It is important to emphasize that profiling is
used in conjunction with other inspectorial clues, such as nerves, vehicle
characteristics, or implausible stories. The volume of Mexican-appearing
people of all legal statuses crossing at any busy southern border port is so
overwhelming that perceived race cannot, without other clues, constitute a
practical rule for initiating time-consuming questioning, but importantly
Anglo-appearance so effectively characterizes normative U.S. citizenship
that it does often function as a "free pass" into the United States. These
practices are a high-volume, border version of the prejudicial policing
described in Naples's chapter in this volume.

The securitization of border crossing has given rise to new systems of
computer simulation-based categorical risk assessment and labeling. It has
not been revealed to the public what risk assessment categories are encoded
in new documents and databases. Risk assessment may involve national
security, but it may also involve issues such as immigration violations,
drug carrying, and monetary transactions. One can assume that travelers
from specific nations are still given higher risk labels for certain issues and
are subject to closer examinations; as a result of this, computerized simula-

tions still hinge on national (and consequently, to some extent, racial) pro-filing. In documentary and intelligence systems, then, we see an increasingly powerful effort by and capacity of the U.S. state to identify and track individuals across spaces of governance, and within transnational flows (on the broad history of this issue, see Torpey 2000; Caplan and Torpey 2001).

At the same time, this trend does not just indicate an undifferentiated Big Brother watching each and every individual in the same way. Instead, trends toward the securitization of domestic, border-crossing, and international issues are likely to be expressed in the specific selection of information and types of people particularly subject to documentary and investigatory surveillance. This may involve national security, but it may also involve issues such as immigration violations, drug carrying, and monetary transactions, as we will see later. Detection technologies, while strengthening the surveillance capabilities of the U.S. state, will not constitute an objective and seamless mechanism of interdiction of "bad people and things," but rather part of the process of securitization already in place and evolving at ports, for example, asking questions such as who or what is selected for special detection technologies. Risk "assessment," in spite of its neutral-sounding name, *imposes* risk (of being delayed or even being indefinitely caught in the U.S. immigration legal system) disproportionately upon the nationals of select groups of countries. It is an inequality-making practice, with historical roots discussed in Salyer's and Akram and Johnson's chapters in this volume and contemporary manifestations delineated in Dole's chapter. This is an emerging situation, about which little information has been made public. From a human rights perspective, close and continuous vigilance is warranted toward the use of new screening technology in practice, starting with the question, Who or what is being selected for special scrutiny?

For many years, border inspectors have unofficially, but pervasively, categorized certain types of people and shipments as "low" or "high risk." What is emerging now is an extension of these informal practices into formal policy under the pressure of securitization. Broadly, this involves designating certain shippers and vehicles/drivers as low risk, low scrutiny, and able to transit inspections rapidly. On the Canadian-U.S. border, there is the NEXUS for pre-clearing border commuters and FAST for pre-clearing commercial and industrial shippers, while on the Mexican border, there is the SENTRI program with Dedicated Commuter Lanes (DCL) for passenger vehicles and, again, the FAST programs for commercial shippers. We know little beyond the formal policy, although this is a subject on which I am now working. Individuals require a background check and a significant annual fee (e.g., $400 for the DCL lanes in El Paso), which favors businesspeople from the binational trade and manufacturing communities and wealthy families, while commercial shippers require a well-documented system of control over cargoes from origin to destination, as well as a background check, which favors large transnational corporations (e.g., the maquiladora sector). By designating certain crossers as low risk and low inspection, and others as higher risk and normal to higher inspection, these policies establish a pattern of unequal treatment and differential chance of legal penalty at the border, even conceding the likelihood that most judgments involved are reasonable.

THE AIMS OF SECURITIZATION

I have said fairly little thus far about the concerns of border securitization—does it focus on migration, drugs, politics, arms? To explore this question, we need to examine the various priorities of the U.S. state and their expression in specific agencies and political stances inside the government. In the aftermath of 9/11, a variety of emergency planning and travel-regulatory law enforcement entities were merged into the Department of Homeland Security, the second largest unit of the central state after the military. On the borders, this involved combining U.S. Customs and the Immigration and Naturalization Service (INS), along with a variety of smaller entities involved in cross-border control of particular substances (e.g., radioactive materials, agricultural goods). There had long been interest in joining these entities to centralize and strengthen border management, but the specific impetus to forcing bureaucracies to sacrifice their immediate identities and interests was the "security" framework. Customs, for example, started out as a revenue collecting and trade regulating organization in the Treasury Department but grew into a law enforcement agency because of the so-called war on drugs. The INS dealt with immigration, though its Border Patrol division was also drawn into the effort to interdict drug smuggling. Their merger in Homeland Security tells us that movement across borders is a crucial moment in securitization, worthy of special organizational focus, and that the other duties of these agencies (which do not disappear in the least) now exist within the framework and priorities of a central security state.

We are thus compelled to explore how these agencies are coming together, and what policies in practice are emerging. Interestingly, inspectors working at primary have long crossed organizational boundaries between immigration and customs, being responsible at land ports for inquiring into both domains (at airports, primary is divided into sequential steps). Thus, the merger of Immigration and Customs just furthers existing practice. After primary, inspectors may refer entrants to specialists in particular legal issues, be they former immigration or customs or agricultural officers, thus also continuing past practice, more or less. But what does it mean that the merger was into Homeland Security? And what of the officers' experience of being forged into a new, single managerial hierarchy, where there had once been independent agencies?

Before the merger, Customs was stronger than the Inspections branch of the INS—better funded, more professional, and with a significantly larger workforce, even when the official staffing at ports was supposed to be even. Preliminary fieldwork suggests that former Customs dominates the new Border and Customs Protection branch of Homeland Security (this leaves aside the INS's former Border Patrol, which retains a certain autonomy in the field [it does not operate at ports], though it is under the jurisdiction of former Customs officials in Washington, DC). In the port of El Paso, for example, the upper leadership is all from Customs, on the entering passenger/private vehicle side as well as the commercial vehicle side.

Interdiction of smuggled drugs is both a cause and a probable consequence of Customs' predominance in Customs and Border Protection. The "drug war" is better funded than immigration control, receiving the lion's share of military and quasi-military investments in border control (e.g., Customs allegedly has the fourth largest air force in the world). Drug seizures provide agencies significant incentives in terms of asset forfeiture. Officers in both former Customs and INS get more personal satisfaction and group glory from drug busts than immigration violations. The latter involve moral ambivalence about punishing working people and family groups that is less often felt about drug arrests; likewise, immigration involves many small infractions of little note while substantial quantities of drugs are detected just often enough to be an attainable goal, although rarely enough to be noteworthy. Tacitly hinting that the antidrug agenda will continue to dominate the priorities and practices in the formative Bureau of Customs and Border Protection (BCBP), El Paso Port Director David Longoria told a city business group in 2004 that he sees immigration charges as a tool to strengthen drug seizures (e.g., exclusion proceedings against drivers and passengers), this being his only mention of immigration and the main point he made about the merger of the two agencies.[1]

The interaction of the antidrug and national security agendas is more difficult to predict. The post-9/11 agenda, as embodied in the creation of the Department of Homeland Security and the subordination of Customs (partly drugs) and INS (immigration) suggests that national security will dominate. The formal statements of every officer with whom I have talked at ports in the last year place national security (prevention of terrorism) as their absolute priority, trumping all other concerns. However, national security interdiction events at borders are likely to be extremely rare events, which most inspectors will never encounter in their careers and ports but must treat as an ever-present but only hypothetical possibility.[2] Large drug busts seem more likely to influence everyday practice than national security events, because they occur often enough for officers to learn from them and also to be rewarded for them. Officers discuss drug interdiction in more concrete and practical ways than they talk about national security, though one must acknowledge the limits on what they can describe to outside researchers. More likely to happen, particularly at land border ports, is that drug and human smuggling will be redefined as key national security threats, that is, they will become "securitized." For example, computerized watch lists are not only used to identify terrorists but vastly much more frequently to interdict people wanted in drug law enforcement and for other legal violations.[3]

There are important connections between national security agendas and the enforcement of immigration laws. After 9/11, immigration laws were the main way that men from Islamic countries were questioned and in many cases held indefinitely or deported (Chisti et al. 2003, and see Dole in the present volume). Anecdotal but probably accurate reports from Mexican border ports indicate that inspectors pull aside and question South Asians and Middle Easterners, often for extended periods of time. At the same time, many immigration violations are not securitized and have no particular emphasis put on them. At best, people are caught because of unsystematic efforts of individual inspectors (for example, noticing nervous entrants). The lack of systematicity is illustrated by the lack of effort to check Ciudad Juárez residents using border visiting/shopper cards ("laser visas") to work without authorization in El Paso. Port authorities insist that this violation *is* systematically policed, but my observation of casual and domestic labor markets in El Paso at this time, combined with a past study (Gilboy 1992), indicate that there is little political will to crack down on extralegal commuter workers at this major border crossing. Gardeners and maids are not a "security" threat, but, whatever their legal status at work, this example demonstrates the limits of border securitization in practice.

In summary, the merger of Customs, Immigration, Agricultural Inspection, and so on, into the Bureau of Customs and Border Protection provides an already existing set of bureaucratic interests and actors with a new and compelling call on the material and ideological resources of the central government (recall, this is what is at the heart of securitization). This is on top of the long build-up in border policing throughout the 1980s and 1990s (see Dunn 1996, Heyman 1999b, Andreas 2000, Nevins 2001, Palafox 2001). The centralization and strengthening of BCBP has the potential to carry with it not only the national security agenda per se but also internal organizational agendas, most likely drug interdiction, and to blur the boundaries between those two phenomena.

This chapter has examined two processes, the securitization of issues and of people, that interconnect in significant ways. The 9/11 attacks raised border control, including ports, to the level of a national security issue. In response, greater scrutiny is being directed at people with the specific potential for acts of terrorism and, more diffusely, with political associations and agendas connected (through computerized watch lists) with the global geopolitical conflicts between the United States and so-called Islamists. Through risk assessment programs, broad social groups (such as men from predominantly Islamic nations) are likely to be targeted for heightened scrutiny when passing through ports. In addition, the securitization of border crossing appears to reinforce drug interdiction. This in turn would widen the range of people subject to added scrutiny at ports to include many U.S. residents and Latin American and Caribbean visitors. In other words, using ports to control specific movements, such as weapons, explosives, or biological agents, or of people with specifically terroristic intentions, is likely to widen from specific counter terrorist measures into the labeling of large groups of people. In addition, an important strategy for ports, to balance growing trade, business, and tourism with the imperatives of national security, is creating unequal paths through inspection, pre-clearing some entrants as low-risk crossers and designating others for more intensive surveillance, again a form of labeling. Labeling of people (as individuals and social groups) is significant because, under the conditions of securitization, it demands attention from inspectors, brings on the use of computer checks and advanced identification technology, and develops more critical premises of interpretation. In other words, securitization alters both the means and the characteristics of surveillance of people when in movement.

Surveillance at all levels promises safety, survival, security—sealing off the domestic civilian population against the most profound fear, that of inexplicable threat. This hope is embodied variously in new detection technologies, modes of documentation and information control, and organization reforms now being deployed at ports. Of course, as this chapter has shown, these surveillance systems are incompletely implemented and often depend on human judgment and traditional border inspection skills. One might assume that as these surveillance systems become more complete and well implemented, they will form an increasingly effective deterrent and preventative force toward external threats (this, of course, assumes that such threats are in fact external and come across borders).

However, a previous study of border databases used in drug interdiction and immigration violations (specifically, to identify past and potential present drug and money couriers and to apply severely punitive aspects of U.S. immigration and entry laws toward them) showed that such efforts have more paradoxical results (Heyman 1999c). They identify and lastingly stigmatize a growing number of individuals, while the underlying social processes (whether push and pull forces in migration, the demand for drugs, or international political conflicts) continue to generate new candidates for crossing U.S. borders, as Massey shows for the case of migration. Instead of solving the problem, one develops polarization between a state with increasing legal and technological capacities for identification and surveillance and a populace with increasing numbers of stigmatized, potential "opponents" of that state. While this outcome remains highly uncertain in the current situation, it is clear that monolithic models of surveillance in the contemporary world (pro and con) need to be approached with a greater attention to practice and process at actual ports.

In turn, the entire set of topics (the securitization of issues and people, the labeling of border crossers, and the growth of surveillance techniques and organizations) suggests that what we are today witnessing is an aspiration toward a thoroughly controlled yet increasingly mobile world. In this world, some people are designated as low risk and free to move within inspection systems (especially identification systems and linked databases) and others are designated as high risk and subject to interdiction whenever crossing designated points like border ports. One might term this "global apartheid," connoting a world in which the privileged travel freely and benefit from the labors of the world's masses, but live in walled-off spaces, carefully protected from the unauthorized incursions of the poor. Whether or not one finds this term accurate, what is at stake are inequalities of power created through differentiated mobility (Heyman 2004). Securitization is as much about maintaining flows of people—businessmen, tourists, rich shoppers, even extralegal maids and gardeners—and of commodities, while attempting to secure the existential separation of the "safe" from the "threatening"—in other words, categorizing and separating types of flows from each other, and subjecting them to vastly different laws and police powers.

In the national security ideal, such a system would effectively maintain the boundaries between the different labeled movements, and would apply just the level of inspection and punishment appropriate to each risk level. The goal of perfectly controlled mobility will likely never be achieved, for reasons explored above, leaving us the negative repercussions of securitization, without all its promised benefits. Instead, the securitization of ports is tending toward a pattern of incomplete but powerful policing, resulting in a highly unequal but also somewhat unpredictable pattern of risk, differing according to national origin, class, political connection and affiliation, and so forth (similar patterns of complex and unequal policing within the U.S. interior are discussed in Naples's and Dole's chapters in this volume). The securitization of ports of entry, then, is a particular view of the world and response to it, demanding domestic unity, raising anxiety, and strengthening central power, yet (following Martínez's analysis) missing the wellsprings of security, tranquility, and human decency that we all seek. In this, ports of entry may be a harbinger of a "securitized" (though perhaps, less secure) world to come.

PART II

Historical Perspectives

3. The Treatment of Noncitizens after September 11 in Historical Context

J. C. Salyer

In ruling on a challenge to the deportation of a number of individuals claimed to be threats to national security, a United States District Court judge in Boston ordered that the noncitizens be released because "the extraordinary circumstances under which these aliens were arrested and detained resulted in an illegal deprivation of their liberty." In the course of the trial it was revealed that individuals had been held incommunicado, without access to counsel, in exceedingly harsh conditions. In his ruling the judge strongly rebuked the Justice Department for its utter disregard for the rights of the individuals detained and for having detained them without proper legal authority.

One might think this court ruling was about the treatment of noncitizens after 9/11,[1] yet this particular trial, *Colyer v Skeffington*, 265 Fed. 17 (D. Mass. 1920), *reversed in part sub nom. Skeffington v Katzeff*, 277 Fed. 129 (1st Cir. 1922), took place in 1920. The court's ruling addressed the excessive and illegitimate uses of power that the executive branch engaged in during the infamous Palmer Raids, in which more than five hundred immigrants were detained and ultimately deported. The Red Scare and Palmer Raids were themselves a part of a much larger process of developing anti-immigrant sentiments in the United States that ultimately converged with fears over national security and culminated in the adoption of a very restrictive immigration quota system under the National Origins Act of 1924. Although the contemporary press attempted to minimize the actions of the Justice Department during the Palmer Raids—in 1924, the *Saturday Evening Post* dismissed them as "nothing but the last symptoms of war fever" (cited in Higham 1988: 233)—the excessively harsh and unfair treatment dealt to immigrants in the 1920s was more consistent with a growing anti-immigrant trend than it was an aberration. Among the factors that produced these new anti-immigrant policies were the interests of industry, conservative labor unions such as the American Federation of Labor, old-line nativist Americans, eugenicists, and the political allies of these groups.

In this chapter, I point to important continuities and changes in how the United States has treated its noncitizen residents in times of perceived threats to national security. Specifically, I compare the federal government's response to the events of September 11, 2001, with the Red Scare of the 1920s and the internment of Japanese Americans during the Second World War. My goal is not merely to observe that parallels exist between now and then but to draw links between the government's actions that followed September 11 and how the United States treated its noncitizens and descendants of immigrants in other periods. The U.S. government's targeting of selected immigrant groups, post-9/11, is not just similar to its persecution of aliens at earlier moments of crisis. It is in some ways directly the heir to the legislation, judicial precedents, and social trends of those earlier times. The questions thus become what explanations and insights can be gained by examining this historical relationship, and what these insights then tell us about the possible course of the future.

There are multiple reasons that individuals consider and reference historical events, such as defining why something in the present is the way it is and serving as precedent to guide actions into the future. It is quite common to present retrospective explanations of a given state of affairs as being the culmination of a teleological narrative that depicts a series of events as expressing the gradual fulfillment of a high moral purpose for the subjects of that history. In the case of the United States, one such narrative would depict the United States as a model to the world of a liberal democracy committed to the rights of individuals as illustrated by events such as the Declaration of Independence, the adoption of the Constitution and the Bill of Rights, the ending of slavery and enfranchisement of former slaves through the Emancipation Proclamation and the post–Civil War amendments to the Constitution, the granting of women's suffrage, the defeats of threats to democracy during the World Wars and in the Cold War, and the addressing of racial discrimination through the civil rights movement. This account claims to be the story of a highly idealistic society striving to realize its ideals of freedom, justice, and equality, at times falling short amid difficult circumstances, but gradually coming closer and closer to achieving moral perfection. Left out of this moral success story are those events that contradict its conclusion—those events that depict race prejudice, injustice, isolationism, and inequality. The result of excluding the countless inconveniently inconsistent events from this grand narrative is the creation of the assumption that they are insignificant transgressions and the promotion of the belief that the ends justify the means, particularly when the ends are themselves considered righteous and good.

An alternative view would consider the historical past in all of its contradictions rather than with the goal of charting an overall historical trajectory. It would consider conflicts and contradictions as opportunities to examine the status quo and correct past mistakes and reshape inherited structures as required. Under this alternative view, examining the nature of events where the national project of freedom, justice, and equality faltered is as vital as knowing the nation's great achievements and milestones on the path to greater liberty.

More specifically, I think it necessary to look unblinkingly at an essential contradiction in the American character and political discourse, regarding immigration. At one and the same time, the United States is both "a nation of immigrants" *and* harbors deep fears about the dangerousness of immigration. Running like a red thread through the last century of American history is the belief that those who choose to immigrate to the United States from elsewhere could in fact be internal enemies. America's immigration history thus contains, on the one hand, events that bespeak a tradition of welcoming those who seek refuge and the promises of a better life, and, on the other, expressions of hostility to immigration, such as obviously racist exclusionary laws, fundamentally unfair enforcement of immigration laws, and the repeated scapegoating of immigrants for a variety of problems.

The examination of the persecution of immigrants in the 1920s and the internment of Japanese-Americans during World War II provide important insights into how and why post-9/11 detentions and deportations occurred and suggest a continuing need for the United States to address and rectify long-standing contradictions between its worthy ideals and its conduct towards its most vulnerable and powerless political minorities. Perhaps the most appropriate starting point is the point when the "traditional" open attitude towards immigration was replaced by restrictive, discriminatory, and exclusionary immigration quota restriction laws.[2] These quota laws, first passed in 1921 and made more restrictive in 1924, have had a long-standing effect on United States immigration policy, as well as the racial and ethnic character of the country. Notwithstanding the significant reform to U.S. immigration policy in 1965, we are still dealing with the legacy of the immigration controls imposed in the 1920s. Perhaps even more significant is the effect the years of debate and the ultimate passage of the laws had in defining who was considered an American. Those in favor of restrictions gave preference to those seen as coming from Anglo-Saxon, Nordic, or Teutonic races; this debate over who would be defined as part of the "American race" made clear that others, including Asians, African Americans, and Jews were considered unequal and subject to different rules. Fear of certain immigrant groups and contempt for their rights can be seen as a driving force in many unfair actions directed at immigrants, from the Palmer Raids, to the Japanese internments, to the mass detentions and deportations that followed 9/11.

THE DEVELOPMENT OF ANTI-IMMIGRANT ATTITUDES AND POLICIES IN THE EARLY TWENTIETH CENTURY

Economic and Social Debates

In the early part of the twentieth century, the relationship of immigrants to the economic system was the principal issue of conflict for immigration policy. Both industrial capitalists and American labor unions had complicated and conflicting relationships with immigrant labor. According to the 1910 census, "immigrants constituted more than 36 per cent of the men engaged in the manufacturing industry and more than 45 per cent of those in mining" (Downey 1999: 272 n.4). The growth of American industry had only been possible because of the huge increase of immigrant labor. From 1820 until 1920, more than 35 million immigrants arrived, mostly from Europe (Calavita 1984: 1). While industry had benefited from immigrant labor and had often used immigrant labor to break strikes and undermine domestic labor movements, industry also feared that immigrant workers would be more radical and provide dangerous allies to the domestic labor movement. Thus, the fortunes of industrial capitalists were closely linked with exploiting the labor of arriving immigrants but also required that these immigrants be rendered docile and controllable.

American labor unions were essentially in the opposite situation. American workers had long argued that unchecked immigration drove wages down, provided industry with strikebreakers, and generally lowered the nation's standard of living. However, unions were, at least in principle, committed to the unity of the working class and did not want to alienate the third of the work force who were immigrants themselves. Labor's position on immigration at the turn of the twentieth century was therefore no clearer than that of industry. There had long been anti-immigrant segments within unions, and with the increase in immigrants from Eastern and Southern

Europe they steadily moved to an even more solidly anti-immigrant position. Even as much of the membership favored solidarity and believed that "the best trade unionists [are] the foreigners" (Calavita 1984: 111), the leadership of the more conservative unions, such as the American Federation of Labor, pushed an anti-immigrant position, in part to gain control over the political radicals within the unions. Samuel Gompers of the AFL argued that new immigrants "could not be taught to render the same intelligent service as was supplied by American workers" (ibid.).

By the turn of the twentieth century, the participation of immigrants from Eastern Europe in the growing number of bitter labor disputes was seen as evidence of their greater radicalism. The New York *Tribune* described striking miners from Eastern Europe as "Huns" and opined that they were "the most dangerous of labor-unionists and strikers. They fill up with liquor and cannot be reasoned with" (cited in Higham 1988: 89). Industry saw a clear benefit in blaming labor unrest on new immigrants from Eastern and Southern Europe who could be cast as more unreasonable and radical. For industry, the central dilemma was the contribution immigrants made as cheap labor versus the gains in labor control to be won by blaming immigrants for "the whole repertoire of capitalism's injustices and irrationalities" (Calavita 1984: 117). Ultimately, industry reconciled itself to supporting and perpetuating the anti-immigrant rhetoric of nativists and eugenicists as explanations for the country's ills while never supporting any actual legal restrictions on immigration.

The fine line that industry attempted to tread became quite clear in the early 1910s, as a number of circumstances came together to stir popular anti-immigrant sentiment and congressional action. First, foreign-born workers who had been shunned by the likes of the AFL came together with more radically socialist American-born workers in the Industrial Workers of the World (IWW, or the "Wobblies") and began to gain political strength—the presidential election of 1912 marked the highest percentage of votes garnered by a socialist candidate in U.S. history. As the IWW attempted to improve their lot through strikes and pickets, public opposition to their activity increased exponentially and blame for their activity was laid at the feet of the immigrant members of the movement. In 1912, the IWW mustered a textile mill strike in Lawrence, Massachusetts, involving 22,000 workers, and gained both wage increases and a forty-eight-hour work week. A New York newspaper warned, in response, "the first considerable development of an actually revolutionary spirit comes today, and comes . . . among the un-American immigrants from Southern Europe" (Higham 1988: 178). Similar activity among lumberjacks in

Washington state led to attacks on strikers by local armed citizens' groups led by Albert Johnson, a local newspaper editor. Energized by these confrontations, Johnson was elected to Congress in 1912 on an anti-Wobbly, anti-immigrant platform (Higham 1988: 178).

Perhaps as important, the findings of the Dillingham Commission on immigration came out in 1910 and 1911 in a forty-two-volume report. The commission was established by Congress in 1907 to conduct a comprehensive investigation regarding immigration and report facts and recommendations from which Congress could determine policy. The most fundamentally important aspect of the report was its division of immigrants into the categories of "old immigrants" and "new immigrants. The "old immigrants" were defined as having come from the "most progressive sections of Europe," such as the United Kingdom and Germany, and having assimilated quickly and diffused throughout the American social and geographic landscape. By contrast, the "new immigrants" came from the "less progressive and advanced countries of Europe" and monopolized the unskilled labor pool, lived in ethnic enclaves, and otherwise failed to assimilate (King 2000: 59–60). Worse still, the report concluded that "the new immigration as a class is far less intelligent than the old, approximately one-third of all those over 14 years of age when admitted being illiterate. Racially they are for the most part essentially unlike the British, German and other peoples who came during the period prior to 1880" (King 2000: 61). In short, the Dillingham Commission attributed most of the social ills that had occurred since the beginning of the 1880s, such as rising unemployment, labor unrest, and urban poverty, to the rise in immigrants from Eastern and Southern Europe who, according to the report, were less intelligent, less able to assimilate, and generally harmful to the American social and economic fabric.

For many Americans with anti-immigrant sentiments, the revival of earlier efforts to impose a literacy test for immigrants seemed to be an apt solution to the problems of increased competition from unskilled labor, increased immigration from the assimilation-resistant Eastern and Southern Europeans, and increased radicalism among workers. Albert Johnson, who had become the chair of the House Committee on Immigration and Naturalization, argued that "these teachings [of 'industrial sabotage'] are coming right along with the influx of more than a million aliens a year. The more illiterate of the aliens, once here, quickly absorb the teachings." Others in Congress felt that a literacy test would weed out "the menace to our free institutions involved in the arrival of people without training in self-government" (Calavita 1984: 92). In what was to ultimately be an unsuccessful exercise of his veto power in 1915, President Woodrow Wilson stated that the bill was unacceptable because the immigration restriction was a dramatic departure from traditional American immigration policy.

From the point of view of industry, however, it was one thing to blame radical immigrants for fomenting revolutionary ideas among otherwise contented native-born workers and quite another to actually impose a measure that would constrict the flow of immigrant labor into the country's factories, mines, and mills. One manifestation of industry's anxiety came in the form of the National Liberal Immigration League (NLIL), a pro-business lobby with a membership that included U.S. Steel and the Susquehanna Coal Company (Calavita 1984: 124; King 2000: 77). The NLIL took a two-pronged approach, arguing that America needed immigrant labor and that immigration restrictions would be a violation of America's tradition of providing asylum for those in need. This dual message of American economic interest being coextensive with American idealism was expressed in a 1912 letter to Woodrow Wilson from the NLIL: "it is as impracticable as it is immoral to slam the door in the faces of honest and healthy immigrants, when there is such a crying need for labor" (King 2000: 317 n.113).

The debate surrounding the imposition of a literacy test illustrates the new levels of intensity and complexity that would be represented when conflicting opinions and interests regarding immigration came to the fore. Isolationists, nativists, antisocialists, and labor overlapped and formed alliances while industry cloaked itself in the language of individual rights and political freedoms and argued that immigrants could assimilate. The question of whether these new immigrants could assimilate or whether they were insuperably different from the "old immigrants" was indeed at the heart of the debate over how many immigrants America could accommodate.

For industrialists, the hope was that implementing successful programs of assimilation or "Americanization" could both make the new immigrants into docile workers and diminish the perceived need for further immigration restrictions. The National Association of Manufacturers and the National Industrial Council, as well as hundreds of companies, supported and ran Americanization programs (King 2000: 100). Henry Ford saw such programs as a perfect complement to his managed, rationalized assembly line and, in 1914, implemented a "Five Dollar Day" plan where workers could qualify for the Five Dollar Day incentive plan only if they demonstrated that they were learning the correct American way to live. The plan required caseworkers from the Ford "Sociology Department" to visit employees' homes to instruct and inspect (Barrett 1992: 1003). The Ford program, like many others, had a mandatory English language school for new immigrant workers at which students were taught such useful phrases as "I am a good American" and were made to act out a pageant in which students descended into an enormous melting pot dressed as caricatures of foreigners and emerged all dressed the same and holding American flags (Higham 1988: 248). A more direct form of Ford's Americanization was demonstrated by his firing of about 900 Greek and Russian workers for missing work to celebrate Orthodox Christmas. Ford explained he was justified because "if these men are to make their home in America, they should observe American holidays" (Barrette 1992: 1003). That Americanization schemes were dictatorial, harsh, and unaccommodating is not surprising in light of the fear of unassimilated foreigners living in the United States. Indeed, Congress's Dillingham Commission had recommended that assimilation include learning English, naturalization, and the abandonment of native customs (King 2000: 64). The hypocrisy of the forced assimilation movement was not lost on everyone: as one critic of the movement observed, "to conserve the inalienable rights of the colonists of 1776, it was necessary to declare all men equal; to conserve the inalienable rights of their descendants in the twentieth century, it becomes necessary to declare all men unequal" (Downey 1999: 257).

Eugenicism: The Scientific Racists Weigh In against Immigration

A far more overtly racist form of anti-immigrant argument came from American eugenicists. Eugenics was premised on the concept that immutable heritable traits control social as well as physical characteristics, and that individuals carrying social or antisocial traits could, through study, be identified and dealt with appropriately. As Madison Grant, a New York lawyer and ardent supporter of eugenics, argued in his widely read book *The Passing of the Great Race* (1916), "moral, intellectual and spiritual attributes are as persistent as physical characteristics and are transmitted substantially unchanged from generation to generation" (cited in Shipman 1994: 124). Based on these concepts, the eugenics project advocated prohibiting the immigration of people who were considered to have undesirable genetic characteristics.

Harry Laughlin, of the Eugenics Record Office (ERO) at the Cold Spring Harbor Laboratory in New York, was perhaps the chief advocate for changing U.S. immigration policy to restrict the entry of "undesirable" individuals from Southern and Eastern Europe. Laughlin believed the United States should consciously define an "American race" which would be based on what Laughlin saw as the original and appropriate immigrants to the United States, mainly immigrants from England and Northeastern Europe.

For Laughlin and other eugenicists, "immigrants from southern and eastern Europe, especially Jews, were racially so different from, and genetically inferior to, the current American population that any mixture would be deleterious" (Allen 1986: 248). A similar message was represented in a widely used textbook, *Applied Eugenics* (1918), which taught, "Looking only at the eugenic consequences, we can not doubt that a considerable and discriminatory selection of immigrants to this country is necessary" (cited in Tyner 1999).

In advocating for stricter immigration restrictions against Eastern and Southern Europe, eugenicists warned that such immigration would cause the degeneration of the American race. It was argued that degeneration would have economic costs, because these arriving immigrants and their offspring would be poor and because they were less intelligent and uneducable. It was also feared that unchecked immigration would result in the deterioration of the national character from miscegenation and because it was believed that the immigrant of "inferior" races would outbreed old stock Americans.

THE RED SCARE AND PALMER RAIDS

> The committee members were not all there; so some of us sat down in one of the rear rooms to wait. We were talking, when about 9 o'clock three men came in through the back door, having guns in their hands, and about the same time the front door was thrown open and we saw some of these men there. The men in charge on the raiding party ordered those in the back room brought into the front room with commands to hold up our hands and to get over there. We held up our hands until a preliminary search for weapons had been made. After that search had been made we were searched; I might mention this, incidentally, that while we were being herded up against the wall one of the men in the room fainted. After the preliminary search for weapons had been made we were searched for evidence which we might have on our persons, which was placed in envelopes with our names marked on them as described by various witnesses. We were then taken down stairs and crowded into vans. . . . After answering the questionnaire and signing it, which most of us agreed to do, we were taken down stairs and assigned to cells. I with ten others was assigned to one cell. I remained in that cell until the afternoon of the following day, which was Saturday, about half past 4.
>
> Testimony of a witness arrested during the Palmer Raids
> (*Colyer v Skeffington*, 265 Fed. 17, 40–41
> [D. Mass. 1920])

The amalgam of these fears only became greater with the outbreak of World War I and the Russian Revolution. In such a climate, immigrants who did not conform were seen as disloyal to their new country and as threats to the political establishment and the economic status quo. With the United States' entry into the war, Congress passed the Espionage Act of 1917 and the Sedition Act of 1918 and the government began to rely on them to suppress criticism of the war, primarily by censoring the speech of pacifists, labor leaders, and communists. Immigrants came under especially close scrutiny, with foreign-language publications seen as so threatening that the Postmaster General required publishers to submit foreign-language newspapers, with translations, to the Postmaster for approval (Hall 1989: 250). Both industry and the government were able to characterize labor unions, protestors, and organizers as subversives harming the war effort. In 1917, members of the IWW were involved in a small number of strikes in industries that were considered vital to the war effort, such as copper mining and timber. In response the Department of Justice raided forty-eight IWW local halls and brought a number of prosecutions against IWW leaders for conspiracy to hinder the execution of the war by trying "to close mines, factories, and munitions plants, and [encouraging] workers not to join the army" (Renshaw 1968: 66). The leaders of the IWW were convicted and received severe punishments of up to twenty years in prison. Other federal and state prosecutions were essentially able to break the union.

With the ending of the war, fear of communists and other subversives actually increased and animosity towards communists, anarcho-syndicalists, and trade unionists reached its high point. In the context of a slumping postwar economy and high prices, general anxiety was exacerbated by a number of bombings allegedly perpetrated by alien subversives, labor unrest, and the distribution of radical literature (Colburn 1973: 424). The Department of Justice promoted the belief that United States was under threat by foreign radicals. After a series of bombings in June 1919, the director of the Bureau of Investigation (the forerunner to the FBI) claimed that they were "connected with Russian bolshevism, aided by Hun money" (Coben 1964: 60). Attorney General A. Mitchell Palmer was able to secure funding for a division to fight radicalism, the General Intelligence Division (GID), by claiming that "reds" were planning "to rise up and destroy the Government in one fell swoop," and he proceeded to use his new power to arrest active immigrant union members (Higham 1988: 229). Also, between 1917 and 1920, Congress extended the grounds on which an alien could be deported, to include teaching or advocating subversion (Immigration Act of 1917), belonging to an organization that entertains belief in the violent overthrow of government (Anarchist Act of 1918), and writing, publishing, or possessing subversive literature (Act of 5 June 1920).

The Red Scare, with its extreme xenophobia and mistreatment of immigrants, reached its peak in the so-called Palmer Raids of 1919–1920. The Palmer Raids were carried out by the GID, under the direction of J. Edgar Hoover, with the purpose of rounding-up and deporting individuals deemed subversive, specifically focusing on groups such as the Communist Party, Communist Labor Party, and the Union of Russian Workers. During the raids, people were arrested without warrants, held without charges, denied access to legal counsel, and were subjected to having their houses and property searched without warrants. Since the government was not relying on arrest warrants, agents often simply arrested everyone at an event who was thought to be subversive, as when 141 men and women were arrested at a dance sponsored by the "Tolstoi Club" (Williams 1981: 562). Individuals were held in harsh conditions, for days, months, and in some cases over a year. Bonds could be set exceedingly high: on 11 November 1919, the *New York Times* reported that 391 members of the Union of Russian Workers had their bonds set between $10,000 and $15,000 (a fortune by the standards of the time). Ultimately, the Palmer Raids resulted in about 550 deportations, and many thousands more were arrested and held for at least some period of time.

In addition to the raids, the press was also at pains to paint striking workers as Bolsheviks or anarchists. The great steel strike of 1919 was described as "a serious outbreak of Bolshevism red hot from Russia" (Calavita 1984: 105–6). One description of thirty-nine IWW deportees was oddly feline in its disdain, describing them as "bewhiskered, ranting, howling, mentally warped, law-defying aliens" (Higham 1988: 229). During the most intense period of the Palmer Raids the opinion of newspapers and the public was strongly supportive of the extreme measures taken by the Department of Justice. Political cartoons of the period tended to urge stronger action on the part of the government. For instance, a cartoon that originally appeared in *The Chicago Tribune* in 1919, captioned "Close the Gate," depicts the United States as fenced with an open gate, labeled "immigration restrictions," through which an immigrant labeled "undesirable" is walking. In place of a head, the immigrant's shoulders bear an anarchist's bomb with a lit fuse (see Figure 3.1).[3] *The New York Times* expressed similar opinions when it lauded the massive dragnet raids of January 1920: "If some of us, impatient for the swift conclusion of the Reds have ever questioned the alacrity, resolute will, and fruitful, intelligent vigor of the Department of

Justice in hunting down those enemies of the United States, the questioners and doubters now have cause to approve and applaud" (quoted in Williams 1981: 563).

The arrests and the manner in which they were carried out did not go completely unchallenged. Following the January 1920 raids, the United States Attorney for the Eastern District of Pennsylvania, Francis Kane, resigned in protest and addressed Palmer in an open letter. He warned, "the policy of raids against large numbers of individuals is generally unwise and very apt to result in injustice" (quoted in Williams 1981: 563). Most notably, two federal district courts considered the legality of the Department of Justice's actions in habeas corpus proceedings, in Butte, Montana, and Boston, Massachusetts. In both cases, the courts issued withering criticisms of the government's actions. In the Montana case, the court ruled that the petitioner was entitled to a writ of habeas corpus because "[h]e and his kind are less of a danger to America than those who indorse or use the methods that brought him to deportation, these latter are the mob and the spirit of violence and intolerance incarnate, the most alarming manifestation in America today."[4]

In setting aside the deportation orders of a group of aliens on due process grounds, in *Colyer v Skeffington* the district court described the various violations that the arrestees suffered at the hands of the Department of Justice. For instance, people attending a communist party meeting were arrested at gunpoint, without warrants, and were searched without warrants. Also, a group of thirty-nine people were arrested while "holding a meeting to discuss the formation of a co-operative bakery." And once arrested people were detained in "unfit and chaotic" conditions and were prevented from having access to legal counsel.[5]

After the hysteria of the Red Scare and the Palmer Raids began to die down by the end of 1920, it became clear to some critics that a dangerous precedent had been set, which would augur ill for the rights of immigrants and other political minorities during the next perceived crisis if left unremedied. In the summer of 1920, former Supreme Court Justice Charles E. Hughes was compelled to warn a gathering of Harvard Law School alumni about the abuses to constitutional rights that had taken place. He stated, "We may well wonder, in view of the precedents now established whether constitutional government as heretofore maintained in this republic could survive another great war even victoriously waged" (Beard and Beard 1927: 671). Similarly, Harvard Law School Professor Zechariah Chafee Jr. warned of the need for further remedial measures, stating, "Unless the methods used by the Department of Justice are severely condemned by

CLOSE THE GATE.

FIGURE 3.1. *Chicago Tribune* political cartoon by Carey Orr, reprinted in the 5 July 1919 issue of *The Literary Digest.*

Congress and the American people they will be repeated in future emergencies" (quoted in Williams 1981: 560).

Unfortunately, there was no severe condemnation, or even investigation, of the Department of Justice and its actions during the period of the Red Scare and the Palmer Raids (Williams 1981: 560–61). Far from being merely "the last symptom of war fever," the Palmer Raids go down in history as a critical phase in defining immigrants as both potential threats to national security and as undeserving of the constitutional rights afforded to citizens. The Palmer Raids also had a strong racial aspect: the focus was on Eastern European immigrants, that is, the "new immigrants" who were deemed unfit by many opinion-makers to be part of the "American Race."

Passage of the Immigration Act of 1924 resulted in 70 percent of the immigrant quotas going to immigrants from the United Kingdom, Ireland, and Germany. This legislation "was purposely designed to build up a northwestern European vision of American identity and nationality" (King 2000: 229–30). If this new immigration policy resulted from a confluence of trends and developments, including Anglo-Saxon supremacy, fear of aliens as dangerous subversives, and belief that immigrants should not enjoy the rights guaranteed under the Constitution, it should not be surprising that these concepts remained key elements, and contradictions, within the United States' immigration policy.

THE INTERNMENT OF JAPANESE AMERICANS

> We are now facing the most disturbing and catastrophic situation, and we have not any solution. The West Coast Defense Commander General DeWitt issued the order of most merciless and ruthless one in all my life. The place we are going for temporary is famous race track, about twelve miles from Los Angeles . . . Moving day was the most lamentable and sorrowful day in all our life on the Pacific Coast—our foundation, built by fifty years of hard toil and planning, was swept away by Army's Order. It was Awful Nightmare! . . .
>
> Entry from the journal of a Japanese-American internee
> (reprinted in Bosworth 1967: 116–17)

> I was too young to understand, but I do remember the barbed wire fence from which my parents warned me to stay away. I remember the sight of the high guard towers. I remember soldiers carrying rifles, and I remember being afraid.
>
> Statement of a Japanese-American internee
> (reprinted in Starn 1986: 707)

After the Red Scare, the next major expression of official xenophobia in a time of national security crisis occurred during the Second World War, when over 110,000 Japanese Americans were evacuated from the West Coast and interned in concentration camps. Of those individuals interned, about 65 percent were American citizens by birth (most of whom were *Nisei*, literally "second generation"); the remaining individuals were Japanese who had immigrated to the United States (*Issei*) but were ineligible for naturalization because of discriminatory anti-Japanese immigration laws. The fact that *Nisei* were interned despite being American citizens demonstrates that rights and privileges attendant to status related to citizenship, immigration, and naturalization have different meanings depending on how society conceptualizes the race of the person whose status is at issue. The rights of a citizen in California in 1942 were vastly different for people of Japanese ancestry than for people of European ancestry.

The internment of Japanese Americans was putatively justified by the need to protect against possible sabotage by enemy aliens who remained loyal to Japan. At a congressional hearing on the issue, the mayor of San Francisco, Angelo Rossi, who was himself of Italian descent, argued, "every Japanese alien should be removed from this community. I am also strongly convinced that Japanese who are American citizens should be subjected to more detailed and all-encompassing investigation. After investigation, if it is found that these citizens are not loyal to this country they, too, should be removed." Rossi saw nothing inconsistent with also arguing that the "evacuation of other axis aliens, other than Japanese, should be avoided unless deemed imperative," because of the "extreme hardship, mental distress, and suffering" it would cause German and Italian aliens (Bosworth 1967: 67–68). The singling out of Japanese for mistreatment based on racial stereotypes was even clearer in the testimony of California Governor Culbert Olson, before the same congressional commission. He argued that the FBI could identify the loyal from the disloyal among Italian and German aliens, but that this would not be possible with Japanese because they all looked alike (Bosworth 1967: 81–82).

In truth, the possibility of interning Italian and German aliens was never considered. A December 1941 report from the general in charge of overseeing the evacuation stated that there were "approximately 40,000 . . . enemy aliens" on the West Coast, when in fact there were approximately 40,000 Japanese aliens, 58,000 Italian aliens, and 23,000 German aliens (Bosworth 1967: 63). Thus, it is clear that both *Nisei* and *Issei* were singled out for persecution because they were considered a national security threat based on racial prejudice. In reality there was no national security or strategic necessity for the massive internment of Japanese Americans. "If it was possible to apply selective internment to suspicious German-Americans or Italian-Americans, the same method could have been applied to Japanese-Americans whose loyalty was in doubt. That it was not is the result of colour prejudice" (Laski 1948: 470).

While the internment of Japanese Americans was perhaps the most extreme, systematic, and inhumane slight Japanese immigrants and their families had suffered, it was by no means unprecedented. Since the time Japanese began to arrive in the United States in significant numbers, at the turn of the century, they had been the target of anti-Asian nativists. Much of the anti-Japanese sentiment in California was rooted in fears of losing economic advantage and demographic superiority. For instance, a 1919 *Los Angeles Times* editorial argued, "If the same present birth-ration were maintained for the next ten years there would be 150,000 children of Japanese descent born in California in 1929 and but 40,000 white children. And in 1949 the majority of California would be Japanese, ruling the State" (quoted in the 9 August 1919 issue of *The Literary Digest*). The precedent that legislation could be deployed to curb the immigration of specific national and racial groups to the United States was first tested against immigrants from Asia. Long before the internments took place, discriminatory laws had been enacted, such as the 1906 exclusion of Japanese students from San Francisco public schools; and discriminatory immigration policies had been put in place, such as the Japanese Exclusion Act of 1924 and the prohibition on *Issei* naturalization. It is fair to say that widespread racial prejudice was reflected in these policies of social exclusion and discrimination and this same prejudice made Japanese Americans uniquely vulnerable to the sort of persecution they suffered during the Second World War.

THE ABUSE OF IMMIGRANTS
AFTER SEPTEMBER 11, 2001

> I have now been in solitary confinement for three and a half
> months and by the time of the next hearing I will have been
> here for four months. If it hadn't been for the Koran and prayer,
> I would have lost my mind or had a nervous breakdown. . . . Why
> am I imprisoned? Why in solitary confinement? And why under
> maximum security measures? I have many questions and no
> answers. What are they accusing me of? Nobody knows.
>> From a letter sent by a detainee held after September 11
>> for an immigration violation
>> (reprinted in Amnesty International 2002: 27)

Following the September 11, 2001, attacks on the World Trade Center and the Pentagon, the Department of Justice targeted noncitizen Muslim, Middle Eastern, and South Asian males for its dragnet of investigation, arrest, and detention. In the process the government used selective and unorthodox enforcement of the nation's immigration laws as a pretext to arrest individuals, to detain them without charges, to hold them incommunicado, to question them without access to legal counsel, and try them in secret immigration court proceedings.

Few would doubt that the attacks of 9/11 warranted a vigorous and searching investigation, followed by rapid but calculated steps to help secure the safety of U.S. residents. Instead, as Zechariah Chafee Jr. had predicted after the Palmer Raids, the nation saw a repetition of the tendency to scapegoat immigrants in the face of emergency. And just as the demonization of Eastern European immigrants as subversives and Japanese Americans as possible saboteurs were preceded by a general undercutting of those groups as welcome members of American society, so the abuses of noncitizens that took place after September 11 was made easier by the preceding years of attacks on immigrants that undercut their claims to be treated equally and fairly (see chapter 4 in this volume).

The advent of the newly Republican-dominated 104th Congress in 1995 marked a decidedly anti-immigrant turn in the history of American immigration policy. This shift was driven by conservative members of Congress, who argued that too many new and undesirable immigrants were taking advantage of a lax system to receive immigration and welfare benefits they did not deserve. Additionally, the first World Trade Center bombing in 1993 and the ongoing "War on Drugs" brought security and crime control issues to the fore of the congressional agenda. As a result, Congress passed the Antiterrorism and Effective Death Penalty Act of 1996 (AEDPA), the Illegal Immigration Reform and Immigration Responsibility Act of 1996 (IIRIRA), and the Personal Responsibility and Work Opportunity Reconciliation Act of 1996 (PRWORA). The overall effects of AEDPA and IIRIRA were to make it far easier to deport aliens with criminal records, even for relatively minor offenses, and to severely restrict opportunities for relief from deportation. These laws also curtailed procedural protections and due process protections for aliens facing deportation, restricted judicial review, and expanded the grounds on which an immigrant can or must be detained pending the resolution of her case. These laws also imposed a strict statute of limitations on the right to file asylum claims. The effect of PRWORA was to significantly restrict access to government benefits, such as food stamps and Supplemental Security Income, to legal immigrants and to essentially bar public benefits (including state and local) for illegal aliens. As a result of the 1996 laws, immigration detainees have been the fastest growing segment of the nation's jail population. This legislation resulted in a 42 percent increase in the number of detainees from 1996 to 1997 (Clary and McDonnell 1998). Additionally, these laws further stigmatized aliens by considering immigrants first as threats to national security and national economic prosperity. In this way the new laws helped blur the line between what had heretofore been civil immigration violations and what was considered illicit or criminal behavior.

After 9/11, it was the policy of the Department of Justice to blur this line as much as possible and to use the contradictions to accomplish what it otherwise would have been prohibited from doing. John Ashcroft's Department of Justice circumvented fundamentals of criminal procedure—for example, arrest and search warrants, providing notice of charges, and allowing access to counsel—just as the Bureau of Investigation had, in its prosecution of deportation cases during the Palmer Raids. Ashcroft made clear that he intended to use the looser standards of the immigration system to circumvent individual rights that are protected in the criminal justice system. On 25 October 2001, Ashcroft told a meeting of the Conference of Mayors that "taking suspected terrorists in violation of the law off the streets and keeping them locked up is our clear strategy to prevent terrorism within our borders." Ashcroft also stated, "if you overstay your visa—even by one day—we will arrest you. If you violate a local law, you will be put in jail and kept in custody as long as possible" (quoted in Salyer 2002). This policy clearly equated individuals who were simply out of immigration status with terrorists and made apparent that the Justice Department's strategy would be to use civil immigration laws as pretexts to arrest and indefinitely detain noncitizens. In practice, this policy resulted in the selective targeting by the Department of Justice of only Muslim, Middle Eastern, and South Asian men. Thus, it was both policy and practice to use wanton racial and religious profiling to persecute a large segment of noncitizen men without any evidence of criminal wrongdoing by those individuals.

It is bad enough that the policies and practices of Department of Justice have violated essential rights and bedrock concepts of fundamental fairness. Yet it should also be borne in mind that very real consequences flow from flouting the rules of American democracy, even when these seem to involve largely abstract principles. There are the consequences to the thousands of people affected by the arrests and detentions—the detainees and their families. That the government engaged in serious and repeated violations of individual rights was even acknowledged by the independent "watchdog" organization of the Justice Department, the Office of the Inspector General (OIG), in a 2003 report on the treatment of detainees. During the investigation, the FBI made little attempt to distinguish between aliens thought to have a connection to the attacks and aliens who were simply out of immigration status (OIG Report 2003: chapter 4). The government violated its own rules by holding individuals without issuing charges, in some cases for over a month (ibid.: chapter 3). The government "clearance" process, requiring the FBI to clear individuals of terrorist suspicion before the immigration service was allowed to release or deport the individual, resulted in individuals being held for even longer than what Immigration needed to investigate their status, with an average added delay of eighty days (ibid.: 51). Some detainees were held in restrictive conditions, confined to cell blocks, and severely limited in their access to legal or family visits or phone calls (ibid.: chapter 7; Amnesty International 2002).

The essential conundrum and test for a democracy is how it protects the rights of political minorities from a hostile majority, particularly when the majority feels threatened. This question is most pronounced when it relates to the rights of noncitizens, who are the most powerless of political minorities. Ideally, in the United States this balance is struck by having legal principles and structures that are antimajoritarian, at least with respect to certain fundamental rights. Problems arise when those charged with maintaining the legal structures, such as the Justice Department, begin to bend the law, either to pander the public opinion or out of genuine fear of some sort of perceived threat. Hypothetically, the courts can and should act as a break on a majority that is running amok but at times of perceived national crisis they have been reluctant to fulfill these duties.

Perhaps it is instructive to remember that the events of 9/11 and their aftermath will become the history and precedent of tomorrow. The question from this perspective then becomes what we can do now to sufficiently condemn the treatment of noncitizens following 9/11 and thus set the correct precedent for the crisis or emergency of tomorrow. The need to remedy the precedents of abuse of government power that have taken place since 9/11 are not only needed to protect the rights of noncitizens but also to reaffirm the vitality of fundamental principles as they apply to everyone.

4. Mexicans of Mass Destruction

National Security and Mexican Immigration in a Pre- and Post-9/11 World

Leo R. Chavez

The September 11, 2001, attacks on New York and Washington, DC, heightened a public discourse on the dangers the United States faces in the contemporary world. President George W. Bush (Bush 2002) developed a general strategy for the national security of the United States, while critics focused on the dangers inherent in the forging of an empire in the modern world (Buck-Morss 2003; Chisti et al. 2003; Hardt and Negri 2001). Nativism reared its ugly head as Arabs, Muslims, and Arab Americans became prime targets of racial profiling and surveillance (Cole 2003a; Volpp 2002, and Dole's chapter in this volume). Americans seemed willing to allow the constitutional rights of foreigners and immigrants to become diminished so long as those of citizens remained intact, a dangerous bargain at best (Cole 2003a; Maher 2002, Naples in this volume). But if there has been one constant in both pre- and post-9/11 public discourse on national security, it has been the alleged threat to the nation (both in the sense of the nation as "the people" and the institutions of the nation-state) posed by Mexican immigration and the growing number of Americans of Mexican descent in the United States. The themes in this discourse have been so consistent over the last forty years that they could be said to be independent of the current fear of international terrorism. However, the events of 9/11 raised the stakes and added a new and urgent argument for confronting all perceived threats to national security, both old and new.

The Mexican threat, though old, still has currency in the post-9/11 world. Consider this quote from Samuel P. Huntington's (2004) alarmist article in the March/April 2004 issue of *Foreign Policy:* "In this new era, the single most immediate and most serious challenge to America's traditional identity comes from the immense and continuing immigration from Latin America, especially from Mexico, and the fertility rates of those immigrants compared to black and white American natives." A year before the attack on the World Trade Center, writing in *The American Enterprise*, Huntington (2000) wrote: "The invasion of over 1 million Mexican civilians is a comparable threat [as 1 million Mexican soldiers would be] to American societal security, and Americans should react against it with comparable vigor. Mexican immigration looms as a unique and disturbing challenge to our cultural integrity, our national identity, and potentially to our future as a country."

Rather than discarding Huntington's rhetorical excesses as bombastic hyperbole, we are better served by attempting to clarify the social and historical context of such pronouncements. How did Mexican immigration and the Mexican-origin population in the United States come to be perceived as a national security threat in popular discourse? In this history, specific themes of threat emerge, become elaborated, and are repeated until they attain the ring of truth.[1] This is a story with a number of interwoven plot lines or narrative themes: the Quebec metaphor, the U.S.-Mexico border as a dangerous and foreign place, the loss or invasion of the U.S. border (and hence nation), population growth and fertility that are out of control, the unwillingness to assimilate, the *reconquista* (reconquest), and national security. I will develop this argument in three steps, critically examining first the Quebec metaphor for the "Mexican threat"; second, the U.S.-Mexico border as a place of danger/invasion; and third, the cost of border surveillance.

The primary data source for this examination is a sample of seventy-six magazine issues (covers and their respective articles) between 1965 and the end of 1999, collected from ten national magazines: *American Heritage, Time, Newsweek, U.S News & World Report, The New Republic, The Nation, The National Review, The Atlantic Monthly, Business Week,* and *The Progressive*. Specific magazine issues were selected for the sample if the cover story included a theme related to immigration in some way. The rationale was that stories that made cover status were about particularly salient social issues at that moment in history. These magazines provide a range of views, from liberal to conservative, and insight into national discourses on immigration, national identity, and citizenship (Chavez 2001).

THE QUEBEC METAPHOR

A master narrative begins to develop in the 1970s: the Quebec metaphor. This theme is found both in visual imagery on the covers of some of the magazines and discursively in some of the articles. The Québécois movement in Canada promoted linguistic (French) maintenance and political separation of the French-speaking provinces from the rest of English-speaking Canada (Saywell 1978). As developed in U.S. national magazines, the Quebec metaphor assumed three essential themes: the Mexican-origin population's inability or lack of desire to assimilate into American life, their population growth and high fertility, and their "reconquest" of land once owned by Mexico. In other words, the lesson of Quebec is a possible future for the U.S. Southwest. In this future, the Mexican-origin population's desire for linguistic separation and political control leads to territorial separation (or a return of land to Mexico), tantamount to an overthrow of the U.S. government and an undermining of its democratic institutions. This extreme outcome, for which little if any empirical evidence is presented, raises the issue of a threat to national security.

The first magazine in the sample that raises the Quebec issue does so very subtly. The cover text of *U.S. News & World Report*'s 13 December 1976 issue alerts the magazine's readers to "CRISIS ACROSS THE BORDERS: Meaning to U.S." The image is a map of North America with two arrows, both beginning in the U.S., one pointing to Mexico and one pointing to Canada. Although simple in design, the telling words are "crisis across the borders." The discourse on Mexican immigration begins by associating transnational flows (the arrows) with problems for the United States. The problem in Canada was Quebec, where many French-speaking residents were pushing for greater sovereignty and even separation from the English-speaking provinces. The crisis in Mexico was more multifaceted: "inflation, hunger, and violence," all of which spelled problems for U.S. investment in Mexico and increased undocumented migration to the United States. Although the connection between the Québécois movement and Mexican migration is vague in the image, the dots between the two arrows become increasingly clarified over the next two decades.

The Quebec metaphor was the focus of *U.S. News & World Report*'s 9 March 1981 issue, which featured an illustrated map of the North American continent, including Mexico. The United States is the focal point of the map, and the stars and stripes of the U.S. flag cover it. To the north is Canada, with symbols of the nation and its people (e.g., Eskimos, Mounties, a man holding a flag of French-speaking Quebec), animals (e.g., polar bears), and economic strengths (e.g., cattle, farming, fishing, oil wells, factories). Tension is created in the image between the Mountie who holds the Canadian flag and the French-Canadian who holds the Quebec flag in one hand and raises his other hand in a defiant, closed-fisted gesture toward the Mountie.

To the south is Mexico, also with symbols of the nation and its people, animals, and economic strengths. There is the colonial cathedral representing the nation and its religious and colonial history. A modern tourist hotel on the Pacific Coast, oil wells and an oil worker on the East Coast, and cattle on the Yucatan peninsula represent Mexico's economic strengths. Mexico's people are represented by a man wearing white peasant clothes sitting in a stereotypical resting pose—usually he is found under a cactus—with legs bent at the knee, arms on knees, head resting on one hand. The sleepy peasant sits in the southern mountain area and is perhaps meant to represent Mexico's Indian populations in the southern states of Oaxaca and Chiapas. A line of men (all the humans appear to be male in the image) emerge from the mountains and walk in a single file toward California. The man in front actually has his left foot ready to step on the red and white of California, at about San Diego. The text tells us that the image is about "OUR TROUBLED NEIGHBORS—Dangers for U.S." The cover's image places both the Quebec "problem" and the Mexican "problem" in the same symbolic space, thus merging them into one unified problem for the United States.

In the accompanying article, we learn about the problems posed for the United States by its neighbors. To the north is the possible political turmoil resulting from the French-speaking Canadians' movement for political independence from English-speaking Canadians. Western provinces also pose a separatist threat should the federal government usurp power at the expense of the provinces. For the United States, economic stability under such political pressures is a concern (p. 38). On the Mexican side, a familiar litany of problems includes poverty, lagging farm production, an "explosive" birth rate, and illegal immigration.

Time's 13 June 1983 issue featured a cover with the headline, "Los Angeles: America's Uneasy New Melting Pot." Los Angeles, as the title of the accompanying article informs, is "The New Ellis Island." The metaphor of Ellis Island is used to bestow on Los Angeles the title of the most important port of entry for immigrants coming to the United States. The report uses various phrases throughout to give a sense that immigration is high. Such phrases include: "Los Angeles is being invaded" (p18); "The statistical evidence of the immigrant tide is stark" (p. 19); and "Even before the staggering influx of foreign settlers" (p. 20). The report focuses on how immigration, particularly from Asia and Latin America, is resulting in dramatic changes in the ethnic composition of the city. Mexicans, however, are distinctive according to the article, in that the southwest was once part of Mexico, and so Mexicans arrive "feeling as much like a migrant as an immigrant, not an illegal alien but a *reconquistador*" (p. 24). The reconquest metaphor refers to the separatist sentiments that are attributed to Mexican-origin people in the United States by analogy with Québécois separatism. Importantly, the article does not provide empirical evidence of a comparable separatist movement organized by Mexican-Americans in the Southwest.

Almost a year later, on 1 April 1985, the then-liberal *New Republic* entered the debate over immigration. The editors stake out a position diametrically opposed to those who would like to restrict immigration (pp. 7–8). They see the immigration debate as one over "who deserves the highest distinction in the world—to be an American, with all the rights of American citizenship." The editors side with advocates of an open door for immigrants escaping poverty and oppression. They criticize the portrayal of Mexican immigration as leading to Balkanization and Southwest's secession, key elements in the Quebec metaphor. Examples of leaders who come in for criticism include House Majority Leader Jim Wright, who worries about "a Balkanization of American society into little subcultures"; Senator Lawton Chiles of Florida, who is quoted as saying, "I think we would not recognize the United States as we see the United States today within a period of ten years if we do not regain control of our borders"; and Richard Lamm, the former governor of Colorado, who fears that immigration will result in "a vast cultural separatism" and that the children of Latino immigrants will grow up not as loyal Americans but might lead "secessionist" riots in the Southwest to "express their outrage at this country."

U.S. News & World Report's 19 August 1985 cover returned to the Quebec narrative by suggesting that the U.S. is losing cultural and political control over its territory. The text announces: "The Disappearing Border: Will the Mexican Migration Create a New Nation?" But it is the image that so artfully and so colorfully tells the story of Mexicans taking over the United States. The cover's image renders the two nations, the United States and Mexico, through the strategic use of colors. Central to the image are large block letters *U* and *S,* colored white. The letters sit in a field of green and rest atop smaller red letters forming the word *MEXICO.* The red of *Mexico* bleeds into the pure white of *US.* This transfusion is made possible by the disappearance of the lines (borders) between the letters. Without the barriers, a one-way flow moves up (north) in the image. The image has little people moving north drawn in stereotypical fashion to suggest Mexicans (Rodriguez 1997).

Inside the magazine, immigration-related issues are covered in no less than six articles. The first is titled "The Disappearing Border," and it sets up the magnitude of the changes wrought by Mexican immigration and profiles the immigrants' socioeconomic characteristics. The article begins by telling a story, a narrative of contemporary Mexican immigration that establishes a "reconquest" theme:

> Now sounds the march of new conquistadors in the American Southwest. The heirs of Cortés and Coronado are rising again in the land their forebears took from the Indians and lost to the Americans. By might of numbers and strength of culture, Hispanics are changing the politics, economy and language in the U.S. states that border Mexico. . . . Their movement is, despite its quiet and largely peaceful nature, both an invasion and a revolt. At the vanguard are those born here, whose roots are generations deep, who long endured Anglo dominance and rule and who are ascending within the U.S. system to take power they consider their birthright. Behind them comes an unstoppable mass—their kin from below the border who also claim ancestral homelands in the Southwest, which was the northern half of Mexico until the U.S. took it away in the mid-1800s. Like conquistadors of centuries past, they come in quest of fabled cities of gold. (p. 30)

What is occurring in the American Southwest is a "reconquest" by Mexicans of land they lost during the Mexican-American War. It is occurring because of the "unstoppable mass" of Mexicans migrating to the United States. The narrative makes it clear that the outcome of Mexican immigration is a transformation of the region's politics, economy, and language. As more Latinos become citizens and vote, they will increasingly influence politics, especially since they are concentrated in nine states that control 71 percent of the electoral votes to elect a President.

Imagined or real, concerns about reconquest and the Quebec metaphor played a central role in the debate that occurred in 1994 over California's Proposition 187, the ballot initiative to "Save Our State" from undocumented immigration. For example, according to Linda B. Hayes, the Proposition 187 media director for southern California, the United States could lose territory a result of the rapid demographic shifts caused by Mexican immigration and, implicitly, the threat of reproduction in the growth of the Mexican-origin population. As she wrote in a letter to the *New York Times:*

> By flooding the state with 2 million illegal aliens to date, and increasing that figure each of the following 10 years, Mexicans in California would number 15 million to 20 million by 2004. During those 10 years about 5 million to 8 million Californians would have emigrated to other states. If these trends continued, a Mexico-controlled California could vote to establish Spanish as

the sole language of California, 10 million more English-speaking Californians could flee, and there could be a statewide vote to leave the Union and annex California to Mexico. (Hayes 1994)

The Quebec narrative surfaced yet again in the *National Review's* 31 December 1997 issue. The cover subtly referenced Mexican immigration. An illustration of Uncle Sam standing in a radiant but empty desert fills the cover. Uncle Sam's red, white, and blue hat sits on the arm of a cactus just behind him to his right. His right hand holds a beige Mexican sombrero as he stares at the reader with an odd, slightly bemused look. The relevant cover text states: "De-Assimilation California Style." The heading and subheadings of the accompanying feature article by Scott McConnell emphasizes the cover's message: "North of the Border, Down Mexico Way: Americans No More?: Can assimilation operate today as it did a century ago? Or is it going into reverse?"

McConnell is identified as a writer based in New York City. The article provides an overview of writings, some academic and some ideological, about attitudes toward assimilation among Mexicans and Mexican Americans, including many who do not live in Southern California. McConnell begins with the assumption that "traditional" assimilation processes are not working in California and therefore must be "revived," primarily because 38 percent of the California's foreign born are from Latin America, and well over half of those are from Mexico. "If assimilation can be revived it has to be revived among Latinos," the author states, although he suggests that the "obstacles are daunting" (p. 32). The problems, according to McConnell, are both economic and attitudinal. Economically, he believes that Latinos face blocked upward mobility because of a high dropout rate and high poverty rates that will continue for generations, although he presents virtually no research to support these arguments.

More problematic is the history of the Southwest, which was once part of Mexico. McConnell notes that "[t]he Latino sense of the United States has always been different" (p. 33), and to prove this point he focuses on the terms *Aztlan, Reconquista,* and *Chicanismo* (Chicano nationalism). The author explains that Mexican-American writers, especially during the 1960s and early 1970s, expressed the attitudes of contemporary Latinos who have not forgotten that the Southwest was once part of Mexico (their mythical "Aztlan" homeland). These writers also believe, according to McConnell, that they do not have to assimilate into American culture but instead are "reconquering" the land they lost through immigration. No evidence is provided on how widespread such views are among multigenerational Americans of Mexican descent. Assimilation, the author concludes, is reversing itself in Los Angeles, where neighborhoods are being "re-Mexicanized," a process he does not define other than to say that people speak Spanish in public and Mexican music is played in the streets. The author concludes that assimilation requires that immigrants and their children use English as their primary language, be politically loyal to the United States, and embrace the ideals of the Founding Fathers as their own. Importantly, no evidence or studies are provided on the use of English by Mexican immigrants and their children, or to examine issues of loyalty to the United States (e.g., military service, acts of espionage), or on what they think about the ideals of American democracy and its economic systems.

A final example of the Quebec narrative underscores its power in the political arena. In the 2003 race for governor of California, Lieutenant Governor Cruz Bustamante ran against the actor Arnold Schwarzenegger. As the world knows, Schwarzenegger won. One of key issues raised about Bustamante was his participation in MEChA (Movimiento Estudiantil Chicano de Aztlan), a college student organization, when he was a student. Opponents characterized MEChA, and thus Bustamante by association, as an organization that advocates taking over of the American Southwest by Chicanos because it was once the mythical homeland of the Aztecs (Arellano 2003). Thus Bustamante, despite his protestations (and his inconsistent voting record),[2] became an Aztec warrior, a separatist, a member of the "Brown Klan," and a militant intent on "reconquering" the American Southwest (Arellano 2003).

The Quebec narrative powerfully encapsulates the threat to national security allegedly posed by the growing Mexican-origin population in the United States. The narrative questions the Mexican-origin population's loyalty in that they are represented as possible enemy agents who wish to redefine U.S. territory as Mexican. Mexican immigrants, and Mexican Americans, are cast as perpetual foreigners, as outside the "we" of the "imagined community" of the nation (Anderson 1983; Chavez 1991). Leti Volpp (2002) refers to such representations as "perpetual extraterritorialization," the idea that certain groups "are always already assumed to come from elsewhere, and to belong elsewhere when their behavior affronts."

THE U.S.-MEXICO BORDER
AS A PLACE OF DANGER/INVASION

A corollary of the Quebec narrative has been the trope of "invasion" and other war metaphors associated with Mexican immigration. In this discourse, the U.S.-Mexico border is characterized as a place of danger in need of militarization and increased surveillance.

This view of the U.S.-Mexico border escalated in severity in relation to attitudes toward Mexican immigration and drug trafficking, hot-button political issues throughout the late twentieth century (Cornelius 2002). In its most extreme form, the border became a "war zone" both metaphorically and in the willingness of U.S. officials and policymakers to deploy military and quasi-military personnel and technology (Andreas 1998b; Andreas 2000; Dunn 1999). As Renato Rosaldo (1997) observed: "The U.S.-Mexico border has become theater, and border theater has become social violence. Actual violence has become inseparable from symbolic ritual on the border—crossings, invasions, lines of defense, high-tech surveillance, and more. . . . [T]he violence and high-tech weaponry of border theater is at once symbolic and material. Social analysts need to recognize the centrality of actual violence and the symbolics that shape that violence."

In the space available here, a few illustrative examples of the invasion/ danger narrative will suffice. On 25 April 1977, *U.S. News & World Report* published a cover with the headline "Border Crisis: Illegal Aliens Out of Control?" The image is a photograph of two Border Patrol agents standing on either side of their vehicle, which sits poised alongside a long chain-link fence topped by barbed wire. A single engine plane flies low overhead. The whole scene sends a message of vigilance and militarization (Andreas 1998b).

The military or warlike imagery of the cover is reinforced in the article. Undocumented immigrants are referred to as "invaders." Invaders are, of course, unwelcome and hostile in their intentions. A nation that is invaded suffers an incursion into its sovereign territory, which could be interpreted as a hostile act, even an act of war. And with invasion comes the fear that one might succumb: "On one point there seems little argument: The U.S. has lost control of its borders" (p. 33). Further emphasizing the siege mentality, we are told, "In some communities along the Mexican-U.S. border, residents are so angry about crime committed by border crossers that they are arming themselves and fortifying their homes" (p. 33). The "fort" image resonates well with the overall war framing. Finally, the border is likened to the Maginot Line the French built between themselves and the Germans before World War II. According to Representative Lester L. Wolff, a Democrat from New York who toured the border, "We really have a Maginot Line. It is outflanked, overflown, and infiltrated. And you know what happened to the French" (p. 33). Once the border is characterized as a war zone that is under siege, "invaded," "defended," and "lost," it is easy to slip from war as metaphor to war as practice.

Three months later, on 4 July 1977, *U.S. News & World Report*'s cover again focused attention on Mexican immigration with the headline "TIME BOMB IN MEXICO: Why There'll Be No End to the Invasion of 'Illegals.'" The image captures of a group of men standing, most with their hands in the air or behind their heads. The scene takes place at night, and a strong light illuminates the men, all of whom have dark hair and appear Latino. A lone Border Patrol agent, barely visible in the background, helps to establish the scene's location: the U.S.-Mexico border. This is the first instance of the word "invasion" on one of the magazine covers under examination, a noteworthy escalation in alarmism. Escalating the militarized image, the invasion metaphor evokes a sense of crisis related to an attack on sovereign territory. Invasions are acts of war that put the nation and its people at great risk.

Exactly what the nation risks by this invasion is not articulated in the image's message. The reader must imagine the risk in much the same way that a horror movie might require the audience to conjure up the monster rather than showing it directly. The war metaphor is enhanced by the prominence of the words "time bomb." Mexico's population, as the article makes clear (p. 27), becomes a time bomb that, when it explodes, will blow up the United States with an unstoppable flow of illegal immigrants.

On 7 March 1983, *U.S. News & World Report* returned to the invasion theme. The cover's text announces, "Invasion from Mexico: It Just Keeps Growing." This cover is momentous in that it not only deploys the war metaphor —but actually names Mexico as an invading country. This is the first instance in this sample of magazine covers in which the words "Mexico" and "invasion" are directly linked. Mexico is now explicitly made an aggressor; the U.S., the sovereign territory under attack.

Newsweek's 25 June 1984 cover text asks, "Closing the Door? The Angry Debate over Illegal Immigration. Crossing the Rio Grande." The cover photo again implies invasion with its depiction of a man carrying a woman across a shallow body of water. The image's directionality of movement goes directly toward the reader's eye. We, the consumers, are the ones at risk from this invasion; *they* are coming toward *us*. The image succinctly captures place (the border), activity (illegal immigration), actors (Mexicans), and directionality (to the United States).

Undocumented immigration to the United States is the subject of this issue's feature story. The public is characterized as deeply concerned with undocumented immigration and yet conflicted in their attitudes and views about what to do about it. As in the *U.S. News & World Report* article published some seven years earlier, we learn the "fact" that "America has 'lost control' of its borders" (p. 18). The report cites President Ronald Reagan, who envisions a nation in grave peril: "The simple truth is that we've lost control of our own borders, and no nation can do that and survive" (ibid.).

The framing of the U.S.-Mexico border as a national security issue, as something that can be "lost" when "invaders" cross it, in the mid-1980s coincided with calls from prominent political leaders to further militarize the border. In 1986, San Diego's sheriff publicly advocated for Marines to be stationed along the border every fifteen or twenty feet, day and night (Meyer 1986). Then-Senator (and later Governor) Pete Wilson also publicly supported this idea if immigration reform were to fail (Gandelman 1986). Duncan Hunter, a member of the U.S. House of Representatives from San Diego, suggested that the National Guard rather than Marines should be stationed on the border (McDonnell 1986). Not surprisingly, the military's involvement has steadily increased since this initial controversy, with National Guard and U.S. Marines regularly deployed along the border (Dunn 1996; Dunn 1999; Reza 1997).

The invasion metaphor was subtly referenced on *The Atlantic Monthly's* May 1992 cover. The image consisted of the words *THE BORDER* placed in the center of the cover, and it used color to define national territories. The upper (northern) half of the words *THE BORDER* were blue on a white field, with a band of red across the top. The lower (southern) half had letters in yellow on a field of green, a central color in the Mexican flag. The text tells us, "In the tense, hybrid world along the U.S.-Mexico border, Mexico's problems are becoming America's problems." The image itself suggests the movement of problems from south to north. Little green bubbles break off the green field of the lower half of *THE BORDER* and float northward. Their unsystematic and uncontrolled flow suggests a chaotic penetration of things Mexican into the United States. —The political geography is one in which the United States becomes infected with the problems of its unruly southern neighbor, a relationship that is made clear in the accompanying article by William Langewiesche.

The article is a firsthand account of Langewiesche's travels on the U.S. side of the border. Through his interviews and observations, we learn about the problems of immigration, poverty, and drug smuggling, all of which flow north across the border. As a place, the border region is not pleasant: "It is also grimy, hot, and hostile. In most places it is ugly. The U.S. side is depressed by the filth and poverty in Mexico. On the Mexican side the towns have become ungovernable cites, overrun by destitute peasants, roiled by American values. The border is transient. The border is dangerous. The border is crass. The food is bad, the prices are high, and there are no good bookstores. It is not the place to visit on your next vacation" (p. 56).

The border is not just unpleasant and dangerous; the author also subtly refers to a variety of military metaphors. A Chicano activist keeps a photographic catalogue of alleged abuses by Border Patrol agents and police officers against immigrants and Latino U.S. citizens. A "barrio" near the Chicano activist's home is decried as "the other war zone," because of poverty and gangs. A Border Patrol officer is quoted as he compares his nightly vigilance against illegal border crossers to the Vietnam: "we didn't win there either" (p. 74). The author describes the high level of technology used along the border to "fight" smuggling, and the various contributions of U.S. military personnel to the antidrug smuggling effort. In remote deserts, the author finds that the Army carries out training exercises designated in part to intimidate would-be drug smugglers. In southern Arizona, National Guardsmen, the reserve army, search vehicles. A frustrated customs agent also compares his work trying to stop the entry of drugs to his Vietnam experience: "It's a civilian version of Vietnam. That makes it the second losing war I've fought" (p. 84). The recurring Vietnam metaphor serves to heighten the level of frustration and anxiety: it challenges us not to lose another war.

The problem of moving from a metaphor of the border as a war zone to acting as if this were actually the case became painfully obvious on 20 May 1997. On that day, a Marine Corporal shot to death eighteen-year-old Esequiel Hernandez Jr., an American citizen who had been herding his family's sheep on a hilltop near his family's home on the U.S. side of the border near Redford, Texas. The corporal and three privates were stationed along the border to help the Border Patrol detect drug smugglers under an agreement with a federal agency called Joint Task Force Six, which was established in 1989. The Marines were to observe and report to the Border Patrol. However, Esequiel Hernandez Jr. carried a .22-caliber rifle and was shooting at rocks as he passed the time guarding his sheep. Feeling themselves under attack, the Marines, who were hidden from view, observed the young man for twenty-three minutes, determined that he was tending his flock, but then killed him when he looked as though he would fire again. Controversy developed over the length of time the Marines watched Hernandez and the fact that Hernandez was shot in the side, not in the chest, indicating he was not facing the Marines as he shot his rifle. In addition, the Marines never identified themselves nor did they render first aid to the dying Hernandez. Medical assistance was not called until the Border Patrol arrived twenty minutes later, but by then it was too late (Prodis 1997).

The harsh reality between the metaphor of a war zone and the actual practice of militarization raises a number issues, including those of human rights (Dunn 1999). At the very least is the incongruence between military personnel trained for war and the job of the Border Patrol, which more often than not involves servicing unarmed civilians seeking work or to reunite with their family. It is not that magazine covers and articles *cause* such violence to occur. However, the broader discourse of invasion, loss of sovereignty, and portrayal of Mexican immigrants as the "enemy" surely contributed to an atmosphere that helped to justify increased militarization as a way of "doing something" about these threats to the nation's security and the American way of life.

SECURING THE BORDER, AT WHAT COST?

In the wake of the tragedy of September 11, 2001, the U.S.-Mexico border again became associated with threat and danger, but with a new twist. The border became the gateway through which possible terrorists might enter. On 25 January 2002, President Bush released a statement from the White House, "Securing America's Borders Fact Sheet: Border Security": "America requires a border management system that keeps pace with expanding trade while protecting the United Sates and its territories from threats of terrorist attack, illegal immigration, illegal drugs, and other contraband" (Bush 2002).[3]

The new threat of terrorism resulted in calls for controlling the border as a means of improving homeland security. As Mark Krikorian, executive director of the Center for Immigration Studies put it, "blocking the enemy's ability to enter our country must be a central objective of homeland security" (Krikorian 2003). That none of the terrorists involved in the 9/11 carnage crossed the U.S.-Mexico border illegally is beside the point. Post-9/11 concerns with "the terrorist threat" and national security have resulted in greatly increased funding for border surveillance and control.

But what are we buying with the large increases in funding for the border surveillance? This question is relevant for both the pre- and the post-9/11 worlds, with the new Department of Homeland Security's efforts to fight terrorism by screening of entering tourists, foreign students, and immigrants. I would argue that what is bought by increased funding for border surveillance is political capital (Douglas Massey, in his chapter in this volume, makes a similar argument). The public can see that "something is being done" about what it believes is a major national problem, the need to control and secure the border from the threat of terrorism, the Mexican invasion, and the separatist threats embodied in the Quebec narrative. But what is the cost?

In their book, *Smoke and Mirrors*, Douglas Massey, Jorge Durand, and Nolan Malone (2002) detail how funding for the INS and Border Patrol increased substantially after the mid-1980s, largely in response to this alarmist discourse about the Mexican invasion and its threat to national security. Massey and his co-authors muster compelling evidence that the Immigration and Naturalization Service and the Border Patrol have not gained in effectiveness in spite of massive increases in funding to control undocumented immigration. Indeed, in a perverse logic, we, the taxpaying public, actually got "more bang for our buck" in the early 1980s, before funding for border control experienced massive increases. As Massey et al. note, by the late 1990s the total INS budget was nearly eight times its 1986 level, and the Border Patrol's budget was almost six times as large, which allowed that agency to more than double the number of its officers. Increases to INS and Border Patrol budgets began with the 1986 Immigration Reform and Control Act, and continued with the 1990 and 1996 immigration law reforms.

Although Americans were spending more money for every unauthorized border crosser that was detained, Massey et al. argue that it has done little to lower the odds of a person in Mexico migrating to the United States. They did find, however, that there was an increase in deaths at the U.S. border, the result of Border Patrol "operations" that make crossing the border difficult at the "safest" places, and thus push clandestine border crossers into ever more remote and dangerous terrain. Massey et al. find that the increase in deaths is correlated to the increased funding levels for the INS and Border Patrol between 1986 and 2000. Their analysis even suggests an increase in the number of unnecessary deaths caused by government border control policies and funding.

Smoke and Mirrors does not deal with the post-9/11 world. However, much of its authors' argument continues to hold weight. Following the 9/11 attack, the "Mood Swiftly Change[d] on Immigration," as one newspaper headline declared (Miller and Anderson 2001). The new "mood" was one that reversed the building momentum in Washington to relax U.S. immigration laws. Shortly after assuming the presidency, George W. Bush began advocating for a legalization program for undocumented immigrants and a guest worker program for Mexican labor (Smith and

Chen 2001). In the immediate aftermath of the 9/11 terrorist attacks, the new immigration agenda put legalization and a guest worker program on a back burner, and focused instead on hiring more U.S. Border Patrol agents and improving surveillance of tourist and student visa holders. These new restrictions on immigration, according to Attorney General John Ashcroft, were "part of an anti-terrorism legislative package delivered to Congress" (Smith and Chen 2001). Not surprisingly, given Massey et al.'s analysis, the post-9/11 response to the threat of terrorism contributed to the already-established pattern of throwing money at what is perceived to be a problem, control of the U.S.-Mexico border.

Were the dramatic increases in spending on border enforcement necessary? To some extent, the worsening economy in the post-9/11 years, coupled with the difficulty of crossing the border, may have resulted in fewer would-be immigrants deciding to come to the United States anyway. About 1.2 million people came to the United States between March 2001 and March 2002, substantially fewer than the 2.4 million who came the previous year (Armas 2003). Immigrants, particularly classic "labor migrants," as are most undocumented immigrants, respond quickly to declines in the demand for labor.

Deaths at the border, as Massey and Durand predict, increased dramatically as a result of heightened border security. Between October 1997 to September 1998, there were 254 deaths of migrants crossing U.S.-Mexico border. Over the same months in 2002 and 2003, there were 339 migrant deaths across the entire U.S.-Mexico border. In short, the immediate post-9/11 years saw a 54 percent increase in border enforcement, a 34 percent increase in migrant deaths at the border, and a negligible increase in apprehensions of clandestine border crossers. Despite the costs, increased funding for border surveillance appears to buy little more than the perception that we are "doing something" about the old threat to national security posed by Mexican immigration and new fear of terrorists crossing the border.

Samuel Huntington's concerns, quoted early in this chapter, fixated on the perceived threat to the nation posed by Mexican immigrants and their children. The issues he raises—a destruction of national identity, an invasion that threatens societal security, and fertility and reproduction, both social and biological—are themes that have been articulated for at least the last forty years in national popular discourse.[4] Indeed, this same discourse helped spawn border surveillance groups such as the Minuteman Project (Chavez 2007). The pervasiveness and the taken-for-granted knowledge/

truth constructed by such a discourse helps explain the characterization of the U.S.-Mexico border as a dangerous place and rationalizes increased surveillance and militarization along the border, a process that received even greater impetus after 9/11 and the fear of terrorism.

Does this discourse, of which Huntington's rhetoric is a part, undermine a legitimate and civil debate over Mexican immigration and the security of the nation? In many respects the answer is yes. It is dangerous to let our fears exaggerate possible threats, because this can distort and blind us to what is observable and knowable. On the one hand, immigration has costs and benefits. Mexican immigrants contribute directly to the nation's economic productivity, pay taxes, and are active consumers. California has a $26 billion dollar agricultural industry that employs mainly Mexican immigrant labor. On the other hand, it costs society to educate the children of immigrants, and yet this is also investment in future workers and problem-solvers. To represent Mexican immigrants and their children as an invading force, as threats to national security and disloyal members of society, akin to "sleeper cells," waiting for the right time to reconquer and destroy the union, and as more of a threat to the future of the United States than the Taliban, serves to disunite us as a people more than the actions of any foreign power. The irony is that such a powerful destructive discourse is cloaked under the guise of national security.

5. The Demonization of Persons of Arab and Muslim Ancestry in Historical Perspective

Susan M. Akram and Kevin R. Johnson

The demonization of Arabs and Muslims in the United States, as well as federal government actions that target Arabs and Muslims in the name of combating terrorism, began years before September 11, 2001 (Akram 1999). Nearly ten years before that day, Lawrence Howard (1992: 1) wrote that the Reagan administration had elevated terrorism "to the foremost foreign policy problem of the nation." Well before 9/11, that policy concern focused almost exclusively on "foreign terrorists," particularly Arabs and Muslims. The demonizing of Arabs and Muslims in the United States also can be traced to popular stereotypes (Said 1996: 28; Yousef & Keeble 1999), years of myth-making by film and media (Shaheen 2001), racism during times of national crisis (see J.C. Salyer's chapter in this volume), and a campaign to build political support for U.S. foreign policy in the Middle East. Since at least the 1970s, U.S. laws and policies have been founded on the assumption that Arab and Muslim noncitizens are presumed terrorists, and have targeted them for disfavored treatment under the law. The post-9/11 targeting of Muslims and Arabs is simply the latest chapter in this long history.

Though directed primarily at Arab and Muslim noncitizens, aspects of the federal government's zealous post-9/11 investigatory response give us reason to worry about potential long-term threats to the civil rights of both citizens and noncitizens. It is therefore a matter of public concern that, before and after 9/11, mainstream media sources have largely kept Arab-American voices out of their coverage of the federal government's surveillance and persecution of Arabs and Muslims in the United States.

Commentators have observed that popular perceptions influence the treatment of racial and other minorities under the law.[1] The U.S. Supreme Court has held that discrimination against Arabs can be considered racially based, and in violation of the civil rights laws.[2] As Natsu Saito (2001: 12) summarizes,

> Arab Americans and Muslims have been "raced" as "terrorists": foreign, disloyal, and imminently threatening. Although Arabs trace their roots to the Middle East and claim many different religious backgrounds, and Muslims come from all over the world . . . , these distinctions are blurred and negative images about either Arabs or Muslims are often attributed to both. As Ibrahim Hooper of the Council on American-Islamic Relations notes, "The common stereotypes are that we're all Arabs, we're all violent and we're all conducting a holy war."

Nabeel Abraham (1994: 155, 180), a leading scholar on the racism against Arabs and Muslims in the United States, identifies three distinct ways in which Arabs and Muslims have been racialized: (1) through political violence by extremist groups based on the Arab-Israeli conflict in the Middle East; (2) by xenophobic violence targeting Arabs and Muslims at the local level; and (3) through the hostility arising from international crises involving the United States. In addition to considering these processes, our chapter examines how the law and its enforcement have contributed to the hostility toward Arabs and Muslims in the United States.

THE SILENCING OF ARABS THROUGH POLITICALLY MOTIVATED VIOLENCE AND INTIMIDATION

Ongoing conflict in the Middle East provokes violence against Arabs and Muslims in the United States, as does the less-well-known intimidation tactics used by some activist organizations. For example, a Rand Corporation study (Hoffman 1986: 11,15) concludes that the Jewish Defense League (JDL) was, for over a decade, one of the most active terrorist groups in the United States. Described as part of a strategy "to eliminate perceived enemies of the Jewish people and Israel" (ibid.: 16), the JDL bombed Arab foreign offices and planted bombs in American-Arab Anti-Discrimination Committee Offices (ibid.: 12–15). According to the FBI (1987: 13), Jewish extremist organizations were responsible for twenty terrorist incidents in the 1980s.[3] Despite FBI documentation, such terrorism was not listed in major hate crimes studies in the United States (Lutz 1987).

Even less well publicized than the anti-Arab violence of extremist groups is the campaign by mainstream pro-Israeli organizations such as the Anti-Defamation League of B'nai B'rith (ADL). Established in the early 1900s as an organization with the laudable mission of fighting anti-Semitism, the

ADL gained a reputation as a leading antidiscrimination organization in the United States. After the creation of Israel in 1948, the ADL's mission expanded to include discrediting or silencing critics of Israel or defenders of Palestinian rights (Lilienthal 1993: 18). The ADL has aggressively engaged in efforts to intimidate Arabs, Muslims, and others with particular views on the Middle East conflict, discouraging them from engaging in political debate. In 1983, for example, the ADL released a handbook that classified some of the most prominent scholars on Middle East issues, as well as humanitarian organizations dealing with the Middle East or Palestine, as "anti-Israeli propagandists." Alfred Lilienthal (1993: 18), an influential historian and journalist, and the author of a two-volume work on the Zionist influence on U.S. government and foreign policy, and himself on the ADL's blacklist, claimed that "many ADL charges against critics of Israel are totally inaccurate, questionable, or based upon half-truths." 'He argues that the ADL often characterizes groups or individuals who criticize Israel or Zionism as "extremists," intent on eradicating Israel or inciting anti-Semitism.[4]

In January 1993, California media reported on an FBI investigation of a San Francisco Police Department officer and an ADL-paid undercover agent that revealed extensive ADL surveillance against Arab activists and organizations. Law enforcement authorities uncovered computerized files on thousands of Arab Americans and on Arab and many other mainstream organizations in the ADL's possession (Paddock 1993: 2). The information included confidential law enforcement files and information from the Department of Motor Vehicles (Jabara 1993: 30–31). The ADL's attorney admitted that the ADL had passed surveillance information to Israel (McGee 1993). The ADL was permanently enjoined from illegal spying on Arab-American and other civil rights groups.[5] The ADL also provided U.S. intelligence agencies with information on politically active Arab groups and individuals that has placed them under heightened government scrutiny (McGee 1993).

The discovery of espionage has contributed to the climate of fear for Arab and Muslim Americans. Such perceptions have been reinforced by the revelation that information provided by the ADL triggered the FBI investigation and arrest of a group of noncitizens, now known as the "LA Eight," for alleged violations of the Immigration and Nationality Act (Jabara 1993: 37) that amount to speech and other nonviolent support of the Palestinian cause. This case, discussed further below, had deep reverberations in Arab and Muslim communities as an illustration of the influence such groups as the ADL can bring on U.S. government agencies to target Arab/Muslim communities, particularly those engaging in political dissent. Our research has shown no public admission of culpability or disavowing of these activities by the ADL. Abraham (1994: 187) summarizes, "The overall effect of the ADL's practices is to reinforce the image of Arabs as terrorists and security threats, thereby creating a climate of fear, suspicion, and hostility towards Arab-Americans and others who espouse critical views of Israel, possibly leading to death threats and bodily harm."

In March 2002, about thirty prominent Jewish organizations including the ADL, the American Israel Public Affairs Committee, the American Jewish Committee, the American Jewish Congress, and the Conference of Presidents of Major American Jewish Organizations formed the "Israel on Campus Coalition" (ICC) with the aim of "promoting Israel education and advocacy on campus."[6] One ICC report promotes a number of "community programs and strategies" to "address problems at local campuses in a systematic way" (Bard 2004: 30).[7] Among the programs endorsed by the ICC is Campus Watch, which monitors Middle East studies programs and publishes "blacklists" of professors it deems to be "anti-Israel."[8] In late September 2002, Campus Watch posted "dossiers" on eight scholars who criticized U.S. foreign policy and the Israeli occupation. Since then, 146 new names have been posted on the Web site, all academics identified as "apologists for suicide bombings and militant Islam."[9] Another ICC initiative was the David Project, a campaign launched at Columbia University to discredit prominent "pro-Palestinian" academics at Columbia, who the ICC claimed intimidated "pro-Israeli" students in their classes. A Columbia University Grievance Committee report found no evidence of anti-Semitism or retribution against students for their opinions. Even so, the controversy resulted in Professor Joseph Massad's canceling of one of his classes and the dismissal of Professor Rashid Khalidi from a New York Department of Education joint program with Columbia that advises New York public school teachers on Middle East issues.[10]

Aside from its campaign to discredit and silence academics on university campuses, the ADL and some other groups have also sought to prevent pro-Muslim and pro-Arab speakers from engaging in public debate. In 2002, for example, the Florida ADL unsuccessfully lobbied the Florida Commission on Human Relations to exclude a Muslim representative from a panel at a civil rights conference (Hanley 2002a:83). Similarly, the American Jewish Committee sought to exclude the executive director of the New York chapter of the Council on American-Islamic Relations (CAIR) from participating in a public forum on multicultural understanding because he was "anti-Israel" (ibid.: 83). The ADL demanded that CAIR's Northern California director be prevented from testifying about hate crimes before the California Select Committee on Hate Crimes.

THE IMPACT OF ANTI-ARAB IMAGES
IN POPULAR CULTURE

Racism against Arabs is not all the work of political activists. Media and film have found a ready audience for dangerous, one-dimensional images of Arabs and Muslims. Jack Shaheen's (2001) review of U.S. film offers convincing evidence of the vilification of Arabs and Muslims by the film industry. Shaheen catalogues hundreds of Hollywood movies in which Arabs or Muslims are portrayed as terrorists or otherwise placed in a negative, often less-than-human light. Muslims are shown as hostile invaders or as "lecherous, oily sheikhs intent on using nuclear weapons" (ibid.: 9). A far-too-common scene shows a mosque with Muslims at prayer, then cuts away to showing civilians being gunned down. Westerners in these movies hurl such epithets at Arabs and Muslims as "assholes," "bastards," "camel-dicks," "pigs," "devil-worshipers," "jackals," "rats," "rag-heads," "towel-heads," "scum-buckets," "sons-of-dogs," "buzzards of the jungle," "sons-of-whores," "sons-of-unnamed goats," and "sons-of-she-camels" (ibid.: 11). Arab women are often portrayed as weak and mute, covered in black, or as scantily clad belly dancers (ibid.: 22–24). Shaheen notes that the U.S. Department of Defense has cooperated with Hollywood in making more than a dozen films showing U.S. soldiers killing Arabs and Muslims (ibid.: 15).

Audiences apparently embrace the demonization of Arabs and Muslims in the movies. Quoting Shaheen (ibid.: 15), "[T]o my knowledge, no Hollywood WWI, WWII, or Korean War movie has ever shown America's fighting forces slaughtering children. Yet, near the conclusion of [the movie] *Rules of Engagement*, U.S. marines open fire on the Yemenis, shooting 83 men, women, and children. During the scene, viewers rose to their feet, clapped and cheered. Boasts director Friedkin, 'I've seen audiences stand up and applaud the film throughout the United States.'"

One-sided film portrayals omit images of Arabs and Muslims as ordinary people with families and friends or as outstanding members of communities, scholars, writers, or scientists. Few U.S. movies have depicted Arabs or Muslims as complex, fully human people, and even fewer have included them in leading roles (ibid.: 34–35). Commentators rarely criticize the unbalanced depiction of Arabs and Muslims (ibid.: 31–33).

Reinforcing the anti-Arab, anti-Muslim stereotypes portrayed in film, public officials have openly directed intolerant speech at Arabs and Muslims, speech that would otherwise be deemed racist if directed at other groups (Abraham 1994: 188–92). In Dearborn, Michigan, in 1985 mayoral candidate Michael Guido distributed a campaign brochure, "Let's Talk About City Parks and the Arab Problem," in which it was claimed that the city's Arab Americans "threaten our neighborhoods, the value of our property and a darned good way of life" (ibid.: 191). In 1981, the governor of Michigan proclaimed that Michigan's economic woes were due to the "damn Arabs" (ibid.: 196).

After 9/11, anti-Arab/Muslim racist comments by public officials rose sharply, including from the highest officials of the U.S. government. The following are just a few examples:

> Former U.S. Attorney General John Ashcroft: "Islam is a religion in which God requires you to send your son to die for him. Christianity is a faith in which God sends his son to die for you." (Eggen 2002)
>
> Louisiana Congressman John Cooksey: "If I see someone come in that's got a diaper on his head, and a fan belt wrapped around that diaper on his head, that guy needs to be pulled over." (American-Arab Anti-Discrimination Committee 2003: 128–30)
>
> Georgia Congressman Saxby Chambliss: "A Georgia sheriff should be turned loose to arrest every Muslim that comes across the state line." (American-Arab Anti-Discrimination Committee 2003: 128–30)
>
> Lieutenant General William G. Boykin, Undersecretary of Defense for Intelligence, of a Somali warlord: "I knew that my God was better than his. I knew that my God was a real God and his was an idol." (Smith and White 2004)

Media personalities, and even some of the most prominent spiritual leaders in the country, have engaged in vitriolic and racist language. According to journalist Ann Coulter (2001), "We should invade their countries, kill their leaders and convert them to Christianity." Jack Cafferty, of CNN's "American Morning" program and "The Cafferty Files," stated, "The Arab World is where innocent people are kidnapped, blindfolded, tied up, tortured and beheaded, and then videotape of all of this is released to the world as though they're somehow proud of their barbarism. Somehow, I wouldn't be too concerned about the sensitivity of the Arab world. They don't seem to have very much."[11] Reverend Franklin Graham stated on national television, "The God of Islam is not the same God. He's not the son of God of the Christian or Judeo-Christian faith. It's a different God and I believe it is a very evil and wicked religion" (American-Arab Anti-Discrimination Committee 2003: 128–30).

RACISM IN TIMES OF NATIONAL CRISES

Periods of perceived national crises in the United States are often accompanied by hostility toward minorities. Such crises have affected not only Arabs and Muslims but also those who are mistaken for Arabs and Muslims. Perpetrators of hate crimes against Arabs and Muslims frequently fail to differentiate among persons based on religion, nationality, or ethnic origin, from Pakistanis, Indians, Iranians, and Japanese to Muslims, Sikhs, and Christian Arabs. The common perception is that Arabs and Muslims are identical and are all eager to wage a holy war against the United States (Joseph 1999: 260, 261; Whidden 2001: 2825, 2850).

The most recent census data show that there are 1.2 million people with ancestries from many Arabic speaking countries in the United States (U.S. Census Bureau 2000). A widely cited study prepared by the City University of New York Graduate Center found that the majority of Arab Americans are not Muslim, and the majority of Muslims are not Arab American.[12] Other studies offer different statistics but concur that Muslims are a minority in the Arab communities in the United States.[13] Nonetheless, the American public as a whole fails to understand the diversity among America's Muslims or that the vast majority of them are "decent, law-abiding, productive citizens."[14]

A public that routinely fails to differentiate between Arab and Muslim, or between terrorist and law-abiding community member, easily generates hostility toward entire communities of Arabs and Muslims. Academics have observed that hate crimes against Arabs and Muslims routinely increase in the United States when Arabs or Muslims are seen as responsible for terrorist acts against Americans abroad. For example, after Lebanese Shi'a gunmen in 1985 hijacked TWA Flight 847 to Beirut, beat an American on the plane to death, and held the remaining passengers hostage, violent attacks against persons of Arab and Muslim origin occurred across the United States (Abraham 1994: 161–62; Baker 1986). Islamic centers and Arab-American organizations were vandalized and threatened. A Houston mosque was firebombed. A bomb exploded in the American-Arab Anti-Discrimination Committee office in Boston, severely injuring two policemen.[15] Later that same year, after terrorists hijacked the Achille Lauro cruise liner and murdered a passenger, an American-Arab Anti-Discrimination Committee office was bombed, killing its regional executive director.[16] Similar outbreaks of threats, vandalism, beatings, and bombings against Arab and Muslim Americans and their community organizations occurred again in 1986, in an apparent response to the Reagan Administration's bombing raid on Libya, and again in 1990 and 1991, as tensions escalated immediately before the Gulf War (Akram and Johnson 2002: 313).

After 9/11, hate crimes and violence against Arabs and Muslims rose exponentially. The FBI reported an increase in anti-Arab hate crimes of 1,600% in the year following the 9/11 attacks. The Council on Arab-Islamic Relations (CAIR) reported an increase of 52% in hate crimes against Muslims and Arabs between 2003 and 2004. CAIR itself processed 1,522 cases of reported civil rights violations and anti-Muslim violence, discrimination, and harassment in 2004, up from 1,019 such reported cases in 2003 (Council on Arab-Islamic Relations 2005; also Hing 2002).

THE U.S. GOVERNMENT AND THE ROLE OF LAW

The law and its enforcement has contributed to the racialization and targeting of Arabs and Muslims (Lopez 2000). Federal government action taken in the name of fighting terrorism has been followed by indiscriminate threats and violence against Arabs and Muslims in the United States, a pattern that began years before 2001 and that has been repeated in the wake of 9/11.

One of the most persuasive theories explaining the relationship between U.S. government policies targeting of Arabs and Muslims within the United States and U.S. foreign policy abroad is that U.S. foreign policy objectives (such as support of Israel and hegemonic designs on the Middle East as a way to secure American oil interests) closely parallel U.S. domestic "demonizing" of Arabs and Muslims. This theory explains why demonizing of Arabs and Arab states has been followed by institutionalized demonization of Muslims and Muslim countries, with the rise of political Islam as the new enemy of U.S. interests. The collection of essays in Elaine Hagopian's (2004) edited volume, *Civil Rights in Peril: The Targeting of Arabs and Muslims*, brings together very persuasive evidence that helps to explain the U.S. government motivation in seeking to prosecute, detain, and remove large numbers of Arabs and Muslims even before 9/11. It also explains the reasons that activists promoting unpopular Arab causes and those advocating political Islam have been particular targets of prosecutions, detentions, and removals. The LA Eight case illustrates this: not all eight are Muslim (Michel Shehadeh and Julie Mungai are Christian) but all advocate a cause—Palestinian liberation—that is almost uniformly shared by the entire Arab world.

The first documented policies in which the federal government specifically targeted Arabs in the United States were part of the Nixon administration's "Operation Boulder." These policies targeted Arabs in the United States for special investigation and surveillance and used law enforcement to discourage their political activism on the Middle East (Bassiouni 1974:v–vi). Ostensibly designed to confront the threat posed by terrorists who murdered athletes at the 1972 Munich Olympics, the president authorized the FBI to investigate people of "Arabic background" to determine their potential relationship between "terrorist" activities and the Arab-Israeli conflict (Gesser 1974: 16–27; Hagopian 1975–76). In one well-known case to the Arab community, the FBI admittedly wiretapped the prominent Detroit lawyer Abdeen Jabara, then president of the Association of Arab-American University Graduates.[17]

Later in the 1970s, President Carter took numerous steps against Iranians in response to the U.S. hostage crisis in Teheran. In the 1980s, the Reagan administration also pledged to combat "terrorism." This policy was followed by the U.S. bombing of Libya, ostensibly to retaliate for Libyan involvement in the Rome and Vienna airport attacks, which the Reagan administration blamed on Libyan leader Muammar Qaddafi. Later FBI disclosures indicated that President Reagan ordered the Libyan bombings despite evidence provided by the Austrian, Italian, and Israeli governments that there was no connection between Libya and the Rome and Vienna attacks.[18]

In the 1990s, after the Iraqi invasion of Kuwait, the focus of the U.S. government's campaign against "terrorism" shifted to Saddam Hussein. The first Bush administration initiated widespread surveillance of Arab and Muslim Americans. The FBI interrogated Arab and Muslim leaders, activists, and antiwar demonstrators across the country. The Department of Justice instituted fingerprinting of all residents and immigrants in the United States of Arab origin, while the Federal Aviation Administration commenced a system of airline profiling of persons from the Arab world.[19]

Foreign policy concerns have loomed large behind policy measures directed at Arabs and Muslims in the United States. The Immigration and Naturalization Service sought to deport noncitizens of Palestinian ancestry at the same time that the federal government attempted to shut down Palestine Liberation Organization (PLO) offices in the United States and at the United Nations.[20]

Large-scale roundups and detentions of Arabs in the United States were planned long before September 11, 2001. In the 1980s, President Reagan issued a secret National Security Decision Directive that authorized the creation of a network of agencies designed to prevent "terrorists" from entering or remaining in the United States.[21] Under one proposal, intelligence agencies would provide the Immigration and Naturalization Service with "names, nationalities and other identifying data and evidence relating to alien undesirables and suspected terrorists believed to be in . . . the US."[22] The Alien Border Control Committee also considered an INS-created strategy called "Alien Terrorists and Undesirables: A Contingency Plan," which would have called for mass arrests and mass detentions of noncitizens from Arab nations and Iran, along with the recommendation to use the immigration laws to remove noncitizens from these nations already in the United States because of their political views.[23] The ideological exclusion and deportation grounds in immigration law historically have been used to target Arabs and Muslims coming to or traveling within the U.S., and, more recently under the amendments of the USA PATRIOT Act, to deny entry and remove persons whose political views are contrary to the positions of the U.S. government.

EFFORTS TO STIFLE POLITICAL DISSENT:
THE CASE OF THE LA EIGHT

Critics long have pointed out that the United States has discriminated against Arabs and Muslims in applying the terrorist and ideological exclusion provisions of the Immigration and Nationality Act (INA), the comprehensive U.S. immigration law (Scanlan 2000: 363–68; Cole 1993). Arabs, particularly Palestinians, are the primary targets of most of the provisions that allow exclusion or removal on the basis of affiliations, political expression, or political views, when the government labels these views or affiliations "terrorist" (Akram 1999: 51; Whidden 2001: 2825).

The federal government's efforts to remove the "LA Eight" illustrate the extremes it resorted to, before 9/11, to deport political dissidents from the United States (Johnson 1997: 865–69).[24] The case began before dawn on 26 January 1987, when officers of the FBI, INS, and Los Angeles Police Department raided the Los Angeles home of Khader Hamide, a U.S. permanent resident, and his Kenyan-born wife Julie Mungai.[25] The couple were handcuffed, told they were being arrested for "terrorism," and taken into custody while police blocked the street and an FBI helicopter hovered overhead. Six other individuals were arrested that morning (Banks 2000: 479).

Both the director of the FBI and the regional counsel of the INS testified before Congress that the sole basis of the government's efforts to deport the LA Eight was their political affiliations. In the words of FBI Director William Webster, "All of them were arrested because they are alleged to be members of a world-wide Communist organization which under the [law] makes them eligible for deportation . . . If these individuals had been United States citizens, there would not have been a basis for their arrest."[26] The evidence underlying the government's charges amounted to a claim that the LA Eight read or distributed literature linked to the Popular Front for the Liberation of Palestine (PFLP). Nonetheless, the district court found that the PFLP was engaged in a wide range of lawful activities—from providing education, health care, social services, and day care, to cultural and political activities (ibid.: 505)—and ruled that the ideological exclusion grounds violated the First Amendment.[27]

While the case of the LA Eight was pending, Congress passed the Immigration Act of 1990, which repealed the provisions allowing for the removal of noncitizens because of their political ideology. The INS then instituted new proceedings against the LA Eight based on charges of terrorism, along with other grounds.[28] The Immigration and Nationality Act permits removal of noncitizens who have "engaged in terrorist activity," defined as having committed "in an individual capacity or as a member of an organization, an act of terrorist activity or an act which the actor knows, or reasonably should know, affords material support to any individual, organization, or government in conducting a terrorist activity at any time."[29] This language authorizes the deportation or exclusion of an individual who has donated money to an organization for its legal, social, or charitable activities if any part of that organization also has engaged in terrorism (Ross 2001; Strossen 1997: 531). In 1999, the Supreme Court ruled that the 1996 amendments to the immigration laws barred judicial review of the claim of the LA Eight that the government had selectively prosecuted them for their political views.[30] Following the Court's decision, the case was remanded to the immigration court. In 2001, the court dismissed the removal charges based on terrorist activity, on the grounds that they were not meant to apply retroactively. Nonetheless, the federal government continued its efforts to deport the LA Eight, even relying on secret evidence to remove two of the eight (Legomsky 2002: 86). In September 2003, the immigration authorities claimed new grounds for removal under the USA PATRIOT Act, for acts of distributing pro-Palestinian literature and raising funds for Palestinian humanitarian causes occurring almost twenty years ago (King 2005). The government brought yet another set of charges against members of the LA Eight for "supporting terrorism" under the newly passed REAL ID Act.[31]

THE SECRET EVIDENCE CASES

Years before 2001, the Immigration and Naturalization Service (INS) selectively targeted Arabs and Muslims through the use of secret evidence—evidence that it refused to disclose to the noncitizen or his or her counsel—to charge, detain, and deny bond or release in removal proceedings. By 1999, twenty-five secret evidence cases were pending in the United States (Akram 1999: 52 n.4).

In the 1988 case of *Rafeedie v INS*, Fouad Rafeedie, a twenty-year lawful permanent resident of Palestinian origin, was arrested and the INS sought to deny his return to the United States based on ideological grounds after he had taken a two-week trip to a conference in Syria sponsored by the Palestine Youth Organization.[32] The INS claimed that disclosing its evidence against Rafeedie would be "prejudicial to the public interest, safety, or security of the United States." The court of appeals rejected the INS position and required application of the ordinary constitutional analysis in determining whether the federal government's national security interests outweighed Rafeedie's First Amendment rights. The court observed that the only way Rafeedie could have prevailed over the INS's secret evidence would be if he could "rebut the undisclosed evidence against him. . . . It is difficult to imagine how even someone innocent of all wrongdoing could meet such a burden."[33]

Following the repeal of the ideological exclusion provisions of the INA in 1990, the INS began a new effort to use secret evidence to detain and deport Arabs and Muslims. The INS relied on new provisions passed in 1996 as authority for its secret evidence strategy. In response to the 1995 Oklahoma City bombings, Congress enacted antiterrorism legislation that has facilitated the targeting of Arab and Muslim noncitizens: the Antiterrorism and Effective Death Penalty Act (AEDPA) and the Illegal Immigration Reform and Individual Responsibility Act (IIRIRA). Both pieces of legislation brought about radical changes to immigration laws and effectively allowed the government to use secret evidence for ideological exclusion and removal.[34] Bolstered by the 1996 reforms curtailing the rights of noncitizens, the INS brought approximately two dozen deportation actions based on secret evidence, claiming that disclosing the evidence would compromise the security of the United States (Akram 1999: 52n.4; Schwartz, Frenzen and Calo 2001: 300).[35] Although the government denies it selectively uses secret evidence against Arabs and Muslims, our research has uncovered only one secret evidence case *not* involving an Arab or Muslim noncitizen.[36]

AEDPA established a special procedure for detaining and deporting "alien terrorists" that permitted the use of secret evidence with certain procedural safeguards designed to protect constitutional rights. The INS, however, never followed these procedures.[37] It instead relied on pre-existing regulations it claims authorize the use of secret evidence in the immigration courts.[38] By so doing, the INS avoided complying with AEDPA's safeguards, which would have otherwise required it to provide an unclassified summary of the secret evidence to the noncitizen and to have a federal court assess the constitutionality of the use of secret evidence. The INS strategy of using the immigration regulations rather than the AEDPA terrorist removal provisions effectively permitted the U.S. government to avoid ever having to prove a charge of "terrorism,"[39] a showing it would not have been able to make in any of the secret evidence cases of the 1990s.

Among the secret evidence cases were those of the "Iraqi Seven," which arose out of the U.S. government's resettlement of Iraqi Kurds after the Gulf War in the early 1990s (Frenzen 1999: 76).[40] The men had all worked for a CIA-funded Iraqi opposition group, and were evacuated from Iraq in 1991 by the United States. The INS commenced exclusion proceedings against them based on alleged visa violations. Fearing persecution if returned to Iraq, the Iraqi Seven sought asylum in the United States. Relying primarily on secret evidence, the immigration judge found them to be national security risks.[41]

As a result of the litigation, the INS released 500 pages of evidence used against the Iraqi Seven (ibid.). James Woolsey, former director of the CIA, was one of the lawyers representing the Iraqis. Besides concluding that hundreds of pages had been erroneously classified, Woolsey testified to Congress that the evidence was based on serious errors in translations, ethnic and religious stereotyping by the FBI, and reliance on unreliable information, including rumors and innuendo. He claimed that the U.S. government made material misrepresentions to the immigration judge. Despite the weakness of the government's evidence, the case was only concluded when five of the Iraqis entered into a settlement agreement withdrawing their asylum claims in exchange for release from detention.

Before 9/11, defendants in secret evidence proceedings had been detained by the INS for as long as four-and-one-half years (Akram and Rempel 2004: 61, n.255). As the cases slowly moved toward conclusion, the government's claims evaporated. No case has included sufficient evidence of terrorism-related charges necessary to justify detention (Akram 1999). The cases were, at best, based on guilt by association, sending the message that being Arab or Muslim or associating with Arab or Muslim causes or organizations is suspect and could subject an individual to discriminatory treatment or even criminal prosecution. Since 9/11, the Secretary of State has designated various groups "foreign terrorist organizations" without providing notice to those organizations (Cole 2003b). The government then criminalizes Muslims' charitable giving to these organizations through a broad interpretation of the statute that makes it a crime to give "material support" to organizations involved in terrorist activities. These charges raise concerns about infringement of First Amendment rights to freedom of association and about prosecuting individuals under statutes that are overbroad and vague (Jonakait 2003–4). The ease with which the federal government may obtain information, arrest, detain, and indict individuals for "terrorism-related" activities and associations has caused Muslims and Arabs in the United States to believe that they do not have the same free speech and association rights as the rest of the population. The effect on Arab and Muslim communities—and, as they perceive it, the intent—is to chill or suppress political and religious speech and association.

This discussion is by no means comprehensive. The surveillance and persecution of Arabs and Muslims by the U.S. government is sometimes a response to public fears about terrorism—fears that are further propagated by the media. In the 1990s, the much-publicized case of asylum seeker Sheik Omar Rahman, later convicted for his role in the 1993 World Trade Center bombing,[42] by itself resulted in changes to the immigration laws narrowing the rights of all asylum applicants (Schrag 2000: 42–44, 134, 137, 148, 162, 164, 217). A 1993 episode of the popular television news show, *60 Minutes*, focused on Rahman's alleged abuse of the asylum system.[43] The story triggered a chain reaction culminating in 1996 asylum reforms, including a summary exclusion procedure by which a noncitizen could be excluded from the country without a hearing.[44]

Since 9/11, security measures are likely to have an enduring impact on the civil rights of all immigrants and some U.S. citizens. The ripple effects of the U.S. government's post-9/11 security fixation on Middle Eastern and Muslim men are many and far-reaching. Here, we conclude by touching upon only one of the issues adversely affected by U.S. national security policy: racial profiling and the threat it poses to the civil rights of nonwhites in the United States.

CIVIL RIGHTS: THE PRACTICE OF RACIAL PROFILING

The federal government's reaction to the events of 9/11 promises to have a deep and enduring impact on civil rights in the United States. Immigration reforms and executive action, which have the appearance of responding to

the acts of terrorism, will remain with us long after the immediate terrorist threat has passed and will adversely affect the rights of all immigrants
and many citizens.

The focus on "Arab appearance" and Muslim identity has revived debate
about the propriety of racial profiling in law enforcement, an enduring
problem for racial minorities in the United States. Before 9/11, the U.S.
public and policymakers had come a long way in a relatively short time
in critically scrutinizing the use of race and perceived racial appearance
in criminal and immigration law enforcement. Prior to 9/11, the use of
racial profiling in criminal law enforcement had been the subject of critical analysis.[45] Presidential hopefuls criticized racial profiling by police in
traffic stops (Berke 2000), and, after the 2000 election, both President Bush
and Attorney General Ashcroft publicly condemned racial profiling.

The argument has been powerfully made that race-based enforcement
of immigration law is also inappropriate (Johnson 2000: 675; Romero
2000: 195). Although the Supreme Court condoned the practice in 1975,[46]
one court of appeals in 2000 held that the Border Patrol could not consider
a person's "Hispanic appearance" in making an immigration stop.[47] The
court ruled that the race-based profile was over-inclusive, pulling in too
many U.S. citizens and lawful permanent residents, as well as allowing for
the arrest of a relatively small number of undocumented immigrants.[48]

Unfortunately, 9/11 resurrected governmental reliance on statistical
probabilities, which are at the core of racial profiling. After 9/11, persons
of apparent Arab ancestry were arrested, interrogated, and detained for
long periods without access to attorneys or family members (Akram and
Johnson 2002: 317–41). A new "special registration" program applied only
to a select few nations populated primarily by Arabs and Muslims. To
many, the reconsideration of the use of race in law enforcement makes perfect sense. Public opinion, at least for a time, has shifted to favor racial profiling in the war on terrorism (ibid.: 352n.336). If the shift proves enduring,
it could have long-term impacts, including encouraging reconsideration of
the efforts to end racial profiling in all law enforcement, thereby affecting
U.S. citizens as well as foreign nationals.

The stereotyping of Arabs and Muslims historically has had a dramatic
impact on immigration law and policy. Separate procedures and the selective enforcement of immigration laws has adversely affected the civil rights
of Arabs and Muslims in the United States. In the case of Arab and Muslim
Americans, as has occurred previously with immigrants to the United
States of Eastern European, Japanese, and Mexican origins (see Salyer's and

Chavez's chapters in this volume), hate speech and dehumanizing media representations prefigured public discrimination and government persecution against members of this group. The most recent "war on terrorism" has built on previous antiterrorist measures. Sadly but not unexpectedly, private discrimination frequently has accompanied governmental action directed at Arabs and Muslims.

In important ways, contemporary immigration law ignores a constitutional revolution that embraced the norm of nondiscrimination against racial minorities, symbolized by *Brown v Board of Education,* over the latter half of the twentieth century (Chin 1998: 1–12). Assuming an extraordinary degree of freedom from any legal constraints and claiming there was no judicial review of any of the executive's decisions, the Bush administration made the federal government's immigration policing and judiciary system a primary domestic response to the threat of terrorism. With few legal constraints, acting in a time when the public was more willing to sacrifice the civil liberties of Arabs and Muslims in the name of national security, the federal government pursued harsh means with little resistance.

The events of 9/11 reveal the limited membership rights accorded persons of Arab and Muslim ancestry in the United States, whether U.S. citizen or immigrant. Various groups in the nation's history have also suffered such treatment. Many of those groups, including African Americans, Asian Americans, and Latinos, continue to strive for full membership in U.S. society. Only time will tell whether Arab and Muslim Americans will ever achieve equality under the law, or which group may replace them as the demons of tomorrow.

PART III

Policing the Borders
of the Security State

6. Security and Insecurity in a Global "War on Terrorism"

Arab-Muslim Immigrant Experience in Post-9/11 America

Christopher Dole

> Today we are facing extreme and most dangerous developments of this paradigm of security. In the course of a gradual neutralization of politics and the progressive surrender of traditional tasks of the state, security imposes itself as the basic principle of state activity. What used to be one among several decisive measures of public administration until the first half of the twentieth century now becomes the sole criterion of political legitimation. . . . A state which has security as its only task and source of legitimacy is a fragile organism; it can always be provoked by terrorism to turn itself terrorist.
>
> GIORGIO AGAMBEN (2002)

With the reordering of America's political, legal, and social landscape in the aftermath of the attacks of September 11, 2001, America's Arab and South Asian Muslim populations became constituted anew as a potential threat to national security. As the movement and mobility of these populations drew intensified scrutiny in the U.S. government's coordinated counterterrorism response, Muslim space in North America was dramatically reshaped and the trajectory of individual lives within it profoundly altered.[1] In an effort to examine the impact of these transformations, this chapter addresses the everyday realities of securitization experienced by Arab and Muslim immigrant men living in the greater metropolitan area of Boston, Massachusetts. What forms of experience became possible under the political, legal, and social conditions that emerged in the wake of 9/11? What are the implications, as Agamben suggests, of security coming to assume a central role in a state's attempt to legitimize itself—especially among the principal targets of the state's security measures? And what lessons can we draw about the making and remaking of political orders from paying close attention to the lives of those in the shadow of "national security"?

In developing an anthropological approach to the study of security,[2] I set the political discourse of national security (as a particular assemblage of bureaucratic structures, institutional practices, and political ideologies) alongside personal and psychological experiences of insecurity.[3] By linking broader political realities with locally constituted personal and psychological experience, I consider how security measures taken in the name of "national security" simultaneously produce and engage a range of personal and psychological instabilities, uncertainties, and insecurities. Focusing on the experiences of Arab-Muslim immigrant men, this chapter illustrates how the state's manufacturing of fear in response to the events of 9/11 has brought back to life a host of insecurities and anxieties that many had experienced in their countries of origin and thought they had escaped by coming to the United States. By paying close attention to these experiences, and the ways that pasts and presents can come to resemble one another, this chapter develops a framework for thinking about the state's response to 9/11 as not merely an extraordinary or excessive response to a singular event. Rather, it takes this lived sense of resemblance and familiarity (between, for instance, the United States of 2002 and Syria of 1982) as a significant commentary on emerging and enduring patterns of political legitimation and state authority.

Complementing Susan Akram and Kevin Johnson's analysis (in chapter 5 in this volume) of the media and political discourses that prepared the ground for the state's post-9/11 security response, this chapter introduces an ethnographic approach to security that attends to the lived experience of being constituted as a target on the domestic front of the United States' "War on Terrorism." In taking such an approach, the chapter examines a set of core social and psychological processes through which "national security" functions and maintains itself. As such, the following discussion illustrates not only the effect of "national security" within a particular community but also the emotions, memories, and experiences that are necessary for its constitution.

"NATIONAL SECURITY"

Despite the long history of Arabs and Muslims in America, the image of the "dangerous" and "sinister" Arab holds a particular place within the American social imaginary, one staged a thousand times over in American film and mass media (as Akram and Johnson make clear in chapter 5). Even seen against this backdrop, something radically new emerged following September 11, 2001. Within hours of the attacks on the World Trade

Center and the Pentagon, a preventive campaign targeting America's Arab and South Asian communities was initiated with the objective of forestalling further terrorist attacks. Within months, and in particular through the enactment of the USA PATRIOT Act, widespread changes were made to criminal, immigration, banking, and intelligence law; the institutional structure of the U.S. government was transformed and the Department of Homeland Security was established; enormous budgetary resources were allocated to the expansion and re-enforcement of counterterrorism campaigns; and international, federal, state, and local law enforcement officials received training in the identification and deterrence of "terrorist activity." Out of this extensive legal, institutional, financial, and military restructuring, a number of dispersed and diverse communities and groups were brought together as a population to be managed and its potential threat neutralized.

Within months of September 11, 2001, thousands of individuals from Middle Eastern and South Asian countries living in the United States would suddenly and unexpectedly disappear from the lives of their families and friends into the labyrinth of U.S. immigration law and its system of deportation centers.[4] By the beginning of November 2001, 1,182 Arab and South Asian men had been detained under a preventive detention program. While preventive detentions continued, the Department of Justice would refuse to release any further information about domestic detainees after 5 November 2001. By December 2003, an additional 1,100 individuals would be detained under the Absconder Apprehension Initiative, a program that expedited the existing deportation orders of some 6,000 Arabs and Muslims. Another 2,870 individuals would be detained through a Special Registration Program directed primarily at Arab and Muslim noncitizens. Although the total number of detentions remains uncertain, an extremely conservative estimate places the number at over 5,000. In each instance, noncitizen men from Arab and Muslim countries were selectively interviewed and required to register; thousands, domestically and abroad, were detained and interrogated for months without access to lawyers; and many have been tried in secret, while others have been denied any trials or hearings.[5]

Those not detained also came under an expansive system of surveillance. Within days of 9/11, government agents were being sent undercover into local mosques, and prominent members of Arab and Muslim communities were being recruited as informants. The FBI, in an early attempt to map Muslim space in North America, directed its field offices to count the number of mosques in their region in order to "set numerical goals for counter terrorism investigations and secret nation-security wiretaps in each region" (Isikoff 2003). Secret wiretaps, as well as secret searches, quickly would be authorized. Meanwhile, rumors of imams acting as informants began to circulate widely. In turn, investigations into Muslim charitable organizations, as well as personal bank accounts, were initiated and the assets of many frozen. Within a year the federal government would introduce a Special Registration Program (the National Security Entry/Exit Registration System, or NSEERS) that required noncitizens from twenty-four predominantly Muslim nations (and North Korea) to register at immigration offices. By the end of 2003, more than 80,000 people living in the United States would be interviewed, fingerprinted, and photographed through this program.[6] During this period, Dearborn, Michigan—the home of America's largest Arab population—would become the first American city to receive its own local office of Homeland Security.

Importantly, the state's reaction has not been monolithic. Alongside detentions, deportations, and surveillance have been a great many calls for tolerance and instances of public outreach to Arab and Muslim communities. Gestures of public support became so widespread that in the first months following 9/11 many Arab and Muslim Americans felt as if their community was, to quote Khaled Mattawa, "being inducted into a kind of collective citizenship ceremony" (Mattawa 2002: 160; quoted in Howell and Shryock 2003). Many people interviewed for this study, however, remained skeptical about the motivations behind these gestures of public support. While some interpreted the political outcry for understanding amidst selective detentions and deportations simply as duplicity—of publicly saying one thing so that secretly they could do another—others saw nothing contradictory. One thirty-seven-year-old Palestinian man, who has since been deported, depicted government calls for tolerance as simply an effort to calm a volatile public so that the state could maintain its monopoly on law enforcement and, when deemed necessary, the use of violence. In either case, emerging from this appearance of contradiction was a sense that the state's actions were unpredictable, and its motivations and meanings ambiguous.

The combination of a coordinated campaign of detention and surveillance targeting America's Arab and Muslim communities, alongside the ambiguity of its intentions and motivations, have created a situation rife with instability, uncertainty, and fear. In an effort to make sense of this situation and its effects within individual lives and communities, in what follows I address two prominent themes that emerged in interviews conducted between 2003 and 2004 with Arab-Muslim immigrant men living in metropolitan Boston.[7] First, I briefly consider the ways that state-sponsored surveillance following 9/11 affected everyday forms of social interaction and obligation. In addition to producing distrust among individuals and widespread feelings of isolation, this disruption of sociability was understood as undermining forms of moral obligation regarded as fundamental to community life. I then consider in some detail the experience of one man whose life illustrates the complex psychological and emotional impact of the state's security response to 9/11. In particular, his account exemplifies the widely acknowledged sense that post-9/11 surveillance and threats of detention within the Arab-Muslim communities revitalized memories of political and personal violence that many had sought to escape by migrating to the United States. In both instances, we see how close attention to individual and interpersonal experience reveals the intimate connection between government security practices and personal and communal insecurity among certain noncitizen residents.

Before continuing, however, I want to draw attention to the problematic status of the category "Arab Muslim." Not only does this category subsume a great diversity of (regional, national, religious, educational, linguistic) backgrounds, but it also serves potentially to reproduce a dangerous set of stereotypes—the racialized conflation of Arabs with Muslims being the most basic. Moreover, by employing "Arab Muslim" as an analytic concept, I adopt a category that is central to U.S. domestic national security policy. As such, I run the risk of further authorizing a set of policies, institutional practices, and forms of knowledge production (organized around the imperative of "national security") whose injurious consequences I seek to examine critically. As analytically and politically problematic as it is, the term "Arab Muslim" was nonetheless recognized as a valid, albeit contested, category of social identity by those interviewed for this study. Furthermore, many of my interlocutors felt that this category captured well their sense of being similarly located within national security discourses and the shared set of experiences this entailed.

THE ADDRESS BOOK: LINKS AND ASSOCIATIONS

The force of the measures taken in the name of national security following 9/11 have been sustained, for those regarded as a potential threat, by fears of being associated or linked to "terrorist activity." The establishment of such a link, many fear, would cast them into a parallel legal system based on secret hearings and evidence, a system into which one disappears and most often re-emerges, if ever, outside of the United States. Moreover, because of the broad ways in which "terrorism" is defined and "associations" determined, it is recognized that most anyone, potentially, could be linked to "terrorist activities." One never knows who in one's life or what chance encounter may establish a link or produce a closer degree of association.

Over the course of research, the address book emerged as a focal point of these anxieties surrounding such "links" and "associations." The address book—in both its paper and digital form (either stored on one's computer, or in one's cell phone)—condensed intense feelings of mutual suspicion and distrust, especially when it came to meeting new people. As a ubiquitous presence within national security and counterterrorism investigations, the address book is that object through which associations are established and investigations expanded, a node within a network of "terrorist" threat where links converge and disperse globally.[8] The customary exchange of phone numbers between new acquaintances (in the parking lot of a local mosque, at a social gathering of fellow Muslims) thus becomes imagined as taking part in a larger, ambiguous drama of "terrorist activities" and "counterterrorism investigations." In conversations about the impact of 9/11, the address book emerged time and again as a potent symbol of how fears of being associated with terrorist activity were transforming social interactions and obligations.

The significance of the address book in relation to these fears of association is captured well in an interview with a thirty-eight-year-old Moroccan man whom I will refer to simply as A. Upon arriving in Boston in 1987, A. had hoped to continue his education in physics, a subject he briefly studied as a university student in Morocco. At the time of our interview, however, A. was working as a custodian at a local research facility and was awaiting a final decision on his citizenship application. I want to quote A. at length because his account not only illustrates the disruption of social relationships and obligations by fears of becoming entangled with the state's surveillance system, but also reveals how deeply the fear of interpersonal relations can burrow into the intimacies of personal experience. In talking about the impact of 9/11 on his life, he explained:

> I don't like to attend a lot of [Muslim] gathering since September 11th. You're just afraid, you don't want to associate yourself with somebody that's involved in "activities." Sometimes you have some dreams, believe me. One day I was dreaming I was getting picked by the FBI because I was just talking to this guy, at the airport or something, and he's like, "How you doing, I'm Moroccan," and I give the guy a "How you doing?" I give him my phone number, he gives me his. . . . And as soon as he walked out, the FBI picked me up. I'm dreaming this you know. . . . And then, the next day I went to immigration for real, this is after I woke up. OK, listen to this. I'm going into immigration, I went inside, and then I heard this guy speaking in Arabic, he was

swearing and stuff, he was mad because the security guard didn't treat
him right. . . . And I turn around. Most people don't just walk away.
But I just didn't want him to get in trouble because he was swearing in
Arabic, thinking they don't understand. And I turn to him, and I say,
"How are you doing, *as-salamu alaykum*." He doesn't speak English
really good he said, and needed somebody to help him translate. I said,
"Ya, I'll do that for you. . . . but you gotta stop, you gotta calm down,
because you can get yourself in trouble. . . . Please calm down and
I'll help you, no problem." But, in a second [*snaps his fingers*] I was
thinking, and I was seeing the dream. I'm saying, "Oh my god, who
is this person?" It's just like your mind is playing on you. See, that's,
that's a type of terrorism.

A.'s experiences reflect a series of widely expressed sentiments. The simple
fear of writing down a new acquaintance's phone number or giving out
one's phone number is but one example of a more general concern about
social interaction—about attending large gatherings of Muslims, making
new friends, or talking intimately with those one does not know well.

Although fears of detention, arrest, and deportation were often the
immediate concerns, their corrosive effects rippled outward. Men like A.
were worried not only for their own safety but for the fate of their families,
who also could be subject to investigation or deportation. Outside the family, where bonds were more easily severed, social life became increasingly
restricted in order to minimize unwanted associations. Such constriction
was especially intense among those whose lives revolved around mosque
communities: visits to the mosque became limited, time spent there was
reduced to formal prayers, and participation in community events more
generally was curtailed.

A.'s account also shows the distinct ways that interpersonal fears con-
ditioned personal experience. For A., assisting a fellow Muslim was a religious and moral obligation, one that was embodied in his spontaneous and
instinctive offer of help. Yet that very offer conjured, equally spontane-
ously, the fear of a loathsome dream fulfilled. A.'s instinctive distrust of
the person before him, someone he would have helped without reservation
in the past, left him unsettled. Not only was he upset by his own hesita-
tion, but he was also troubled to realize that the anxieties of security that
had seeped into his dream life were now shaping his waking life. Despite
his fears, A. did ultimately help. For others, however, the fear of being
drawn into potentially suspicious relations—or simply the fear of drawing
any attention to oneself—forestalled the sorts of interpersonal obligations
regarded as central to Muslim communal self-identity.

This disruption of sociality simultaneously articulates within existing social and cultural structures to produce particular patterns of social isolation that, in this case, have a pronounced gendered component.[9] Although domestic "counterterrorism" measures, and the Special Registration Program in particular, explicitly target men, the disruption of social interaction described by A. has produced distinct feelings of extreme isolation among many women. A middle-aged woman who would only say she came from a Middle Eastern country, for instance, described how, after 9/11, regular trips to visit friends and friends' visits to her home were dramatically reduced and her network of non-Muslim friends was greatly restricted. While many neighbors expressed sympathy for her and her family's situation, their visits also became less frequent and, simultaneously, she limited her visits to them in order not to impose unwanted discomfort (or potential suspicion). As a result, she describes becoming overwhelmed by feelings of tremendous isolation, loneliness, and depression. In this context, mosque visits became the center of her social life. Even there, however, the past congeniality of the designated women's space became highly charged and its flow of interaction stilted.

Although experiences of extreme isolation were particularly intense among women who did not work outside the home, and while the impact of state-sponsored surveillance on women's lives took multiple forms,[10] across the interviews women stressed the importance of sociability and hospitality as forms of moral practice. If we acknowledge the significance of such social relationships and obligations in binding the community together, then we can understand the particularly corrosive effects of the climate of suspicion and mutual distrust fostered by state surveillance. By creating an environment in which one has to be continually vigilant about what one says, divulges, and insinuates to the members of one's own community, the "war on terrorism" thus permeates the social intimacies that constitute community life.

THE PASSPORT:
THE INSECURITIES OF NATIONAL SECURITY

While fears about being associated with or linked to "terrorist activities" have disrupted social and communal relations, the ways in which these fears are reproduced within a broader framework of national security have simultaneously rendered uncertain individual lives. As an inverted reflection of a desired sense of absolute national security, personal insecurity has come to characterize a range of experience, from tangible fears of being deported or having loved ones deported, to fear over losing one's job, to a general sense of not knowing what to expect next. And there was recurrent acknowledgment among the men I interviewed that these experiences were both recognizable and familiar. That is, as interviewees struggled to make sense of their unexpected feelings of fear and anxiety, conversations persistently engaged personal and familial histories of political violence. This section thus turns to the ways that national security operations evoked past experiences of state violence thought to have been escaped by coming to the United States.

In order to examine how one's present becomes problematic as it engages an escaped past, I want to consider at some length the story of a thirty-year-old Jordanian man whose account captures the lived experience of being constituted as an object against which a state's legitimacy is established. At our first meeting, in 2003, M. (as I will refer to him) was driving a taxi and living alone in a small apartment in Boston. While our initial meeting was convivial enough—chatting about Jordan, his desire to return to school, the cost of living in Boston—the intensity of his situation only became apparent over subsequent conversations. Although his appearance and behavior gave no indication, he talked at length about how he had never felt "stable" or "secure" in his life, feelings that had recently come to a head. In particular, our initial encounter occurred not long after he underwent special registration, an event around which converged a complicated nexus of problems.

Despite months of mass detentions, deportations, and wildly spreading stories of others entering for special registration and not exiting, M. reported unafraid to the John F. Kennedy Federal Building for special registration. Upon entering, he sat down with six young agents. The lead agent, as M. described the encounter, was seemingly sympathetic, yet conducted the interview with expected bureaucratic disaffection. Midway through, one agent abruptly left the room, visibly frustrated. A few minutes later he returned with a U.S. marshal and M. was informed that he would need to go with the marshal for further questioning.

> When the U.S. marshal came down, and he said, "You really have to come with me," I'm like "uh-oh." "Where is he taking me, am I getting out today or what?" That's the feeling. When you hear "U.S. marshal," you know this is a big thing going on here. Cause those guys are hired for one reason only, you know what I mean. I don't know why I had to be one of the, you know, "concerns."

M. left, with the marshal, to another floor and to another office. In silent transit, his anxieties grew, for he had experience with "going with people" like this already.

What that guy was telling me like, "you'll have to come with me." That kind of reminded me of something in Jordan. This "you'll have to come with me," [and] this [feeling of] "uh oh." . . . In Jordan, there is no law, there is no things, there is no . . . In Jordan, they can do a lot against you without you even doing nothing. And I suffered this kind of thing in Jordan, that's why I hated it, that made me leave the country.

His recognition of the familiarity of the phrase "you'll have to come with me," and the sense of trepidation that accompanied it, brought forth a troubling period in his life. In tracing M.'s narrative present, one is drawn into a constellation of tragic loss, state violence, and distress that makes concrete and specific the ways in which "national security" gains force by engaging feelings of personal and psychological insecurity in those who are, rightly or wrongly, targets for scrutiny.

At age fifteen, while still living in Amman, Jordan, M.'s father died of lung cancer. As M. describes it, he experienced his father's death as a consuming absence within which he felt adrift. Lost were his father's affection and authority, and in this void emerged a struggle for a new familial order. He was too young, according to his eldest brother, to manage the auto-parts shop bequeathed to him by his father, and so the family (now under the eldest son's protection) took over the business. When M. emerged from formal schooling, ready to take over his shop, he found his brother with legal documents, signed by their mother, transferring M.'s inheritance permanently to his brother. Left with little to occupy him, still hurting from his father's death and the shifts in power that followed, he took to idle wandering. It was here that he began to encounter the police:

This is what happened in Jordan. Let's say you live in Dorchester, and then the police see you hanging out in . . . let's say, what's the highest class area in Boston? Let's say, for example, Beacon Hill, or maybe Belmont or Newton, and the police see [you], they will stop you, and will ask you from Dorchester "what the hell are you doing here, what are you planning to do, *you'll have to come with us.*"

And extending an earlier quotation,

In Jordan, they can do a lot against you, without you even doing nothing. And I suffered this kind of thing in Jordan, that's why I hated it, that made me leave the country. That was another reason that I left the country. Because I had been so much insulted by the police. [. . .] They can swear you, swear your family, swear your mother. They can beat you, beat you to death in Jordan.

The death of M.'s father, the sorrow and family disorder that followed, his lack of hope for a future and anger over being deceived by his brother—

hurting over having, in effect, lost a brother—and the "punishment" he received for idle wandering and joblessness fused together into an affective knot, a deadlock that he called "depression," and whose resolution would come only through escape. Over his desire for escape also settled a regional instability, with its own enduring state of emergency, in which his future's promise was unimaginable beyond a repetition of the present. Amid this uncertainty and in an effort to escape the depression, he took to the streets, an effort that frequently ended in confrontations with the police. In each instance, an impending beating was announced with "you'll have to come with me/us," a phrase he came to loathe and associate with a state's use of violence to maintain order. Despite the geographic, temporal, and cultural distance between the streets of Amman and the Federal Building of Boston, the two merged as he left the interview room with the U.S. marshal.

Upon arriving at the marshal's office, M. decided that frankness was best. He knew he had nothing to hide, although he also was aware of the difficulty of proving what one does not know. After much questioning, the marshal broke off the interview, requesting M.'s passport. As M. tells it, assuming the marshal's voice, "I'm the one who has your passport now, and this passport is going to be safe. Nobody is going to touch it but me. It's not going to be lost. We're going to contact you really soon." Unlike his confident entrance into the Federal Building, he walked out troubled, yet with an enormous sense of relief. Amid this relief, however, moved memories of the troubled years of his youth, the arbitrary beatings, the loss of his father, and a further collection of familial memories that spanned generations.

Whereas the phrase "you'll have to come with me" created a link between his premigration feelings of loss and idleness, the loss of his passport extended deeper into his and his family's past. For M., the experience of having his passport confiscated forged an unanticipated connection to the stories of his grandfather's passport that he had grown up listening to, a passport that had long been an emblem of familial suffering and an artifact of colonial violence. In 1939, in the waning years of what became known as the Great Revolt, M.'s grandfather was shot through the heart by British colonial forces stationed in Jerusalem. In his dead grandfather's breast pocket, as the story went, remained a passport with a neatly shorn bullet hole. In 1948, the remaining family was forced out of Jerusalem to an encampment in Jordan, and then again in 1967 to Amman. Carried along among their limited belongings, with each move, was the grandfather's despoiled and voided passport. By the last resettling, the passport had assumed a haunting spectrality in the family. Although the passport was packed away and rarely saw the light of day, it lingered on the edges of stories and in the silences of recollection. It persisted as a symbol of the familial chaos instigated by colonial authorities in the name of maintaining order, and a material reminder of the state violence that brought an early death to M.'s grandfather.

As with other interviewees, M. was drawn to America not merely for economic reasons, but also because of its promises of stability, order, and safety. Such a setting offered the possibility of recovering from the lifelong impact of pervasive political conflict and the persistent tendency of authoritarian states to rely on violence to maintain social and political order. In coming here and starting anew, M. sought to put behind him his melancholic sense of loss and depression, the familial disorder, the sense of aimlessness, and the regional volatility that materialized in multiple instances of police brutality. In the ambiguity and uncertainty that came to define M.'s life after 9/11, however, the present became radically open and unstable, and dimensions of a past that were thought of as long left behind reopened to the present. Alongside the loss of his passport and its connection to his grandfather's death, the dread that accompanied "you'll have to come with me" and his overall feeling of nervous anticipation (of arrest, of deportation, of disappearing) brought back to life the affective knot from which he sought escape.

Over the months that followed his special registration interview, these memories and recollections intensified and came to overshadow his daily life. Moreover, his ever-impending deportation stood as a looming threat of return to a place from which he escaped. At the time of our final interview, after several phone calls and inconsistent explanations, his passport was still gone (or "safe"), he was unable to leave the country, and he remained in an indefinite state of uncertainty.

> Whether I get approved or don't, just let me know what the hell is going on, because I need to know what's going to happen so that I can do my future plan. Cause you know, at a certain age, you don't want to waste so much time of your life, you want to have some stability, and you want to know where you're going to be next year.

He summed up his situation in these terms: "After [all this], I don't know, am I going to stay here, am I going to go back, are they going to kick me out, are they going to deport me? Even if you stay, you are always in fear." For M., as with other interviewees, state-manufactured instability and insecurity have created an opening through which disturbing and unsettling dimensions of one's past return. In this process, people's relationship to the present is problematized and their orientation toward the future made wholly uncertain.

The climate of fear, suspicion, and uncertainty emerging from and systematically produced in the wake of 9/11 has been experienced by many as a reliving or repetition of the forms of violence they fled in coming to the United States. M.'s case clearly illustrates this repetitive quality of Arab-Muslim encounters with national security. (When A. referred to his unsettling dreams as a form of "terrorism," for instance, he did so by invoking premigration memories of fear and anxiety that coincided with a cousin's detention and interrogation by Moroccan police.) As these examples depict, the extent of the war on terrorism is therefore not merely limited to a series of specific, known, visible state responses. Quite the contrary, the actual presence of FBI and secret service agents in people's homes has been regarded by many as an understandable response by authorities. Rather, the war's front is infinitely expanded and more deeply embedded through its production of a negative space or void of uncertainty, ambiguity, and unknowability in which one's future becomes unpredictable. It is here that the measures taken in the name of national security fasten to a troubling set of affective associations and insecurities that span personal, familial, and political disorderliness and insecurity.

THE FUTURE OF AN ILLUSION (OF SECURITY)

In approaching security ethnographically, I have emphasized the lived experience of individuals entangled in particular ways within a discourse of "national security." While there are assuredly others who are also bound within this discourse (e.g., the U.S. marshal who interviewed M., or the security guards who searched A. upon his entrance into the Federal Building), I have focused on those who have received particularly intense scrutiny, because of their status as Arab-Muslim immigrant men, within the security operations initiated in the wake of 9/11. In examining the forms of life that these discourses and operations have made possible, I thus return to a question posed at the outset: What lessons can we draw about the making and remaking of political orders from paying close attention to the lives of those in the shadow of "national security"?

In the accounts of those subjected to surveillance and threats of detention or deportation, "security" and "insecurity" becoming aligned in distinct ways. The multiple connotations of the term "security" are illustrative here. On the one hand, we can understand "security" as referring to the assemblage of state-sponsored institutions, practices, and ideologies dedicated to protecting the safety of the nation's population and its property. This is the conventional connotation of "national security." On the other hand, we can also understand "security" as indexing the existential, embodied sense of wholeness and emotional stability—of a unified, bounded self with a continuity of memory—that one associates with normative notions of the "secure" or "stable" person. Framed in these terms, a primary task of the first form of (national) security is the protection of this second sense of (personal) security. The stories that I have recounted, however, reveal an alternate configuration. That is, the system of surveillance and selective deportation initiated after 9/11 has systematically produced personal and community insecurity among those subjected to targeted attention. "Security" and "insecurity," in this respect, are mutually conditioning.

While difficult questions remain concerning the relationship between the insecurity of a select few and the security of others, as well as the processes that keep the latter largely unaware of the former (Fischer 2007), it is apparent that the manufactured ambiguity and uncertainty of "national security" that defined counterterrorism campaigns (for those who were their targets) parasitically attaches to personal and psychological experiences of instability and insecurity. And as we have encountered, this method of ensuring "national security" was seen by many as a government's attempt to prevent terrorism by producing its own forms of terror. A., for example, was terrorized by dreams of arrest and detention that damaged his personal relationships. Indeed, among those interviewed for this study, "terrorism" and "counterterrorism" were not depicted as clearly distinguishable phenomena. Rather, for those whose lives take shape in the shadows of surveillance and fears of detention or deportation, what links "terrorism" and "counterterrorism" is the ease with which one can slip into the other. Where A. acknowledged this in the feelings that his dreams had become terroristic, Agamben, in this chapter's epigraph, put it more bluntly: "A state which has security as its only task and source of legitimacy is a fragile organism; it can always be provoked by terrorism to turn itself terroristic" (2002).

Particularly striking in this regard were the ways that interviewees described the experience of being the object of state-sponsored security measures as both recognizable and familiar. In the methods of surveillance and intimidation employed by the state in its response to 9/11, interviewees recognized the very forms of state violence that had been employed to subdue political dissent and opposition in the setting where they had grown up. Importantly, this recognition of familiarity was not merely the result of an abstract observation of resemblances. Instead, in that most had either directly or indirectly experienced these forms of state violence, it took the form of a collection of bodily and emotional responses that emerged amid intense uncertainty and insecurity. We thus can understand this recognition of familiarity as establishing a continuity of personal suffering that draws together a series of disparate political settings (Jordan, Lebanon, the United States, Morocco, Syria, and so on) and, in the process, offers a revealing commentary on the genealogy of the state's methods for ensuring security.

In particular, this sense of continuity—such that an authoritarian state like Syria, known for its violent suppression of dissent, can be seen as resembling the United States—raises critical questions about the exceptionality of the security measures taken in response to the attacks of 9/11. Should we view such instances of state surveillance, threats of detention, and the cultivation of insecurity simply as an exceptional response to a singular event? Ethnographic accounts of state violence elsewhere would suggest, rather, that this singular event merely exposes what typically exists either unrecognized in the routines of everyday life or segregated into areas that remain out of view (see Taussig 1992, 1997). The experiences of Arab-Muslim immigrant men who find themselves captured in the discourse of "national security," and the continuity of personal suffering and state violence that this establishes, would suggest just such a reading of the state's counterterrorism response to the attacks of 9/11. And given the history of the state subjecting citizens to what had previously been reserved for the noncitizen, this would also suggest that we take great care in how we approach the expansion of state authority and policing through the targeting of noncitizens.

In the end, this framing of security and insecurity must take care to avoid portraying those interviewed for this study as passive victims. Indeed, my interlocutors expressed significant concern about the potential of this research to do just that. While social lives were disrupted, they certainly were not destroyed. Alternative tactics of relating and speaking took shape in response to shifting strategies of state surveillance. For many, too, self-dignity was considered a vitally important religious ideal, and the status of victim implied dignity's loss. At times, interviewees went so far as to blame themselves for not sufficiently educating the American public about Islam before 9/11, presuming that such education might have prevented much of the anti-Arab and anti-Muslim backlash. The long-term consequences of 9/11 within Muslim and Arab communities, however, raise once again the problem of victimhood. In the wake of 9/11, America's Muslim and

Arab communities have entered the political stage to a far greater extent than ever before—with increasing calls to vote, to publicly condemn terrorism, to be politically active, to have a collective voice heard in federal and state legislatures, and to work with other non-Arab and non-Muslim organizations. Given the contemporary structure of America's political field, however, the available path to political influence being offered takes the form of a race-based identity politics. Insomuch as such identity-based politics rely on assuming the position of victim of injury, as Wendy Brown has observed (1995), how are America's Arab or Muslim communities to enter into the American political scene otherwise than by claims of victimhood? More basic still, considering the heterogeneity of backgrounds, what sort of community is going to coalesce through such a process? And how might new forms of solidarity also institute expanded sites for surveillance and control? While it must remain for future research to examine these political binds further, the present discussion suggests that addressing such questions requires that we take into account the lived experiences and memories of state violence against which a political order seeks to sustain its legitimacy.

7. Policing the Borders in the Heartland

Nancy A. Naples

Citizenship is achieved in particular local contexts and is an ongoing accomplishment that cannot be understood by exclusive focus on law and immigration policy. Examination of local social regulatory practices reveals the complex and contradictory ways different individuals and groups are incorporated into the wider polity and how gender, race, and class are woven in and through these practices.[1] While the border between Mexico and the United States is the site of the most pronounced and aggressive policing of U.S. citizenship, other sites of both formal and informal social regulatory practices shape the everyday lives of migrants as well as long-term residents in many other parts of the country (see, for example, Zúñiga and Hernández-León 2005).

The specific analysis presented here is based on a twelve-year ethnographic study of a small rural town I call Midtown, Iowa, which has experienced a radical increase in the in-migration of Mexican and Mexican Americans[2] for work in an expanded food processing plant. As a consequence of active recruitment by the plant owners and informal networking, Mexican and Mexican-American workers and their families migrated to the town beginning in 1990.[3] The increased presence of Mexicans and Mexican Americans as permanent residents altered the ethnic composition of this formerly ethnically homogeneous town. While it is the actions taken by the plant owners that started the process of social restructuring in this one small Iowa town, the daily practices of local police and other state actors furthered the process by which the Latino newcomers were permitted or, in many ways, prevented from becoming full members of the community. The economic and demographic changes provided the basis for a longitudinal ethnographic study of the relationship between economic restructuring and the social restructuring of class, gender, and race-ethnicity

Following the feminist geographer Doreen Massey (1994: 138–139), I view "localities" as *"constructions* out of the intersections and interactions of concrete social relations and social processes." With this situated approach, it is possible to analyze how global economic and political processes, national and state policy, and local practices and social interactions work together in complex and sometimes contradictory ways to *regulate citizenship.* By placing the analysis within a community context, I explore the relationship between citizenship practices and the market, state, local social institutions, and informal community interactions. By shifting the standpoint to the everyday life experiences of immigrants, migrants, and others who are the targets of state interventions, certain less visible features of state activity and the contradictions of this activity are brought into view.[4]

SHIFTING THE STANDPOINT ON THE STATE

The analysis in this chapter argues for a broadened definition of the state that captures the multiple arenas through which residents are incorporated into the U.S. economy, society and polity (and how community processes, migratory patterns, and resistance strategies may inhibit incorporation). This process of incorporation occurs at the local community level and involves ongoing social regulatory activities that circumscribe the ways in which new residents can make claims as permanent members of specific locales. These local social regulatory activities and interactions construct the racialized, gendered, and class-specific grounds upon which Mexicans and Mexican Americans can earn a living wage, access social provisions, and gain a political voice to protect their status as legitimate members of the local polity. Furthermore, the social regulation of settlement, mobility, communication, and social interaction interact with one's ability to achieve full membership in a particular locale, which is firmly linked with the expression of, and access to, citizenship rights.

The history of Mexicans and Mexican Americans in the United States is influenced by a complex pattern of colonization, proletarianization, agricultural industrialization, and disparate migratory flows. Economic restructuring contributes to a shifting international division of labor that is reshaping the racial-ethnic composition of communities across the United States. Mexicans have been particularly hard hit by processes of displacement and wage depreciation in regions across their country. As a consequence of their displacement from other regions, coupled with the development of low-wage food processing and related industries in the rural Midwest, Latinos are forming a growing proportion of migrants to the Midwest (Stanley 1994). As a result, rural communities in the Midwest with a traditionally white European-American population have been forced to confront their own racism and manage ethnic tensions previously seen as the problems of urban areas or rural communities in the South, Southwest, and West.[5]

Much has been written about the experiences and incorporation of Mexicans and Mexican Americans in the West or Southwest (Acuna 1981; Boswell and Jorjani 1988; Chavez 1992; Fernández-Kelly 1983; Douglas Massey 1987; Montejano 1986; Robinson 1993; Thomas 1985). Less is known about the more recent immigration and migration of Mexicans and Mexican Americans in the rural Midwest (Millard and Chapa. 2001; Zúñiga and Hernández-León 2005). Ethnographic attention to the experiences of incorporation for immigrants and migrants to the rural Midwest provides an opportunity explore the complex ways citizenship is achieved as well as contested (see also Lamphere 1992; Millard and Chapa. 2001; Oboler 2006; Rocco 2006). The arrival of nonwhite residents in these small rural towns often leads to heated discussions about the efficacy of economic development activities and anger at the state agencies for promoting such strategies. However, the incorporation of different racial-ethnic groups into the rural community also increases awareness of the local manifestations of global political-economic forces (Naples 1994). The contradictions are frequently played out in community-level responses to state intervention as they influence processes of racial formation. In addition to the local economic development corporation, other sites of social regulation and contestation include the police, state licensing agencies, schools, and health and social services, as well as employment practices, housing provision, gender relations, and language.

Following a discussion of the local constructions of community and citizenship in the field site, I explore the process of economic development and shifting recruitment strategies of the local employer. I then analyze the contradictory effects of immigration law enforcement and other formal and informal social regulatory processes in terms of the politics of settlement, mobility, communication, and social interaction. I conclude with a discussion of how these class-based, racialized, and gendered patterns contributed to the social regulation of citizenship in rural Iowa.

THE LOCAL SOCIAL REGULATION OF CITIZENSHIP

Resistance to the civic, social, and relational incorporation of Mexican and Mexican-American residents in Midtown is firmly entrenched in housing practices, police surveillance, health and social services, and translation services, as well as the social regulation of interpersonal relationships, especially teenagers' associational and dating behavior. These community-based social regulatory processes led to limited contact between Latino and non-Latino residents; shaped interactions between police, educators, service providers and Latino clients; and compromised associational possibilities and relationships among residents in a variety of settings.

Community-based constructions of, and responses to, racism and ethnic tension vary across different parts of the United States. New Latino residents to the rural Midwest rarely have access to advocacy organizations and other formal groups established in other locales to protect the rights of workers or community residents who experience discrimination, harassment, or lack of access to vital health and social services. Since most long-term residents in these towns hold onto a firm distinction between those who belong and those who are considered outsiders, "newcomers" frequently face a great deal of resistance when they begin to make claims in different arenas (Naples 1996). One significant way outsiderness is constructed is through the visual marker of race-ethnicity. Racial-ethnic differentiation inevitably places anyone who does not (visually, at least) appear to share the same racial-ethnic background at the margins of small town life. Class position, language, and associational patterns such as marital status and household structure are also markers of belongingness in rural Iowa.

The widely held belief in agrarian ideology serves as a powerful discursive frame that informs the social regulation of citizenship in rural Iowa. By "agrarian ideology," I mean a privileging of family farmers, especially those who adhere to a traditional gender division of labor and who have a multigenerational history in the region. This formulation of community identity and belonging makes it difficult for anyone who moves into the region for work in a factory or other low-wage nonfarm employment to become an accepted part of the community (Naples 1994, 1997). Those residents who do not own farms in the community but play central professional roles such as doctor, educator, or clergy are also granted high status within the community, a consequence of class relations within these small towns.[6] Those who perform nonfarm work at minimum wage or who are receiving public assistance are therefore further marginalized within the town's somewhat collectively held class-based ethos.

The privileged position of the middle class farm household with the traditional gender division of labor masks the many inequalities that have long characterized rural Midwestern communities. These patterns of class, gender, residency, and race-based inequalities serve as the grounds for denying "membership" in the community to those from non-farm working-class backgrounds, single mothers, or new residents, as well as anyone else constructed as "an outsider." Those who dare to speak out against inequality and discrimination are further marginalized (Naples 1997). Many more keep silent for fear of reprisals from their neighbors who are invested in seeing only the positive benefits of rural life. Consequently, agrarian ideology serves as a social regulatory frame that inhibits the full incorporation of many white European-American residents as well as Mexican and Mexican Americans.

As a consequence of these powerful frames, those within the marginalized segments of the town may never acquire the designation of legitimate community member (Naples 1996). However, certain changes in the political environment may create the grounds for shifts in designations that result in reincorporating some newcomers or disenfranchising other longer-term residents. For example, when the Immigration and Naturalization Service (INS) raided Midtown, some of the longer-term residents began to incorporate as "community members" the Latinos who held legal residency or citizenship status but were picked up in a raid and detained at the regional INS office in Omaha.[7] Further, as the composition of the Latino community shifted from predominantly single male workers to two-parent families, Anglo residents softened somewhat in the negative attitudes they expressed, although mistrust of Latinos' long-term commitment to Midtown remained strong. White European-American residents often commented: "Well, many have strong family values." In keeping with the privileging of a heterosexual two-parent family form, when longer-term residents are divorced or turn to welfare for economic support they frequently experience alienation from the perceived "community-at-large." Ironically, this heteronormal construction of family serves as one dimension upon which Mexican and Mexican-American residents find acceptance.

REGULATING SETTLEMENT

The politics of location are especially revealing of the contradictory features of social regulatory practices. Lack of affordable housing was one of the most consistently mentioned problems in the community. The mayor, city councilmen, social service providers as well as almost every other resident interviewed stressed that Midtown did not have an adequate supply of affordable housing. Furthermore, they did not see how the town could absorb the new workers who were earning minimum wage in the food processing plant and could not afford to pay for the limited housing in the community. Owners of rental property took advantage of the housing shortage to increase rents and alter rental practices. In response to this perceived need, the economic development corporation worked to establish an apartment complex financed by the Farmers' Home Administration (FmHA) that would provide low- to moderate-income housing for sixteen families.

In the meantime some workers commuted up to fifty miles to work in the plant. A number of residents were concerned about the problems posed by workers from out-of-town who do not have a sense of "pride in the community." However, when workers and their families were able to find housing in the community a process of segregation and discrimination was put firmly in place. The director of the local social services agency reported that when a low-income family qualified for a housing subsidy landlords often refused to make the required repairs to their buildings in order to pass HUD inspection: "[S]ome of them [eligible for HUD assistance] . . . found a house, but then the landlord refuses to do anything to pass inspection and so there it is, they're stuck again." Furthermore, she reported that in response to the expansion at the plant some residents were buying housing and charging "outrageous prices for rent." For example, she explained, "They have some trailers down here in the trailer court. I mean, they're new trailers—but they're talking $400.00 a month rent and they're furnished and everything, but, still if you work at [the plant] up here for [minimum wage], there's no way they can afford that." Some landlords also took advantage of the workers' needs to share housing with one or more other families. Rather than charge a flat monthly rent, some owners were charging the Mexican and Mexican-American renters a monthly fee per adult in the home.

Half of the Mexican and Mexican-American workers and their families found rental housing in a trailer park. The trailer park was located on the edge of town and provided housing for predominantly low-income families. Some members of the community believed that the trailer park is the home for unemployed people who are "not really desiring of a job." Others see it as a place where there are a lot of problems connected with a supposed low-income "lifestyle." As one white community resident explained, "It's just the traditional, the minimum-wage workers, that's their lifestyle and that's really what you expect." However, the owners of the trailers did little to correct problems renters found with their homes, and the quality of the housing in the trailers continued to deteriorate over the course of our field work. Sister Theresa, one of the two Catholic nuns who commute to

Midtown and provide support for low-income residents, complained about the bad condition of the trailers: "Some of those trailers should be burned down. When you go in there, it is just like you are almost outside." Another informant explained, "I think if you went down and wanted to rent one, they would probably rent you one. . . . They are in bad shape. They have the water shut off to them now. . . . But there has never been any upkeep on those trailers at all. Nothing. . . . There were holes in the floors and ceilings. They are just terrible."

The economic development groups in Midtown and the neighboring town of Southtown have placed housing high on their agenda. However, the director of the local Housing Authority who is charged with facilitating the development of low-income housing reported having trouble finding landlords who will take the low-income rental certificates.

> I am having trouble . . . trying to get property owners, landlords to register with our office, that way, if someone comes in, not a property manager, but we can give them a list of people to contact. So far, that is a slow process. I think they are afraid that we will try to force them into doing things. I don't know. . . . There are some vacant houses that I have contacted the owners to try to get them to turn those into rentals and they don't want to bother. They would rather just leave them sit than do anything with them. It is frustrating. Someone drives around and sees an empty house, there is an empty house but there is not much we can do unless the owners themselves decide to do something.

The housing segregation and discrimination furthered the social regulatory process and broadened the stigma placed on all low-income residents. The interaction between state and federal programs to assist those living in poverty and community processes to exploit and marginalize these residents left many Mexican and Mexican-American families with few housing options and household arrangements available to them (also see Bullard, Grigsby, and Lee 1994). Ironically, commuting to their jobs at the plant, as well as sharing limited housing with several adults or extended family members, served as markers of their marginality as well as a presumed lack of commitment to the local community. In this way, the social regulation of settlement served to sustain the belief held by many Anglo residents that the Latinos were not interested in full incorporation into the town.

REGULATING MOBILITY

Many Mexican and Mexican-American residents interviewed complained that their mobility and access to the small number of public spaces was circumscribed by their fear of unpleasant interactions with white residents. Their fears were further fueled by a 1992 INS raid that contributed to the deportation of a number of workers and subsequent out-migration of many more who did not feel safe remaining in Midtown. Erin Landers, one of the plant owners and a longtime resident of Midtown, reported that the resident who was suspected of calling in the INS believed, as did many other Midtown residents, that all the workers were undocumented:

> [P]eople who are biased think all Mexicans are illegal. Matter of fact, they use that term. [They say]: "We want you to get these illegal aliens out of here." And unfortunately when Immigration came in and checked some documents, even though we followed all the procedures and everything appeared to be in order, there were a few whose documents were illegal and that was a real valuable learning experience for us because we learned even more what to look for and I probably drive Immigration nuts because now I call to verify every document just to be safe because I just don't want to encounter any more problems.

The INS "raided" the town in spring 1992. INS officials waited in the parking lot outside the plant and picked up Mexican and Mexican-American residents walking along the streets and playing in the schoolyard. Landers, a life-long resident of the area, believed that a local white resident who resented the Mexicans and Mexican Americans contacted the INS. Landers described the raid as follows:

> Immigration did what they were asked to do. They came in and literally raided our business. They had vans surrounding the building and people on the roof and it was absolutely a terrible experience and they came on shift changes. They knew our shift hours and the people from first shift that were leaving. We even saw them stop and handcuff one of the individuals who was an American citizen who happened to be Hispanic. . . . [T]hey grabbed him out of his car, handcuffed him, put him in their vehicle, . . . and ran a check on him and [he was] scared to death saying: "I'm a citizen! I'm an American citizen!" And these folks spoke English—they'd learned that in the home, but they were scared to death they were going to be sent back to Mexico and shouldn't have been.

The tension created by this and subsequent raids in Midtown generated a sense of anxiety among everyone, including those with United States citizenship and working papers. Since legal residents had also been picked up in the raids and driven to Omaha before they were released without transportation home, their fears were well founded.

The INS raids, subsequent deportations, and ongoing investigation served to regulate the lives of all Mexican and Mexican Americans living in Midtown. INS intervention also made visible the shifting construction of the "outsider" in Midtown (Naples 1996). While INS activities served to confirm white European-American residents' fears that there were, at least initially, many undocumented Mexican workers in the plant, it also highlighted the fact that many other workers were "legitimate" members of the community. In addition to the growing acceptance of the Mexicans and Mexican Americans on the part of some Anglo residents, several white residents also reported an increased awareness of the oppressive features of INS interventions. For example, Bernice Poster, who was born in the area and now runs a small business in Midtown, described how her consciousness shifted when she tried to help a young Mexican man who was unfairly arrested and deported after he recovered from an accident. She explained, "I used to think that they [INS] were the good guys, that they were doing a good job. But after what I've been through [in trying to help a young Latino] and seen I think they're all a bunch of rats. I've seen how they treat the Mexicans and no one should be treated like that. They're like the Gestapo." A similar, and in many ways, more interesting shift in consciousness occurred in response to perceived unfair treatment of the Mexican and Mexican-American residents by the local police. Here the local police, all of whom are residents of the town, were constructed as separate from "the community" in much the same way as the INS agents.

The fear of deportation and harassment by INS officials occurred alongside ongoing harassment by local police. Even many white European-American residents reported that the police targeted Latinos to a greater extent than the white youth who were often the cause of certain problems. Some reported that the Latinos were arrested for drinking when white residents would be escorted home or ignored. In the first half of the 1990s, the white residents were, for the most part, unaware of the extent of police harassment. As the contact between the white European Americans and Latinos increased, the awareness of police harassment grew. Sympathetic white residents have complained about the unfair treatment and a few have established alliances with some of the Mexican and Mexican-American residents. As another manifestation of the contradictions inherent in social regulatory practices, the increased police surveillance of traffic violations led to an increase in the number of young white European-American residents who were pulled over for traffic violations.

As the number of Latino youth increased, Anglo community members worried about the importation of urban problems such as gang activity, use of drugs, and interracial violence. After one incident in which a fight broke out between a Latino and an Anglo teenager, the high school and park became objects of white ethnic community concerns and police surveillance. The police chief explained, "We have had some racial tensions and some racial problems at school and basically we just put officers over there to make sure there is no violence or anything like that." He explained that the school officials called in the police when the fight broke out. He said that he now sends police officers over to the school "towards the end of the school day when people are getting out and then we monitor the traffic and the parking lot." He believes that their presence will deter further outbreaks of violence.

Since there are few places for young people to congregate after school, both Latino and Anglo youth gravitate towards the park. During summer 1998, a fight broke out between an Anglo teenager and a Latino youth that led to widespread fear about the so-called racial tensions in the community. While most European-American adult residents we spoke to about the incident in the park blamed the Latino youth, both Anglo and Latino youth told a more nuanced story. Anglo teenager Tim Brown explained, "a sophomore beat up a Mexican kid because he drove by . . . the park and the Mexican threw a ball at his car or something and he pulled in and was asking him why he did it and the Mexican kid got up in his face and he spit in it and that was it. He just knocked him out and that was pretty much all there was. He didn't get into any trouble because the Mexican kid started it by throwing the ball at his car, which that is how it is." This incident seemed to ignite the fears of many white European-American residents that the Mexican and Mexican-American youth were engaging in "gang activity." Many parents forbade their children from going to the park. In a 1998 interview, Tim Brown explained that as a result of the park incident, white residents felt run out of the park. From the accounts we received by Anglo and Latino youth, this perception reflects Anglo fear of the growing Latino presence in the town. According to Tim, "During the summer, it used to be that we'd go up to the park and play basketball all the time, but really the park in the summertime now is pretty much all Mexicans and they have pretty much run all the white kids out of playing basketball, but we still do some. It has changed that way because there are a lot more now than there ever was and when they get a big group there, there is more racism against white people than there would be there by themselves." Of course, the Latino teenagers tell a somewhat different story about the park incident and other interactions with Anglo community members. They define the Anglos' reaction to their presence in the park as a result of racism and their dislike of Mexicans and Mexican Americans. Ironically, Anglo fear of the Latino youth contributed to their circumscribing their own children's mobility and use of the park.

State licensing agencies also play a key social regulatory role. One of the main sites in this regard is the Department of Motor Vehicles (DMV). Public transportation is generally unavailable in rural communities. Consequently, most residents require access to motor vehicles for work, grocery shopping, attending church services, or visiting health clinics, and so on. Consequently, the DMV plays a central role in providing the means by which residents of rural communities can sustain their lives. Obtaining a legal driver's license is even more essential for the Mexicans and Mexican Americans who are often stopped by local police with little or no cause. However, even those possessing legal birth certificates and working papers report problems when they apply for a license to drive.

Anna Ortega's experience illustrates the problem. Ortega, who is a bilingual United States citizen, was successful in her fight to protect other Mexican Americans from discrimination by DMV officials. She effectively mobilized the political power of the Mexican-American community in her hometown of Laredo, Texas. Ortega reports: "[The DMV] tried to take away the U.S. citizenship cards from the Tejanos. I had to bring the judge over and complain. I had to call Immigration. I even had to call the mayor of Laredo, Texas, to tell him what was going on here—that they were picking up our birth certificates saying that they were fake and that we were illegal aliens." Ortega's story highlights the value of two key resources for the migrants to Midtown: English-language proficiency and ongoing links between the migrant and settled Mexican-American community in other areas of the United States.[8]

REGULATING COMMUNICATION AND ASSOCIATION

During field trips to Midtown in 1991, white European-American residents were especially vocal about the Mexicans' and Mexican-Americans' lack of English language proficiency. Many believed that it was simultaneously a sign that these "newcomers" did not want to be a part of the community and a lack of their educational ability. And yet key community actors initially resisted the idea that they should provide English as a Second Language (ESL) courses or hire a Spanish teacher for the local high school. Each of these strategies would cost the town money and, they argued, the Mexicans and Mexican Americans were not going to remain long in Midtown.

Progressive clergy who initially spoke out in support of the new residents were frequently chastised by parishioners who wanted to deny the community's racism, ethnic tensions, or poverty. Steps taken by local officials to address the specific needs of non-English-speaking residents, such as the hiring of translators for emergency services or ESL teachers for "limited English proficient" students, were often compromised by the limited Spanish proficiency of translators and ESL teachers. Maryann Manor, the wife of one of the ministers, was among the community residents who attempted to address the problem (which she defined as a mutual inability to communicate). She spoke a little Spanish and organized a study group for other community members who wanted to learn the language. Manor reported that she and two other community members approached the plant owners with the idea of offering an ESL course to the workers at the factory, but the owners refused the offer.

Workers stated that the plant did not employ a translator. The management called upon bilingual employees to help them communicate with the non-English speaking workers. In 1991, Landers explained why they had not translated the employee handbook and how the workers learned about the plant's policies and employee benefits: "[B]ecause it is fourteen pages long, compressed print. Yeah. So what we do there, when they are hired, when I interview them I go over the things that are in the handbook so they are aware of our policies and benefits and, you know, all of their requirements. Ah, and if they don't speak good enough English then I have somebody that is bilingual help me to translate that and that works real well." However, some of the workers interviewed who did not speak English reported that they were unable to understand how their pay was calculated or the procedures for overtime. Workers who knew more English helped their coworkers, as Efren Palacios explains: "Your companions who are more advanced and know some English [explain the rules, the contract, etc.]. There is one guy who works with me and who helps. There is always a companion who is there to help. If there is a Mexican who needs help with filling out an application, someone goes and tells a companion and they go to help with the application." Lack of English proficiency compromised the workers' ability to advocate for their rights in the workplace. When asked what the workers did if they had a complaint, Palacios explained: "Well no, no one complains. No one knows who to go to or any of that." Most of the Mexicans and Mexican Americans also discussed the ways that lack of English proficiency left them vulnerable in their daily interactions with non-Spanish-speaking members of the community. As Manuel Gomez put it, "We don't know English. We don't know how to read it or speak it so as to defend ourselves."

Several Mexicans interviewed believed that neither the interpreter nor the ESL teacher (who also acts as an interpreter when called upon by city officials) were providing accurate translation. According to Medina:

> Everyone knows that I don't like the way they interpret. I tell
> them what I can and what I can't, well so be it. I don't want them
> to say something else. Because I know they say one thing and one
> understands that they're not saying it the way it is. If I say it, I'm going
> to say it like this, even if it's not good, but you're saying it the way you
> want it said. They, no, they say other things that aren't so. Friends of
> mine have told me that they told them to say one thing and that they
> said something else. And they said, "Hey! That's not what I said!" so
> they know it's not right. I don't like them to interpret.

During the period 1992–94, one bilingual community worker from Texas lived in Midtown who, Medina believes, was not used as an interpreter by the city because he was of Mexican descent "'cause the police think . . . he'll help the Mexicans."

Public officials claim that there are few capable bilingual residents who can serve as translators and ESL teachers, that the limited pool forces them to choose less-than-adequate personnel. Others insist that the services are more than adequate, while still others resent the need to provide such services. Bilingual Latino residents claim that the translators typically hired by public agencies do not communicate effectively to Spanish-speaking residents and often make significant mistakes when interpreting to public officials and health care and service providers. Depending on the context, these mistakes are of more or less consequence, with the most serious problems occurring when these translators are used in court.

Language is a crucial site of contestation in which long-term residents and newcomers negotiate their relationships to the community and to each other. This process of negotiation goes beyond the limits to communication that language differences pose. In fact, many white European-American residents react to the Latinos who speak Spanish among themselves in public spaces with fear. Teenager Martha Glass reported that "if they [the Latinos] are at the park or something and they are talking in Spanish, they [the police] go up to them and they say that they are saying that they are going to do something. This one kid, he waves to the cops to say hi, and is pulled over and they started yelling at him for doing that. At the park, if the Hispanics are talking and standing around, people think they are talking about them." Martha articulated this fear herself when she described her reaction to a group of Latino high-school students talking among themselves in Spanish. Although she does not speak Spanish, she assumed that these young people were talking about her and her friends: "Some of the Hispanics are kind of rude sometimes and they are talking in Spanish about us and I told them if they wanted to say something, they should say it to my face or don't say it all and they came over and started yelling at us."

The struggle over language and communication ran through interactions with employers, coworkers, city employees, and other community residents. Not surprisingly, language barriers and cultural differences posed key challenges to school personnel. School officials and teachers often reacted with fear when Latino students spoke to each other in Spanish. A number of high-school students reported that Latinos have been suspended for speaking Spanish in school. As the above examples illustrate, community members who were in positions of power frequently tried to control the mode of expression and association of the young Latino residents. These attempts were especially directed at controlling gender and race relations. These attempts also had some contradictory consequences for white European-American residents, as well.

The social regulatory practices that shaped the possibility for achieving citizenship and full membership in Midtown included surveillance and informal regulation of gender, class, and racial-ethnic relations. Interracial dating was particularly disturbing to those interested in maintaining the divisions between segments of the community from different class and racial-ethnic backgrounds. Concerns about interracial dating and marriage were articulated by educators, social workers, parents, and clergy. Joan Lamm, who had been a teacher in Midtown High for six years, summed up her fears as follows:

> Culture differences are real interesting too because, um, the man's approach to women in Mexico is much different than it is here. And it's very confusing to the high school students . . . Well, you will find groups of Spanish-speaking boys talking together about the girls [and the girls] . . . are flattered by this, but actually . . . [the boys] are not speaking in a flattering way, OK. So they, I don't know, they have a tendency that they're real charming to the girls, but they're not. The approach is not the same as an American boy's would be and sometimes the girls are a little confused and hurt by this.

Lamm, who did not speak Spanish, feared that the young boys were saying "things in Spanish that would translate to whore or slut, or things that were derogatory." The fear of Latino male sexuality and aggression formed a powerful discursive subtext in the interviews with white European-American women residents. Anglo community members viewed Latino men through the stereotyped notion of "machismo," which is said to be characterized by, among other things, "extreme verbal and bodily expression of aggression toward other men, frequent drunkenness, and sexual aggression and dominance" (Hondagneu-Sotelo and Messner 1994), thus contributing to their surprise when Latino adolescents and men did not exhibit these qualities.

Rarely did the white European-American residents mention the Mexican and Mexican-American women.[9] Due to the recruitment strategies of the plant owners and gendered migratory pattern of Mexican and Mexican-American labor, the first wave of workers comprised men between the ages of sixteen and forty. During the second wave a number of women migrated to work in the plant or to accompany their husbands. The third wave includes a larger percentage of families with men and women and their children. As a consequence of the migratory time sequencing and gendered division of household labor, the men are more visible to the wider community. Furthermore, several other factors contribute to the Latinas' public invisibility at this stage of migration. These factors are related to the patterns of settlement, mobility, and communication mentioned above. For example, many of these women did not have access to transportation, nor does Midtown offer the food products they desired. Families pooled resources and traveled weekly to Des Moines, a distance of two-and-one-half hours, to purchase groceries from a store that stocks Mexican food and other Mexican products. Lack of facility with English also contributed to their limited interaction with other community members.

Initial research indicated only reluctant attempts in the early 1990s to deal with perceived differences. Many white European-American residents contrasted the ideal-typical traditional resident with the newcomers. And, of course, the Latinos were viewed as not measuring up for a variety of reasons. The racism implicit in many comments about the Mexicans and Mexican Americans was couched in discussions of the white residents' fear of a rise in the cost of education and social services, a growing underclass, and increased crime (also see Hagan and Palloni 1999). By the end of the 1990s, a number of significant shifts had taken place. Since a growing proportion of Latinos were remaining for longer periods than in the early 1990s, their presence was now viewed as a permanent feature of the community. Furthermore, as the Latino children entered the schools, they formed friendships with Anglo children, thus breaking down divisions between residents of different racial-ethnic backgrounds.

This analysis reveals how the social regulation of citizenship changes over time and is influenced by the extent to which diverse community members legitimate or deny community membership to "newcomers." The power to control settlement is one of the most potent strategies for circumscribing citizenship claims and other modes of incorporation (Doreen Massey 1994; Rose 1993). Clearly, that power is most vividly observed at the border between Mexico and the United States. However, the increase in new destinations for immigrants and the growing surveillance strategies that local communities now employ in post-9/11 efforts to prevent terrorism require community-based research designed to explore the interdependence of dominant groups with those kept on the margins (Millard and Chapa 2001; Zúñiga and Hernández 2005). bell hooks (1990) highlights this contradiction in analyzing the dynamics of domination and resistance in the segregated community in which she grew up. She also reminds us that such marginalized places can also serve as sites of resistance and "a space for radical openness which allows the creation of a counter-hegemonic politics" (hooks 1990, summarized by Rose 1993: 156; see also Evans 1979; Fraser 1989). Despite the potential of such physical marginalization for radical challenge to the dominant class and racial-ethnic group in Midtown, the diversity of the Mexican and Mexican-American community, different migratory patterns, and out-migration of many workers and their families undermines the radical potential of their marginalized status.

The most obvious arena for regulating the mobility of immigrants is in the policies and practices of the INS (now ICE). ICE controls entry through federally defined immigration quotas and border patrol activities. Immigration quotas and border patrol policies are developed in direct dialogue with the labor needs of businesses and their lobbies. Yet in some instances ICE activities directly circumscribe the efforts of certain employers to exploit a low-wage and relatively powerless work force. In the early 1990s, INS actions posed such a challenge to the owners of the food processing plant when it deported a large percentage of their workforce.

The Mexican and Mexican-American factory workers worked in the least desirable jobs in the plant and faced verbal and behavioral abuse by supervisors and white coworkers. Initially Latinos in Midtown were treated as one homogenous group by the employer as well as the Anglo residents. However, actions taken by the INS reshaped the composition of the Mexican and Mexican-American community as well as the town's relationship to the different segments of the Latino population and the recruitment practices of the local employer. The mode of incorporation subsequently changed in response to both state intervention and increased community awareness.

The regulation of communication also shifted as a consequence of the

INS investigation. In addition to adjustments made by the plant owners (e.g., translation of employment manuals and presence of bilingual workers to act as translators during each shift), two ESL teachers were hired to work with students in the elementary and high schools. However, as research assistant Erica Bornstein (1994: 21) reports: "One remedial-ed teacher told me the ESL teachers were not helpful in determining the children's prior education or family history, and thus students were frequently placed in the wrong grades." The provision of ESL classes has improved since this 1994 field trip. However, a shortage of competent ESL teachers and translators who are trusted by the Latino residents was evident as late as December 1998.

The regulation of association across gender, race-ethnicity, and class also contour the social construction of citizenship in a local context. As a consequence, the social regulation of dating, sexuality, and emotional expression are experienced differently by men and women and is further differentiated by race-ethnicity and class. Of course, these patterns are also fluid, shift over time, and are shaped by the modes of incorporation and racialization processes that are part and parcel of economic and social restructuring.

Rather than viewing the state as a static entity with clearly defined policy arenas and citizenship as a formal legal category, this analysis defines the state and the social regulation of citizenship in dynamic relationship with those who are targets of specific state interventions. The Latino and Anglo residents whose perspectives form the basis for this analysis experience the power of the state as fluid, ever changing, and woven throughout their social lives. The identity of citizen is also constructed in relational terms. For example, even Latino community members with formal citizenship rights feel themselves marginalized by informal social regulatory processes of racialization (see also Oboler 2006). As Anna Ortega, a United States citizen who moved from Laredo to Midtown, explained, "But a lot of the Americans think that because we're brown everybody comes from Mexico and it's not like that you know. Because you can be Mexican, Hispanic, and you can come from Texas; you can come from Chicago . . . You can be born and raised in California . . . [They think]: They're from Mexico. They're all illegals." As I note in my analysis of the "outsider phenomenon" in rural Iowa,[10] Ortega distinguished herself from the white European-American residents, whom she defined as "Americans." Community social regulatory processes create a boundary between those defined as the "real" Americans (namely, white European Americans) and other Americans. Local formal and informal regulatory practices serve to construct and maintain these boundaries which are reinforced by ongoing material practices, ideological constructions, and institutional arrangements. These local practices and processes contribute to the social regulation of citizenship in powerful and often invisible ways that draw on and contribute to popular and state government demands for increased policing of the geographic border between the United States and Mexico. Furthermore, the policing of citizenship contributes to a racialized and class-based definition of who belongs or who deserves entry into the United States and once here, who can be incorporated into the polity. In fact, as a result of these social regulatory practices, many of those who do not fit the narrow definition of "American" feel themselves outside the category despite their legal status as citizens.

8. An Anatomy of Mexican Repatriation

*Human Rights
and the Borderlands of Complicity*

Tricia Gabany-Guerrero

This chapter examines the contradictions in U.S. policies toward the deportation of Mexican laborers. The critical sources for this analysis are institutional ethnographies of the deportation process, including reports by deportees and by the governments of both the United States and Mexico.[1] Institutional processes unfold according to the logics of particular states and constituencies. The implementation of policy is often left to the discretion of an administering agency, which must operate within the law but may develop operational logistics that are not discretely mandated by specific legislation. Through institutional ethnographies, we can reconstruct the disparate processes involved in deportation from the United States and repatriation into Mexico. We incorporated data from a nongovernmental organization (NGO) in Ciudad Juárez, Mexico, La Casa del Migrante (CDM),[2] which collected information on individual deportees' experiences with U.S. and Mexican government institutions as part of a deportee intake process.

This chapter situates its findings in the context of the largely invisible human rights and security problems that plague current U.S. immigration policies. By examining the process of deportation from the perspective of the deportee—one who is forcibly engaged in binational institutional relationships—the consequences of increasingly security-conscious U.S. policies become visible. As Susan Akram and Kevin Johnson argue in chapter 4 of this volume, the situation of without-status immigrants has worsened drastically in the past ten years. Immigration lawyers are virtually helpless to defend without-status immigrants, who have been redefined as criminals. Citizens of both the United States and Mexico are kept largely unaware of the practices that occur after out-of-status immigrants are apprehended. This chapter draws attention to a growing crisis for immigrants and their advocates, while U.S. employers and consumers benefit from the low cost of unorganized laborers whose freedoms dwindle under the pressures of national security.

THE CRIMINALIZATION OF UNDOCUMENTED MEXICAN IMMIGRANTS

A succession of increasingly restrictive policies at the federal, state, and local levels in the United States—made worse when the United States shifted administration of immigration from the Department of Justice to the Department of Homeland Security (DHS, specifically through ICE, Immigration Control and Enforcement)—has forced adults and children to be detained in prisons with criminals and has portrayed migrants as a threat to national security. Current definitions of the law reduce the capacity of judges to grant exceptions and diminish powers of appeal and circumstance. With increasing insistence and reach, reports by organizations like Amnesty International, Human Rights Watch, Witness, and a few dedicated nonprofits in the United States and Mexico have denounced human rights abuse in the process of detention and removal.

U.S. employers are encouraged by authorities, increasingly at the state level,[3] to comply with increased restrictions on immigrant labor. While some U.S. employers comply with the intent and letter of immigration law, others engage in a dance of complying with the law and simultaneously undermining it, in order to maximize profit by minimizing labor costs. Even with a rise in nationalist employment tendencies, the goal of minimizing labor costs is unlikely to change given the economic crisis in the United States.

The precariousness of immigrants' legal and human rights in the United States became evident in a recent case in which undocumented workers (predominately women) were arrested, removed, and incarcerated in Texas, New Mexico, and New England without regard for their children or dependents. In New Bedford, Massachusetts, far from the U.S.-Mexico border, the Insolia Company, a United States military contractor, was the target of an ICE raid in March 2007. Senator Edward Kennedy (2007) described the aftermath for the families of those who were imprisoned:

> On Sunday afternoon, in the basement of Our Lady of Guadalupe in New Bedford, I saw first-hand the pain and suffering of the families and community ripped apart by the actions of the Department of Homeland Security. In my 45 years of public life, this was one of the most heartbreaking scenes I have ever witnessed. Babies were

screaming for their mothers. Wives were desperately searching for information about their husbands. One father tearfully described the agony and sleeplessness of his young children who couldn't understand why their mother had disappeared. Shock, confusion and despair were the order of the day . . . the workers were rounded up and immediately transported by DHS to Texas and other states, far from their families, without even an opportunity to say goodbye. The DHS knew that many of these workers had children at home, but they did not do nearly enough to protect them. As a result, children came back to empty homes; at least one nursing baby went to the hospital with dehydration; and hundreds cried themselves to sleep, wondering where their loved ones were and why they had disappeared.

Of the more than 250 workers in detention, a judge ruled that 60 should be temporarily released, as they were the only caregivers for dependent children. Children caught in these circumstances may or may not be under threat of detention and deportation, as they or their guardians have to prove legal status in the United States.

The deportation of Mexicans from the United States is an uncomfortable topic fraught with contradictions that strain political relations between neighboring countries that share an intense history and one of the longest borders in the world (Durand and Massey 2003). Unknown to many U.S. citizens is the episode during the 1930s in which more than one million Mexicans were deported, even though many adults and children were U.S. citizens (Balderrama and Rodríguez 1995). This virtual purging of Mexican Americans and Mexicans from several communities in California merited notice in 2005, when the state of California issued an "Apology Act for the 1930s Repatriation Program."[4] According to Camilla Guerin-Gonzales (1994: 98):

> When they arrived in Mexico, both repatriated women and repatriated men found themselves in economic trouble. The large numbers of repatriates and the absence of effective coordination of their relocation within Mexico made the transition for most of them extremely difficult. While the U.S. and Mexican governments had often cooperated in carrying out formal repatriation, they had little control over the flood of Mexican Americans and Mexican immigrants fleeing the U.S. on their own because they feared deportation or starvation. Mexican women, men, and children who took part in formal repatriation programs joined a stream of returning immigrants who could not establish that they were in the U.S. legally. In 1929, seventy-nine thousand Mexicans returned to Mexico. Another seventy thousand left in 1930. The largest number, one hundred twenty-five thousand, left for Mexico in 1931, including seventy-six thousand men and forty-

men, according to statistics gathered by the Mexican

to 2008 the number of Mexicans reported to have
om the United States to Mexico rose from 490,546 (Ramos
oo) to 592,031 (Instituto Mexicano de Migración 2009), the topic
deportation is not prevalent in the academic literature and empirical
research concerning the Mexican experience of deportation is virtually
nonexistent. Notable exceptions (outside of general discussions and legal
reviews) are De Genova's (2002) theoretical discussion, a sociological study
of Salvadoran deportees conducted with an NGO in El Salvador (Phillips,
Hagan, and Rodriguez 2006), and a limited study of immigration policies
affecting legal residents in Texas (Rodriguez and Hagan 2004).

RESEARCHERS, METHODS, AND BORDERS

Ciudad Juárez, Chihuahua, is the largest Mexican city on the U.S.-Mexico
border. With a population of more than two million people, it dwarfs El
Paso, its U.S. neighbor. Responding to the dearth of scholarly research
about deportation, we developed an institutional ethnographic research
project at The University of Texas at El Paso to investigate the Mexican
deportation experience through a partnership with La Casa del Migrante.
This chapter is based principally on the research conducted in Ciudad
Juárez from 2000 to 2002. The U.S.-Mexico border presents geographical
and citizenship advantages for research that are not possible elsewhere in
the United States or Mexico. Here a border-dwelling, U.S.-based researcher
is relatively free to cross national borders without threat of deportation
by either the United States or Mexico. Border dwellers have historically
held this privilege, but the distinct advantage of holding a U.S. passport is
nowhere more clear than at the entrance to Mexico after crossing one of
the Rio Grande bridges between El Paso and Ciudad Juárez.

After crossing the downtown bridge from the United States into Mexico,
there is a checkpoint with a stoplight. The driver of each vehicle must hit
the stoplight's button to see if it turns red or green. A green light means
that the vehicle and its passengers may pass through without any search
or questions. A red light means that the driver will be subjected to a series
of questions, with a full vehicle search if illegal or contraband items are
suspected. Whether one is allowed to cross into Mexico's ten-kilometer
border zone is not so much about people as goods—Mexican officials are
primarily keen to prevent the importation of items that are either illegal

or in violation of customs regulations. Aside from traffic on the bridge, the experience of crossing into Mexico may take all of five minutes.[5] The ease of border crossing from the United States into Mexico has developed further implications with the growth in the covert importation of automatic weapons into Mexico.

Going from Mexico to the United States is more time consuming, even if one is a U.S. citizen. All border crossers must provide evidence of citizenship or a visa; vehicles are extensively monitored and searched at random. Before 9/11, the process of returning to the United States after a day of research in Ciudad Juárez was relatively easy. After 9/11, extensive searches of vehicles, official interrogation, separation of family members (men/boys in one line and women/girls in another), and the resultant long lines of traffic made research on the Mexican side more difficult. After conducting six hours of research, one could expect at least a three-hour return trip to the United States Yet a U.S. researcher could cross legally and conveniently, even if delayed by traffic and lines.

The situation of Mexican researchers crossing into the United States is completely different. A border crossing card does facilitate crossing, but as security tension mounted after 9/11, increased suspicion produced daily delays that could last between four and five hours. To arrive in the United States by 9 A.M., a Mexican would need to be at the border station between 4 and 5 A.M. Crossing on foot was the preferred form of entry, as random searches of vehicles could produce extensive delays.[6]

In 2000 and 2001, U.S. deportation procedures followed two approaches: (1) near the border a policy of "catch and release" allowed undocumented Mexican laborers to be captured by the U.S. Border Patrol and "released" back to Mexico through nightly "deposits" at selected border entry points; and (2) (largely in the interior of the United States) undocumented Mexican workers were processed as criminals and held in U.S. criminal detention centers before deportation.[7] At this time, the "catch and release" policy prevailed at the U.S.-Mexico border. While ICE (2006: v) touts the end of this practice as a major achievement, nightly deposits of people at the border still constitute an ongoing humanitarian crisis for local NGOs.

The official numbers of deportees through the El Paso–Ciudad Juárez metro area increased to a reported 271 deportees per day during 2001 (98,215 total), but reports from official sources in El Paso indicated that the number from all points of origin was closer to 150,000 per year. While the impact of these large numbers of undocumented workers on the metro area is another subject that merits much more research, its effects can be discerned at a local level through the challenges confronted by the CDM staff.

CDM accepts homeless adult male migrants or deportees for a period of up to two weeks; it screened prospective beneficiaries through a rigorous interview to determine the authenticity of their claim to be migrants. The screening interview data provided the basis for this study. By reviewing and analyzing the data provided by CDM for 23,584 migrants collected during the period from 1990 through 2001, we identified trends in human rights abuses, deportation, and larger issues with respect to deportation in the Ciudad Juárez metro area (Gabany-Guerrero 2002).

DEPORTATION PRACTICES

Observing the intake interviews conducted by volunteer staff at CDM, it became clear that detention and deportation placed extraordinary stress on the deportees. Environmental factors in the Chihuahuan high desert plateau also had an impact on deportee health, a fact that was not always understood by CDM's volunteers. Bloodshot eyes, which frequently were interpreted by volunteers as potential indications of drug abuse during the intake interview, were more likely the result of desert dust, windstorms, and air contamination on the border. Deportees also appeared dehydrated and exhibited confusion, forgetfulness, nervousness, and anxiety. As a result, the research project proposed that CDM volunteers provide immediate hydration and electrolyte support for migrants, including saltine crackers and purified water, at least fifteen minutes before the intake interview.

The process of adult deportation from the United States has changed since this research was conducted, but reports from Ciudad Juárez have substantiated that the conditions of deportation at the border remain largely unchanged. Upon arrest in the interior of the United States, adults are immediately separated from children. As reported by deported men in interviews and database records from CDM,[8] human rights abuses occur at all stages of arrest, detention, and deportation, but the most severe levels of abuse were reported in the interior of the United States and not at the border. This conclusion is supported by Phillips, Hagan, and Rodriguez (2006), who have documented increases in immigrant detentions and violations of human rights (excessive force) against deportees. They also found that the rate of violence against deportees is higher for immigrants detained by local rather than federal authorities and for deportees who do not have legal representation.

According to the deportees' narratives, adult deportation included being blindfolded and usually driven (not flown) to the border from points of detention other than El Paso (most frequently California, Washington,

Oregon, Colorado, Arizona, New Mexico, and other points in Texas). Deportees reported being released at the border with no identification and no information about where they had been released (i.e., they did not know that they were in Ciudad Juárez). The deportees interviewed at CDM were released by the U.S. Border Patrol under the bridges of the Rio Grande/Rio Bravo in the early morning twilight hours between 2 and 4 A.M. (Gabany-Guerrero 2002). Deported men, disoriented, hungry, and thirsty, were not received at the border by any Mexican officials or the Instituto Nacional de Migración.

Those whom we interviewed at CDM had found their way from the public plazas where they could have fallen victim to assault by either authorities or thugs, to this small homeless shelter. Because the CDM was located on the outskirts of town, deportees found the site through a mixture of luck, fliers posted in the central part of the city, and the advice of Ciudad Juárez residents. Those who found the shelter and were accepted were fortunate, as only forty beds were available per night. The migrants accepted at CDM were required to find a job in Ciudad Juárez within twenty-four hours of entry in order to maintain shelter. Medical doctors visited the shelter once per week and food was prepared by volunteers from donations.

We conducted structured interviews with deportees who wished to participate in the study after twenty-four hours of residence.[9] The interview was structured to include information about the process of deportation and general questions about how the migrants interpreted their cultural capital, their tastes in music, languages spoken, and their formal education and trades they had learned. When asked about their immediate goals, 45.7 percent stated that their principal goal was to return to their place of origin; 26.2 wanted to cross again to the United States to joint with family members. One particularly troubling narrative was told by a father and his son, no more than twelve years old, who related their story switching from fluent English to fluent Spanish in the interview at the CDM shelter. The father had been deported after living in the United States for more than fifteen years because he had not processed his immigration papers.[10] At the time of apprehension, the boy was with this father and said that he refused to have the INS separate them. Even though he was a U.S. citizen, the boy decided that it was better to be deported with his father than to risk what would happen to him in the United States as a ward of the state.

The plight of undocumented children is even more severe. Research recently conducted by María Eugenia Hernández Sánchez (2007: 100) has documented that when undocumented children are detained, whether as part of a family apprehension or alone, they are separated from family members and processed apart from adults. Children are handed off from one agency to the next, going through no fewer than five agencies and seven interviews in the United States and Mexico. In the United States, children apprehended by the Border Patrol are sent to either Child Protective Services (under DHS) or ICE, where they are detained, at times behind bars. The children each received a small juice and a granola bar during their stay of up to twenty-four hours at the border detention center. In the border immigration office of ICE, the children were interviewed again and at that point might sleep in the same room with unrelated adults. Hernández Sánchez (2007: 83) notes that the children virtually always discussed the condition of the bathrooms and described the lack of privacy. Many children were unaware that once they were fingerprinted, they were *procesados* and had a criminal record in the United States.

At this point either the children are taken directly to the border office of Desarrollo Integral de la Familia (DIF, the official Mexican government family welfare agency) or turned over to the Mexican Consulate. Although the Mexican Consulate staff do not necessarily see the children, the Consulate serves as the primary link between the children, their families, and U.S. agencies. Surprisingly, the Mexican Consulate is required to pay the U.S. government for access to a database that provides information about Mexican detainees (adults and children) or deaths. From there, the Instituto Nacional de Migración meets the children at the border. The Procuraduría en Defensa al Menor is in charge of the children's paperwork and determines whether or not a child is to be released into an adult claimant's custody. If there is no adult authorized to take custody, the child is then placed with the DIF (required if they are 0–8 years old). The DIF houses the deported children with other children who may have emotional or legal problems. The DIF may send children over eight years old to Casa YMCA in Ciudad Juárez, which only has enough beds for twenty children (Hernández Sánchez 2007: 78). Hernández Sánchez clearly documents the active role that children attempt to have in determining the outcomes of their situations. Hernández Sánchez (2007: 24) effectively documents that children learn to negotiate with authorities early in the process and play an active role in attempting to affect their own outcomes. Children are placed under severe pressure to respond to questioning in at least two interviews per agency and do not have access to legal representation except at the intervention of the Mexican Consulate. Especially in the case of children who were U.S. citizens with Mexican parents who were deported and unlocatable—in spite of claims by Mexican parents attempting to recuperate their children—children might be placed up for adoption to surrogate parents. My analysis reinforces Hernández Sánchez's view that children are not solely the hapless victims of immigration policy enforcement but active agents (albeit severely limited by their legal status in both states). Both children and adults use varying forms of capital (cultural and economic) to influence the outcomes of their respective situations, but it must be recognized that they are subsumed within the processes of two powerful nation-states and hence their room for maneuver is very limited.

While it is unclear exactly how many Mexican children are deported each year from the United States, a report by the DIF and UNICEF (2004) noted that up to 7,100 were deported in 2005 and 34,692 in 2008 (Instituto Nacional de Migración 2009). Ciudad Juárez and Ojinaga (now virtually part of the El Paso/Ciudad Juárez metropolis) were the two border locations where the majority of deportations of minors occurred. In fact, very little is known about the accuracy of reports regarding Mexican children who are deported; their numbers may remain underreported by U.S. agencies and a comprehensive international analysis has not been conducted. DIF reported that the number of Mexican children deported at the U.S. border with Sonora, Mexico, alone increased from 6,000 cases in 2005 to 9,000 cases in 2006 (Prensa Latinoamericana 2007).[11] At these two border points alone, therefore, an estimated 15,000 Mexican children are deported per year.

POLICY CONSIDERATIONS

While researchers know more now than was known ten years ago about the human rights violations that occur in the arrest, detention, processing, and deportation of irregular immigrants from Mexico, the need is great for more study, especially with regard to women and children deportees. There are, however, several very specific and direct areas where changes in U.S. and Mexican policies would correct current human rights violations.

First, a binational task force on children and families that conforms to United Nations resolutions on the treatment of children should be formed. This task force should review current policies and practices with respect to the deportation of children and families and institute binational accountability for record-keeping and reporting, as well as standards for the treatment of children and families.

The issues surrounding Mexican-United States migration are the result of inadequate and incomplete attention by U.S. and Mexican policymakers, who have tended to embrace neoliberal rhetoric and have ignored in-depth analysis of migration circuits. U.S. and Mexican policy discussions have not addressed the serious ramifications of migration for both nations, and the U.S. and Mexican congresses appear to have been derailed from serious immigration reform by nationalist rhetoric. Major issues with the previous formal worker agreement (the Bracero Program) have not been resolved, and thousands of aging Mexican workers who toiled in the fields of the United States during and after the Second World War have not received the Social Security compensation that was withdrawn from their paychecks and promised to them more than sixty years ago. These injustices must be redressed before a new migratory labor agreement is reached.

Lest any new guest-worker agreement repeat such injustices and for immigration reform to be truly "comprehensive," greater provision must be made to bring both authorized and unauthorized immigrants under the vigilance of labor laws and labor unions (as Douglas Massey suggests in chapter 1). Current H2B visa policy does not provide for labor law compliance. In a recent case in Connecticut, Guatemalan workers were legally contracted in Guatemala to work for Imperial Nurseries in North Carolina but were shipped (against their will) to Connecticut and held in servile conditions (Masis 2007). If this can happen to legally contracted workers, imagine what is possible for those without documentation. Indeed, my own ethnographic research in Connecticut has revealed that indigenous women from Mexico and Guatemala were employed by Imperial Nurseries at the same place and transported on a daily basis from Springfield, Massachusetts.

U.S. employers may be individual farm or green industry operators or vertically integrated corporations, such as Imperial Nurseries; both participate in the creation of a job market that requires labor contractors. Both the individual operator and the corporation participate in the transformation of wage laborers to indentured laborers or sweat industry workers in the twenty-first century. The individual operator claims that local labor sources are unreliable and unwilling to work, and therefore the importation of Mexican laborers is justified. While individual operators secure housing, Mexican laborers (especially in rural areas) are tied to the operation both physically and legally. Workers are available on a twenty-four-hour basis to milk the cows, attend to the harvest, protect the transplants from freezing ,and serve the needs of the employer. These conditions are part of the larger "anatomy of deportation," outlined in this chapter, insofar as the undocumented status of the worker serves to reinforce her or his dependence on the labor contractor and the U.S. employer. Undocumented workers are in such supply that the threat of deportation is sufficient to quell labor organization. Further cementing the worker's lack of options is the debt she or he has incurred to cross the border and prepare the legally required employment paperwork.

In addition, to consider a new migratory labor agreement without reinvestment in Mexico's rural and indigenous regions is a major mistake. The growing gaps in Mexico's economic development must be addressed in an equitable and sustainable way so that some of the benefits from Mexico's economic growth go to the poor. Perhaps not since the Porfiriato has the gap between rich and poor been so visible. As a researcher who works specifically in the State of Michoacán, one of the Mexican states with the longest history of sending economic immigrants to the United States, I have observed a surprising phenomenon that contradicts the image of absolute rural poverty: I call it the "Hummer Syndrome." Poverty is on the rise in Mexico while the rich get richer. The conspicuous consumption of Hummers has risen—an increase of over 179% from 2005 to 2006 alone (Canada Newswire 2006)—with the spectacular rise in wealth of the upper class. The increase in disparity between economic groups in Mexico that has been developing over the last ten years is complicated by recent increases in organized crime activity, which have reached unbearable levels in historically migrant-sending communities. In interviews conducted in summer 2009, I found that the infiltration of organized crime networks into the daily lives of working-class families has created a sense of desperation that threatens the stability of civil society and may create further impetus for migration.

Specifically with regard to deportation, if ICE must continue to deport Mexicans, then the process should conform to international human rights standards (see the introduction to this volume) and strive to respect culturally acceptable limits for Mexicans. The multiple immigrant statuses of individuals in Mexican families, who have migrated to the United States in the past twenty years, is a serious consequence of fluctuating immigration policies (Hernandez 2005) and women's participation in the guarantee of their children's labor protection through specific migratory reproductive strategies. The separation of families with different immigration statuses will create humanitarian and human rights violations of unprecedented numbers and an entire generation of virtually orphaned and displaced children who may become the victims of heinous crimes in child trafficking and violence. Greater weight must be accorded throughout to the international legal principle of protecting the best interests of the child. Children should never be separated from their parents in the process of deportation; this is a violation of humanitarian concerns of the highest levels. Children are currently forced to defend themselves before a myriad of agencies and institutions without any resources or parental guidance. They are required to defecate virtually in public in front of unknown adults, required to sleep in the same room with unknown adults, given inadequate food and beverage rations, and exposed to both adults and children who may have been accused and convicted of crimes.

Most of the processes described in this chapter are not easily visible to the public. It is unlikely that immigration policy changes proposed in the United States will address the concerns raised here unless human rights scholars and activists document and report the conditions of undocumented workers. Foundations bear the responsibility as well for providing the means for nonprofit agencies and universities to create partnerships for research and civic engagement to change the course of U.S. immigration history and to create a space for recommendations that extend beyond the often blindsided view of policymakers in both the United States and Mexico.

The Mexican government is equally responsible for the care and reincorporation of their deported citizens. There is no government official waiting under the International Bridge at 2 A.M. to receive the next group of blindfolded deportees. There is no poster there saying, "Welcome Home, *Paisano*, Hero to the Nation, Payer of the International Debt and Supporter of your Hometown!" Deportees are not issued identification cards, phone cards, or even given a map of Ciudad Juárez or a list of homeless shelters where they might find a bed for the night. These are migrants who have spent most of their adult lives working for the nation, and they have returned hungry, disoriented, tired, angry, and bewildered. Because the Office of Mexican Immigration closes at 3 P.M., there are no services available to these returnees. Either the Mexican government should negotiate the times and places of repatriation or provide twenty-four-hour staff to receive the deportees. Anything less invites serious long-term problems for Ciudad Juárez in absorbing migrant labor, promoting the revolving door that spits the deportees back across the border or the underground economy of violence and illicit trade that is the only place where deportees can currently find a job. In sum, the negotiation of a new immigration agreement or worker policy with Mexico needs to consider the complete circuit of migration, and the agencies responsible must conform to international human rights standards. Without this, migrants and their advocates will continue to be challenged to confront one of the most serious crises in the shared histories of our two nations, the impact of increasingly restrictionist immigration policies and their enforcement in the United States which is changing the terms and conditions of life for undocumented workers.

PART IV

Beyond U.S. Borders

9.   Discourses on Danger and Dreams of Prosperity

Confounding U.S. Government Positions on "Trafficking" from the Former Soviet Union

Alexia Bloch

Five Ukrainian women tortured with boiling oil and held in a windowless basement prison, one for up to six years, are preparing to return home today after being rescued through an IOM administered helpline for victims of trafficking. . . . The women, trafficked to Turkey and forced to provide sex to male clients against their will, were rescued 1 August near the resort town of Antalya by the Turkish gendarmerie. The gendarmerie acted after one of the trafficked Ukrainians contacted IOM's 157 helpline requesting rescue. . . . They are now eligible for IOM sponsored voluntary reintegration assistance in their home country. This includes medical, psychological, and legal assistance, family and housing allowances and either education or business grants. (IOM 2005)

The story is shocking. Young women, duped or forced into travel to a foreign land, are made to live as sex slaves, tortured for attempting to escape, for minor transgressions, or for no reason at all. The lucky ones are rescued from this shadowy underworld by the heroic actions of law enforcement agencies and nongovernmental organizations. Rescue narratives like this one strike a deep chord, for no moral person would want to turn a blind eye to such appalling acts of dehumanization committed for profit. And indeed, these stories are part of a burgeoning literature on human trafficking that would lead us to believe that there are tens of thousands of women across the world who are waiting to be saved from similarly deplorable conditions.

Yet it is unclear the extent to which these stories, disturbing though they are, are representative. Such narratives elide the fact that some women who migrate in order to engage in sexual work do not necessarily seek to be "saved," and may well escape from the safe houses arranged for them in order to return to brothels or the street. Still, images of naïve women victimized by criminals dominate public discourses about trafficking (Soderlund 2005). These rescue narratives are disseminated by a range of NGOs, but also in media, including documentaries with names like *Sex Slaves* (CBC 2005) and *Trafficking Cinderella* (Niaglova 2001), and in widely distributed feature films such as *Lilya 4-Ever* (Moodysson 2002). However well intentioned, they misrepresent a complex situation. While human rights violations of the sort described above should be addressed, antitrafficking rhetoric incites public outcry about the plight of involuntary migrants without providing a clear picture of the context and diversity of contemporary labor migration. Not all migrants are trafficked, and the distinction between "voluntary" and "involuntary" is not as useful as these rescue narratives might suggest (Kempadoo and Doezema 1998; Watanabe 1998).

I first became aware of the extensive impact of labor migration on local communities of the former Soviet Union in the 1990s, in the course of research I conducted in central Siberia and the Russian Far East (Bloch 2003a; Bloch and Kendall 2004). One morning in 1993, I found a crowd in the village post office gathered around a woman and her suitcase of goods—t-shirts, lingerie, children's clothing, and men's dress shirts—all items that were virtually unavailable in the town shops. At that time trips to Israel, North Africa, China, and particularly Turkey, with its relatively open borders, were arranged through city travel agencies booking "shopping tours."[1] Women were the primary entrepreneurs of this type and they often combined a few days' vacation with the aim of pursuing wholesale textile purchases for resale back home. Over the decade that followed, these novel border crossings gave way to other, more long-term, gendered forms of labor migration. Today, migrants seeking work beyond the former Soviet Union tend to turn first to opportunities in Western Europe—particularly in Germany and France, where wages for even illegal employment ranged from U.S.$800 to $1200 per month in 2003 (Ghencea and Gudumac 2004: 74). Options in these countries are limited, and especially for women there are far more accessible prospects for work in Israel, Turkey, China, South Korea, and Japan.

Transnational migration from the former Soviet Union emerged initially in the early 1990s as the Soviet Union relaxed restrictions on foreign travel to capitalist countries. Then with the fall of the Soviet Union, borders, such as China's, opened to former Soviet tourists and business people alike (Wishnick 2004; Matloff 1998). As Russia was pressured by the International Monetary Fund to engage in "restructuring" in 1993–94, nearly 120,000 firms were transferred to private hands and often closed.

Hundreds of thousands of workers lost their jobs. Women were fired in disproportionate numbers, and by 1992 they comprised 71 percent of the unemployed (Barr 1994: 167–168). This situation, largely defined by U.S.-backed structural adjustment policies imposed on Russia in exchange for receiving billions of dollars in foreign aid, has not changed significantly in more recent years. In seeking to improve desperate circumstances, post-Soviet women and some men began pursuing small-scale trade, moving goods—predominantly clothing—from Turkey, China, and the United Arab Emirates, among other places, to home communities for resale (Zhurzhenko 1999; Aktar and Ögelman 1994). Thus, the large-scale problem of unauthorized border crossing from the former Soviet Union can be clearly linked to the dire economic situation brought about by U.S.-backed structural adjustment policies (Blanchard, Froot, and Sachs 1994).

Along with the shuttle trade, labor migration in other forms grew throughout the 1990s. The structural adjustment policies advocated by U.S. government advisers such as Harvard economist Jeffrey Sachs continued to lead to the closure or severe downsizing of many formerly state-owned factories and organizations deemed "inefficient." Widespread unemployment led to jarring poverty. Russian government statistics on countrywide poverty levels for 1992 suggest that more than one-third of the population was living in poverty, with only slight changes in the late-1990s. Despite these dire figures, strikingly, women's chances of living in poverty relative to men's chances fell between 1992 and 1995. In 1992 households headed by women were 3.8 times more likely to be impoverished than those headed by men, while in 1995 households headed by women were just 2.7 times more likely to be impoverished (Russian State Statistical Bureau, cited in Census Brief 1998). One might consider how cross-border labor migration of women could be a significant factor in the decrease in women's poverty.

Following the 1998 economic crisis in Russia in which the country defaulted on its World Bank loans and the ruble was drastically devalued, labor migration both into and out of Russia increased (see Massey, this volume, on patterns of migration following economic restructuring). In some areas nearly one-quarter of working-age adults left their communities (Ghenchea and Gudumac 2004: 41), traveling from struggling areas of rural Russia, Moldova, and Central Asia to find work as domestic servants and day laborers in economically vibrant regions such as Moscow (Moşneaga and Echim 2003: 224).[2] While men predominantly found work in construction, women found work in other realms of an emerging service economy, such as apartment renovations, domestic work, hospitality, and entertainment spheres or sex work (Tiuriukanova 2002). Despite these more regional possibilities within the former Soviet Union, post-Soviet women and men are increasingly involved in transnational labor migration as they seek ways to make a more viable living (Malysheva and Tiuriukanova 2000; McDonald, Moore and Timoshkina 2000; Bloch 2003b).

While the portrait of labor migration I describe above suggests a process involving choices made by individuals, the popular media more often equates women's emigration from the former Soviet Union with the coerced movements of people, or "trafficking." Trafficking has been defined in a wide range of ways, and it continues to be much debated since any definition has political leverage, potentially affecting the legal treatment of male and female migrants. One scholar's helpful definition makes a distinction between two elements, the *process* of recruitment and the *context* of work, explicitly describing "trafficking" as

> [a]ll acts involved in the recruitment and transportation of a woman within and across national borders for work or services by means of violence, or threat of violence, abuse of authority or dominant position, debt bondage, deception or other forms of coercion . . . [and] the extraction of work or services from any woman or the appropriation of the legal identity or physical person of any woman by means of violence or threat of violence, abuse of authority or dominant position, debt bondage, deception or other forms of coercion. (McDonald, Moore, and Timoshkina 2000: 8)

Unfortunately, explicit definitions of trafficking are rare in the popular media. The term "trafficking" is instead used in a manner that bluntly invokes a sense of outrage in readers and a sense of pity for the victims of apparent offences. The blanket term manages to bury the reality of labor migration for many people, and also creates a type of moral panic around migration involving sex work. One example of this appeared in a 2004 *New York Times Magazine* feature article, "The Girls Next Door." The article stated that the United States had become a major importer of "sex slaves," and it pointed to sources estimating there to be 10,000 to 50,000 women in "captivity" in communities stretching from New Jersey to Oregon (Landesman 2004: 32). Peter Landesman's article has been widely discredited on the basis of poor sources, fabricated data, and shoddy analysis invoking moral panic (*Mother Jones* 2004; Schafer 2004a, 2004b).[3] However, the moral panic incited by the article—featuring "victims" in need of rescue from "trafficking"—is not unique and is echoed repeatedly in a wide range of media, including journalistic accounts, popular films, and documentaries (e.g., Specter 1998; Malarek 2003) (see Soderlund 2005 on the role of the U.S. media in framing discussions on trafficking).[4] At another level, discourses on trafficking are now being widely disseminated world-wide as the United States Agency for International Development and inter-national agencies such as the Organization for Security and Co-Operation in Europe extend their antitrafficking initiatives.[5]

The prevailing discourses on trafficking provide support for conserva-tive positions about women as a class in need of protection from "criminal elements," and also derail serious discussion about how women and men are in fact involved in labor migration and how their efforts are increas-ingly policed at international borders. Sources like *The New York Times Magazine* article often fail to take into account the ways that apparently trafficked people exhibit agency. Worse, invoking "trafficking" turns atten-tion away from how women and men are engaged globally in labor migra-tion in a wide range of spheres that is frequently underpaid, exploitative, and lacking social benefits.

Based on my ethnographic research among labor migrants in the for-mer Soviet Union, I argue that labor migration is fraught with potentially exploitative relations, but that women and men often willingly choose this option over other dehumanizing conditions they face in home communi-ties.[6] Focusing on "trafficking" can distract us from critical efforts to trans-form the conditions of unemployment, deskilling, and political stalemates that drive migrants to search out opportunities, albeit ones fraught with compromises. An ethnographic approach to this topic encourages us to turn attention to the particular contours of labor migration and thereby to avoid homogenizing the experience of labor migrants (Abu-Lughod 1993).

This chapter consists of three primary sections. I first consider some problems with the data on "trafficking." In the second section, I discuss the role of the United States Agency for International Development (USAID) in shaping discourses about "trafficking" across the globe, including in the former Soviet Union, and particularly in the Russian Far East.[7] The final section focuses on recent ethnographic material gathered in the Russian Far East among NGOs and tour agencies interacting with labor migrants. Overall, I seek to demonstrate the ways in which U.S. policy initiatives to police trafficking are problematic. U.S. policies supporting structural adjustment measures directly contribute to the extreme poverty that has engulfed households and communities since the 1990s. Incongruously, however, U.S. policy initiatives also seek to control and prevent unau-thorized border crossing, a movement of people primarily related to labor migration and to negotiating a way out of poverty.

"TRAFFICKING," DEFINITIONS, AND DATA

Forced or coerced migrations are certainly a matter for international concern. However, the extent to which all cases labeled as "trafficking" fit this category is unclear; many instead could be seen as cases of labor migration. Sources concerned with trafficking rarely specify the wide range of situations that are labeled as trafficking or explore the social relations surrounding labor migrations. In particular, the rhetoric of needing to "save" women from criminal elements demands a homogenization of the complex forces compelling people to leave their home communities in search of work and the mechanisms that enable them to do so.

First, the actual number of people who are in fact trafficked, including in the region of the former Soviet Union, is unclear. Figures offered are dramatic but frequently are presented without an explanation of the methods for gathering data and the process of analysis. The wide variation in numbers invoked by a range of sources suggests a lack of concrete data. In 2001, USAID (2001: 1) estimated that between 700,000 and 4,000,000 women, children, and men were trafficked each year worldwide, a figure that USAID (2005: 3) later revised to 600,000 to 800,000. Neither report indicates how these figures were established. In a report published by the International Organization for Migration, the authors write that in the late 1990s two-thirds of the estimated 500,000 women annually "trafficked" for prostitution to 40 to 50 countries across the world came from Eastern Europe and the former Soviet Union; again there is no indication of how these numbers were arrived at (McDonald, Moore and Timoshkina 2001; Hughes 2000). In another report published by the Moldova Center for Preventing Women Trafficking (CPWT 2001)—an NGO created in 2000 with the support of the U.S. Embassy in Moldova—the authors note that between 600,000 and 1,000,000 people were absent from Moldova in 2000; the organization estimates that 70 percent of these migrants were women, and that most of them were trafficked. None of these sources gives a clear indication of how "trafficked" individuals were differentiated from labor migrants.

Numbers related to trafficking are beginning to be challenged by a few scholars who suggest that the term "trafficking" is too widely invoked and therefore not useful for understanding a truly complex situation (Doezema 2000; Jahic and Finckenauer 2005). As recent research attests (Ghencea and Gudumac 2004; Ünal 2006), in the context of the former Soviet Union, labor migrants are crossing borders by boat, train, bus, and plane to take up work that they overwhelmingly seek out, independent of any coercion from employers, pimps, or agencies. However, repeatedly the NGO and USAID literatures paint a black-and-white picture of victims of trafficking. In one case, a report writes of Odessa as a "key junction for trafficking" where "in the first half of 2002, 688 women deportees arrived on the twice-weekly ships from Turkey" (Blumberg and Shved 2002: ix). This report suggests that the 688 people identified as deportees were trafficked, but this is not substantiated.

My qualitative interview data with more than fifty migrants in Istanbul indicates that many of the women arriving in Odessa, and crossing other international borders as well, see themselves as labor migrants rather than as people who are trafficked. Post-Soviet migrant women in Istanbul told me that Odessa is one of the key routes for women working as short-term labor migrants as they travel—usually individually, but sometimes with friends—between Turkey and their home communities, particularly in Belarus, Moldova, and Ukraine. Sometimes women return repeatedly to Turkey to pursue short-term arrangements as hostesses or exotic dancers in nightclubs, but at least as commonly they are returning from jobs as domestic workers where they care for children and the elderly, as well as clean and cook for households. On average in 2006 these jobs paid $500–$600/month—at least ten times what they could earn back home—and women generally seek to prolong their relatively lucrative stays in Turkey for as long as possible. It is not uncommon that they get deported when stopped by Turkish police for working without proper visas. Labor migration, even without a work permit, does not automatically constitute trafficking.

In Moldova, a post-Soviet location that has figured heavily in recent discussions of trafficking, the idea that all labor migrants are trafficked is also being questioned, with some scholars suggesting that 90 percent of those absent from the country should be considered as simply labor migrants (Moşneaga and Echim 2003). Valeriu Moşneaga and Tatiana Echim estimate that 10 percent of all labor migrants out of Moldova are involved in "sexual migration," but they are not necessarily victims of trafficking (2004: 224).[8] While the imposition of harsh economic restructuring in this region has pushed thousands of women and men to seek employment abroad, far from the majority appear to have been trafficked. More importantly, as argued by the NGO Global Alliance against Trafficking in Women (www .gaatw.net), antitrafficking stands taken to address the mistreatment of migrants widely result in repressive laws and international agreements, when instead antitrafficking measures should be "ensuring safe migration and protecting rights of migrant workers." As in other locations across the world, antitrafficking campaigns in the former Soviet Union appear to be about controlling the migration of women in search of work rather than about insuring safe working conditions or a higher standard of living in home communities.

USAID AND POLICING BORDERS

A wide range of international organizations—including the Asian Development Bank (www.adb.org), the International Labour Organization (www .ilo.org), the International Organization for Migration (www.iom.int), the United Nations (www.un.org), UNESCO (www.unescobkk.org), the Organization for Security and Co-Operation in Europe (OSCE) (www.osce.org), and USAID—has dedicated significant resources to antitrafficking measures. While the OSCE is the world's largest regional security organization with 55 member countries, USAID has emerged as the most influential state body promoting the global policing of what it considers to be trafficking. USAID publications reflect the ways that labor migration is widely being confounded with the more ominous sounding, and arguably much less widespread, "trafficking" in humans.[9] In a March 2004 report, for instance, USAID sources note that "[t]rafficking in persons is a pernicious and brutal abuse of human rights that affects nearly every country in the world. Its victims are most often poor and vulnerable women and children forced into degrading sexual or economic exploitation" (USAID 2004: 1). USAID Web sites repeatedly invoke the need to protect "vulnerable women and children" from becoming "victims" of "trafficking." As is common in the popular discourses on human trafficking, the USAID materials consistently link "women and children" as subjects to be protected. This conjoining of "women and children" as a category of victims elides the agency that many would argue adults, in contrast to children, inherently possess. Furthermore, by linking "sexual" and "economic" exploitation to trafficking these discourses leave little room for the discussion of labor migration.

In spite of the vagueness of the term "trafficking," since 2000 a number of specific measures have been legislated by the U.S. Congress and implemented by the U.S. State Department to curtail trafficking (Soderlund 2005). In 2000 Congress passed the Victims of Trafficking and Violence Protection Act (TVPA), increasing the U.S. role in both defining trafficking and policing it. This legislation empowers the State Department to rate countries annually on their efforts to combat trafficking and apply economic sanctions to those countries deemed to be inattentive; each year these ratings are published in the *TIP Report*.[10] Between 2001 and

2004, the USAID budget for antitrafficking efforts more than quadrupled. Funding directed toward field missions, regional bureaus, and the Women in Development office—all engaged in antitrafficking efforts—grew from $6 million to more than $27 million (USAID 2001: 3, 2005: 7). Likewise, the OSCE, another major player in antitrafficking efforts, has also significantly increased its financial commitments in this realm.[11] While the OSCE has operations in Central Asia, the Caucasus, Eastern Europe, and Southeastern Europe, USAID has field missions and regional bureaus extending throughout the world, with five geographic concentrations: Central and Southeastern Europe and Eurasia; Asia; Africa; Latin America and Europe; and Women in Development (WID), a section that has its own subsidiary programs in each of the regions. Worldwide, USAID manages programs funded by the U.S. Department of State and the United Nations Development Program and therefore significantly defines global discourses on trafficking and, by extension, labor migration.

In bringing together an examination of USAID positions on trafficking with my recent ethnographic findings, I hope to destabilize what have come to be truisms about "trafficking." Discourses on trafficking invoke moral frameworks in which migrants are viewed as either villains—"illegal" migrants who breach the security of nation-states—or "victims" of opportunistic criminal networks. There is little consideration of those labeled as "trafficked" as first of all labor migrants. To take this position would require policymakers to consider the ways that transnational migration is part of a global transformation of flexible labor forces serving new forms of capital, often working for the benefit of nationalist interests (Ong 1999; Glick Schiller 1999). Casting women and children as victims enables the U.S. government to pose as safeguarding the world, even as it promotes the structural adjustment programs that have led to such widespread impoverishment and unemployment in places like the former Soviet Union.

DREAMS OF PROSPERITY AND DISCOURSES ON DANGER

In turning to recent ethnographic research conducted in the former Soviet Union, namely in the Russian Far East, this chapter considers how migrants are in fact enmeshed in an array of social relations that both compel and enable them to seek work as labor migrants. As part of a multisited project on post-Soviet women's transnational labor migration (2002–2005), I conducted more than fifty interviews with migrants and carried out a wide number of informal conversations with sex workers and two other migrant populations—domestic workers and petty traders. This research has focused on how women interpret their experiences as transnational labor migrants. In addition to participant observation and semistructured interviews with migrants, this project also included interviews with representatives of a range of nongovernmental organizations—including three addressing trafficking in women, and four providing social services to displaced persons or migrants—and with tour agencies in Moldova, Turkey, and the Russian Far East.

One theme that emerged from my research is the dissonance between the aims of local nongovernmental organizations, supported by USAID, and the dreams driving migrants to seek work abroad. While the dominant discourses promulgated by USAID feature the dangers of migration and situate migrants as victims, my data indicates that women are not simply naïve, but often are making informed decisions about labor migration. Furthermore, these dreams of prosperity must be historically and locally situated in order to understand both the opportunities and constraints to which emigration is a response (see, e.g., Constable 2003; Brennan 2004).

Migrants' decisions to seek work abroad are facilitated by their interaction with an extensive web of people (see also Busza, Castle, and Diarra 2004). At the most direct level, relatives and friends become drawn into a remittance economy. Households rely heavily on regular monthly wire payments of U.S.$50–$100 for a wide range of needs. Some migrants' remittances pay for utilities or contribute to children's postsecondary education, while others support grandmothers left at home to care for grandchildren and look after their food and well being, or save money for a future apartment. All these community hopes then compel women to look for possibilities abroad.

While my primary focus in this larger research project is on migrants' narratives about their labor migration across a wide geographical expanse, at this point I wish to turn to the networks of actors in the Russian Far East—particularly tour agencies and NGOs—and their roles in enabling or discouraging women's migration. The livelihoods of various tourist and employment agencies, as well as NGOs, are linked to people's migration strategies. The "irregular migration" along the borders of Russia involves Russian NGOs who apply USAID ideologies of the dangers of trafficking; these NGOs are supported financially by USAID in this application-by-proxy of U.S. policy initiatives.[12] In contextualizing women's labor migration in this way, we can better avoid silencing migrants' own accounts of their journeys and at the same time emphasize how global shifts of political economy influence local migration patterns.

HISTORICIZING BORDER CROSSINGS AND
SEXUAL MIGRANTS IN THE RUSSIAN FAR EAST

Women's labor migration out of the former Soviet Union is part of the massive global shift in primary destination and source countries as the global economy has led to a new array of concentrations of wealth and poverty (Ehrenreich and Hochschild 2002). Until the early 1990s, the only inflows of temporary migrants to the Soviet Union were from countries like Vietnam, Angola, and China; migrants arrived on student visas and frequently combined studies with casual labor and business aspirations (Duong 1995). There was no legal way for citizens of the Soviet Union to leave the country for temporary labor migration. Until the early 1920s, however, prior to the Soviet Union's virtual closure of its borders, there had been flows out of the region. For instance, a range of scholarship, as well as popular media and fiction, has reflected on the ways in which women from places like Ukraine and Russia had currency as migrant sex workers or entertainers for at least 100 years, dating to the late nineteenth century. In contexts as varied as India, Turkey (Béller-Hann 1995), Manchuria (Murakami 1999: 136), and South America, "white Russian" women found employment as hostesses, performers, and sex workers. At the turn of the nineteenth century, when there were widespread migrations out of Europe, Jewish women from Ukraine and Russia made up a distinct group of sex workers in South American capitals such as Buenos Aires (Levine 1994; Guy 1990).

In some cases, desire for women from the region of the former Soviet Union has been linked to ideological sympathies and modernist imaginings, equating women's perceived forthright and unconstrained sexuality with a certain type of "modernity." In Indian cinema, for example, the figure of the Russian circus entertainer was historically tied to a sort of nostalgia for popular socialist ideals (for example, the 1970 film *Meera nam Joker*). However, as in the past, the current appeal of women from the former Soviet Union in many locations worldwide appears to have little to do with ideals of equality, and more to do with the sign of "whiteness" as sometimes exotic and sometimes familiar, and the willingness of these women to engage in a wide range of sex work in exchange for relatively low wages and the possibility of emigrating abroad (Golden 2003; Béller-Hann 1995; Hann and Béller-Hann 1992).

In the Russian Far East today, Russian citizens, and women in particular, frequently traverse the nearby Chinese border or the more distant South Korean and Japanese borders as they pursue opportunities to earn a living as entertainers, hostesses, or sex workers. Even as far away as Moldova, women consider labor migration to Japan or South Korea where they have heard wages for entertainers can be considerably more than the $400–$600 per month they can earn in Istanbul (personal correspondence, 2005). The extent of the options for women migrants is reflected in just one issue of the Vladivostok newspaper *Dal'Press* (July 2003, no.28), a significant resource for people seeking employment locally or abroad.[13] The following is a selection of the more than fifty advertisements appearing under the classified section "show business":[14]

Japan: Girls 18–30 years old for clubs throughout Japan. Dance training provided.

Korea: Girls 19–30 years old for famous clubs in Seoul and Pusan. Fast processing of necessary documents (22 days). Daily interviews. Performance collectives especially encouraged to apply. http://www .scanna.ru (p.71)

Sakura Entertainment, Japan: Work in prestigious clubs as singer* professional dancer* musician* topless dancer*. Work visa. Dependable partners [in Japan]. Speedy processing of paperwork. For an interview call or e-mail mailto:sakura@neiv.ru (p.71).

The more of this ad you read, the more you will understand that you need to work in South Korea, Japan or the U.S.A. Do you know that only our firm guarantees once you send in your documents you will receive work that pays at least $1000U.S.? Visas also provided. We invite regional representatives to collaborate with us (p.72).

'Garant-Service' invites applications to work in Korea: women and men . . . Family pairs get a discount. Loans also available. Japan, England, U.S.A, Canada, Australia, Egypt, Ireland, Europe. Student programs. Japan, Korea—dancers, hostesses, topless, performance collectives, contracts from three to six months. Selection done by photograph. Fast processing. E-mail . . . (p.74).

The employment agency 'Perspective' invites girls 18–29 years old to work in Japan. Show-collectives, dancers are welcome. Interviews will be held with Japanese clients July 19 at 1pm. We invite regional repre- sentatives to collaborate with us (p.74).

Vladturbizness invites girls 18–30 years old to apply for work as danc- ers and hostesses in clubs in Korea, Japan, Spain, Cypress. Dancers and show-collectives apply to work in China. Speedy and free processing! Men and women 25–50 years old, apply for work-study in South Korea, Spain, Italy, England, America, Canada, and South Africa. Loans avail- able, guarantees and visa support (p.74).

These advertisements reflect the transnational nature of the entertain- ment and sex work industries more broadly, including in the United States and Canada (McDonald, Moore, and Timoshkina 2000), Japan, Korea, and Western Europe. They demonstrate that local (Russian Far East) businesses, complete with municipally issued licenses indicated in each ad, are widely engaged in arranging visas and employment for women in the region. The advertisements also suggest how these agencies collaborate with Japanese, Korean, and Chinese recruiters, among others, to make necessary arrangements for their clients' employment. The e-mails and Web sites included serve to legitimate the businesses and in fact are a means for potential dancers to research the firms before pursuing employment possibilities. While the advertisements raise as many questions as they answer—for instance, how much does one need to work to earn the U.S.$1,000 guaranteed in one ad?—they reflect the ways in which the recruitment of men and women for a wide array of sex work is not simply a matter of criminal activity or naïve victims. As scholars have demonstrated in a range of locations (Brennan 2004; White 1990; Brock 1998), there is a pool of people who are in fact seeking out employment in the realm of entertainment and sex work. In appealing to the various groups of people seeking employment (couples and artistic collectives) the advertisements further disrupt images of lone women as innocent victims in need of protection that are prevalent in dominant discourses on trafficking. To understand this better, we also need to consider the involvement of intermediaries in transnational labor migration of women from the Russian Far East.[15]

MANAGING THE BORDER IN THE RUSSIAN FAR EAST

Tour Agencies

In the border region of the Russian Far East, the role of NGOs and tour agencies-cum-employment agencies in mediating travel has recently taken on increased importance.[16] A whole industry of agencies facilitate outmigration by arranging short-term visas and transport—by bus, train, boat, and charter flight (Erokhina 2000). In some cases quasilegal organizations promise employment opportunities abroad for high pay that do not turn out to be so lucrative (Malysheva and Tiuriukanova 2000). In many cases, however, women are able to secure work contracts that they find satisfactory. In interviews in 2003, a number of women emphasized that work abroad represented opportunity for them. Zoia, a woman from Blagoveshchensk, a small city north of Khabarovsk that borders China, explained to me that she worked in 2002 as a "hostess" in South Korea on a year contract arranged through a tour agency. Zoia made enough to buy herself an apartment and furnish it. Given the few opportunities for employment in her city, without her year in Korea Zoia would still be living with her parents, something she found anathema to her sense of independence.

Women like Zoia often consult friends and acquaintances who have themselves returned from work abroad to seek information about the best locations to work, the least expensive ways to arrange travel, and the most reliable agencies for arranging visas. In many cases, young women also described to me how they themselves had traveled regularly to China in the mid-1990s when they did "shop-tur", or "shopping-tourism"—tourism mixed with petty wholesale trade. While the "shop-tur" practice has become less significant since the 1998 economic crisis and the Russian government's imposition of steep trade tariffs, women and men still draw on the resources of tour agencies-cum-employment agencies (such as those placing newspaper advertisements like the ones above) to arrange employment and visas for travel to neighboring countries.

These agencies advertise widely in the Russian Far East, and they are also a visible fixture along city streets. In Khabarovsk in summer 2003 at the river ferry terminal, which served as the primary departure point for travel across the Amur River to China, five different tour agencies had small offices set up in what looked like boxcars and temporary buildings. Each one sported its own sign, "Shop-tur" and "Fuyuan." The trip to Fuyuan in Heilongjiang Province, located just across the Amur River, was one hour by boat. A day trip cost about U.S.$20 and a two-day trip, $80. The charge for two days included the Chinese visa—U.S.$25—a hotel, and the return boat ticket. While men and women from the Russian Federation were welcome to make day trips without a visa, longer visits required a visa. Officially, the visa for China was only issued to women over 25, but men of any age were eligible. Apparently, as in several Middle Eastern countries such as the United Arab Emirates since the early 1990s, this was a Chinese attempt to slow the flow of young Russian women seeking work across the border.[17]

At one tour agency, Raduga, I was told that in summer the agency sends one boat each day across the Amur River to China, departing at 8 A.M. and returning at 8 P.M.; only a handful of people travel in the summer months—sometimes as few as four or five. However, in the fall, when children are preparing for school and parents are purchasing clothing from the petty traders, passengers usually number thirty to forty. Prior to the 1998 economic crisis, petty traders sought to make the long trek by air from Khabarovsk to Turkey to buy wholesale textiles thought to be of higher quality than those available in China. Today traders are once again turning to the more affordable goods available just across the border in China.

At the Raduga agency and two others I visited, they told me they only arranged for daytrips and passengers always returned; I was told that other "less reputable" [neveryne] travel agencies would take passengers who might remain illegally in China to seek work. The women labor migrants I consulted with spoke of arranging work abroad by contacting one of these less reputable organizations, which could arrange the desired work visas. Even when employment options are arranged through friends or acquaintances, obtaining visas can be a problem. In 2003, for instance, South Korea and Japan decided to curtail their "entertainment" visa category indefinitely, and spheres of employment in South Korea and Japan officially became restricted for those on a "working holiday" visa that was not issued to citizens of Russia.[18]

This blurring of the lines between "tour agency" and "employment agency" is not surprising in the Russian Far East, given that both spheres involve negotiating the nearby border.[19] For the people living on it, this border currently represents opportunity. As one young woman reflected, "I have lots of girlfriends who have worked several contracts in clubs in China, Japan, and Korea; one of them is even getting married to a South Korean. . . . I would like to take up a job as hostess, but my husband won't allow it; he won't let me go abroad" (personal communication, July 2003). Young women in Khabarovsk and Vladivostok frequently expressed such aspirations in interviews. When compared to their other options in poorly paid positions, working abroad in the entertainment sphere seemed potentially lucrative, and it meant a chance to expand one's horizons. Opportunity was very much the dominant aspect of women's accounts of their migration experiences, and stood at odds with the discourses on danger that I encountered at the NGOs of the Russian Far East.

NGOs

From the perspective of NGOs in the Russian Far East, labor migration is fraught with dangers that far outweigh any benefits. Winrock International, a nonprofit with thirty-five locations worldwide that promotes causes ranging from reforestation to antitrafficking,[20] also has a presence in the former Soviet Union (FSU). Since the mid-1990s, its primary work has been in Ukraine, but it has steadily expanded throughout the region, opening an office in Khabarovsk in 2000, and in Kishinev, Moldova, in 2004. The assistant director of the Khabarovsk office explained to me that Winrock International's programs had significantly grown in the three years it had been in Khabarovsk (personal communication, July 2003). The Khabarovsk office, like other Winrock International sites in the FSU, is funded primarily by USAID. Winrock International maintains the office and staff of five, and it oversees grant monies aimed at supporting antitrafficking educational campaigns. In 2001 the organization administered ten grants of U.S.$5,000 each for projects meant to educate the public about trafficking. In 2002 they were awarded sixteen grants of U.S.$15,000U.S. each for similar work.

My interview with the assistant director confirmed what scholars have indicated about feminist and human rights organizations in Russia overall, that they are overwhelmingly supported by international funding, with 90 percent of their budgets supplied by Western agencies (Sundstrom 2002: 222, 227). Based on her research focusing on over 100 women's organizations in seven regions of the Russian Federation, Lisa Sundstrom (2002: 222) establishes that 67 percent of women's NGOs received foreign funding at some point, and 42 percent were entirely dependent on foreign funding in 1999–2000. Similarly, in 2003 the funneling of USAID monies for antitrafficking efforts in the Russian Far East clearly played an important role in transforming local civic organizations and defining their mandates (see Hess, this volume, for a related point about U.S. policy and its repercussions in China). None of the sixteen NGOs that received grants from Winrock International in 2002 had previously focused their efforts on any aspect of labor migration or trafficking. In one case a person awarded a grant was a dean of a newly established psychology institute, and herself trained as a psychoanalyst. In another case, Tsiunami, one of the organizations awarded a grant in 2002, was created several years earlier as an environmental watchdog. In 2003 when Winrock announced its grant competition, two of the three people in the organization decided their expertise—small business person and psychologist—would position them to write a competitive proposal to fund a set of workshops on the dangers of trafficking.

The types of workshops created by each organization funded by Winrock varied depending on their profiles. For instance, Tsiunami designed its two-day workshop so that most of the hours were spent on developing job skills—how to interview well, dressing for success, and so on. (In fact, Tsiunami was partially operating its workshop in a space shared with a nanny agency, "Mary Poppins," owned by one of the Tsiunami organizers). Workshops were conducted in Vladivostok and in surrounding towns, and in addition to advertising on radio and in newspapers such as *Dal' Press*, Tsiunami located participants by handing out flyers and contacting youth organizations and local Centers for Employment [*tsentr trudoustroistva*]. When the workshops were held in villages men sometimes also participated and were not turned away, even though the material on trafficking was specifically targeted at women. Although USAID funded the workshops via Winrock International, the source of this funding was not something interviewees in the organizations found problematic. They did say that while the explicit antitrafficking component of the workshops was interesting, people seemed to participate in spite of this section of the workshop rather than because of it. In Tsiunami's case, a two-hour module focused on the dangers of trafficking drew on materials made available by Winrock, in particular a set of "myths of migration" to be addressed in each workshop (Tsiunami 2003).[21]

These so-called "myths of migration" assumed migrants to be extremely naïve. They included statements such as, "It is okay to work illegally"; "You need to find a rich man to marry abroad—that is the ticket to the good life"; and "If you go and work for a few months as a prostitute, you can get rich." In a sort of Socratic method, the organizers sought to have participants critically consider their own thoughts on commonly held myths of migration. Tsiunami organizers told me that in each of the sessions at least one person walked out during this section. From the condescending nature of the flyers advertising the antitrafficking portion of the workshop, it was easy to imagine that there might be a disjuncture between the aims of the organizers and the aims of those attending. One flyer handed out on streetcorners stated in bold letters,

> Finding work abroad—it's a chance to earn money and see the world, but first and foremost you should know that each year 4 million people become victims of trafficking . . . a huge number of women are exported from Russia for the purposes of illegal exploitation in Korea, Japan, and China. . . . We don't want to frighten you; we are only trying to protect you from danger! (Tsiunami flyer 2003)

The flyers and the "myths of migration" employed in USAID-funded workshops reflect how a growing number of foreign-supported NGOs in Russia tend to be detached from the majority views of the local public.[22] While potential labor migrants have heard of the possible difficulties they could encounter, their knowledge of successful migrations in their communities compels them to dream of relative prosperity only attainable by becoming part of the growing remittance economy with incomes from Japan, Korea, and China. As researchers in other locations have argued (Busza et al. 2004), NGO efforts to deter migration might be better spent on creating viable economic alternatives at home and establishing meaningful resources for migrants who do choose to go abroad. While an information campaign has merit, it does not address the root of the problem, that there are inadequate economic opportunities in home communities and virtually no labor regulations in place to protect labor migrants in destination countries.

As of fall 2000, local administrations in the Russian Far East were debating a series of laws addressing transnational "prostitution." The legislation proposed in Khabarovsk included outlawing tour agencies and employment agencies involved in recruiting migrant laborers for work abroad (Glava Administratsii 2000). In summer 2003, NGO representatives said Victor Ishayev, the governor of the Khabarovsk region, was serious about such legislation, but Sergei Darkin, the governor of the Primorsk region—in which Vladivostok is located—was not supportive. As of 2006 the proposed legislation had still not been passed. In taking a stand against trafficking in such a form, local power structures would also be making a difficult economic decision. As in other locations where local economies rely heavily on sex work and entertainment (Wonders and Michalowski 2001), there continues to be widespread ambivalence about legislation that would have detrimental economic impacts. In the Russian Far East such legislation would prevent the region from securing significant market gains at a time when local administrations are scrambling to be savvy about new market possibilities and especially trade with their immediate Pacific Rim neighbors.

As long as there are few opportunities in home communities, women will most likely be willing to take the risks involved in becoming labor migrants in neighboring and more distant countries such as Turkey and in western Europe and North America. As migrants, their ability to traverse historically confining borders and to send resources back to home communities frequently outweighs the potential dangers (see Massey, chapter 1 in this volume). The multitude of intermediaries prepared to assist labor migrants with transport, visas, and arranging employment have become a significant part of the legal and gray economies in many locations throughout the former Soviet Union. NGOs that are just at the start of long-term antitrafficking campaigns funded from abroad may have a tough time finding an audience. Migrants' dreams are not easily dismissed with the discourses on danger imported from afar.

As scholars we can contribute a critique of the trafficking discourses in an effort to demystify diverse processes of labor migration. Instead of invoking evil forces taking advantage of innocent victims, social scientists can turn attention to the realities of labor migration for thousands of people (see Massey, chapter 1 in this volume, for other concrete suggestions for research). Such an investigation requires an untangling of the multiple actors engaged in facilitating and deterring men's and women's transnational migrations. It seems ironic that at the very time that capitalism globally has come to be defined by flexible labor forces, the supply of which require fluid transnational borders, USAID and other international organizations have positioned themselves to police the borders so many women and men long to cross. Hopefully, more extensive scholarship focused on migrants' experiences of labor migration can influence policymakers to reassess the enormous resources currently focused on trafficking, and to instead concentrate on improving migrants' working conditions in destination countries and livelihoods in sending communities.

10. "We Are Not Terrorists!"

*Uighurs, Tibetans, and
the "Global War on Terror"*

Julia Meredith Hess

The research for this chapter began with the question of how U.S. policies implemented in the wake of September 11, 2001, were affecting the policy of other states. I was particularly interested in China, as it affects the lives, status, and activism of the Tibetans with whom I generally work. While it is true that Tibetans in China are being persecuted as "terrorists" post-9/11, I found much more evidence for the targeting of another ethnic minority, Uighurs. Uighurs[1] are a Turkic-speaking, predominantly Muslim ethnic group in China's northwest province known as the Xinjiang Uygur Autonomous Region (XUAR). Before September 11, 2001, China consistently downplayed Uighur separatist activities and did not publicize actions to counter Uighur dissent in Xinjiang. However, soon after 9/11, the Chinese state mounted an international campaign to label all Uighur separatists "terror groups." The Uighur human rights situation worsened, marked by increasing repression, including arrests, the repatriation of Uighurs to countries neighboring China, detention, torture, and execution. My goal in this chapter is to show the transnational scope of discourse, in this case discourse that privileges the language of "terror" and "terrorism." I argue that the Chinese state has used the discursive framework of the Global War on Terror (GWOT) to reframe policy that was already in place prior to the events of 9/11. The diffuse set of statements, initiatives, and policies linked with the GWOT can in no way be held to blame for the Chinese government's hostility to and repression of Uighur strivings for greater autonomy. That shabby chapter of China's human rights record predates 9/11: Chinese governments have long held Uighurs to be potential challengers to state authority, whether labeled as "ethnic nationalists," "counter-revolutionaries," "separatists," or, now, as "terrorists" (Human Rights Watch 2005a: 6).Yet the Chinese state has taken advantage of the

U.S.-promoted discourse of a global war on terror to frame Uighur dissidents and other activists as "terrorists," providing the state with a justification for accelerating their crackdown on the Uighurs and driving greater numbers to flee from repression.

Like the other essays in this volume, my argument here attends to how 9/11 has both altered conditions for international migration and also served as a pretext for governments to pursue preexisting agendas toward its immigrant and minority populations with increased force (see the introduction for an overview). The U.S. response to 9/11—as a global state of emergency permissive of exceptions to any and all human rights norms in the pursuit of alleged terrorists—creates more permissive conditions for *other states*, in this case, China, to escalate their rhetoric against even peaceful separatist movements (such as the Uighurs) and to harden an already established policy marked by hostility, surveillance, and repression (Kelly 2003).

There are approximately 8.5 million Uighurs in Xinjiang. Outside of Xinjiang there are some 600,000 Uighurs, most in Central Asia and Turkey. First, I will discuss the situation of Uighurs in Xinjiang, then move to a discussion of how Chinese state policies are affecting Uighur migration from Xinjiang. The last part of the chapter will consider how state policies, increased migration, and the development of a transnationally linked activist community of Uighurs may foment Uighur nationalist ambitions. I will refer to Tibetan cases for comparison throughout. In conclusion, I comment on the burgeoning transnational campaign to highlight the situation of Uighurs in China and its relationship with the now decades-old struggle for international attention for the Tibetan cause.

REPRESSING DISSENT: CHINA AND ITS OTHERS

Both Uighurs and Tibetans are among fifty-six recognized ethnic minority groups, or national minorities [*minzu*] in China. The range of inclusion in the Chinese state of these different national minorities is highly variable. Both Uighurs and Tibetans claim historical independence from China. In contrast, the Chinese state counters that both Uighur and Tibetan areas have long been integral parts of China. An in-depth discussion of these claims is beyond the scope of this chapter but has been the subject of many accounts (for the Tibetan case, see Goldstein 1989, 1999; Shakya 1999; Smith 1996, for the Uighur case, Gladney 1997, 2004b). However, even when the Han Chinese managed political dominance, they never attempted to colonize Tibet or Xinjiang until after the communist revolution of 1949.

The province of Xinjiang is located in Northwest China and shares a border with eight states, including Kazakhstan, Kyrgyzstan, Tajikistan, Afghanistan, Pakistan, and India. Prior to the 1949 revolution, Xinjiang had achieved independence a number of times and was known in its latest incarnation as the East Turkestan Republic (1944 to 1949). As in Tibet, the Chinese Communist Party (CCP) implemented reforms slowly at first, but by the mid-1950s Chinese reform in Xinjiang was marked by policies designed to overwhelm and stamp out ethnic markers that defined Uighur culture and identity.

The collapse of the Soviet Union in the late 1980s and the subsequent birth of independent republics in Central Asia prompted the development of many Uighur groups agitating for independence or more autonomy from the Chinese state. Many of these groups were nonviolent, but some did advocate violence. During the 1990s there were several bombing incidents within the province of Xinjiang and in Beijing that were attributed to violent Uighur factions. "According to a Chinese government report published on 21 January 2002, which listed 'terrorist' incidents in the region over the past ten years, the most recent explosion allegedly carried out by a 'terrorist' group took place in April 1998 in Yecheng and the only other recent incident of violence imputed to 'terrorists' since 1999 was the murder of one court official in Kashgar prefecture in February 2001" (Amnesty International 2004: 6).

Nevertheless, shortly after 9/11 the Chinese implemented a "Strike Hard, Severe Repression," campaign against Uighur separatists. Marking little distinction between violent and nonviolent tactics, the Chinese detained and imprisoned thousands of Uighurs. Xinjiang is the only province in China that can apply the death penalty for political offenses. According to Amnesty International (2004: 2):

> The Chinese government's use of the term "separatism" refers to a broad range of activities, many of which amount to no more than peaceful opposition or dissent, or the peaceful exercise of the right to freedom of religion. Over the last three years, tens of thousands of people are reported to have been detained for investigation in the region and hundreds, possibly thousands, have been charged or sentenced under the Criminal Law; many Uighurs are believed to have been sentenced to death and executed for alleged "separatist" or "terrorist" offences, although the exact number is impossible to determine.

Though estimates are difficult to come by, it is certain that since the late 1990s thousands of Uighurs have been detained and arrested. Human Rights

Watch (HRW) reports that "a scholarly paper from a Ministry of Justice compendium, shows that in 2001 9.2 percent of convicted Uighurs—one out of eleven—were serving prison time for alleged 'state security crimes.' This probably amounts to more than 1,000 Uighur prisoners" (Human Rights Watch 2005a: 70). Amnesty International (2004: 5–6) reports that "[i]n March 2003, Han Zhubin, China's then procurator-general, published statistics which revealed that in the five years between 1998–2002, procuratorates nationwide approved the arrest of 3,402 individuals and prosecuted 3,550 people on charges of 'endangering state security.'" Moreover, "Given the intensification in the official crackdown on the 'three evil forces' of 'separatism, terrorism and religious extremism' in the region, it is likely that the numbers of arrests and prosecutions have increased significantly since then (ibid.: 6). Uighur exiles estimate that these number in the tens of thousands (ibid.). A March 2003 U.S. Department of State report totaled the number of executions at 4,000 (U.S. Department of State 2003b).

The Chinese state is using the United States' war on terror as a justification for launching an international campaign to repress Uighur separatism in Xinjiang. Prior to 9/11, the Chinese downplayed Uighur separatist actions in the region and "tried to manage it discreetly through state-to-state negotiations with Turkey and Pakistan" (Christofferson 2004). However, subsequent to the September 11th attacks, the Chinese have highlighted acts of violence by Uighurs, lumping them together with nonviolent acts and groups. This international campaign intentionally conflates separatism and nonviolent dissent with "terrorism." (Compare chapters 4 and 6 in this volume, by Akram and Johnson and Dole, respectively, on how Arabs and Muslims are profiled as terrorists in the United States.)

RELIGIOUS PERSECUTION

Uighurs converted to Islam beginning in the tenth century and by and large practice Sufi and Sunni Islam, distinct from so-called Wahabbist or more dogmatic and rigid sects of Islam. The breakup of the Soviet Union encouraged the development of oppositional movements all over Central Asia. "The pro-independence groups in Xinjiang are overwhelmingly ethnonationalist movements—that is, they are articulated along ethnic lines, not religious ones. This appears to be the case among both religious and secular groups" (Human Rights Watch 2005a: 12). However, according to HRW and Amnesty International, repressive policy measures enacted by the state target religious activity. According to Amnesty International (2004: 2–3, n.9), the government has increased restrictions on the religious rights of the Muslim population in the region, banning some religious practices during the holy month of Ramadan, closing many mosques and independent religious schools, increasing official controls over the Islamic clergy, and detaining or arresting religious leaders deemed to be "unpatriotic" or "subversive." Regional authorities have also launched political campaigns to "clean up" cultural and media circles and some government departments in Xinjiang to rid them of "undesirable elements."

HRW (2005a: 28–29) documents both overt and covert policy directed toward Uighurs in XUAR. The 1994 Regulations on Religious Activities "echoed the national regulations" (29). In 1998 and 2000 increasingly strict regulations were passed, calling for particular scrutiny and focus on religious leaders and the religious activities of CCP members in Xinjiang. These policy changes reflected "an effort to 'step up the struggle against national separatism' and to 'root out reactionary religious behaviors'" (30). In July 2001, a series of amendments to the 1994 Regulations were adopted which further tighten religious restrictions in Xinjiang.

The 2001 amendments severely tighten the already restrictive provisions of the 1994 Regulations on Religious Activities in five main areas. These are:

- narrowing the scope of "normal" religious activities;
- the extension of the "anti-separatist" clause, previously applied only to the clergy, to *all* "citizens who profess a religion["];
- increased control over registration and operations of religious organizations;
- tightened control over religious publications; and
- heavier sanctions and penalties. (Human Rights Watch 2005a: 32)

Notable in the HRW description of the development of restrictions on religious freedom in Xinjiang is that the CCP associates religious affiliation and practice with political dissidence, not only among the population at large, but also within its own ranks. It may be that through zero tolerance for ethnonationalist expression or activity in Xinjiang and Tibet, the state has unwittingly provided the impetus for the revival of religious institutions in the more open reform period after the end of the Cultural Revolution in the 1980s. This reflects not just a shift in resistance tactics to a less policed or scrutinized sphere, but the complex interconnections of social, political, economic, religious, and ethnic social relations and institutions. Knowing the role of religion and religious leaders in all sectors of Tibetan society makes it unsurprising that religious affairs and activities are controlled by the state as well as being venues of political expression.

THE TIBETAN CASE: SUPPRESSION OF RELIGIOUS AND ARTISTIC FREEDOM

In Tibet, the majority of political prisoners are monks and nuns (Congressional-Executive Commission on China 2005), monasteries and the activities of monks and nuns are tightly controlled, and political dissidence often takes on ritualistic attributes (see Schwartz 1996). Increased repression of religious activities in Xinjiang, on top of increased repression of political activities, will undoubtedly serve to politicize religious activity and expression.

In Tibet, a popular religious figure associated with a large-scale religious revival, Tenzin Deleg Rinpoche, was accused of carrying out a 2002 bombing in Chengdu, the capital of Sichuan province, with a number of associates. In 2003, Tenzin Deleg, along with Lobsang Dondrup, was found guilty of the bombing in a closed trial that the late United Nations High Commissioner for Human Rights, Sergio de Mello, said, "[did] not appear to have met minimum standards" (World Tibet Network [hereafter WTN] 2005a). Both Lobsang Dondrup and Tenzin Deleg were found guilty and given a death sentence. Lobsang Dondrup's was carried out immediately; he was executed on 26 January 2003. Tenzin Deleg was given a two-year reprieve. After almost two years of intense international pressure, including campaigns orchestrated by the International Campaign for Tibet and Amnesty International, Tenzin Deleg's death sentence was commuted to life in prison (WTN 2005a).

A Tibetan writer, Oser, published a book of essays entitled *Notes on Tibet*, which the Chinese state banned in September 2003. Subsequently, Oser was removed from her post as editor of the Tibet Autonomous Region Literature Association and stripped of her government-issued housing and benefits. What follows is a short excerpt from her poem "Secrets of Tibet," which was dedicated to Tenzin Deleg Rinpoche, Bangri Rinpoche, and Lobsang Tenzin and circulated widely on the Internet. Referring to Tenzin Deleg, she wrote:

> With a pack of tricks, they finally trapped him after 9/11.
> Magnificent way to accuse him, in the name of "anti-terrorism,"
> punishing one to warn many. They said he hid bombs
> and pornography, as well as planning five or seven bombings.

I remember, half a year before he was locked up, he was very sad:
"My mother passed away, I am going into a one-year retreat for her."
Such a sincere follower of the Buddha,
how could he be involved in bombing and killing?[2]

The case of Tursunjan Emet, a Uighur poet, shows the way the state strategically labels activities and conflates terms in order to criminalize activism. Emet was arrested after a performance at a Kashgar concert hall on 1 January 2002 (Human Rights Watch 2005a: 19). According to Amnesty International (2004: 8),

> A local Chinese Communist Party official reportedly clarified that his poem "attacked government policy regarding ethnic minorities" and that "he wanted to destroy the unity between Uighur and Han." He reportedly added that "we regard this as *terrorism in the spiritual form*, but we want to educate not punish him." No further details about the poet or his fate have become available. Amnesty International is concerned that the vague term "spiritual terrorism"— not concretely prescribed, let alone defined, in China's criminal law— appears to have been used in this case as a pretext for arrest.

According to a report published in *China Rights Forum*, the Chinese media reported that in 2002 the Xinjiang party secretary declared a crackdown on "'separatist techniques' that included many modes of expression universally recognized as fundamental rights and freedoms: 'news media,' 'literature works,' 'arts performance,' and 'distributing . . . leaflets, letters, and posters'" (Becquelin 2004: 6). Among the targeted activities were "[u]sing works of literature . . . to disseminate dissatisfaction." According to this same report, by March 2002 authorities had burned tens of thousands of books, including *A Brief History of the Huns and Ancient Literature*, which officials viewed as fomenting separatism. Also burned was *Ancient Uyghur Craftsmanship*, a 1998 book which detailed "centuries-old techniques of papermaking, candle-making, carpentry, carpet and silk weaving" (Becquelin 2004: 7).

The Chinese have also passed laws that accelerate the shift to all-Chinese education in Xinjiang. Introducing Chinese from Primary three, and teaching all courses at Xinjiang University in Chinese, "some scholars have argued that the language policy as currently implemented 'implicitly categorizes the Uyghur language as disloyal'" (quoted in Becquelin 2004: 7).

Similarly in Tibet, writers have been imprisoned. The PEN Tibetan Writers Abroad Centre passed a resolution on 19 June 2005 calling on China to free all Tibetan writers "who are under arrest, in prison or who are deprived of their political rights and right to movement." Specifically the resolution named five writers currently in prison for "spreading negative political ideology in their writings." The names of the writers are Geshe Je Tashi Gyaltsen, Jamphal Gyatso, Tsultrim Phelgye, Lobsang Dargye, and Toesam Zangden (WTN 2005b).

In February 2004, seven Uighur acrobats who were part of a state-sponsored troop from Xinjiang contacted Uighur exiles while touring in Canada and sought asylum. A juggler named Dilshat Sirajidin stated, "We performed for the government and they used us to create this image of ethnic unity. We didn't have a choice. We had no right to oppose." According to a newspaper article, "Uygur Internet forums and chat rooms were awash with news of the defections. It brought with it cheers and congratulations and a strange new lease of life among the Uygur in diaspora who plod on relentlessly in the hope of getting the wider world to pay attention to the plight of their brothers in China" (Sullivan 2004).

STATE POLICY AND UIGHUR MIGRATION

Repression of Uighurs in Xinjiang has led to migration out of the region. Uighurs often flee to Kazakhstan and Kyrgyzstan, where there are large established communities of Uighurs native to these states. Uighurs also flee to Pakistan, Nepal, Europe, and the United States. There is concern among human rights organizations that Uighurs in Nepal and Pakistan are being forcibly repatriated to China after having received recognition of their status as refugees from UNHCR (Human Rights Watch 2005a). There are cases of Uighurs in Kazakhstan and Kyrgyzstan who have disappeared and who are feared to have been forcibly returned.[3]

There is a small community of exile Uighurs in the United States, numbering around 1,000 individuals. While it is unclear if China's crackdown on Uighurs is leading to increased emigration of Uighurs from Xinjiang, it is quite certain that post-9/11 actions taken by the United States and by China are having an impact on Uighurs outside of Xinjiang.

In August 2002, the United States succumbed to pressure from China to place the East Turkestan Independence Movement (ETIM) on a list of recognized terrorist organizations. In September 2002, the United Nations endorsed this categorization of ETIM. The U.S. government came under criticism that they had taken Chinese assertions about the ETIM at face value. In response, U.S. officials stated that they had "independent evidence" supporting Chinese assertions. According to Amnesty International (2004: 18), "Since this listing was confirmed, official rhetoric has intensified

in the Chinese media against 'separatists, terrorists and religious extremists' in the XUAR as China has sought to interpret this move by the USA
and the UN as an endorsement of its crackdown against all forms of dissent
in the region."

According to an article in the *Far Eastern Economic Review* by Susan
Lawrence, there are indications that the U.S. government has grown wary
of China so readily associating all Uighur organizations with terror (Lawrence 2004; also Becquelin 2004). Erkin Alptekin, the son of the former
president of East Turkestan, Isa Yusuf Alptekin, was received in Washington despite the displeasure of the Chinese state. According to Lawrence,
"Washington's dismissal of China's concerns regarding Alptekin is striking because it comes at a time when the joint commitment of China and
the United States to fighting terrorism is often cited as a key factor in
their improved bilateral relations." Furthermore, "Most conspicuously, in
December (2003) when China released a list of four organizations and 11
individuals it claimed to be Eastern Turkestan terrorists, the U.S. declined
to endorse it" (Lawrence 2004).

Among those detained by the United States in Guantánamo, Cuba, there
were approximately twenty-two Uighurs who were captured in Afghanistan. These Uighurs are among some 300 who were reportedly captured
during the war in Afghanistan. The Uighurs in Guantánamo forcefully
call attention to the quandary the United States faces in reconciling international concern for human rights, the interests of its "allies," and its
"war on terror." When the United States announced that it was considering extraditing the Uighur detainees back to China, human rights groups
and advocates raised an alarm based on summary executions and torture
experienced by other Uighurs who had previously returned to China. The
United States did allow a delegation of Chinese to come to Guantánamo in
September 2002 to interrogate the Uighurs, allegedly allowing the Chinese
to use "'stress and duress' techniques such as environmental manipula-
tion, forced sitting for many hours, and sleep deprivation, some of which
allegedly occurred on the instruction of the Chinese delegation" (Amnesty
International 2004: 19). After a military tribunal declared that the Uighurs
were not terrorists but simply "in the wrong place at the wrong time,"
it ordered them released (Savage 2005). Finally, in early 2006, five of the
Uighurs were sent to Albania, where they are being housed in a refugee
camp. The remaining Uighur detainees, among many other detainees,
remain in a kind of limbo in Guantánamo.

The fate of the seventeen Uighurs who remain has vexed the administrations of both George W. Bush and Barack Obama. Although the Uighurs

were captured in Pakistan, their accounts of the training they received convinced investigators that they were not enemies of the United States, but were rather receiving training in order to aid in their struggle against the Chinese state. They were thus not declared "enemy combatants." There has been difficulty in finding a country to accept them, as most states are not willing to take on the anger of the Chinese state that would result from welcoming them. While the Obama administration said that it would be willing to resettle the Uighurs on U.S. soil, Republicans raised concerns about jeopardizing the safety of the United States if former detainees are allowed to resettle in the United States (Clark 2009). In June 2009, the Pacific-island nation of Palau announced that it would accept the seventeen Uighurs. Subsequently, Bermuda announced that four of the seventeen had been resettled there (BBC News 2009). As of this writing it is not clear if or when the remaining Uighur detainees will be transferred to Palau.

Actions taken by the United States, China, and the United Nations subsequent to September 11, 2001, are having a marked effect on Uighur migration, asylum, and refugee claims. In an interview, Nury Turkel, the president of the Uygur American Association, said that U.S. State Department reports outlining Chinese repression of Uighurs in Xinjiang is having a favorable effect on Uighur asylum claims in the United States: these justify the claim that Uighurs have a "well-founded fear of persecution" under the Chinese state. Thus, although there is more scrutiny for all asylum seekers and longer waits for all processes under the Bureau of Citizenship and Immigration Services, according to Turkel, Uighurs now have the highest rate of acceptance of asylum claims in the United States, principally because the U.S. State Department's own information on Chinese actions in Xinjiang compels the government to give Uighurs asylum.

Tibetans have also been affected by the increased scrutiny of asylum procedures in the United States. The Tibetan population in the United States increased dramatically in the United States in the 1990s after the passage of legislation that provided immigrant visas for 1,000 Tibetans and their immediate families (Hess 2009). Beginning in 1995, the United States began to give asylum to Tibetans previously settled in South Asia (WTN 1995). Increased scrutiny of asylum seekers after 9/11 led to the arrest of a Tibetan woman, Sonam Chodon, who claimed she was a nun fleeing persecution from China. She was detained upon arrival at Dulles airport in 2003 and subsequently received the support of Tibet activists, the media, and even a U.S. senator who claimed that U.S. policies were too harsh and that asylees were being unnecessarily detained. She was indicted for passport fraud after it was determined that her passport was not legitimate. In an news article about Sonam Chodon's case, Assistant Homeland Security Secretary for Immigration and Customs Enforcement Michael J. Garcia is quoted as saying, "We are a welcoming nation, obviously. . . . We have a very broad and generous asylum policy for people who legitimately meet those standards." Further, the article states,

> Garcia acknowledged that immigration agents have been tougher in enforcing the law since Sept. 11 but said that process started in reaction to the first World Trade Center bombing in 1993. Ramzi Yousef, who later was convicted in that attack, entered the United States as an asylum seeker in 1992. "If I could have rolled back the clock and we could have prosecuted Ramzi Yousef for fraud, he'd be a failed asylum seeker rather than the mastermind of the World Trade Center bombing," Garcia said. (Markon 2005)

Garcia's commentary on Sonam Chodon's case lends weight to the assertion that these government policies were in place prior to 9/11 but have been pursued with added vigor since 9/11 (see chapter 2 in this volume, by Josiah Heyman). What is lacking in the government's response to Sonam Chodon's case of "passport fraud" is the acknowledgment that many asylum seekers have no other choice but to use false documents in order to leave their country of origin, or whatever intermediate country they are leaving, in order to enter the country where they are seeking asylum. Asylum seekers are generally marginalized people, many of whom would find it impossible to leave their countries or gain access to the United States by legitimate means. That the passport Sonam Chodon presented to authorities had been used before by others should not be a surprise to immigration officials. Further, use of a fraudulent passport does not invalidate an asylum claim for Tibetans in Nepal. (Nepal has been repatriating recently arrived Tibetan refugees back to China; the long-settled Tibetan population has also experienced increasing restrictions on religious freedom [Tibet Justice Center 2002; Hess 2006]). The activist response to Sonam Chodon's case is a testament to the responsiveness of the Tibet movement in the United States. Uighur exiles, as we will see in the next section, are using similar campaign-style activism to inform the world of the situation in Xinjiang, and they are starting to see some results.

"WE ARE NOT TERRORISTS!": UIGHUR TRANSNATIONAL ACTIVISM IN DIASPORA

One fundamental issue highlighted by this research is that there is no clear definition of "terrorism." Definitions differ in terms of recognition of the acceptability of the use of violence by civilians against the state. In other words, can there be legitimate violence against a state? In the United States, the State Department, the Central Intelligence Agency, Homeland Security, and others operate under different definitions of "terrorism." There is currently pressure for the United Nations to develop a universally acceptable definition of terrorism (UN Office on Drugs and Crime 2006). States take advantage of this lack of clarity to categorize people they wish to repress. In this case, since the launch of the U.S. war on terror, China has sought to take advantage of this murky area and has used "separatist" and "terrorist" interchangeably. As we have seen, the Chinese state is widening the net, increasingly labeling all forms of Uighur and Tibetan expression and practice—religious, cultural, and artistic—as political, and thus related to terrorism. As one Uighur stated, "[Before September 11, 2001,] we used to go around saying 'China abuses the human rights of Uighurs!' Now we go around saying, 'We are not terrorists!'" (Gladney 2004b).

In Xinjiang itself, I suggest that the Chinese state's repression of all Uighur dissent will continue to foment the development of Uighur nationalism in exile. Not only will the crackdown in Xinjiang result in a population stifled by fear and more likely to continue to seek out extralegal channels of expression, but it will also encourage emigration. China's policies will also encourage Uighurs in exile who left for reasons not necessarily related to politics to identify themselves as Uighur, come to recognize the benefits of an independent Uighur state, and to engage in political acts.

Outside of the confines of the Chinese nation-state, exiles and refugees whose homelands are part of China are creating alliances and are working together to frame their issues in the terms of discourses that are increasingly global. Nury Turkel, the president of the Uyghur American Association, described for me the similarities and differences between the Tibetan and Uighur situation with respect to China as well as in terms of international recognition and support. In both Xinjiang and Tibet, the Chinese government provides incentives for Han immigration and pursues policies that lead to cultural degradation and loss: for instance, policies that require Han Chinese to be the primary language in schools are attacking the linguistic basis of Uighur cultural identity. Turkel said that while Tibetans have a lot of international support, this is not true of Uighurs. While North Americans and Europeans generally have positive views of Tibetans, they have not heard of Uighurs. The Dalai Lama is a Nobel Prize winner, an international icon associated with nonviolence, and over the last twenty years has achieved increasing recognition from world leaders.

Uighurs have no such charismatic figure to lead an international political campaign. The international media attention garnered by Tibetans has meant that the Chinese readily respond to international pressure related to Tibet. Uighur activists are learning from the Tibetan example and are also working with Tibetan activists. Highlighting the similarities of the status of Uighurs and Tibetans in China works to reinforce the idea that the Chinese state systematically abuses the human rights of its ethnic minority citizens. Furthermore, diasporic Uighurs are clearly learning from Tibetans how to respond to Chinese actions, how to frame their responses in language that receives a favorable response from media as well as international activists and other allies.

Recent scholarship has attended to the role of the Internet in disseminating information and creating virtual venues for far-flung people to discuss issues related to identity formation, activism, and political ideologies (McLagan 1996; Bernal 2003). Others have examined the proliferation of conceptual frameworks and ideologies as they circulate globally, including "human rights" and "democracy" (Appadurai 1996; Cunningham 1999; McLagan 2003). In "Computing for Tibet," Meg McLagan (1996) documents the emergence of electronically published information and its role in the Tibet movement. Since that time, Tibetans in diaspora and others have used the Internet to disseminate information about what is happening in Tibet.[4] Tibetan youth from India, Europe, the United States, and Canada use chat rooms and message boards to discuss political topics, identity issues, education, romance, and gossip.[5] Tibet support groups and other human-rights groups have orchestrated campaigns using the Internet in very effective ways.[6]

Uighurs in diaspora are developing a presence on the Internet. There are a number of Web sites that seek to educate about the human rights of Uighurs in Xinjiang and the history of East Turkestan.[7] There are sites dedicated to the independence movement.[8] There is a site with a message board where people post messages in both Turkic and English.[9] Like the Tibetan sites, people talk of politics and also of the complexities of diasporic identity:

> When someone say "hey this girl is from China", when I talk about Eastern Turkestan and nobody around me has ever heard of that, I feel so humiliated. I really can not find right words to describe that kind of feeling. I guess only an uiyghur can understand this humiliation and pain.
>   I always think how many of us have ever asked ourselves what our people really want. We shape the issues the way we think they should be. Uiyghurs have no freedom, no rights? That is absolutely true. But

how many of our people in that situation really think they are being persecuted, and have realized the importance of independent nation? And how many of you really take some time to understand the lives of the people in E.T. [East Turkestan]? Many overseas uighurs left E.T. long time ago, and are influenced by the concepts of democracy and human rights. In my opinion, it is hard to understand how people think and what they need when you are long-isolated from that particular cultural context. How can be the people eager for democracy when they are constantly being endangered by the need of survival?

I used to blame Uiyghurs in E.T. as ignorant and hopeless, but the more I understand them, the more greatful [sic] I became for them. Because they are the people who have been attaching our land, and keeping everthing [sic] on and on. Without them, we are nothing.[10]

This young Uighur woman is clearly reflecting upon both the constructionist and representational aspects of forging a Uighur diasporic identity, a process that embodies a number of tensions. The first is the difficulty of expressing "Uighur-ness" in a society where few have even heard of Uighurs, their problems, and the contentious relationship with China. Second is the tension between Uighurs living in Xinjiang, who face the reality of living within the Chinese state on a daily basis, and exile Uighurs who are exposed to discourses of "democracy and human rights" and who are developing separatist ideologies, even as they themselves are geographically displaced from their "homeland." Finally, while we see the development of an exile-driven nationalistic movement, we also see the simultaneous development of a notion of purity of suffering or an authenticity of experience related with Uighurs in Xinjiang.

Anna Tsing's (2000) critique of anthropological treatments of globalization includes her assertion that attention to global "flows" does not pay enough attention to the role of individual or collective agency in creating the movement of global phenomena. My aim in this chapter is to provide a glimpse at how several groups of actors are both responding to and creating transnational flows to represent their own identities and political goals (see chapter 9 in this volume, by Alexia Bloch, for another example of this kind of work). I contend that the ways actors conceptualize their own identities and use technologies such as the Internet to build transnational coalitions (that go beyond the confines of their ethnic, religious, political, or other axis of identity) reveal a great deal about new configurations of subjectivity as well as global and transnational processes.

Uighur exiles, connected through an increasingly effective transnational network of organizations, receiving and creating information through a variety of media—newspapers, online venues—will reinforce Uighur nationalist identity and activism. Moreover, with the rapid expansion of the Internet in China and despite strong efforts by the Chinese government to control and censor information, some of this information will penetrate into Xinjiang, shoring up Uighur aspirations for autonomy or independence.

In an interview, a Uighur living in the United States remarked that the Chinese have a way of shooting themselves in the foot. Not only will increased repression in Xinjiang encourage the flowering of transnational Uighur resistance, but as we have seen, it has direct policy impacts as well. Uighurs are increasingly gaining political asylum in the United States. Uighurs are learning how to present their case effectively in the international media, rebutting Chinese claims about history of the region, current policy and highlighting human rights abuses. In March 2005, on the eve of Condoleezza Rice's visit to persuade the Chinese to convince North Korea to give up its nuclear weapons program, the Chinese released a prominent Uighur political prisoner, Rebiya Kadeer, reportedly in exchange for the United States' not sponsoring a resolution condemning China's human rights record at the United Nations. While this "exchange" can be criticized as a limited concession by the Chinese that ultimately demonstrates no substantive change of human rights policy, it illustrates the increasing recognition by human rights activists, journalists, and the U.S. State Department of the situation of Uighurs in Xinjiang. The pressure of these activists, journalists, and the U.S. State Department led the Chinese state to take some action. Ironically, it may be that while Uighurs have had the burden of claiming to the world that they are "not terrorists" in the wake of 9/11, they have also started learning the art of garnering attention for their cause. Exile Uighurs are consciously linking their case to that of the Tibetans and forging links with Tibetan organizations and learning from their international campaign. The release of Rebiya Kadeer shows that their tactics may be beginning to pay off. Kadeer is now in the United States, giving talks about the treatment of Uighurs in Xinjiang. One Uighur, who was quoted as saying prior to September 11, 2001, "We have given up on independence, we just want to migrate!" (Gladney 2004a), may also ironically find himself increasingly politicized in diaspora. In this way, state repression not only affects those who live under oppressive policies; it can also foment nationalist and patriotic commitment among diasporic populations.

11. The Impact of Plan Colombia on Forced Displacement

María Teresa Restrepo-Ruiz and Samuel Martínez

> I believe the rights included within the Human Rights International Law did not originate in the world of the ideas directly, but have come from people's suffering and experience, an experience defined by having seen the damage provoked by events that cause feelings of anger, powerlessness and pain.
>
> ALBERTO MARTOS-SAUQUILLO[1]

> The person who is displaced from the countryside to the city has to leave everything and flee just with what she is wearing—if she can—in order to save her life. Almost in every case, the person left behind small properties and few goods that had been gotten through the hard work of many years. Many times, the booty of the aggressors is constituted by properties passed down from generation to generation, with all that this means for the tradition, culture and the strong family bonds. Material goods and spiritual referents of cultural identity are knocked down in a moment. (Acevedo 2000)[2]

Today, Colombia has the highest number of people experiencing internally forced displacement of any country in Latin America, and in the world it is second only to Sudan in its population of internally displaced persons (IDPs) (Global IDP Project 2004). More than 3.7 million of people—upward of eight percent of Colombia's total population—have had to flee from armed conflict and political violence and relocate themselves within Colombian territory since 1985 (Human Rights Watch 2007). In 2003, 904 out of 1,100 municipalities in Colombia were affected by forced displacement (Global IDP Project 2004). And the incidence of forced displacement rose still further from 2003 to 2005, according to the nongovernmental Consultancy for Human Rights and the Displaced (Consultoría para los Derechos Humanos y el Desplazamiento, CODHES).

In the Colombian conflict, forced displacement results directly from indiscriminate attacks by rebels or by government or paramilitary forces, the terror spread by nearby massacres, selective killings, torture, and threats,

as well as from the impact of minefields and the fumigation of coca planta-
tions funded by the U.S. government through its Plan Colombia, legislation drafted with the aid of the Colombian government and signed into law
by President Bill Clinton in 2000. Forced displacement disproportionately
affects politically marginal groups, impoverished peasants, ethnic minorities (the indigenous and Afro-Colombian communities), women, children,
and the elderly (Red de Solidaridad Social 2001, cited in González Bustelo
2001; Mesa de Trabajo Mujer y Conflicto Armado 2002).

Even as Colombia has experienced one of the longest internal armed
conflicts and most severe human rights crises in the world, the U.S. government has granted this South American country unprecedented monetary
and military aid, with little public debate within the United States. After
the approval of Plan Colombia by the U.S. Congress in 2000, Colombia
became the third largest recipient of U.S. military aid in the world after
Israel and Egypt (Adam 2006). Counting aid provided by the U.S. Agency
for International Development ($3 billion) alongside the $4.7 billion now
spent on Plan Colombia, Washington has since 2000 dedicated a total
of $7.7 billion to antinarcotics and anti-insurgency efforts in Colombia
(Mondragón 2007: 42). In a short visit in November 2004 to Cartagena,
Colombia, U.S. President George W. Bush said, "This war against narco-
terrorism can and will be won, and Colombia is well on its way to that
victory."[3] However, after six years of Plan Colombia, neither the traffic
in illicit drugs nor the humanitarian crisis created by U.S.-backed efforts
to suppress that traffic appears to be improving (Mondragón 2007: 43).
Notwithstanding any changes in the balance of conflict at the military
front lines, we stand by our analysis of Plan Colombia's impact as it stood
at the time when this chapter's final draft was completed (late 2007), our
perspective being framed in particular by concern about the counterproductive effects that Plan Colombia had had on the IDP crisis in the years
preceding.

Growth in the number of IDPs has been an unintended human by-
product of recent U.S. administrations' reliance on militarized rather than
political solutions to conflict. In this chapter, we explain how Plan Colombia
has assaulted the human rights to life, safety, and subsistence of millions of
Colombians and thus worsened the problem of internally forced displacement. Through promotion and support for Plan Colombia, the U.S. national
security agenda has negatively impacted uncounted communities in Colombia, and now threatens to expand its negative consequences across the whole
Andean region. The pursuit of U.S. official policy objectives by primarily
military means has yielded dubious gains while worsening already grave

threats to security for millions of Colombians, forcing many to flee their homes and land and seek safety somewhere else within the national territory or neighboring countries. Among the "seismic shocks" set off by U.S. policy initiatives in places around the world (of which Martínez writes in his introduction to this volume), none are more devastating than the conditions of danger and insecurity created by U.S.-sponsored counterinsurgency and antinarcotics warfare in Colombia.

In the first section of the chapter, we focus on forced displacement, its causes, and the human costs of displacement for those affected by it. The second section focuses briefly on Plan Colombia: the process of its creation, its logic and assumptions, as well as the evolution of its aims and strategies as it has been implemented. In the third section we examine the impact of Plan Colombia on forced displacement and ponder the particular responsibility borne by the United States for worsening this crisis.

WHAT "FORCED DISPLACEMENT" REALLY MEANS

Colombian organizations of IDPs have defined "displaced person" as follows: "any person that had been obligated to migrate within the national territory. She or he has abandoned her place of residence and economic activities because her physical integrity and freedom have been threatened as a result of any of the following situations that are caused by men: internal armed conflict, internal disturbances or tensions, generalized violence, massive human rights violations and any other circumstance derived from the preceding situations that may drastically disturb the public order."[4] This definition is shared at the international level[5] and finds expression also in the term by which IDPs are most commonly referred to by Colombians: *los desplazados* (the displaced).

The real causes of this phenomenon are called into debate by certain alternative terms by which some Colombian activists and scholars prefer to speak of the IDPs: the "uprooted" or "exiled" *[desterrados]* and the "dispossessed" *[despojados]*, who collectively constitute an "exodus" or "banished" group (Molano Bravo 2000). For these politically engaged intellectuals, the term "displacement" is misleading in so far as it connotes nothing more than a change of place. The alternative terms that they prefer make it clear, by contrast, that internal displacement is an event that people have to face because others have economic and political interests in their land and want to take it, using violence and terror.

In this context, the epigraph from Juan Camilo Acevedo with which we begin our chapter draws attention also to a fundamental reality: victims of forced displacement have experienced multiple violations of their human rights. Therefore, even as we use the internationally accepted standard term "IDP," we wish also to underscore the need to adopt a critical view of the language through which we speak of this reality, rooted in the realization that the rights infringements experienced by Colombia's IDPs generally neither begin nor end with their uprooting and geographical dislocation.

Daniel Pécaut (2000) asserts that Colombian IDPs enter into a state of "statelessness" comparable to that experienced by European refugees during and after the Second World War. They are plucked out of their familiar social milieus and deprived of the support provided in their places of origin. They become economically destitute, being obligated to leave their goods, land, and animals, and forced to seek safety in places unknown to them. According to Human Rights Watch (2007), "Those who are internally displaced are generally worse off than the poorest members of their host communities, with two-thirds living in inadequate housing with no access to basic sanitation, according to studies by the International Committee of the Red Cross, the Catholic Church, and the University of the Andes. Only one in five displaced persons receives medical care, and some 300,000 displaced children do not have access to education, the Geneva-based Internal Displacement Monitoring Centre reported in June 2006." Feelings of disorientation and impotency may flow from the sheer senselessness of their displacement, which typically occurs not because of their political affiliation or points of view but simply because they were living in a zone of conflict that one or another armed group wanted to dominate. Although in theory people facing forced displacement enjoy the same rights as all Colombians and can demand respect for their rights and provision of their entitlements, IDPs have been deprived of a regular place of residence and in practice hold restricted means of political participation. Another factor affecting the exercise of citizenship of Colombians IDPs is what Pécaut (2000) calls a social-psychological framework of limited-time orientation. Many IDPs not only consider themselves to be in temporary residence but must also move continually from town to town to survive economically; others have to move within the city where they have taken refuge—in Bogotá, for instance—when they are targeted once again by paramilitaries or guerrillas.

Arguably, the dispossession of political rights is a process that begins even before people are displaced. Pécaut (2000) explains that historically Colombian peasants have had to depend on the protection of political and armed groups. These groups impose their rules through excessive and arbitrary force. The realization that tomorrow they might fall under the control of the opposing force creates a strong pressure to maintain the lowest possible political and civic profile even before being displaced.

However, as Donny Meertens (2001) argues, the displacement experience is heterogeneous and it is not accurate to assume that all people facing displacement are politically inactive. She shows how different levels of collective identity, organization, and political consciousness influence the role of women IDPs. Those women who had some political and community roles before displacement tend to identify themselves as leaders after being displaced. Other factors that influence the level of political participation of Colombian women IDPs are the degree of urgency, danger, and psychological trauma associated with their displacement. Women who witnessed massacres or the deaths of relatives, spouses, children, or neighbors tend to seek to live invisibly after they are displaced and do not often participate politically in any way in their places of refuge. As Meertens (2001) and Osorio (2000) point out, many people facing forced displacement are constructing new urban forms of life on the basis of collective action. They are rebuilding their identities and territories through the formation of new social networks. Among the organizations seeking to assert the rights of IDPs to greater levels of state support, many are led by women. All seek to put pressure on the government by making their voices heard and refusing to disappear from the political scene.

WHY FORCED DISPLACEMENT OCCURS IN COLOMBIA

An essential starting point for understanding the repercussions of Washington's recent Colombia policy is that the United States is interfering in a situation that has already been unstable for decades. Forced displacement is not something new in Colombian history. Historically, forced displacement in Colombia has been used as strategy of war. During the period known as "La Violencia" (1948 to 1956), a bloody civil war between the main political parties (Conservatives and Liberals) uprooted more than two million people and cost the lives of 300,000 Colombians (Obregón and Stavropoulou 1998). Similarly to what is happening today, the people most likely to be displaced were peasants living on land favorable for agricultural production or any other means of resource extraction (Rojas and Romero 2000). As Jorge Rojas (2000) explains, forced displacement has been not just an unavoidable side-effect of war. It has sooner been one of war's main aims, encouraged by economic interests as well as military strategy.

Subsequent to the era of La Violencia, Colombia has experienced more than fifty years of intense political violence. Since the 1960s, the Colombian army has been fighting the insurgent groups the Revolutionary Armed Forces of Colombia (FARC-EP) and the National Liberation Army (ELN). In the 1980s, right-wing paramilitary groups emerged, with the support of the military and rural landowners, to confront the FARC and ELN. The drug-trafficking phenomenon contributed immensely to the escalation of the armed struggle and to Colombian political instability. The widespread use, by insurgents and paramilitary armies alike, of profits gained from illicit drug production and trafficking to bankroll military operations has widened the conflict, as the two sides have fought for control over fertile potential coca-producing land.

As in all civil wars, the principal victims have been civilians. In this context, forced displacement is only one of many egregious human-rights violations to which the civilian population has been subjected. Political assassinations, torture, forced disappearances, massacres, kidnappings of civilians and members of the military, forced recruitment of children and youths by any of the irregular armed actors, and rape of women in conflict areas are other grave features of Colombia's present human-rights crisis (Human Rights Watch 2007). A major failing of Law 975, enacted by the Colombian government in 2005, to bring about the demobilization and dismantlement of armed paramilitary organizations was that it did not require the identification of the totality of assets of former paramilitary group members nor demand the effective turnover of all assets gained through illegal means (Human Rights Watch 2005b). Thus, the amnesty that has been accorded by this law to the soldiers and officers of the counterinsurgent paramilitary groups holds out a bleak prospect for IDPs: land, seized at gunpoint by the paramilitaries, will probably never be returned to its rightful holders (Ambrus 2007: 17).

This tragic and complex situation grows also out of deep and enduring social and political inequities, which, together with the absence of the State in a large part of the national territory, have created conditions ripe for armed struggle. Add the lure of massive quantities of drug dollars to the war coffers of both insurgents and paramilitaries, and the result is a self-perpetuating cycle in which each group in the conflict seeks to obtain or keep control of areas rich in agricultural and natural resources and uses violence as instrument to achieve it.

At the same time as territorial domination became a principal objective of the armed groups, both insurgents and paramilitaries have often preferred "taking the water away from the fish" rather than directly confronting the enemy. This strategy focuses on undermining the enemy's social base, by converting all people and social organizations within enemy-held territory into potential military targets. By getting rid of the people who might be supplying various goods (food, transportation, etc.) to the enemy, a disputed territory may be made untenable by the adversary at a much lower cost in casualties to one's own soldiers than would be incurred by attacking frontally.

In attempting to synthesize all these factors, Mabel González (2001) explains that forced displacement occurs most in contexts where several factors coexist: human rights violations, armed conflict, social conflicts (for instance, workers' organizing), implementation of large economic development projects, and illicit crop cultivation. The causes of forced displacement include unresolved conflicts rooted in social inequality, economic exploitation, and political marginality. Thus, what is now happening in Colombia differs from past crises of displacement mainly in the magnitude of the phenomenon; the number of regions and actors involved in forced displacement has increased along with the geographical expansion of the armed conflict (Fajardo 2000).

There can be no doubt, in short, that the conditions for conflict predate massive U.S. support for militarized "solutions" to the drug-trafficking and anti-insurgency crises. The internal displacement crisis predates Plan Colombia and, as a result of coercive Colombian government policies, it might still be happening even if Washington had never sent Colombia massive amounts of military aid. Yet the next sections of the chapter demonstrate that U.S. support for attempts to suppress Colombia's insurgent groups through armed force—a strongly favored use of Plan Colombia aid—has worsened the IDP crisis and has yielded only limited results in resolving armed conflict. What limited gains are won on the battlefield are more than offset through the loss of life and the problem of internal displacement and refugees made worse as the United States favors military over political approaches to this long-standing and complex conflict.

PLAN COLOMBIA

Plan Colombia has its origins in the administration of President Andrés Pastrana Arango (1998–2002) and the second Clinton administration (1997–2001).[6] In 1999, Thomas Pickering of the U.S. Department of State and antidrug "czar" Barry McCaffrey visited Bogotá and offered to President Pastrana to increase U.S. aid greatly if he developed an integral plan to strengthen the armed forces, turn back the economic recession, and combat drug trafficking. At the end of 1999, the Pastrana administration handed over to the U.S. government the version of the bill that President

Bill Clinton would ultimately approve and pass on to the U.S. Congress. It is significant that Plan Colombia was originally written only in English and not translated into Spanish until 2000; the United States was therefore not only the Plan's initiator but it was the Colombian government's only interlocutor in negotiating the Plan's content. Pastrana would later be accused, by Colombian Senator Piedad Córdoba, of violating article 341 of the Colombian Constitution, in negotiating directly with the United States without prior approval of the Colombian Congress.[7] Presumably, it was of less importance to Pastrana what Colombian society in general, much less the people living in the areas most to be affected, might think.

It might be said that Plan Colombia represents but the latest and largest form of Washington largesse to the Colombian government and military. The two countries' "good and cooperative relations" have been dampened only by the flagrant links of the administration of President Ernesto Samper (1994–98) to the Cali drug cartel. Yet Plan Colombia towers over any prior aid package that Colombia, or any other South American country, had ever before received from the United States. According to Adam Isaacson (2003), Plan Colombia has each year provided over seven times more aid than Colombia received in 1997.

Plan Colombia may be said to continue the established U.S. policy since the 1980s of prosecuting the "war on drugs" as one pillar of Washington's evolving national security strategy. That illicit drugs constitute a threat to North Americans' well-being seems indisputable, when one considers that more 40 million U.S. citizens are addicted to cocaine or heroin. Beyond that threat, Plan Colombia fits with the U.S. strategic aim of destabilizing leftist—and, hence, presumptively anti-U.S.—insurgencies, in the Colombian case by breaking down the massive subsidy that narco-dollars have provided to the FARC and ELN (Ramírez 2004). Therefore, in the eyes of many officials in Washington, combating the production and trafficking of illicit drugs in Colombia not only strengthens one friendly regime but builds a bulwark against leftward political tendencies continent-wide.

One immediately evident feature of Plan Colombia is that it overwhelmingly favors military over political solutions. Of the $3 billion of U.S. aid to Colombia between 2000 and 2004, roughly 2.5 billion were destined for military and policing programs, and $637 million for economic and social programs.[8] According to the Center for International Policy's analysis, the percentage of U.S. aid to Colombia going to economic and social assistance has fluctuated from 1997 to 2007 but never exceeded 23.7 percent of the total amount of Plan Colombia aid and in many of those years has fallen far short of that percentage (see Table 11.1 and Figure 11.1). In principle,

TABLE 11.1. Plan Colombia Aid, 1997–2007
(million USD)

	Military and police assistance programs (% of yearly total)		Economic and social assistance programs (% of yearly total)		Grand Total
1997	86.6	*(100)*	0	*(0)*	86.6
1998	114.3	*(99.6)*	0.5	*(0.4)*	114.8
1999	306.6	*(97.2)*	8.8	*(2.8)*	315.4
2000	743.6	*(76.3)*	231.4	*(23.7)*	975
2001	236.9	*(99.4)*	1.4	*(0.6)*	240.2
2002	398.9	*(77.5)*	115.5	*(22.5)*	516.2
2003	624.4	*(82)*	136.7	*(18)*	760.7
2004	614.8	*(82)*	134.5	*(18)*	690.1
2005	597.8	*(81.6)*	134.7	*(18.4)*	777.2
2006	632.2	*(82.7)*	132.2	*(17.3)*	733.8
2007	615.9	*(82.3)*	132.2	*(17.7)*	756.5

SOURCE: Center for International Policy (http://ciponline.org/colombia/aid table.htm).

NOTE: Figures for 2007 are estimates.

Plan Colombia envisions diverse approaches, organized around four central components: (1) a politically negotiated solution to the conflict, (2) economic and social recovery, (3) initiatives against narco-trafficking, and (4) institutional strengthening and social development. Other key strategic aims of Plan Colombia included the elimination of 50 percent of illegal crops through aerial fumigation in five years, provision of support to alternative development programs and voluntary eradication of illegal crops, protection of the nation's oil infrastructure, and aid to internally displaced people and for environmental programs, funds to local governments, improvement of the justice system, and protection of human rights. The numbers cited above tell a different story, however, as U.S. aid has gone mainly to strengthening the military and police, with much smaller amounts being destined to the whole gamut of political and economic reforms that many experts consider pivotal to resolving Colombia's conflicts. All this makes some Colombians, especially in the civil society sector, say that Plan Colombia escalates rather than diminishes the armed conflict and human rights crisis.

Even so, the initial version of Plan Colombia, approved by the Clinton

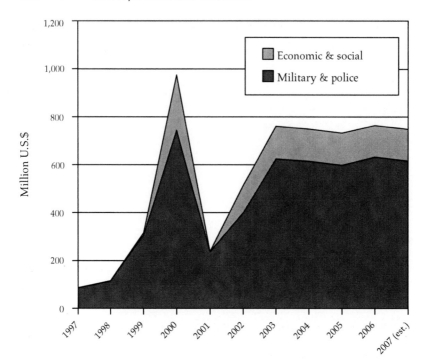

FIGURE 11.1. Plan Colombia: Economic and social versus military aid. Reproduced from "Just the Facts: A Civilian's Guide to U.S. Defense and Security Assistance to Latin America and the Caribbean," Washington Office on Latin America and Center for International Policy, http://www.ciponline.org/facts/co.htm.

administration and Congress in 1999, did not allow this aid to be used in fighting insurgent groups. McCaffrey (2000: 15, cited in Isaacson 2003) himself said that "as a matter of Administration policy, the United States will not support Colombian counterinsurgency efforts." In principle at least, U.S. officials did not permit the Colombians to use their U.S.-donated helicopters, guns, or specially trained brigades against guerrillas or paramilitaries, unless such action was part of an antidrug mission.

After the 9/11 attacks and with the beginning of the "Global War on Terrorism," the U.S. and Colombian governments easily surmounted that limitation. In 2002, the Bush administration and Congress enacted a bill permitting Colombia to use all past antidrug aid for "a unified campaign against narcotics trafficking [and] against activities by designated terrorist organizations," such as the FARC, ELN, and the main paramilitary organization, Autodefensas Unidas de Colombia (AUC) (Isaacson 2003: 15).

Under Plan Colombia, the war against drugs and fighting the insurgency have become one and the same aim. In this way, this plan presupposes that the sole motive of armed conflict in Colombia is control over narco-trafficking, taking out of the analysis the economic, social, and political roots of both the armed insurgency and the spread of illicit-crop cultivation, and centering U.S. aid as a result on strengthening the Colombian military and police and the forced eradication of illicit crops.

THE IMPACT OF PLAN COLOMBIA ON FORCED DISPLACEMENT

Plan Colombia has worsened harm to hundreds of thousands of people who live in the areas most affected by the forced eradication of illicit crops through aerial fumigation and the increasing militarization of antidrug and counterinsurgency operations.[9]

The United Nations Office on Drugs and Crime (2004) reported that the hectares of Colombian land planted in illicit crops decreased by 30 percent in 2001 and 2002 and by another 16 percent in 2003. At the same time, increases in coca production were discovered in other regions of Colombia and in Colombia's Andean neighbors, Bolivia and Peru. The CODHES 2003 report on fumigations and displacement maintains that what is occurring is a classic "push-down/pop-up" dynamic, familiar to law enforcement officials worldwide, in which coca cultivation has not been abandoned but simply transferred to areas where it had not previously taken root. Colombian commentators have called this "the balloon effect": when illicit crops are eradicated in one area, production moves to a different place. In 2002, reductions in coca cultivation were observed in the regions of Putumayo, Guaviare, Caquetá, Norte de Santander, Meta, and Cauca just as increases were seen in Amazonas, Nariño, Vichada, Vaupés, Guanía, and Arauca (Ceballos 2003: 7). In 2003, UNODC (2004) reported that there were more regions where illicit crops were being cultivated than in 1999; cultivation expanded from twelve departments in 1999 to twenty-three in 2003. BBC News (2006) confirms that this trend has continued in more recent years: while aerial fumigation succeeded in diminishing coca production in the regions sprayed, by expanding the survey area U.S. government researchers found an extra 26 percent of land under coca cultivation. The same study also found production was more dispersed.

While the effectiveness of Plan Colombia's antidrug strategy is questionable, one clear consequence of forced eradication is that it expands the geographical spread of armed conflict, along with coca production, bringing grave consequences for people in the affected regions and generating

TABLE 11.2. Internally Displaced Persons (IDPs),
Colombia, and Plan Colombia Aid, 1999–2005

Year	Number of IDPs	Aid (million USD)
1998	—	114.8
1999	288,127	315.4
2000	525,000	975
2001	720,000	240.2
2002	950,000	516.2
2003	1,244,072	760.7
2004	2,000,000	690.1
2005	2,000,000	777.2

SOURCES: http://codhes.org/Info/Cifra/Dpto_Recp_Pers_1999.pdf;
UNHCR, *Statistical Yearbook 2005* (http://www.unhcr.org/cgi-bin/
texis/vtx/statistics/opendoc.pdf).

new flows of internal refugees. Insurgents and paramilitary forces move
with the illicit crops and, as these groups spread, they use violence and
forcibly displace peasants and indigenous groups in order to obtain more
land for coca and poppy crops (Ceballos 2003: 8). At a later stage, insurgents
and paramilitary forces may fight among themselves for the land, catching
any remaining civilians in the middle. The forced recruitment of children
and young men, threats, disappearances, selective killings, and massacres
spread terror and send civilians fleeing for their lives to other parts of the
country or into neighboring countries, particularly often Ecuador. One
CODHES study (Ceballos 2003: 11–16) reports a close correlation between
the number of hectares of coca and the number of killings in any given
region.

Plan Colombia has worsened the country's forced displacement crisis,
first, by inadvertently spreading coca cultivation to new regions and across
a wider expanse of territory than it occupied prior to the Plan's aggressive
pursuit of forced eradication. More generally, Plan Colombia has worsened
the armed conflict by prescribing a primarily military response to political problems rooted in poverty, inequality, economic insecurity, and low
levels of health, educational attainment, and other measures of human
development. Far from lessening internal displacement, the advent of Plan
Colombia coincides with a dreadful upturn in the magnitude of the IDP
crisis (see Table 11.2).

Aerial Fumigations and Forced Displacement

Another way in which Plan Colombia bears clear responsibility for increasing rates of forced displacement is its support for eradicating coca cultivation chiefly via aerial fumigations. Marcela Ceballos (2003) estimates that from 1999 through 2002, 35,000 families were forced to flee their homes as a direct consequence of fumigations. In its report of April 2004, CODHES (2004) pointed out that in 2003 alone a total number of 27,044 people fled areas where fumigations were taking place. Though the total number of new IDPs decreased nationwide, rates of forced displacement increased in the regions where fumigations were concentrated. In regions of the south, including Putumayo and Nariño, forced displacement rose to levels three times higher than before Plan Colombia (Ceballos 2003: 27).

The testimony of one displaced farmer evokes the on-the-ground reality of aerial fumigation:

> I have problems because my family is dispersed. When we went away from the *monte* (highlands) almost all of us felt sick. My wife and one daughter are with me and they are sick. The rest of my family is separated from us. I'm trying to resolve this problem, we are separated and sick. I had a little *finquita* (small farm) with cassava, corn, and some coca plants. We are indigenous people and our law allows us to have [coca] crops, but we grew them to subsist because there is nowhere we can look for subsistence. Those plants always have given [good] results because we have to sell the rest of our products at a very cheap price. Those who manage the [coca] market get more benefits than the *campesinos* (peasants). We grow it and take it to the town, but [those] who benefit from it are others. The problem is that we are cultivating and the fumigating airplane comes and kills all we have. I left my *finca* abandoned. The fumigations kill everything, dry out all the crops, and everything becomes, like, yellow. So, what can one do? It is not possible to live there. There were massacres and one gets scared for the family. I want to live feeling tranquil.[10]

Such testimony contrasts with the assurances of the Colombian and U.S. governments that fumigation with glyphosate is safe and has insignificant adverse consequences for people; many experts have joined their voices with the IDPs in denouncing the alarming impact of aerial fumigations. Critics of Plan Colombia's fumigation practices include not only the peasants and indigenous people who have suffered its consequences but also Colombian and Ecuadorian environmental and human rights organizations, local and national governmental offices such as the Defensoría del Pueblo (the Colombian state human rights ombudsman's office), and Colombian and North American scientists.[11] The immediate consequences of fumigation with glyphosate include human health problems, especially of the skin, vision and digestive system; illnesses and deaths of farm animals; contamination of water sources; and the extermination of legal crops, which has created a significant food crisis in the fumigated regions.

Elsa Nivia (2002), an agronomical engineer, has raised several concerns in relation to the glyphosate compounds used in aerial fumigations. Though the label of Roundup (Monsanto's commercial name for glyphosate) used in Colombia says that it becomes inactive immediately when it falls on soil, researchers affirm that in some soils it can be freed and move easily for short periods of time (Cox 1995). That observation is in keeping with the many denunciations presented to the Defensoría del Pueblo regarding the total destruction of legal food crops as consequence of Roundup applications. Nivia (2002) also points out that glyphosate is very soluble in water and can contaminate ground water at various levels. In many countries, Roundup is categorized as a fertilizer that causes poisoning in human beings, its most frequent toxic effects being skin and eye irritation, nausea, dizziness, vomiting, allergies, and respiratory and heart problems.

Moreover, the kind of glyphosate used in Colombia with Plan Colombia funding is Roundup Ultra, which differs from standard Roundup in the quantity of each active element used. Glyphosate is used in aerial fumigations in Colombia in a concentration twenty-six times higher than is allowed in U.S. agriculture. According to Nivia (2002: 393, 397), each doubling of the glyphosate dose multiplies its biological action by four, meaning that exposure to glyphosate as applied through Plan Colombia has a potency 104 times higher than the dose recommended for agricultural use in the United States. Making matters worse, coca-growing areas in Colombia are often fumigated two to four times, piling higher any toxic effects. Nivia (2002: 398) concludes that what scientists know about glyphosate can explain why so many negative accounts, involving human beings and farm animals being poisoned and legal crops—such as plantain, maize, and cassava—being wiped out, have emerged from the regions where the Plan Colombia aerial fumigation program is being implemented.

It is important to note that there are alternatives to aerial fumigation with glyphosate, which would avoid all its negative impacts on agriculture and human health. In 2000, the peasants and indigenous groups of Putumayo signed agreements with the Colombian government to eradicate coca manually and cultivate alternative crops. María Clemencia Ramírez

(2003) reports that in 2002, the Pastrana administration decided without explanation to terminate manual eradication, even though this program was showing promising results, and commence aerial fumigation in Putumayo. Food security projects, meant to complement the coca eradication, were in their initial stages or had not been started at all, leaving many of the department's residents not only exposed once more to aerial fumigation but feeling they had been deceived into cooperating with a program through false promises of lasting benefits for farmers.

Colombian and U.S. authorities dismissed these reports as being little more than complaints originating with narco-traffickers and insurgents. In response, environmental and human rights advocates point out that assurances of glyphosate safety for humans are based on studies made of its use in the concentrations and conditions found in the United States, and not on the compound being sprayed by Plan Colombia (Pérez 2001, cited in Nivia 2002). As Ramírez (2004: 11) suggests, perhaps the larger problem is that the success of the initiative against narco-trafficking is measured solely in technical terms—by the number of hectares with illegal crops that are eradicated—rather than in human rights terms that reflect the Plan's effect on people's security and quality of life.

From a human rights standpoint, the most immediate concern must be that the Colombian and U.S. governments desist from further pursuit of Plan Colombia's failed strategy of suppressing both the traffic in cocaine and the armed insurgency through military means. The cost in lives and rights has been colossal, and the gains in drug-trafficking prevention and reclaiming control of the country from the insurgents have been questionable.

In the unlikely event that the Colombian government were to choose a radical change of course and reengage the insurgency in peace talks, there would of course still be millions of IDPs whose whole way of life has been disrupted and would still stand in need of restitution. Here, again, a rights-based approach would suggest a quite different course of action from what the Colombian government has followed to date. Instead of the "social assistance" model on which the Colombian authorities have based their outreach to IDPs, rights-based restitution would view government assistance to IDPs not as a form of charity but an entitlement, and hence not discretionary but obligatory in character and not partial but comprehensive in its aims and scope.

Even though Colombia's Law 387 of 1997, which defines the state's response to the IDP crisis, sets as a goal the "restitution of rights" to each

IDP, the law did not make clear exactly what is meant by that. "Restitution" is a bold expression that can become useless and empty if its contents are not specified. An analysis of Colombia's IDP policy, presented by the UN High Commissioner for Refugees (UNHCR 2004), concludes that real solutions to the IDP crisis can emerge only from an approach that recognizes the full complement of human rights. Specifically, the UNHCR's analysis suggests that the Colombian state undertake a multifaceted program aimed to guarantee realization of the following goals (Restrepo-Ruiz 2005: 46–47):

1. people own and exercise their right to live in a safe environment without having their lives in danger;

2. people know the truth: who displaced them, the reasons that led to their displacement, and what happened to their property and assets;

3. people see justice: wrongdoers are prosecuted and punished, . . . [IDPs] have their goods returned or compensated;

4. people have the means for their personal development, for living with dignity, which implies having a life's project that makes them self-sufficient;

5. people can exercise their political and civil rights without any kind of discrimination by authorities, civilians or illegal groups, and

6. people's culture is respected and protected.

In a volume dedicated to studying the global repercussions of U.S. policy on human geographical mobility, it is important, finally, to sound a warning that U.S. government officials are not only touting Plan Colombia as a success but suggesting that similar programs be implemented not only in the Andean region but in places as far away as Afghanistan (States News Service 2007). In 2001, the Bush administration launched the Andean Regional Initiative as a complement to Plan Colombia, promising regional cooperation against narco-trafficking, "a direct threat to our public health and national security" (U.S. Department of State 2001). The U.S. government sees the Colombian crisis as one that will be difficult to contain within Colombian borders; hence it envisions the likelihood of conflict ultimately being internationalized across the Andes. Nowhere is the possibility raised that promoting a mainly military (rather than political and economic) response to the conflict may be one of the reasons why the problem never goes away and now seemingly threatens to spill over Colombia's borders. In the same declaration, the U.S. government says that "we need to work with the neighboring countries and provide with support for their efforts to

contain the violence in Colombia. These efforts should focus on strengthening their capability to confront lawlessness in border areas, preparing for
possible refugee flows, and assisting in alternative development programs"
(ibid.). The Colombian experience of U.S. aid suggests that, with a "friend"
like this, enemies may well be redundant; the plan behind the Plan beyond
Colombian borders seems to be "get ready for more widespread chaos."

12.   Challenging U.S. Silence

International NGOs and
the Iraqi Refugee Crisis

Kathryn Libal and Scott Harding

> Bandaid assistance and token resettlement might make Ameri-
> cans feel less guilty about the destruction and suffering this war
> has caused, but it will not be sufficient to make a difference in
> saving the lives of the vast majority of innocent civilians whose
> lives are still at risk.
>
> BILL FRELICK,
> director of refugee policy, Human Rights Watch

> We're proud of our record (on refugee resettlement) and we
> plan to build on it. At the same time, we must guard against
> the possibility that hiding among the refugees are people who
> are neither refugees nor Iraqis, for that matter. Security as
> well as sanctuary has to drive our refugee policy.
>
> AMY KUDWA,
> Department of Homeland Security spokesperson

Ignoring warnings that waging a war in Iraq would lead to entrenched conflict and the displacement of tens of thousands of people, in 2003 the administration of George W. Bush embarked on a project for "regime change" and "democratization" with little consideration of the human costs involved. The Iraq war has created a flow of forced migrants, both within and across national borders, numbering more than four million people, approximately 15 percent of Iraq's population.[1] This ongoing dislocation dwarfs original expectations among humanitarian organizations and is considered the largest forced migration in the region since the Palestinian diaspora was created. Iraqis now constitute one of the largest displaced population in the world (U.S. Committee for Refugees and Immigrants 2008). Some suggest that after internally displaced persons (IDPs) are taken into account, Iraqis make up the largest uprooted population in the world (Oliver 2007).

The displacement of Iraqis and the overall destabilization of Iraq have been generated largely by a misguided and harmful U.S. policy of unilateral intervention, in which the social consequences of the war for Iraqis appear less important than achieving U.S. strategic goals. Despite the unpopularity of the Iraq war among the U.S. public, the Bush administration was able to effectively shape public perceptions of the conflict. As a result, the dominant discourse in the American media and Congress has been on the human and financial costs of the war and tarnished international prestige *for the United States.* Yet while Congress and presidential candidates wrangled over benchmarks for progress and timelines for U.S. military withdrawal, a man-made disaster marked by massive human displacement unfolded.[2] Despite some economic and social progress, the U.S.-led war has undermined not just security but also social development, public health, and economic growth in Iraq, further fueling the refugee crisis.

Of equal concern has been the belated response and limited role of the United Nations and, most importantly, the U.S. government, in developing policies and programs for Iraqi refugees and IDPs. Due to the failures of U.S. policy, humanitarian organizations have had to assume primary responsibility for addressing the needs of displaced Iraqis. In the case of Iraq, these NGOs—often frontline providers for vulnerable populations in wartime—were initially caught unaware by the scale of the displacement. Several years into the crisis, these organizations remain underfunded and ill-equipped to tackle the humanitarian disaster.

Efforts to provide temporary assistance to Iraqi refugees in neighboring countries, such as Jordan and Syria, have also been beset with challenges posed by the war and U.S. policy failures. This is compounded by the inability of Iraq's neighbors to confront the consequences of absorbing more than two million refugees without formally recognizing them or seeking extensive international assistance. While Jordan and Syria had indicated a greater willingness to accept international assistance by late 2007, by that point the crisis was so pronounced that most refugees remained vulnerable and unable to meet basic needs related to housing, food, education, and health care.

Despite the massive human displacement caused by the conflict, until late 2006 the Iraqi humanitarian crisis attracted little media attention. Most analysts appeared more concerned with tracing U.S. policy, the rise of ethnic and sectarian conflict, and questions of Iraq's political future, rather than the lived social consequences of the war. While more attention was placed on the struggles of displaced Iraqis in 2007, news coverage remained impressionistic and sporadic. Most press emphasized human interest stories of those few refugees who resettled in the United States and Europe, rather than the barriers faced by millions of refugees and internally displaced Iraqis. Moreover, few journalists connected the humanitarian consequences of the war to U.S. policy decisions. Even the U.S. antiwar movement has ignored the displacement crisis, emphasizing instead the economic costs of the war and claims to support U.S. troops through withdrawal from Iraq. As of this writing, with the advent of the Obama administration and the turning of attention toward a renewed military effort in Afghanistan, the Iraqi humanitarian crisis has once again receded from public view; coverage of the situation in Iraq, when it occurs, tends to emphasize a purported "return to normalcy" in places like Baghdad.

As the flow of Iraqis across national borders intensified, their plight was increasingly politicized. Despite the severity of the crisis in Iraq, those refugees seeking third-country resettlement have few options (Marfleet 2007, Sanders and Smith 2007). Nearly all "settler countries" of the West (the United States, Australia, Canada, and European states) have been reluctant to grant asylum and resettlement to Iraqis in meaningful numbers. U.S. and Western refugee policy currently excludes large numbers of Middle Eastern and other Muslim refugees, allegedly to maintain national security (Sperl 2007). Thus, Iraqi forced migrants find themselves vulnerable on multiple fronts—unable to seek permanent resettlement in significant numbers in the West, blocked from fuller integration within neighboring countries, and at risk of being repatriated back to Iraq despite an ongoing civil war.

In this chapter we outline humanitarian and human rights consequences of the U.S. invasion and occupation of Iraq. First, we contextualize the displacement crisis by tracing how U.S. foreign policy contributed to the current humanitarian disaster. Against this background we turn to the much less-examined topic of advocacy for Iraqi refugees and highlight the efforts of international NGOs to compel the United States and the international community to comprehensively address the displacement crisis. This analysis is based on documentary evidence from nongovernmental and official sources and approximately thirty interviews with staff and officials from NGOs, the UN High Commissioner for Refugees (UNHCR), and Congressional staff members working on immigrant and refugee policy.[3] Our research shows that while NGOs have been the most important actors calling for accountability for displaced Iraqis, even they are constrained by the politics of humanitarian assistance in the United States and Middle East. Finally, we highlight the Bush administration's failure to take responsibility for the human costs of the U.S. invasion and consider the effects of public apathy in the United States about the impact of the war on Iraqis.

U.S. MILITARISM AND UNILATERALISM

Eliminating the threat of Iraq's alleged weapons of mass destruction and securing the human rights of Iraqis were primary justifications for the 2003 U.S. invasion of Iraq. In reality, gaining access to Iraq's enormous natural resources, establishing a client state to counter the power of Iran, and prosecuting the "war on terror" have formed the foundation of this failed policy. For some sixty years U.S. policy toward Iraq, whether as allies or antagonists, has been shaped by the same strategic concerns driving its overall Middle East policy: the desire to maintain regional stability and secure access to natural resources. Following World War II the need for oil assumed prominence in U.S. military and strategic planning. As foreign oil gained greater economic importance, the United States began planning direct military intervention to control access to the Persian Gulf. Unilateral military planning and intervention to control global oil deliveries have thus become the norm in U.S. policy in the region (Klare 2002).

U.S. involvement in Iraq dates to the late 1950s, when the Eisenhower administration supported Abdel Karim Kassem, a former general who took power in a coup. In spite of his harsh repression of political dissent, Kassem received U.S. backing until 1963, when a CIA sponsored coup brought the anticommunist Ba'ath Party to power (Johnson 2004). Saddam Hussein was among those party members said to have participated in the systematic murder of hundreds of doctors, teachers, and other professionals in the coup (Morris 2003). Five years later when the Ba'athists gained complete control in Iraq it was due in part to the support of President Lyndon Johnson and the CIA (Johnson 2004).

For decades, U.S. policy emphasized stability in Iraq rather than human rights concerns. Prior to Iraq's 1990 invasion of Kuwait the United States tolerated Saddam Hussein's brutality, especially during the 1980s when it reestablished diplomatic relations (Hiltermann 2007). This was an era of intense domestic persecution and human rights violations and destabilizing external actions taken by Iraq. Yet through both trade agreements and military support, the Reagan administration promoted close ties. U.S. trade with Iraq totaled $1.5 billion in the late 1980s, and included exports of items with dual-use applications helping to fuel Saddam Hussein's military (Colhoun 1991). The Reagan administration also manipulated information about Iraq's use of chemical weapons against Iran and its own Kurdish population, undermining UN and Congressional efforts to sanction Iraq and help save thousands of lives (Hiltermann 2007). As Scott Harding (2007: 299) notes, "the United States practiced an 'enabling' foreign policy—one that facilitated and condoned internal repression in the name of meeting U.S. strategic interests." While the United States was not the only country to tolerate Saddam's brutality for its geopolitical needs, its fixation on containing Iran and the spread of Islamism undermined concerns for the well-being of Iraqi citizens. Whereas the Bush administration's use of unilateralism and militarism has often been criticized, prior U.S. emphasis on realpolitik has also contributed to today's Iraq quagmire. Ethnic and sectarian rivalries in Iraq have been fueled by decades of earlier U.S. backing for authoritarian regimes. Arguably, the U.S. record of ignoring systematic and brutal violations of human rights to further U.S. interests is another reason why the United States faces opposition to its current military occupation. Thus the 2003 invasion of Iraq and subsequent military campaigns waged by the U.S. are only the latest in a series of interventions that have resulted in "blowback" against American foreign policy (Malone 2006).

Following its intervention in the 1991 Gulf War, the United States used its military dominance to engage in unilateral intervention via air and missile attacks against Iraq throughout the 1990s. Coupled with U.S.-led efforts to enforce UN economic sanctions, and a separate U.S. trade embargo, these policies had a cumulative negative impact on most Iraqi citizens. Exacerbating an already repressive state, U.S. policies undermined Iraq's physical infrastructure and economic progress, worsened hunger and poverty, and created a widespread health crisis contributing to hundreds of thousands of excess child deaths (Mertus and Hallward 2006).[4]

Based on a "neoconservative" policy of unilateralism, the Bush administration used the events of 9/11 to sanction a newly aggressive American militarism. Khalidi (2004) argues that the Iraq war represents the first in a new category of U.S. interventions. Calling the U.S. invasion a "novel departure"—essentially a war of choice—he links it to the 2002 National Security Strategy that articulated a doctrine of U.S. preemption (which is contrary to the norms of international law). Intervention in Iraq also created conditions to end the economic embargo, a first step toward allowing U.S. companies access to Iraqi oil concessions. Iraq's proven oil reserves are the second largest in the world, while its estimated oil may be twice as large (Klare 2002, Engdal 2004).

Whether the overthrow of Saddam Hussein was indeed unique, or similar to other U.S. military interventions, it has clearly caused massive destabilization. Within Iraq, it has aggravated social divisions and fueled sectarian conflict, hindered basic community functions, further undermined social development, and created a massive refugee and displaced population with broader regional implications (Byman 2007). Ironically the human rights of Iraqis, so often touted as the motivating force behind American policy, have again become collateral damage in a larger struggle for global dominance.

THE HUMAN COSTS OF THE IRAQ WAR

The U.S. reliance on military intervention and billions of dollars in security and development aid to achieve political stability in Iraq has thus far failed. One analysis of weak and "failed states," based on economic, social, political, and military indicators, ranked Iraq second worst in the world in terms of vulnerability to violent *internal* conflict and social dysfunction (Fund for Peace and *Foreign Policy* magazine 2007). Iraq scored lowest on several key "indicators of instability": group grievance, factionalized elites, human rights violations, the nonaccountability of the security apparatus, and chronic and sustained human flight. An annual survey of levels of perceived political corruption ranked Iraq third worst in the world (Transparency International 2007), with U.S. officials suggesting that one-third of U.S. aid to Iraq has been lost or stolen (Cave 2007).

While the ongoing U.S. military occupation complicates Iraq's political process, by late 2007 there was little evidence of political reconciliation or progress on key policy issues. The existence of a civil war, failing state institutions, and deep ethnic, religious, and tribal cleavages compromise future stability. Throughout 2007 much of the country was engulfed by kidnappings, retaliatory killings, and sectarian violence. Though estimates of civilian deaths vary widely, the Iraqi government claimed about 150,000 civilians had been killed between 2004 and 2006 (Oppel 2006), while other research suggests a civilian death toll since 2003 of approximately 600,000 (Burnham et al. 2006). The UN, using information from the Iraqi government, hospitals, and health care officials, found that 34,352 civilians died in violence in 2006 alone (UNAMI 2007a).

In general, lack of adherence to human rights standards remains a pervasive problem in Iraq, demonstrated by ongoing extrajudicial executions, targeted and indiscriminate killings, kidnappings, and hostage taking. Life in central and southern Iraq is "characterized by pervasive extreme violence, serious violations of human rights, and a general lack of law and order" (UNHCR 2007a: 9). The UN found that "the sheer scale of violence directed against Iraqi civilians is unparalleled to any other emergency in the world today" (UNAMI 2007b: 1).

U.S. military operations, combined with ethnic cleansing and other targeted violence by Iraqis, have had a devastating impact on social development, health and well-being. The social fabric of communities has been radically transformed, as many members of religious minority groups and families of mixed Shia and Sunni backgrounds have fled. In trying to establish security and reduce the generalized violence, in 2007 the U.S. military began seeking to create "civilian havens" (Dagher 2007). In particular, neighborhoods in Baghdad were segregated into separate Shia and Sunni Arab enclaves controlled by various local militia, U.S.-backed Iraqi security forces, or the U.S. military. Barricades and security checkpoints control access in and out of many neighborhoods, making it difficult for Iraqis to navigate the city to work, attend school, receive health care, or get food and other vital services. The U.S. and Iraqi security forces profile Iraqi men, collecting fingerprints and retinal scans when they enter or leave many Baghdad neighborhoods. One Iraqi from Ghazaliya lamented, "One road in and one road out, that's it . . . Iraq is a prison, and now I live in my own little prison" (as cited in Dagher 2007). Some analysts thus suggest that in order to reduce violence, the United States implemented a policy that deepened the ethnic and sectarian Balkanization of Iraq. This decision thus poses substantial challenges to long-term peace-building and reconciliation in Iraq.

The enactment of a "Baghdad Security Plan" and a U.S. military "surge" in early 2007 appears to have helped reduce the level of violence, killings, and attacks on civilians and security forces. While more than 5,500 civilians died from violence in Baghdad province alone in the first quarter of 2007, according to government ministries (Susman 2007), by October the number of civilian deaths fell to approximately 1,000 a month (Buckley and Gordon 2007). Despite any apparent gains, violence against women and professional groups like academics, rising intolerance against minorities, and sectarian violence in those areas with diverse ethnic and religious groups still remained especially problematic (UNAMI 2007a). Moreover, even as violence apparently declined in late 2007, lawlessness remained endemic in central and southern Iraq.

While obtaining accurate data on key social indicators is difficult, the overall health and well-being of much of the Iraqi population is precarious. Despite some economic progress, the U.S.-led war has created a deepening disaster for Iraqis in terms of social development and public health. A comprehensive survey of living conditions in 2004 found deteriorating physical and social conditions (UNDP 2005). Electrical, water, and sewer systems were deeply compromised and unreliable, further endangering health. Following that study, conditions in Iraq further declined. By 2009 unemployment ranged from 25 to 40 percent (Brookings Institution 2009).

According to the Iraq government's own data, between 20 and 25 percent of Iraqis lived in poverty, based on a measure of those living on less than $2.2 per day, and a majority of the population depended on food rations (Iraq Ministry of Planning and Development Cooperation 2008). "Iraq's per capita GDP, at current prices, has improved since 2003. However, the rate of inflation is high and food and fuel subsidies have declined. Thus, actual living standards in 2007 are below those of 1980" (2008: 41). A lack of medicines, equipment, and personnel imperiled an already fragile health service system. Physicians became a particular target of violence, leading 20,000 doctors (more than one-half of Iraq's physicians) to flee the country (Brookings Institution 2009).

Children remain especially vulnerable to the effects of continued conflict: from 1990 to 2005, Iraq had the highest increase in infant mortality—150 percent—of any country in the world (Save the Children 2007). Child mortality rates, which soared during the 1990s as UN sanctions and the impact of previous wars took effect, have not improved since the ouster of Saddam Hussein. Only 30 percent of Iraqi children are estimated to have access to clean water (UNICEF 2007). A recent report found that one in eight Iraqi children died in 2005 before their fifth birthday; more than half of these deaths occurred among babies less than one month old (Save the Children 2007). Reflecting a lack of clean water and a breakdown of the sanitation system, a cholera outbreak was reported in late 2007 (UNAMI 2007c).

Food security remains an urgent concern for Iraqis in central and southern governorates. In 2006, the World Food Programme (WFP) found that 15 percent of Iraqis (some four million people) were food insecure and in dire need of different types of humanitarian assistance, including food, despite the rations they received from the government (UN World Food Programme 2006). The 2006 survey also "indicated that a further 8.3 million people would be rendered food insecure if they were not provided with a PDS ration,[5] compared to 3.6 million people in the previous survey" (UN World Food Programme 2006).

These data provide a snapshot of the hardships confronting most Iraqis, yet a more pernicious sense of isolation and dread pervades much of the country. In late 2007 the UN noted that "continual fear from violence from all sides including, armed sectarian groups, criminal rackets, various militias, as well as during operations by security and military forces is a daily reality for civilians" (UNAMI 2007c: 3). The International Committee of the Red Cross also described the "immense suffering of the entire population." Echoing the findings of other observers, the group found that engaging in the mundane pursuits of everyday life—walking to school, shopping, riding the bus—were now matters of life and death (ICRC 2007). Fear of everyday violence in Iraq is particularly acute for women and girls, limiting their freedom of movement and ability to go to work or school (Amnesty International 2005; Susskind 2007). Of particular concern is the long-term mental health impact of pervasive violence, especially on Iraqi children, an issue that has received scant attention (UNICEF 2007; MedAct 2004; Greene 2005).

The disintegration of Iraq's key social institutions (especially in the central and southern governorates) and endemic conflict in Baghdad and other regions has forced Iraqis to leave their homes in massive numbers. The displaced are increasingly vulnerable and lack critical protections, whether they are IDPs in Iraq or refugees in neighboring countries. The UN found that many Iraqi IDPs cannot access needed medicines, adequate housing, or work (UNAMI 2007c). Moreover, some relief workers worry that those Iraqis who are too poor to move at all remain the most vulnerable. The UN and other independent observers have been unable to assess the extent of suffering by Iraqis who cannot leave their homes and communities. Indeed, measuring the scope and magnitude of the humanitarian crisis remains a challenging task that is being carried out by NGOs, some government and UN agencies, and various experts and academics.

THE JORDANIAN AND SYRIAN CONTEXT

The impact of the refugee flow into neighboring countries, especially Jordan and Syria, has been profound (Sassoon 2009). Currently an estimated 1.2 million Iraqi refugees reside in Syria, making up approximately 7 per cent of the population. Jordan has approximately 450,000 Iraqis, approximately 10 per cent of its total population (UNHCR 2009). These figures are staggering—even the wealthiest countries would have difficulty absorbing such numbers proportionate to the size of their populations.

Two central obstacles prevent most Iraqi refugees from meeting their basic needs: the lack of international funding for humanitarian assistance—especially from the United States as the initiator of the war—and the reluctance of host governments to develop comprehensive programs to allow Iraqis to work, seek health care, and enroll children in local schools. In a review of international relief efforts, Amnesty International (2007: 3) concluded that "despite an increasingly critical situation, contributions from other countries aimed at sharing the responsibility of the crisis remain seriously inadequate." A July 2007 meeting of regional governments, the United States, NGOs, and UN agencies failed to produce any meaningful agreements and highlighted differences between key actors over how to address the refugee problem. These disagreements further inhibited countries like Jordan and Syria from garnering sufficient international support for refugee services.

With the international community slow to act, Iraqis have been compelled to rely upon host country governments for most assistance. These states are ill-equipped to address refugees' needs in the short or long term due to a lack of internal capacity in the form of state and private institutions. According to Refugees International, "The national education, health, water and sanitation systems of host countries are facing the challenge of meeting the needs of a rapidly expanding refugee population, and it is therefore the government agencies that provide these services that are in most need of international support" (Refugees International 2007a).

Both Jordan and Syria are developing countries and have difficulties meeting the economic needs of their own citizens. Even without vulnerable Iraqis residing in enclaves in Amman and other cities, Jordan has high rates of poverty, unemployment, inflation, and foreign debt, and it suffers a shortage of critical resources, especially water (Hunaiti & Al-Tayeb 2005).[6] The UNDP found that the first Gulf War, the impact of September 11, and the 2003 U.S. invasion of Iraq adversely affected the lives of Jordan's poor (UNDP 2004). A limited infrastructure and industrial base have combined to make Jordan highly dependent on tourism and international support, with U.S. foreign aid comprising a substantial portion of state revenues. Jordan's aid-dependent economy has been deeply affected by the cessation of special agreements with Iraq that subsidized oil costs.[7] The government is increasingly worried that continuing conflict in Iraq will spark terrorism or sectarian violence among Iraqi refugees in Jordan.[8] Moreover, its government does not want to create a "pull factor" by giving the impression that Iraqis can settle in Jordan permanently and has thus been reluctant to offer any services to Iraqi refugees. Jordan claims that in the past several years the "costs" it has borne related to Iraqi refugees amounted to approximately $1 billon per year (Jamous 2007).

It is difficult to assess how well Iraqis are faring in Jordan and Syria due to the complexities of identifying and serving this population. Unlike "traditional" refugees in distinct refugee camps, most Iraqis remain relatively invisible, residing in the urban centers of Amman and Damascus. Their intent on keeping a low profile due to fears of deportation or discrimination by the local population has made accurate assessment of their numbers and status challenging. Interviews with NGO staff in Jordan suggest that Iraqi families have used informal networks of support from other Iraqis, as well as worked in the underground economy (especially male youth), sold personal possessions, and relied upon savings for survival. One in five Iraqi households in Jordan is female-headed and tends to have low levels of education and inadequate income. Reflecting their tenuous status in Jordan, most families are dependent on income transfers from Iraq and personal savings. "This makes a large segment of Iraqis in Jordan at risk of becoming vulnerable with the depletion of savings, or deterioration in the security situation in Iraq that may affect the transfers of funds that support a significant portion of the Iraqi community in Jordan (Fafo Institute for Applied International Studies 2007: 3–4).

Until the end of 2006 most Iraqis could gain entrance into Syria legally for three-month stays that could be renewed once. Throughout 2007, as the numbers of Iraqis grew and Jordan began turning back refugees from its borders, Syria gradually tightened its visa requirements. Until late 2007, the majority of Iraqis in Syria were "out of status," without current visas, which was tolerated by the government (Amnesty International 2007). Then in October 2007, Syria announced it was closing its borders to Iraqi refugees and only Iraqis with visas would be allowed to enter. The government also plans to encourage Iraqis whose visas have expired to return to Iraq, while Iraq has begun offering cash to families that return. Syria ostensibly tightened its policies due to receiving little international support for refugees. Even if Iraqis have visas, most cannot obtain work permits and must rely upon limited government assistance and informal work to survive. Humanitarian assistance provided by the United Nations and a limited number of local and international NGOs provides support for only a small number of refugees. According to Amnesty International (2007: 12), many Iraqis interviewed in summer 2007 "had received no food aid even though their savings were exhausted."

Overall, Iraqis remain vulnerable to deportation, arrest, and eviction from temporary homes in Jordan and Syria, raising the need for other countries to assume a larger role in serving Iraqi refugees. To date, however, the United States and European Union, those most capable of providing material support and absorbing large numbers of refugees, have downplayed the extent of the problem and only recently begun to offer increased humanitarian aid. Even where the Bush administration entered into bilateral agreements to aid specific countries, such as Jordan, the level of assistance has been inadequate.

RECOGNIZING THE REFUGEE AND IDP CRISIS

Prior to the U.S.-led invasion, NGOs warned of a humanitarian disaster marked by mass displacement of Iraqis. At the time, several relief organizations formed a joint task force to deal with an expected flow of refugees. Funded by the U.S. Agency for International Development, organizations like the International Rescue Committee, International Medical Corps, World Vision, Save the Children, and Mercy Corps met to plan and coordinate humanitarian assistance in Iraq (and elsewhere) after the invasion was launched. The UN estimated more than a half-million Iraqi refugees would flee the country once fighting began, while some U.S. officials also prepared for a large exodus (UNAMI 2007a). At the time Gil Loescher (2002: 12) warned that lack of contingency planning and coordination among the U.S. government and military, UN agencies, and humanitarian NGOs would hinder any relief efforts for displaced Iraqis.

Following the start of the war, however, this displacement did not develop. While looting, crimes of retribution, kidnapping, and other "invisible" acts of ethnic and religious cleansing occurred, the hallmarks of "humanitarian crisis" did not immediately occur following the overthrow of Saddam Hussein. Thus, despite a growing insurgency, U.S. and international efforts to "reconstruct" Iraq included funding to assist the tens of thousands of "returnees" who had fled Iraq in the Hussein years and whom the United States expected to pour back into their homeland from Jordan, Syria, Turkey, and Iran. While some return migration occurred—the U.S. government estimates 250,000 people—a significant number of Iraqis were already fleeing the country or being displaced within Iraq. Yet, until 2006, State Department funding for NGOs prioritized the needs of returning Iraqis (U.S. Department of State 2006).

Given the steady flow of Iraqi refugees by 2005, it remains puzzling why it took so long for the global community to recognize the mounting problem. Numerous NGOs were operating in Iraq and many of these organizations had earlier planned for a refugee emergency. The oversight seems due in part to the fact that prior to the upsurge in displacement in 2006, few organizations were actually tracking IDP and refugee flows. One exception was the U.S. Committee for Refugees and Immigrants. Their annual survey found that nearly 900,000 Iraqi refugees existed at the beginning of 2006, an increase of more than 500,000 people from the previous year (U.S. Committee for Refugees and Immigrants 2006). By the end of 2005, according to UN agency estimates, more than one million Iraqis were also internally displaced (UNHCR 2007c).

Today, NGOs and the UN relate the same basic narrative about the humanitarian situation in Iraq: the swell of refugees and displaced persons only became apparent following the bombing of the Al-Askaria shrine in Samarra in February 2006. The mainstream media has echoed this account, suggesting further that the bombing and ensuing collapse of security actually triggered the mass exodus and internal displacement. Others, however, say that a surge in refugees to neighboring countries was evident a year earlier.

In any case, the bombing awakened human rights and humanitarian organizations to the developing disaster. In spring 2006 Human Rights Watch led a fact-finding trip to Jordan, Lebanon and Syria. Later that year, Refugees International initiated its own investigations in those countries. The findings of these "field visits" prompted these NGOs to shift significant resources for investigation and advocacy from other regions to Iraq and its neighboring countries. Their reports, in turn, have catalyzed other NGOs, the UN and the United States to begin to address the consequences of Iraqi displacement. Amnesty International and Human Rights First joined these earlier efforts, mobilizing resources to initiate advocacy campaigns.

Despite these efforts, international NGOs still struggled to make this largely invisible and unpopular problem visible in the West. In March 2007, Refugees International complained that "no Iraqi, U.S. or UN institution is taking the displacement crisis seriously enough to mount an effective response" (Refugees International 2007b: 6). Nonetheless, the sustained advocacy of these NGOs had some impact: Media campaigns and lobbying of Congress and the UN helped to rejuvenate debate on questions of humanitarian relief and refugee resettlement policy. Since the November 2006 release of a Human Rights Watch report on Iraqi refugees in Jordan, there was also a noticeable increase in mainstream media coverage of the refugee issue in the United States.

Another critical step for U.S.-based NGOs was the development of active coalitions to pressure for more humanitarian assistance and better resettlement policies for displaced Iraqis. In May 2007, Refugee Council U.S.A organized the first meeting of an Iraqi Refugee Work Group of U.S.-based NGOs to "better facilitate broad-based advocacy" on the Iraqi refugee crisis.[9] Members of the group met regularly to coordinate media and lobbying efforts, attend Congressional meetings on the refugee crisis, and "build grassroots support for the growing needs facing Iraqi refugees and IDPs."

The coalition began to build the capacity to form consensus around policy goals, advocacy targets, and public education strategies. For example, members effectively pressured for increased bilateral assistance from the international community to Jordan and Syria. In addition, they actively lobbied Congress and the Bush administration to resettle greater numbers of Iraqi refugees in the United States and commit more resources for refugees. By late 2007, both the U.S. Senate and House of Representatives had draft legislation concerning refugee admissions and humanitarian assistance and advocates were testifying frequently before Congress. Despite these gains, such efforts seemed insufficient to address the scope of the displacement crisis.

STATE OF DENIAL

Until early 2007, the State Department and U.S. lawmakers largely ignored the mounting numbers of refugees and IDPs, tending to attribute most displacement to the legacy of the deposed Iraqi regime. Following the 2006 Congressional elections, when Republicans lost majorities in the House of Representatives and Senate, Democrats opened hearings on various dimensions of the war, including the plight of refugees and IDPs.

These hearings marked a key shift in the way the war and its consequences were being addressed in U.S. politics and reflect in part the work of different NGOs. At a special session on Iraqi refugees in early 2007, Senator Edward Kennedy noted that the U.S. bore a "heavy responsibility" for what he called an "extraordinary human tragedy" (U.S. Senate 2007: 4). He and other senators criticized the Bush administration's neglect of the issue and urged greater efforts to assist and resettle vulnerable Iraqi refugees. Kennedy asserted that the U.S. "should work urgently with Iraq's neighbors, especially Jordan, Syria and Lebanon, who are bearing the greatest refugee burden. Prompt action is essential to prevent destabilization of the region and to relieve suffering and save lives."

According to a senior congressional staffer, after this hearing NGOs capitalized on their relationships with Congress to increase pressure on the State Department. These groups successfully persuaded congressional staff to monitor media coverage of the humanitarian crisis as a basis for developing policy initiatives. Recognizing growing Democratic opposition to the war, NGOs were careful to portray the displacement crisis as a bipartisan concern. As a result of this advocacy, the State Department began to meet regularly with members of Congress and their staff on this issue.

But at UNHCR meetings held with NGOs and U.S. government representatives in spring 2007, the Bush administration continued to claim that the refugee problem "predates the current conflict."[10] When UNHCR held ministerial meetings in Geneva on the Iraq refugee crisis, Paula Dobriansky, undersecretary of state for democracy and global affairs, admitted that "Iraqi displacement is a serious problem." But she also repeated references to the "sizable number of Iraqis during the time of Saddam Hussein who left" and called on the international community to address the "humanitarian concern" through "coordinated action" (U.S. Mission to the United Nations in Geneva 2007). Dobriansky's understatement contrasted sharply with urgent calls from NGOs and the UNHCR to develop a comprehensive program for assistance and resettlement for a growing population of refugees.

The Bush administration began to implement a limited number of humanitarian programs for refugee assistance, both within Iraq and in neighboring countries. The State Department lobbied the Syrian and Jordanian governments to accept the assistance of international NGOs, who would partner with local humanitarian organizations such as the Red Crescent Society. In a policy shift in late 2007, the State Department dedicated more resources to fund NGOs working in Jordan and Syria, another indication of the impact of advocacy by these groups.

Nonetheless, human rights advocates remained critical of administration efforts. Kristele Younes of Refugees International charged the Bush administration with denying the humanitarian disaster because it would be "interpreted as acknowledging failure in Iraq" (Refugees International 2007c). Bill Frelick of Human Rights Watch urged President Bush to use the "bully pulpit" to pressure Americans to welcome thousands of refugees to the United States (Frelick 2007). He called on the administration to work with the Arab League, European Union, and the UNHCR to establish a voluntary resettlement program in the Middle East and Europe. "The U.S. government needs to acknowledge that it has a particular responsibility toward Iraqi refugees because of its military intervention in Iraq." (Frelick 2007: 4). Doing so, however, would require that the United States provide much higher levels of financial support to host countries than it normally allocates for humanitarian emergencies.

The amount of humanitarian assistance provided by the U.S. for the refugee crisis remains grossly inadequate. State Department officials assert that from FY 2003 to 2006 the United States allocated more than $800 million to support UN agencies and NGOs working with refugees, IDPs, and returning Iraqis (U.S. Senate 2007: 6–7). To put this figure in perspective, at the same time the United States was spending more than $250 million *per day* on the war in Iraq. One week of U.S. war spending was more than the total annual budget for UNHCR operations worldwide (Couldrey and

Morris 2007: 3). Analysis done by the UN Office for the Coordination of Humanitarian Affairs in 2007 confirmed how "under-funded" relief efforts were: "Iraq is the second least funded (per affected person) of the 15 most severe humanitarian crises" in the world (United Nations 2007). Such facts did not sway Congress to provide adequate funds for Iraqi refugees and IDPs.

U.S. denial of the displacement disaster is also evident in debates over refugee admissions and resettlement. Historically resettlement to the United States has been an important part of U.S. refugee policy. A 2006 policy statement to Congress underscored the symbolic importance accorded this idea: "Throughout its history, the United States has maintained a rich and vibrant tradition of offering refuge to those who have suffered or fear persecution . . . The ability to offer resettlement as a durable solution to some of the world's refugees is a critical responsibility in a highly visible policy arena" (U.S. Department of State et al. 2006: iii). Despite this portrayal, resettlement targets and actual admissions fell significantly since the Bush administration took office.[11] Reflecting a little noticed but important policy shift, U.S. refugee admissions programs were increasingly driven by dual goals: balancing "humanitarian commitments" with "national security" (U.S. Department of State et al 2007: 3). Invoking the specter of the "hidden terrorist" passing himself off as a refugee serves as a powerful bogeyman to justify restricted access to the United States. Since the Iraq war began, resettlement targets for the Middle East and South Asia decreased dramatically. Targets fell from 15,000 in FY 2002 to a low of 3,000 in FY 2004. Arguably the work of humanitarian groups and UNHCR to draw attention to Iraqi refugees has forced the State Department to boost its admissions ceiling for refugees from the Middle East and South Asia; up to 28,000 refugees were allowed to be admitted to the United States from the region in FY 2008.

More specifically concerning Iraq, the Bush administration's efforts to resettle refugees were negligible. Between FY 2003 and 2006, only a few hundred Iraqi refugees were admitted into the United States. The State Department justified this low number because it stopped processing Iraqis due to security threats following September 11 (2007: 42). In FY 2007, 1,608 Iraqis were admitted, reflecting a move to allow up to 7,000 of the most vulnerable Iraqis (religious minorities or those who had worked with Americans in Iraq). In FY 2008, 13,823 Iraqis were resettled to the United States, far fewer than advocates and the United Nations had pressed for admitting (U.S. Department of State 2009: 8).

The Bush administration continued to deny the scope of the refugee crisis and the U.S. role in creating the disaster in Iraq. A report on proposed refugee admissions for FY 2007 illustrates this, by minimizing the impact of refugees on Iraq's neighbors. Moreover, the State Department continued to stress the repatriation of Iraqis to their home country, ignoring the severity of current conditions in Iraq (U.S. Department of State et al. 2007). However, in November 2007 the UN warned against attempts by Iraq and its neighbors to facilitate repatriation. UNHCR claimed that the material and security conditions in Iraq were still too uncertain to warrant large-scale return of Iraqis (UNHCR 2007b).

WEAK PUBLIC SUPPORT FOR IRAQI REFUGEES AND IDPS

Despite the prominence the war in Iraq has assumed in the United States, the Iraqi refugee issue gained visibility only toward the end of the Bush administration. Most public debate about refugee support in Congress and the media focused on passing legislation to allow those who worked as translators and support personnel for the U.S. government to resettle in the United States. It has been more challenging to sustain public interest in the millions of other displaced Iraqis. U.S. public opinion remains firmly against the war in Iraq, while a small, robust antiwar movement continues to influence U.S. policy. Nonetheless, the broader American public has been largely detached on the refugee issue, a phenomenon with tragic consequences.

While some respondents for this study cited "compassion fatigue" for such disengagement, others worried that racism and xenophobia fueled public apathy. Advocates for Iraqi refugees recognize the current limits of American public support for those displaced from the war and argue that only through grassroots public education and active lobbying would more just refugee policies be developed. But the obstacles to such mobilization are formidable. Lack of understanding of the Middle East, rising anti-Americanism, fear of terrorism, and xenophobia all shape public responses to the war. Ambivalence about the fate of American soldiers who fight against an "enemy" difficult to define also influences perceptions of Iraqis as "other" and therefore undeserving of assistance. As a member of one faith-based refugee advocacy group noted, congregations are more likely to be "moved" when people like them (i.e., Christians) are being oppressed.

The absence of public pressure to impel American policymakers to establish comprehensive programs for refugees has remained a key barrier to reforming U.S. refugee policy. As troubling is the blend of nationalism, racism, and fear that informs some public responses to the prospect of accepting Iraqi refugees for resettlement. Refugee advocates realize that in the current climate of a U.S.-led "War on Terror," many Americans are reluctant to have Iraqis, or any refugees or immigrants from the Middle East, settle in their communities. According to one advocate, "We have to be careful how we phrase things. We talk about Iraqis coming to the United States . . . as victims of war, as families, as highly educated, skilled people. [But] many communities see al-Qaeda coming to their neighborhoods. It's hard for people who are misinformed or non-informed to really make the distinction."

The UN High Commissioner for Refugees, António Guterres, has asserted that a political solution in Iraq is essential to resolving the displacement crisis (UNCHR 2007d). A solution to Iraq's political impasse, however, has been exceedingly difficult to achieve and sustain given the nation's pervasive political, religious, and ethnic divisions. While the premature repatriation of refugees may be politically expedient for Iraq and its neighbors, it will solve none of Iraq's underlying problems. Indeed, wide-scale refugee return to a fractured society may exacerbate conflict in Iraq, due to the government's lack of legitimacy and weak infrastructure. Refugees and IDPs returning to Baghdad thus far find few supports to meet their material needs and no mechanism to redress grievances regarding lost property and lack of adequate housing (Gordon and Farrell 2007).

Clearly the challenges that displacement have created for peace-building and reconstruction in Iraq should have given pause to the Bush administration in its march for "regime change" in 2003. The U.S. role in the Iraq war raises troubling questions about the gap between the rhetoric and reality of human rights. The Bush administration invoked human rights protection as one of its justifications for Iraq invasion in 2003. However, the ramifications of the war and U.S.-led attempts to rapidly reconstitute an Iraqi state malleable to U.S. interests undermine such claims to secure Iraqis' human rights.

Despite the Bush administration's claim to have been tackling the Iraqi displacement crisis, its policy on refugees was marked by deception and denial. Further, the "restrictionism" that typifies Western policies created to control unauthorized immigration has also been evident in the U.S. approach to refugee resettlement. Julie Peteet underscores that "a more restrictive, state-centric global consensus to prevent refugee movements has emerged as states close their borders" (2007: 6). For example, congressional efforts to provide higher resettlement targets and sufficient humanitarian aid for Iraqis have been tardy and relatively narrow in intent. Human rights organizations have been hesitant to accuse the United States of violating international humanitarian and human rights obligations, instead engaging the Bush administration and Congress through a mix of education and advocacy to establish better policies. Recognizing limited public awareness about the scope of the Iraq humanitarian crisis and the barrier of nationalism to building grassroots support, human rights groups and NGOs remain critical actors in pressing for accountability and change in U.S. refugee policy.

Yet while these groups decry the small number of Iraqis allowed to resettle in the West, they also recognize that large-scale resettlement of Iraqis is untenable in the current anti-immigrant climate. In response, global refugee policymakers grapple with protection and support for displaced populations like Iraqis within or near conflict zones. Analysts of forced migration point to the risks of "containing" refugees and IDPs within so-called safe havens or safe corridors inside embattled states or neighboring countries. Despite the specific international laws, the rights of the displaced to basic protection have been neglected in such settings. In Peteet's view of the Iraq humanitarian crisis, the lack of international response signals "a gradual shift from a concern with refugee rights to increasing invisibility and exclusion on a selective basis" (2007: 9).

Daniel Byman has pointed out that the United States has failed to appreciate how morality and strategy are inextricably bound vis-à-vis the Iraq displacement crisis. He claims it is "both morally abhorrent and strategically ill-advised to abandon" Iraqi refugees, yet thus far "U.S. efforts to help these refugees have ranged from feeble to nonexistent" (Byman 2007). While the United States and the international community have mobilized some resources to support Iraqi refugees and IDPs, overall funding and services have remained insufficient. Host state and NGO capacity to assist the displaced is also inadequate.

The U.S. unilateral military intervention in Iraq—whether to prosecute a "global war on terror," to secure access to resources, or both—has had catastrophic effects for Iraqis and the region. European states have been reluctant to host refugees or provide them substantial resources, citing the now common claim that the United States broke the "Pottery Barn rule" in foreign policy. The notion that "you broke it, you fix it" may signal to the United States how destructive its policies in Iraq have been. Even if the conflict in Iraq is resolved, demands on neighboring states will remain for years to come; many refugees will remain reluctant to return to a society divided by political conflict and violence. A viable resolution of the Iraqi displacement crisis will thus require a sustained multilateral approach, with the United States taking a lead role. Such a shift in U.S. policy, one that recognizes the needs of multiple actors, will not come easily. Without added pressure on the U.S. and international community from a range of organizational and individual actors to address these realities, Iraqis will continue to suffer and regional instability will increase.

Conclusion

Samuel Martínez

Taking the essays as a whole, at least three overarching points of concern to students and advocates of migrant rights may be identified:

U.S. foreign policy has contradictory global effects on migrants. The hundreds of millions of dollars spent each year by the United States on efforts to suppress the international trafficking of women and children are one sure sign of the good intentions of U.S. legislators. This "war on trafficking" forms the background to the chapter by Alexia Bloch in this book. Bloch raises a concern, however, widely shared among migrant rights advocates, that in fighting trafficking the United States is combating a problem largely of its own and other governments' creation. Rather than curbing unauthorized entry, the erection of heightened security barriers around U.S. borders has only deflected immigrants into the grip of smugglers. Well-intentioned efforts to punish trafficking are therefore bound to be much less effective than it would be to act upon the root cause of the phenomenon, by reforming an immigration and border enforcement policy that makes working with a smuggler the only reliable means for an impoverished immigrant to come to the United States even to fill those dead-end jobs that U.S. citizens are not taking in the numbers required. Unfortunately, the U.S. response to trafficking, though amply funded, has followed the same "get tough" law enforcement mold as the border tightening policies that created ripe conditions for trafficking in the first place.[1]

Bloch also brings forward a—to date underresearched—gender dimension to this volume's analysis of how U.S. foreign and immigration policies shape the circumstances under which migrants seek to cross borders today.[2] Unstated assumptions about women's nature coincide with Christian morality in framing women as favorite objects of humanitarian concern; at the

237

same time, these gendered framings of the global human trafficking crisis implicitly reject the possibility that a woman might exercise free will and judgment (and still choose to be a sex worker) rather than remain in an economically dire situation in which she cannot help herself or her family. The law enforcement and social services paradigms of intervention against trafficking, in which sex entertainment workers are assumed to stand in need of "rescue" and "rehabilitation," leave no room for more pragmatic government approaches such as legalizing the sex trade, which might bring these women out of the shadows and enhance their power to resist exploitation independently and on their own terms.

Worse, by focusing exclusive attention on the victim-perpetrator dyad, the dominant discourse surrounding trafficking fails to touch unfreedom's root causes, which disproportionately hamper women's effective freedom. Restrictionist immigration and border control policies, which drive migrants into the smuggler's grip, find a silent but remorselessly effective accomplice in the free-market restructuring of various countries' economies, which has increased female rates of poverty and with it heightened women's vulnerability to the blandishments of slavers posing as labor recruiters.

Looking beyond immigration policy per se, we find that U.S. initiatives overseas have similarly contradictory effects. The chapters by Alexia Bloch and María Teresa Restrepo-Ruiz and me, for example, point to evidence that the human impact of free-market reform and suppression of the illicit drugs trade has been worsened by U.S. support for economic "shock therapy" and militarization of the antidrug agenda. In the states of the former Soviet Union, structural adjustment policies favored by the United States and international financial institutions have worsened the gender inequality and economic deprivation that place women at risk of leaving home for sexual work (and potential exploitation) abroad. In Colombia, U.S.-sponsored forced eradication of coca cultivation and military suppression of illegal narcotics manufacturing have aggravated conditions of danger and uncertainty from which rural people must move in order to regain physical security and the economic resources with which to survive. Of course, the United States government cannot be held responsible for poverty, economic upheavals, or civil wars overseas. Even so, it may be asked whether the U.S. leadership has done what it can to resolve such conditions by peaceful and political means, prioritizing the human rights of people in "target" countries of U.S. concern, and thus lessening the pressure to leave home felt by millions of people in other nations. In other words, there is a distinction to be drawn between "blaming" the United States *for* human rights crises (and hence reducing these to the effects of U.S. policy) and faulting the United States for aggravating existing threats to human physical and economic security across a range of foreign policy domains.

After 9/11, measures taken in the name of U.S. national security have significantly worsened this picture. As Christopher Dole's chapter vividly evokes, post-9/11 security measures have spread insecurity among the citizens of selected other nations in the name of providing greater security to U.S. citizens. In the aftermath of the 9/11 attacks, the U.S. government imposed widely reported control measures—involving official registration, unlimited secret detention, and deportation—on Muslim Middle Eastern and South Asian males, and targeted their communities for intrusive official investigation and surreptitious surveillance (for more details, see Salyer's and Akram and Johnson's chapters in this volume). Following the attacks of 9/11, more than 1,200 people were arrested and placed in "preventive detention" in connection with terrorism investigations, based principally or solely on their Muslim religion or Middle Eastern/South Asian ethnicity or national origin (Cole 2003a: ch.2). Information about their identities, their whereabouts, and the charges against them were withheld from their families, the press, and the public. Broader and more openly discriminatory still was the government's "special registration" program, NSEERS (National Security Entry/Exit Registration System), under which males age sixteen to forty-five from twenty-five Middle Eastern and South Asian countries were required to register and be fingerprinted, photographed, and questioned under oath by INS officers. Of the 82,880 men who complied with special registration by 1 June 2003, 13,434 were placed in deportation proceedings for visa violations (Cainkar 2004: 218–19). Out of more than 200,000 registered (including those processed at ports of entry), none were charged with terrorism.

These are but the most flagrant and obvious dimensions of the post-9/11 "securitization" of immigration.[3] Since 9/11, all obstacles to entry of immigrants from the global South have been heightened, with harmful consequences for would-be legitimate entrants and their families. Frontier surveillance, restrictions against unauthorized entry, bureaucratic-legal obstacles to obtaining visas, and criteria for granting asylum all have been toughened. A series of little-known and seemingly benign technical innovations in the processing of asylum claims has insidiously eroded legitimate applicants' chances of establishing the existence of a credible threat to their safety in their home countries (McCarthy 2003).[4] The REAL ID Act of 2005, according to J. C. Salyer,[5] "contains a number of measures . . . requiring the asylum applicant to obtain corroborated evidence for all claims or prove such evidence is unavailable," and mandates immigration judges to determine "the accuracy or inaccuracy of all statements whether they are relevant to the asylum claim or not." Obviously, insisting that asylum seekers enter the United States with authentic permits and identity documents[6] and holding all their statements to an absolute standard of truth are unreasonable criteria for admission: refugees must in many cases adopt false identities to evade capture by the governments that are persecuting them and they are particularly prone to make inconsistent statements and minor errors, due to the psychological disorientation that may ensue from the traumatic circumstances of their persecution at home. The discernable trend of these changes in asylum processing and determination is to push U.S. refugee policy back to its Cold War status: an aggressive complement to foreign policy aims, admitting refugees preferentially from enemy states and in no more than the numbers predefined as acceptable.

Internationally, U.S. leadership on human rights has been diminished, with negative consequences not just for U.S. prestige but for political and religious dissidents in other countries, who may in turn end up swelling the ranks of asylum seekers arriving at ports of entry in the world's liberal democracies. The U.S. prioritization of security over human rights protection and its willingness to turn a blind eye to human rights abuses inflicted by governments overseas in the name of antiterrorism has regrettably provided a ready-made pretext—the imperative of winning the "war on terror"—for rights-abusing states, such as China, Thailand, and Malaysia, to clamp down more forcefully on political dissent and minority rights militancy, as Hess's chapter in this book vividly shows. While it should be repeated that we are not blaming the United States for other countries' rights clampdowns, concerns can be raised about whether the U.S. government is providing the example and the leadership that the world needs in the migrant rights field. As Subhash Kateel (2007), cofounder of the immigrant rights group Families for Freedom, has said about the bad human rights example set internationally by the United States post-9/11, "Really bad ideas from the United States get even scarier when they are exported to other countries."

Even so, post-9/11 U.S. government actions have extensive precedents and deep historical roots. Far from a new phenomenon or historical aberration, today's securitization of immigration and attendant abuses of migrant rights have precedents in earlier generations, draw to an important degree upon established bureaucratic-legal foundations, and follow preexisting social prejudices. For example, the mechanisms and strategies used to detain captives of the U.S. "Global War on Terror" as "enemy aliens," outside the reach of the protections of U.S. law, are strikingly similar and in some ways directly repeat the means previously used to contain the northward flow of boat people from Haiti (Martínez 2003).[7] As we are reminded by the chapters by J.C. Salyer and Susan Akram and Kevin Johnson, by looking historically we learn how ineffective as well as unjust it has been in the past for the U.S. government to respond to national security crises by making a scapegoat of entire nationalities.

The three historical chapters in Part II are in striking agreement, first, that anti-immigrant backlash has always been unleashed across conventionally defined "racial" boundaries. Even the Eastern and Southern Europeans who were mainly targeted by the Palmer Raids were derogated by politicians, scholars, and opinion-shapers of the early twentieth century as racially distinct from and incapable of assimilation into white America. That the descendants of those immigrant nationalities are today treated as white underscores the conventional and arbitrary, rather than biological and inevitable, character of the distinctions in question. Accordingly, a second conclusion sustained by all three chapters is that anti-immigrant backlash, even though always triggered by a perceived sense or mood of national emergency, has also always been in a sense prepared for, over a span of decades, by public expressions of racism and exclusionism, in the press and other elite communication organs. History thus reminds us that words can have effects that hurt people. In the years before 9/11, cultural scripts had been deployed by U.S. opinion-shapers to demonize Middle Eastern Muslims as "terrorists" (Akram and Johnson in this volume) and create fears about the U.S. border with Mexico being "out of control" (Chavez in this book). Observing that past public dialogues on immigration have had real and frightening material consequences for immigrants, this book constitutes a call for policymakers to engage in debates about immigration with the utmost sense of responsibility.

Chief perhaps among those "really bad ideas" that the United States' example is propagating internationally is the misperception that building a wall between neighboring states and otherwise escalating border vigilance to near-emergency proportions is going to bring the unauthorized entry of immigrants to a halt. As the Democratic presidential candidate Bill Richardson quipped in 2007, "If you build a 12-foot wall, people will get 13-foot ladders."[8] The official "get tough" approach toward immigration antedates the 9/11 attacks by many years (Chavez, this volume); aspects of this policy have also long stood demonstrably in contravention of internationally-recognized human rights norms. As Chavez notes, the buildup of surveillance and apprehension resources at frequently crossed points of the U.S.-Mexico border has had the effect of pushing immigrants to cross at less guarded but more dangerous and remote areas, producing a spike in migrant border deaths since the mid-1990s (Eschbach, Hagan, and Rodríguez 2003). Having been redirected into solitary desert wilderness, unauthorized entrants are now more vulnerable than before to assault, more frequently get lost and die of thirst in the desert, and incur more danger from prolonged exposure to sunlight, heat, or cold. Counting deaths on both sides of the border, one advocacy group estimates that more than 3,000 migrants have lost their lives crossing the U.S.-Mexico border since the 1990s.[9] Considering twenty years of clampdown has produced only declining marginal returns in immigrant apprehensions per dollar spent on the Border Patrol (Chavez, this volume), it must be asked whether border enforcement alone can ever diminish unauthorized entry or is worth this price in human lives.[10]

During the 1990s, monitors from Amnesty International (1998) and Human Rights Watch (1992; 1995) issued a series of pathbreaking reports documenting abuses committed by the U.S. Border Patrol, including beatings and sexual assaults. There have also been several cases of border crossers being shot by Border Patrol agents, with the agents often claiming later that the border crosser was throwing, or reaching for, a rock. Human Rights Watch has also documented how the U.S. government often fails to investigate and punish abuses by its border guards. The dramatic growth in the size of the Border Patrol in recent years has only exacerbated the problem of effective oversight. Officials from the Office of the Inspector General have complained of severe understaffing that makes it impossible for them to investigate all complaints of border abuses.

Inspired by the widespread perception that the United States stands under threat from an uncontrolled immigrant invasion, armed anti-immigrant militants have taken the surveillance and policing of the country's border with Mexico into their own hands, magnifying the potential for abuse. According to a Witness/American Friends Service Committee (2005) joint investigation,

> The militarization of the U.S.-Mexico border, already well underway in the 1990s, took on a new intensity with the advent of the "War on Terror" and its accompanying rhetoric of fear. Overnight, migrants forced north for economic reasons were painted as something far more sinister: potential terrorists. Groups that had long denounced those crossing the southern border in frankly racist terms latched onto a new way to rally broader opposition. A patriotic call went out for new

"Minuteman Patrols" to defend the borders, starting with Arizona's Cochise County on April 1, 2005.

While the response of border vigilantes may seem extreme, the "terrorist card" has been played more frequently since 9/11 by anti-immigrant activists who frequently speak in mainstream media, heating up the already inflammatory rhetoric surrounding unauthorized immigration:

Anti-immigrant activists have used the terrorist threat to stir up popular xenophobia, racism and fear of immigrants. Mark Krikorian, for example, president of the Center for Immigration Studies, quotes Deputy Defense Secretary Paul Wolfowitz and other high Administration officials to bolster his case that the "home front" must be our first defense against terrorism. . . . These activists argue that since we can't defeat the terrorists on the battlefield in conventional warfare, U.S. citizens and their government must find new ways to respond to this "asymmetric warfare." Shutting down the borders and shoving out the "illegals" is the most effective and logical first step. "Immigration control is to asymmetric warfare what missile defense is to strategic warfare," Krikorian asserts. . . . The militarism of this new immigration/ anti-terrorism policy is also on display at the Department of Homeland Security (DHS), where DHS Under Secretary Asa Hutchinson described the visa process in September 2003 as a "forward-based defense" against terrorists and criminals. . . . [A]ccording to [Republican Senator Sam Brownback (Kansas)], all citizens can enlist in the War on Terror. "While the battle may be waged on several fronts," says the Senator, "for the man or woman on the street, immigration is in many ways the front line of our defense." (Barry 2005: 29–30)

RHETORIC AND REALITY

If the U.S. Congress was genuinely concerned with enhancing U.S. citizens' security via immigration reform, then one of its first steps would be to accord more, not less, protection to immigrants' rights, including even the undocumented. To begin with, widespread distrust of governmental authorities worsens any security threat that might exist among immigrant populations themselves. "In the aftermath of Sept. 11," for example, "Arab-Americans have a greater fear of racial profiling and immigration enforcement than of falling victim to hate crimes, according to a national study financed by the Justice Department" (Elliott 2006). That is exactly what the constitutional and immigration law expert David Cole (2002) predicted in the immediate aftermath of the 9/11 attacks. This outcome was not inevitable but could have been avoided had the government carried out its post-9/11 investigation in ways that were less obviously discriminatory, scattershot, and intrusive for Middle Eastern and South Asian communities. After having been collectively treated as if they were suspected enemies of the United States, the members of the ethnic/religious communities who could be most helpful in rooting out any violent Islamic extremist plot are now understandably hesitant even to make contact with law enforcement, lest they themselves end up being thrown into indefinite secret confinement in an immigration jail. Christopher Dole's chapter on the personal post-9/11 experiences of Arab and Muslim men in Boston eloquently dramatizes that sowing insecurity, even among a numerical minority of racially/nationally-defined immigrants, in the long term cannot but have a counterproductive effect on the security of the large mass of U.S. citizens, to the degree that it creates resentment and suspicion toward government even among those Middle Easterners and South Asians who are firmly a part of the U.S. social fabric. In hindsight, the post-9/11 state-sponsored witch hunt against Arab and Muslim immigrants and citizens was a false first step toward bringing all residents of the U.S. to stand united.

The chapters of Part III, "Policing the Borders of the Security State," coincide in finding that the dominant, law enforcement–centered paradigm of security also conjures a largely false sense of security among members of the U.S. mainstream (in racial and class terms) by spreading fear and *in*security among particular racial, national, and citizenship "outsiders." The authors of these chapters also agree that creating a simulacrum of security for the citizen majority by spreading fear among noncitizen minorities inevitably also has spillover effects on members of populations purportedly shielded from state persecution by their "white" ethnic identity or legal residency. The use of racial profiling, for example, creates an uneasy feeling of being under watch even among Middle Eastern and South Asian Muslim Americans who are legally authorized to live in the United States, while official harassment of Mexican Americans and Central American immigrants via low-tolerance policing at the local level renders community relations tense all around, as Naples's chapter in this volume demonstrates. Over all noncitizens hangs the ultimate sanction of falling into the shadows of a secretive immigration detention and deportation process and being possibly separated from livelihoods, homes, and families built through years of effort in the United States.

An anecdote may help show further implications that the health and safety of immigrants may hold for U.S. citizens, and suggest why it would be in the general public interest to extend even to irregular immigrants the same workplace rights and protections enjoyed by all citizens. On 24 May 2006, a front page story of *The Hartford Courant* reported that a crew of roofers, "apparently fearful of detection by immigration offi-cials," spent a half-hour trying "to administer their own form of first aid to an injured co-worker, who had fallen 30 feet off [a] steeply pitched roof" (Becker and Altimari 2006). A neighbor witnessing the scene eventually called 911. The injured worker, a young Ecuadorian, was hospitalized in intensive care. His coworkers were detained and processed for deportation. This episode was a small tragedy, much like others that happen almost every day. Yet it points to the seed of a potentially much larger problem. With the threat of global pandemic periodically on the horizon, it carries increased danger to the public that unauthorized immigrants might fail to seek prompt medical care, largely out of fear that it could result in being reported to Immigration and Customs Enforcement (ICE).

The danger, it should be emphasized, comes not from the immigrants—in the case of avian influenza, for example, they do not carry the flu into the country but merely stand in peril of contracting it from the poultry they work with—the danger comes rather from get-tough immigration policies that drive these workers to the margins of U.S. society.[11] Though exact numbers are not available, it is known that "a sizable percentage" of the 216,000 immigrants working in U.S. poultry processing—people whose cooperation would be critical to any government effort to halt the spread of an avian flu outbreak—lack valid work documents (Aho 2006).[12] The days that a sick poultry worker might delay in seeking medical care out of fear of being reported to the police could constitute a lost opportunity to isolate the infected individual before she or he spreads the flu to other humans. Considering that rapid diagnosis and quarantine may be the best line of defense against new strains of flu, what more vital human security concern could there be than bringing workers out of the shadows by regularizing their residency and work status? Such public health implications exemplify the urgent need to expand the U.S. immigration debate to consider the real human security issues impinged upon by unauthorized immigration. In general terms, the most prevalent and serious human security threats are not those introduced into the United States by unauthorized immigrants; the threats stem rather from an immigration policy that is out of touch with the need for immigrant workers in certain industries (and poultry processing is only one example) in order to remain competitive in a global marketplace. In closing its eyes to the mismatch between immigration policy and labor market demand, Washington effectively confines many millions of undocumented immigrants to a legal netherworld and tacitly permits employers to expose their workers to workplace hazards of all kinds with impunity.

Injecting a greater measure of realism into the immigration debate will take a lot of work, for regrettably the evidence is strong that U.S. citizens have on the whole been convinced by the get-tough rhetoric of the anti-immigration lobby. There is at least a tacit recognition on the part of many U.S. citizens that immigrants come to the United States in the main to work and that even the unauthorized play a vital role in the economy (Cornelius 2002: 169). A *Washington Post*–ABC News poll taken in mid-December 2005 asked whether illegal immigrants who are working here should be given the opportunity to keep their jobs and eventually apply for legal status, or be rounded up and deported to their native countries. Three in five Americans said undocumented workers should be given the opportunity to stay and become citizens (Balz 2006). Even so, the same poll found that four in five Americans think the government is not doing enough to prevent illegal immigration, with three in five saying they strongly hold that view, and revealed that 56 percent of Americans believe that illegal immigrants have done more to hurt the country than to help it, with 37 percent saying they help the country.

Behind unsubstantiated generalizations about whether or not immigrants truly take only the jobs that citizens refuse to do or represent a net burden on state resources, other basic questions go completely ignored in the U.S. immigration debate. Seen from a political-economic standpoint, perhaps the most obvious of these unasked questions is, Why have the jobs that "Americans won't do" (but immigrants will) grown so rapidly in number in recent years? In other words, Why are many jobs that used to be done by U.S. citizens seemingly no longer acceptable to them? It seems likely that many of these jobs have been "degraded" (Green 2003) or "downgraded" (as Carole Nagengast puts it in her afterword to this volume) in part as a result of the same accelerated economic restructuring and lifting of government regulations on commerce that have stimulated higher than ever rates of South-North migration. In other words, the same freeing up of market forces that has dislocated workers from secure, if relatively unrewarding, livelihoods in far-flung parts of the world has also produced an increasing demand in the United States and other industrially advanced economies for cheap, unregulated labor. Economic dislocations, North and South, respond to similar profit-driven imperatives for producers either to compete more effectively for a share of increasingly globally integrated markets or face the prospect of going extinct.

Yet "globalization" is perhaps too pat a justification for adopting a more liberal immigration policy. In many sectors of the U.S. economy, it may well be true that without cheap and compliant immigrant labor, rising costs of production would eventuate in imports seizing a larger share of the market from goods made in the United States. (Those immigrant poultry workers mentioned above are probably one example: it is likely that without their willingness to work for low wages imported meat would start taking the place of U.S.-raised chicken on supermarket shelves.) Yet in other businesses immigrants could be replaced with U.S. citizens with little effect beyond increased labor costs. (If the immigrant roofers who took that nasty fall in Connecticut were replaced with higher-paid U.S. citizens or authorized immigrants, for example, it seems likely that both home builders and home buyers would simply adjust to marginally higher prices; roofs would still be installed, repaired, and replaced without undocumented immigrant workers, because roofing installation is not a service that can be imported from abroad.) It may not be knowable with existing data to what extent immigration responds to the former versus the latter kind of demand. It is uncertain, in other words, how many immigrants help U.S. businesses win out against potential or actual foreign competitors, and how many supply cheap labor that just enables some businesses to earn a surplus profit or underbid other U.S.-based competitors. It can be said in principle that globalization places uneven constraints on different sectors of the economy, depending on their vulnerability to foreign competition. "Global competition" does not constitute a sufficient justification for each and every U.S. employer to switch to immigrant labor; much less does it condone undercutting trade unions and lowering wages to below poverty level.

The picture becomes even more complex when one considers that even those undocumented roofers (whose employment is not strictly speaking mandated by global market competition) also help lower consumer prices and keep inflation low. The issue of immigration's effect on consumer prices evokes the difficulty of tallying up the immigration "balance sheet" for U.S. citizens. Doubtless, most U.S. citizens gain more from the lower prices and added economic activity made possible by immigration than they lose by ceding lower-end jobs to these immigrants. Yet keeping inflation low and large business corporations' profits high—the two economic benefits to which immigration most indubitably contributes—can only be one criterion for deciding the quantity and kinds of immigration that the United States wishes to promote. While it is essential to tally the economic balance sheet of immigration's impact, it is questionable whether such calculations should trump other, nonquantifiable concerns, of a social and moral character.

Perhaps the most obvious question in this regard is, How low do we wish to let the cost of labor go in the United States? To do no more than accord certain immigrants rights to live and work in the United States, as proposed (around early 2007) by immigration liberals in the U.S. Senate, would no doubt be a victory for migrant rights: it would create safer and more predictable conditions for the entry of large numbers of immigrants who would otherwise have to entrust their safety and freedom to a smuggler in order to take up the jobs waiting for them in the United States. But if liberalizing immigration comes with few added worker-rights protections but simply permits the entry of more workers prepared to accept below-poverty-level wages, then it could also be predicted to worsen economic inequality. The question of how much more inequality U.S. citizens should put up with has been neatly sidestepped in the U.S. immigration debate, but it should be a central policy concern.

Of particular interest in this connection is the recommendation made by Douglas Massey in chapter 1 to overlay a more liberal immigration policy with invigorated labor and worker safety regulation, by directing federal resources away from unproductive attempts to suppress immigration and channeling these resources instead into workplace inspection and code enforcement. The aim would be "to assure employers' compliance with minimum wage laws, social insurance legislation, occupational safety and health regulations, tax codes, and mandated fair labor standards. This enforcement strategy has two advantages for the receiving society: it lowers the demand for immigrant workers by preventing employers from using them to avoid expensive labor regulations, and it prevents the formation of an underground, clandestine economy that puts downward pressure on the economic and social well-being of natives and immigrants alike" (Massey, this volume).

TOWARD A POLITICALLY PROGRESSIVE POSITION ON THE IMMIGRATION DEBATE

It is observations and recommendations of this kind, linking immigration trends to larger developments in the U.S. and global economies, that have been most sorely lacking in the U.S. immigration debate, and it is in this connection where the paucity of voices from the political left in this debate has been felt most. Immanuel Wallerstein (2006) has said that the slogan of the left "seems to be protect our rights, property, and jobs, not the rights, property, and jobs of the entire world." The claim is made that the stance of the left on immigration is therefore no less hypocritical than that of right-wing free-marketeers who "claim that goods and capital should move freely, but . . . tend not to extend this market principle to the movement of people" (Wallerstein 2006). Wallerstein is correct insofar as the tacit assumption behind much of the immigration debate has been that U.S. citizens must either drive out immigrants en masse or simply accept that the lower tier of U.S. workers will gradually fill with immigrants whose need for income obligates them to accept awful terms and conditions of work, bringing predictable negative effects on wages, work conditions, and standards of living. Realistic, politically progressive policy recommendations seek to overturn this assumption, by proposing that we are not necessarily forced to choose between the welfare of U.S. citizens and the rights of aliens.

The standpoints developed by the contributors to this book aim to break the left's silence and make the case instead that upholding workers' and migrants' rights is good for immigrants and for U.S. citizens equally. This does not mean turning our eyes away from immigration's negative effects on host country labor (as immigration liberals wish us to do). It is virtually inevitable that some host-country workers stand to gain from immigration while others stand to lose. As concluded by the authors of a widely cited (but perhaps less widely understood) policy evaluation, sponsored in the mid-1990s by the National Academy of Sciences: "although immigration yields a positive net gain to domestic workers, that gain is not spread equally: it harms workers who are substitutes for immigrants while benefiting workers who are complements to immigrants" (Smith and Edmonston 1997: 140). We will have learned nothing from the last decades of free market reform around the world if we do not realize that adjustment to the free flow of long-bottled-up factors of production brings about economic dislocation, visiting pain upon some and gain to others and, hence, raising the need for those who bear the costs of adjustment to get help beyond what the market can provide. Freeing up the movement of the labor factor of production would eventuate in upheavals in the host countries like those that tearing down walls around consumer and financial markets has brought, in the name of free market reform, to dozens of developing countries. Those negatives can be anticipated and partially mitigated through government policy.

Permitting freer immigration while taking steps to compensate for the increased economic inequality that it—much like any other free-market reform—would generate: that proposal is not a utopian vision but a strategic goal around which achievable policy measures can be planned. Far from trading off the rights of immigrants and citizens, the progressive standpoint is that both immigrants and low-income U.S. citizens should benefit from government policy aimed at ensuring a living wage, economic security, and workplace safety to all, such as protection for union organizing, invigorated enforcement of workers' safety laws, and provision of universal health care insurance. Perhaps under those circumstances the growth in the number of jobs that "Americans won't do" would actually begin to reverse. And just as important, perhaps under those circumstances the question of who does what job might begin to seem less urgent, as immigration turns into gain for host-country and immigrant workers alike. At least one radical implication flows by way of the solidarity that many of this book's contributors show with the downtrodden, the vulnerable, and the exploited: many of the contradictions of U.S. immigration policy would be diminished (though not eliminated) if that policy were to be reformed with primary concern for the rights and well-being of those whose labor creates the wealth of society, instead of mainly responding to the priorities of those who extract profit from the labor of others.

In the international sphere also, the U.S. free-market reform agenda and the "wars" on drugs and terrorism are worsening already worrisome trends in human geographical mobility. As the leader of the world's financial establishment, the United States is largely responsible for, and has it in its power to modify, those policies of the dominant international financial institutions that generate upheaval in the lives of people in many distant nations—such as the International Monetary Fund's imposition of draconian national budgetary cuts and removal of tariff protections as a condition for international loans to already desperately poor nations. (Indeed, in the wake of the global financial crisis of late 2008, former IMF economists are beginning to wonder what it might be like for the United States to taste its own structural-adjustment medicine [Lachman 2009].) Granted, a more just global economic order might not set loose any fewer migrants than are on the move today; the world economy would still tend toward progressively greater incorporation of all people on the face of the planet, putting ever more people at risk for leaving home as labor migrants. Yet U.S. policy initiatives to mitigate poverty and expand economic alternatives abroad might at least diminish the desperation to emigrate that currently exists in countries undergoing difficult transitions to free market economies, a desperation that motivates many people to accept even the most coercive circumstances of emigration and worst kinds of jobs abroad.

Similarly, the projection of military force is proving ineffective in dealing with the illicit drugs trade and international terrorism—whether the fighting is done by the U.S. armed forces or by other nations' armies, using U.S.-manufactured weapons and paid for by U.S.-sponsored arms sales programs—and has displaced millions of people from their home places and livelihoods, most dramatically but not solely in Iraq and Colombia (as detailed in chapters 11 and 12). That kind of tragedy is certainly avoidable and of the United States' own making, and hence susceptible to concerted pressure on the U.S. government in the future to strive instead for social and political rather than military responses to global problems.

These insights underscore this volume's guiding principles, the need to examine international migration through a global political-economic lens and the importance of seeking out connections between immigration and the other political, economic, and social issues and trends that may be more responsive than rates of immigration are to public policy. Our aim is not to provide definitive answers but to introduce hitherto little-remarked international and intersectoral dimensions into the public immigration debate. Evaluation of these concerns may well lay beyond the expertise of scholars and policymakers of any one academic disciplinary background, suggesting in turn the need to make our scholarly/activist approach ever more broadly multidisciplinary, a goal toward which this book represents just one step.

The decisions taken by leading U.S. bureaucrats and the executive and legislative branches of the U.S. government have effects that resonate in the lives of people overseas, who may number several times more than the entire United States population. U.S. influence, in setting people in motion and in shaping the circumstances under which they leave home and cross international borders, goes well beyond immigration policy per se. On issue after issue, the United States—albeit at times with even altruistic intent—has in recent decades exerted the wrong kind of influence, as judged from the vantage point of working people struggling for a means to escape poverty, attain greater security of life and livelihood, and aspire to the comforts of an advanced industrial way of life, things which U.S. citizens tend to take for granted. As food price subsidies and tariffs that protect local industries are eliminated and spending on education and state-provided health care is slashed, in the name of freeing markets, food producers and factory workers in their thousands are displaced from secure employment and many of them swell the ranks of the world's international migrants. Promoting militarized responses to crises, of illicit drug production, terrorism, refugee flows, and minority rights movements, only produces more people whose only hope for survival and peace lies away from their home places. Like the proverbial miner's canary, the plight of the world's international migrants today gives signs that we inhabit a toxic political and economic world order. Can U.S. leadership be held accountable for what it is and is not doing to improve this state of affairs? At fewer than 300 million people, U.S. citizens are a relatively small fraction of the world's people. Yet they potentially wield a hugely disproportionate influence over the fate of the world's other billions, through their democratic right to reshape U.S. policy in a human rights mold. What faces them is not the alternative of either blaming the United States for all human rights crises around the world or resigning themselves to all aspects of international migration being part of a global pattern beyond any government's influence. Instead, a middle ground can be found in which U.S. policies are judged first and foremost according to their potential for enhancing and assuring the livelihoods and chances of survival of millions in the affected countries. The aim would not be to discourage immigration (people who are climbing the social and economic ladder are as much prime candidates for international migration as those who are experiencing economic and political instability) but rather to enable immigration of the kinds and numbers judged necessary. Both moral judgment and broad calculation of self-interest suggest that U.S. workers stand to gain from an international order under which immigrants can exercise real choice about when to emigrate and under whose auspices they will travel, can cross our borders safely and with dignity, and can live in the United States free of fear, coercion and unacceptable exploitation or conditions of work.

Afterword

Migration, Human Rights, and Development

Carole Nagengast

On 18 May 2006, Moisés Cruz Sánchez, age forty-five, was shot to death by two still officially unidentified gunman as he emerged from a café with his wife in the town of San Juan Mixtepec in the southern Mexican state of Oaxaca. As of spring 2007, nobody had been arrested nor did there appear to be an open investigation. Moisés Cruz was a Mixtec, a member of one of Oaxaca's sixteen indigenous groups. Mixtec-speakers live in hundreds of towns and villages in the Mixteca region of Oaxaca and most govern themselves according to customary indigenous law *[usos y costumbres]*, as provided in the Oaxacan Constitution. Huge numbers of Mixtec speakers are among the millions of Mexicans, many of them without papers, who have migrated to the United States. They have left their home communities for broad structural reasons having to do with the global expansion of the market economy and the highly segmented labor market in both Mexico and the United States. Paradoxically, U.S. and Mexican foreign and domestic policies have contributed to poverty and lack of economic opportunities in Oaxaca, indeed throughout Mexico (see Massey in chapter 1; Besserer 1999; Gil 2006; and Nagengast, Stavenhagen, and Kearney 1992), hastening the departure of large numbers of migrants, especially from rural areas.

Moisés Cruz was much concerned with the effects of massive migration on the personal well-being and human rights of his family, friends, and neighbors of his hometown of San Juan Mixtepec, and he worked tirelessly to defend them against those who would exploit them on both sides of the border. He was also deeply concerned about the development of his community and served it as municipal president and in other positions in the indigenous cargo system that is so well known to anthropologists. He also assumed activist roles in several binational organizations of indigenous

Oaxacans in the United States and in Mexico. These include El Frente Mixteco Zapoteco Binacional, La Asociación Benito Juárez, El Comité de Defensa Popular Mixteca, El Centro de Desarrollo Rural Indígena, and La Red Internacional de Indígenas Oaxaqueños (Besserer 1999). Cruz was an active member of the Partido de la Revolución Democrática (PRD), the prominent national political party of the Mexican left that in the presidential election of 2006 posed a serious but ultimately unsuccessful bid to unseat the neoliberal National Action Party (PAN). It was no doubt because of his outspokenness and visibility around development and human rights and against corruption in Mexico that Moisés Cruz was assassinated. However, his was truly a binational existence and activism and he is sorely missed on both sides of the border.

In this afterword I focus my remarks on two main concerns taken up by Moisés Cruz: the violation of migrants' human rights and how the policies that cause those violations contribute to development in the United States and, less systematically but no less importantly, to de-development in Oaxaca, Mexico. The latter is in spite of the significant contribution made to the economy of Mexico by migrant dollars, some $13.2 billion in 2003 (Orozco 2004). I conclude by offering some concrete steps academics, concerned U.S. citizens, and policymakers can take to help migrants, whether from Mexico or elsewhere, to protect their human rights in the United States, even if the systemic changes Douglas Massey recommends in chapter 1 to all migrant receiving countries are not immediately realized.

DEVELOPMENT AND MIGRATION: INTERNATIONAL STANDARDS

The United Nations 1986 Declaration on the Right to Development specifies that human persons, not nation-states, should be the central subject of development and the active beneficiary of development.[1] The Declaration also reinforces the idea that *sustainable* development occurs only through respect for and protection of human rights. As for migration, a 2004 United Nations resolution on the topic takes it as given that migration brings many (largely unacknowledged) benefits to receiving countries as well as to migrants, their families, and their communities of origin.[2]

International law also provides an "International Convention on the Protection of the Rights of All Migrant Workers and Members of Their Families" (ICMW).[3] The ICMW was adopted in 1990 and entered into force in 2003. It has been ratified by thirty-four countries, including Mexico and many other migrant-sending nation states, but neither the United

States nor other migrant receiving states in the northern hemisphere have ratified it. The Convention starts with the principle that all migrants, regardless of their legal status in the country of residence, are entitled to certain fundamental rights (see "What Rights Do Migrants Have?" in the introduction to this volume). It guarantees equality of treatment and working conditions for migrants. It specifies that migrants, regardless of legal status, enjoy basic freedoms, due process, and the right to privacy, and it guarantees such things as migrants' right to transfer their earnings and their right to information about their rights. Even though the United States has not ratified the Migrant Convention, it has ratified the International Covenant on Civil and Political Rights and other core human rights treaties.[4] These international agreements make few or no distinctions between the rights enjoyed by citizens and noncitizens.[5] Therefore legal scholars agree that the Convention on the Rights of Migrants applies equally to regular and irregular migrant workers—that is, those with and without legal documentation.

I do not know if Moisés Cruz was aware of the United Nations declarations, conventions, and legal definitions of migrant rights and development or, if he did, whether he thought them relevant to the situations he and his fellow migrants and activists faced and continue to face on both sides of the border. To be sure, international law may reflect the hegemony of Western Enlightenment philosophies that migrant workers from the global South might not view as completely relevant to their predicaments. However, I have a hard time thinking that migrant workers would take exception to the provisions of the ICMW. The Web pages of binational migrant associations often contain links to the Universal Declaration of Human Rights and to international human rights nongovernmental organizations like Amnesty International and Human Rights Watch. To the degree that human rights are recognized and enacted both through their legal and formal definitions and through the action of ordinary people everywhere, they define what people find acceptable or not in various realms of their material, social, cultural, and economic lives. As such human rights are a sign of the ethical standards that guide peoples' existence. Ideally human rights are also reflected in government policies at the local, regional, national, and international level, but this turns out to be rarely the case. Even in states with a strong liberal tradition, a strong judiciary and a fundamental commitment to individual liberties, the human rights of migrants are not well protected. If anything, average people in the global north have been encouraged to think that migrants have few rights in a receiving country.

MEXICO AND U.S. TRADE POLICIES

With these general ideas about migrant human rights as a preamble, let us now turn to a brief consideration of Mexico's role in the global economy and the part the United States played in creating that situation. While some Americans are angered that so many illegal migrants are working in the United States, critics of U.S. and Mexican economic policy say these policies created the exodus in the first place. Starting in the early 1980s, the United States mandated Mexico's adoption of the neoliberal model of privatization, free trade, and fiscal austerity as the price for U.S. investment in Mexico. In some respects (currency stabilization, low inflation and interest rates, a trade surplus with the United States, and a more or less balanced budget) Mexico's economy did well in the ensuing years. In other respects, however, neoliberalism was disastrous. Adjusting for inflation, Mexico's gross domestic product and net job creation have been flat for more than twenty years, and the costs to the country's poor and middle class have been staggering (Dickerson 2006).

Migrants have been coming to the United States from Mexico for decades, but the mass influx that now numbers close to twelve million only started in earnest in the mid-1990s. Economists cite a variety of economic and demographic factors that fueled the accelerating tide, but most agree that the 1994 North American Free Trade Agreement (NAFTA), which opened Mexico's markets to subsidized U.S. agriculture, was the largest contributor.[6]

Thirty percent of Mexican farm jobs were lost as a direct result of NAFTA, a figure that translates into 2.8 million farmers and many millions more family members. Entire villages in the Mixteca region of Oaxaca, where San Juan Mixtepec is located, have been demographically decimated as *campesinos* (peasant farmers) flocked to Mexico's cities (Kearney 1996; Besserer 2004). Today, more than half of the country's 106 million people live in dire poverty. Half of the labor force—20 million people—work in the informal economy as day laborers, street vendors, unauthorized taxi drivers, and the like. The drafters of NAFTA knew that the poorest of the poor would be adversely affected but expected that many of the displaced campesinos would find jobs in then growing maquiladora industries, which produce for the export market. Those jobs never materialized in part because the competition for maquila jobs was immense to begin with and because as the 1990s progressed the maquilas faced ever-increasing competition from China. Global capital and jobs move easily; workers do not.[7]

Neoliberal policies simply were not able to deliver the jobs to poor

Mexicans in the numbers needed. While investments were supposed to have been made in Mexico's rural areas that would have provided new incentives for potential migrants, these too lagged way behind. Even though migrant remittances have injected billions of dollars into rural Mexico, the largest part has been used to improve the infrastructure of towns (e.g., to build roads and houses) but little to build the productive base. Towns and pueblos in the Mixteca region of Oaxaca like San Juan Mixtepec (Besserer 2004), San Jerónimo Progreso (Kearney 1996), and Santa María Tindú (Gil 2006) have been hollowed out as huge numbers of working-age people go north, many to return only occasionally for ritual occasions or men for a year at a time to fulfill civic or religious obligations.

Because of the increased dangers of crossing the border and because schools in the Mixteca are extremely poorly financed and staffed and typically only go to the sixth grade, most often Mixtec women and children remain in the United States to work and attend school during the periodic absence of men,[8] even once corn-, bean-, and squash-producing land lies fallow. In short, the net affect of NAFTA thus far has been to contribute to the de-development of rural Mexico (Dickerson 2006).

Pamela Starr, a Latin American analyst for the Washington-based Eurasia Group, says that it is disingenuous for the United States to invoke NAFTA policy to require small Mexican farmers to compete with American farmers who are heavily subsidized by the government. "An essential part of any migration program designed to reduce the flow [of illegal migrants] needs to have U.S. efforts to help Mexico develop its own economy. The U.S. has two options; It can import Mexican goods, or it can import Mexican workers."[9]

UNDOCUMENTED WORKERS IN THE UNITED STATES

Let us now turn to the United States, the top migrant receiving country in the world (United Nations 2002). The essays in this volume ably detail and discuss U.S. immigration policy and what appears to be its often-unfair application (see especially the chapters by Salyer, Gabany-Guerrero, Chavez, and Naples). In short, migrants past and present have suffered disproportionately for seeking and finding jobs in the United States. Nonetheless, and in spite of significant attention to their plight in mainstream media, there is widespread public opposition to irregular migrants and a growing call for a new immigration policy that heavily penalizes those who violate its provisions, as Chavez discusses in chapter 4.

Without attributing causality, it is important to point out that there are some negative social and economic consequences to citizens and legal residents of unregulated migration. These include increasing social stratification and the intensification of labor market segmentation, the effects of which may be exacerbated when there are large and increasing numbers of irregular migrants (United Nations 2002: 36, para.120–21; 120, para.400). Migrants may indeed depress the wages of local workers, although this mostly affects high school dropouts who are already in the lowest paying, low-skill occupations (ibid.: 32, para.109). Migrants with irregular status may constitute unfair competition for regular workers, provoking resentment and endangering social cohesion. Finally, in the worst cases migrants may enter the underground economy or become involved in criminal activities.

In spite of these serious problems, to which there are no easy solutions, study after study suggests that labor migration has long been important to development in the United States. While migrants make up less than 11 percent of the population, they constitute more than 14 percent of the labor force and more than 20 percent of the lowest paid workers (Urban Institute 2003: 1). Migrants have generated significant growth in both the population and the labor force since 1990, thus providing a strong driving force to the economy.

About 60 percent of irregular migrants in the United States are from Mexico. They are employed in animal slaughter and processing; as sewing machine operators; in manufacturing, landscaping, and construction; and in restaurant and other service-sector jobs. Of course they continue to work in agriculture in large numbers. The industries that rely on irregular migrants often violate wage, hour, and overtime payment laws, as has been well documented in this volume and elsewhere (see, e.g., Passel, Capps, and Fix 2004). A 2000 U.S. Department of Labor Survey found that 100 percent of poultry processing plants that employed irregular workers, mostly in the South, did not comply with federal wage and hours laws. Half the garment manufacturing businesses in New York City were out of compliance with Fair Labor Standards and remarkably few agricultural enterprises strictly obey the law. Further, irregular workers often work in extremely dangerous jobs, with minimal or no compliance with safety standards. A 2004 study found that thousands of irregular migrants are hurt every day at work and that a Mexican migrant worker dies every single day on the job because of unsafe conditions (Pritchard 2004).

In sum, irregular migrants work longer, harder, and under harsher conditions and for far lower wages and fewer benefits than native-born North American workers or legal immigrants can or will. The average income per person born in the United States was $24,000 in 2005; a legal migrant averaged $20,000, while an unauthorized migrant earned but $12,000 (Passel, Capps, and Fix 2004: 69).

Contrary to popular belief in the United States, by far the largest portion of the migrant population is employed, does not engage in criminal activities, and does not tap into the welfare system. Of the some 12 million irregular migrants in the United States, almost eight million, or two-thirds, are workers and the rest are mostly children and women who care for children at home. As for providing education to the children of irregular migrants or health care and pensions to the elderly, the children of irregular migrants are *already* the poorest educated of all children in the United States. Forty-seven percent of migrant children drop out of school before finishing middle school (ninth grade); the majority enter the work force between the ages of fourteen and sixteen because their families need the wages (Fry 2005; Passel 2006). While clearly some migrant children finish high school and some go to college in spite of the hardships they and their families face, it is not always easy to understand Americans who regard this a bad rather than a good thing, other than supposing that migrants take places in college that would otherwise go to their children. There is no evidence to support this supposition.

Many Americans believe that migrants exhaust the medical system. Migrants must be young and healthy to do the work they do, they generally do not suffer as many long-term chronic illnesses as do native-born citizens and therefore use fewer medical services than most native born. But because migrant families are on the average young and women are in their prime childbearing years, and they rarely have medical insurance of any kind, babies are often born in emergency rooms. Migrants also receive medical care for acute illnesses in emergency rooms. That is a function of poverty and not legal status. Finally, less than 1 percent of all irregular migrants, a statistically insignificant number, collect social security or old age pensions. On the contrary, huge numbers of irregular migrants contribute millions of dollars every year in taxes withheld to a social security system from which they will never reap benefits (Passel 2006).

There is very suggestive evidence to indicate that migrants rejuvenate declining industrial areas throughout the United States and elsewhere in the global North. They introduce new life and commercial enterprises; they introduce diversity and often a new tax base. They also meet labor shortages and help prevent inflation by increasing demand for goods and services. They supply skills that are locally in short supply, and they provide incentives for capital accumulation and thus create new jobs (ILO

2004: 30, para.104 & 31, para.108). For example, there is good evidence that regular and irregular migration to the Los Angeles area has had just such advantageous effects since 1990 (Streitfield 2006).

Finally, the Texas Comptroller reported in December 2006 that the 1.4 million undocumented immigrants in Texas provide a net economic gain to that state, generating more revenue for the state than the state spends on them to provide services. "This is the first time any state has done a comprehensive financial analysis of the impact of undocumented immigrants on a state's budget and economy," says Texas State Comptroller Carole Keeton Strayhorn, "looking at gross state product, revenues generated, taxes paid and the cost of state services." The report concludes that the 1.4 million undocumented immigrants in Texas in FY 2005 contributed $17.7 billion to the gross state product of Texas, and that undocumented immigrants produced $1.58 billion in state revenues, exceeding by nearly half a billion dollars the $1.16 billion they received in state services.[10]

In sum, the evidence on the effects of regular and irregular migration on the United States is mixed, but it does suggest that migrants bring significant financial, social, and cultural development to the entire U.S. economy and that the benefits outweigh the disadvantages (ILO 2004: 35–36, paras.116–119). If this is true, then government officials might want to protect migrants' fundamental human rights not only to adhere to international law but also to enhance development in the United States.

Nonetheless, when confronted with evidence of what migrants contribute to the economy and the human rights abuses committed against them, many North American politicians, media pundits, and citizens resort to conversation stoppers, such as "We can't reward people who break the law," or "The better treatment we give them, the more of them will come." Even though problematic assumptions underlie these statements (as discussed by Naples, Chavez, and other contributors to this volume), many Americans want to penalize the men, women, and children who pick their fruit, build their houses, and wash their dishes. They say they want more of those jobs to go to the native-born unemployed and more of the money now being used to educate and provide health care for migrants to go towards their own pensions, to provide health insurance for their own children, and to improve their own lives. Further, many citizens around the country have voted to implement laws that are intended to deny social benefits and health care to migrants who are unable to produce proof of legal status. Some seek to expel the children of migrants from schools and prevent their parents from renting or buying houses. Texas now has a bill before its legislature that would decrease or even deny social benefit to children born in the United States to irregular migrants. After Colorado state law targeted undocumented workers, growers found that the resulting farm worker exodus left crops rotting in the fields. Colorado is now drawing on convict labor to bring in harvests on private farms, a solution that is surely short-term.

Should immigration restrictionists—who want to penalize the workers rather than seek structural reform—get what they wish for, serious economic problems would result. If the border were even more stringently policed, it is unclear who would clean those chickens or wash those dishes, unless we imagine that poultry farms and packaging plants will go out of business and the jobs exported. That would not bring local advantage to anyone in the United States. We have already seen that migrants use a disproportionately low percentage of social welfare dollars and bring large benefits to the United States. With 12 million of them, they also have a lot of buying power in the areas in which they live.

WHY CITIZENS ARE ANTIMIGRANT

The United States is faced with a perceived need to choose among alternatives many find unattractive: deporting the lot of them and damn the consequences, instituting a guest worker program, or stretching the law to fit economic convenience. However, Massey in chapter 1 argues convincingly that international migration is virtually inevitable in a global economy. I would like to make a few general observations about the American economic system, which I think skews popular perceptions such that citizens and policy makers perceive only problems where they might see opportunities.

First, at least until late 2008 the American economy seemed to be booming. The stock market was up and the unemployment rate was down. While all seemed well economically, there have been disturbing signs for some time visible to those who cared to look. For example, the 2007 *Forbes Report* indicated that largely as a result of economic shifts associated with globalism, the richest 400 people in the United States now have more than $1 billion each. Together, this small group controls total assets of $1.25 trillion. This, *Forbes* points out, represents a sizable increase in the amount of income and wealth controlled by ever fewer people.[11] At the same time, there are also huge and growing numbers of poor people as income from labor has been replaced by income from profits, which has been distributed from low-wage workers to high wage earners. If the *income* of the United States is divided into thirds, the top 10 percent owns one-third; the second third is controlled by the next 30 percent; the bottom 60 percent owns the final third. If the *wealth* of the country is divided into similar thirds, the wealthiest 1 percent own one-third, the next wealthiest 9 percent own the second third, and the poorest 90 percent have the final third (Schweickart 2002).

Whatever the exact figures, it is widely recognized that the traditional middle class, the great bulge in the middle, the so-called backbone of the United States, has shrunk dramatically over the past several decades. The median annual gross salary in the United States was about $24,000 per worker in 2004 ($43,000 for a family), a sum that no longer allows a middle-class life style in most parts of the country. For example, with respect to the conversion of publicly subsidized housing in New York City from rent-protected status that once catered to teachers, firefighters, and artists to expensive luxury apartments, a real-estate broker is quoted as saying, "Middle class has changed from being teachers and policemen to being white-collar sales and managerial junior-partner type jobs. If you are making $200,000 a year in New York—and nowadays that's middle class—you can well afford to be paying [the projected] $4,500 a month in housing costs" (Hamilton 2006). Teachers, nurses, and firefighters can no longer afford a middle-class live style in New York or other large cities.

The upward distribution of income in the United States has largely been driven by deliberate policy decisions. Dean Baker (2006) of the Center for Economic and Policy Research argues that both trade and immigration policies intentionally subject workers at the middle and lower ends of the wage distribution to international competition, while leaving the highest paid workers protected. Many once-middle-class jobs have been exported, a result of both policy decisions and globalization, as Samuel Martínez discusses in his introduction to this volume. The middle class has been scooped out, and as jobs have been exported, fewer and fewer people are finding employment that allows middle range life styles. It is not so much that migrants take jobs that Americans will not do; it is that they take jobs Americans once held and which once enabled them to live middle-class lives, but no longer allow that lifestyle because they have been down-graded in terms of wages and working conditions.

My second observation that seeks to explain or at least contextualize citizen enthusiasm for penalizing migrants has to do with health care. The soaring cost of health care disproportionately affects lower- and middle-income workers. A majority of the nine million native-born children in the United States who are now without medical insurance come from what we used to call the working class. That is, they have at least one parent who is employed full-time. Nonetheless, their working parent cannot afford health care premiums (Mendoza 2006).[12] Thus native-born poor and working-class people and migrants, also poor and working class, use emergency rooms to treat acute illnesses that should be treated in medical clinics and they compete for ever scarcer Medicaid dollars.

Third, many older North American workers who thought they would have retirement packages are being told their pensions have been canceled. Fewer and fewer middle class jobs have health insurance associated with them and many people are being told that if they want to keep their present positions they must take pay cuts. Many have taken such cuts.

Finally, since September 2001 U.S. citizens have been afraid of another terrorist attack. This fear was worsened by later attacks in London, Madrid, and elsewhere, and no doubt by an ever-increasing sense of insecurity as a result of the U.S. war in Iraq and the larger "Global War on Terror." As the numbers of American and Iraqi dead and wounded mount, there is dread in the air. The influx of drugs and even the possibility that terrorists might enter across the southern border intensify that dread. Since 9/11 the overall level of xenophobia in the United States has been on the rise. A good deal of it is directed toward those perceived to be "Arabs," Muslims, or from the Middle East generally, and toward anyone with dark skin who speaks English with an accent (see chapters 3 and 5 by Salyer and Akram and Johnson, respectively). Much of it spills over to Latinos. Residents of the border region say that the U.S. Constitution has been implicitly suspended as Border Patrol agents enter and search peoples' houses without warrants, stop drivers and pedestrians at will, verbally and sometimes physically abuse brown-skinned people—some citizens and some not. Intimidation has created a general sense of anxiety and unease, they say, in Spanish-speaking communities, especially in the southwest (Nagengast 2002).[13]

The U.S. Congress did not pass an immigration bill in 2006 for political reasons, but it did authorize a new 700-mile long wall. The militarization of the border has been stepped up as additional National Guard troops armed with M-16 automatic rifles have been deployed. It is hard to predict future Congressional action, but there may not be in the near future any regularization of immigration status for those migrants already here. Nor is there in sight a guest-worker program or additional safeguards to protect workers from exploitation and abuses. In other words, it is likely to be business as usual, at least for the foreseeable future. Migrants will come; some will be captured and sent back, but enough will get through to bring in the harvests, pluck the chickens, and keep the construction industries going. The government does not have the will to regulate the comings and

goings of migrants, perhaps because many politicians implicitly understand the relation between a poorly regulated low-wage sector, increasing
development, and human rights abuses. Or as Josiah Heyman argues in
chapter 2, increased border surveillance may be masking social discomfort
with the fuzziness of the U.S.-Mexican border.

There may also be a link between the war on migrants and the so-called
war on terrorism in the United States. Fearful citizens strike out at the clos-
est targets because they have not been educated to look beyond media representations (see chapter 4 by Leo Chavez). They have not learned to search for
the causes of international migration, terrorism, and human rights abuses.
The U.S. Congress agreed with President George W. Bush in September
2006 when he said the United States needs "a new kind of thinking" to
combat what his administration has defined as a growing terrorist threat.
Terrorists, some of our political leaders say, are people who hate democracy.
Therefore, even in the face of Supreme Court rulings to the contrary, it
has been made legal in the United States to subject people who have been
defined as unlawful enemy combatants to treatment that, while harsh, falls
short—at least it was claimed until the Obama administration began releasing the details of the previous administration's practices in 2009—of cruel,
inhuman, and degrading treatment and torture. Human Rights and civil
liberties organizations were deeply skeptical, and for good reason, it turns
out.[14] Moreover, according to a study published in the *Archives of General
Psychiatry*, the effects of psychological torture and "moderate pressure"
are as severe and long lasting as physical torture (Bakalar 2007). Not only
is brutal and ruthless treatment of foreign prisoners deemed acceptable
by the United States, there is also a presumption of guilt rather than an
assumption of innocence implied in this, as, for example, when Congress
agreed by a narrow vote to the acceptability of holding people indefinitely
in detention camps, such as at the U.S. base in Guantánamo. As of this
writing some have already been held without charge for years. If and when
prisoners are brought to trial, they may be denied access to evidence against
them. The U.S. government has made violations of essential human rights
acceptable and raised them to the level of appropriate tools of democracy. It
is unclear how much popular support there is in the United States for these
abridgements of fundamental human and civil rights and international
law. Douglas Massey, quoting Joppke (1998b), points out in chapter 1 that
a strong liberal tradition of human rights and individual freedoms is not
sufficient to protect any foreigners from the depredations of an oppressive
state unless there is a strong and independent judiciary. Even that would
appear to be insufficient in this case.

As the syndicated columnist Rosa Brooks (2006) said in a somewhat different context, "If a hammer is your only tool, then everything looks like a nail." Governments everywhere often fail to address the problems of ordinary people with anything *but* a hammer. Both the "War on Terror" and low-intensity conflict being waged in the United States against "illegal immigration," are being lost because national leaders ignore scholars who tell them that approaching either phenomenon purely as a act of aggression can only worsen the root causes—which are mainly political in the case of terrorism and economic in the case of unauthorized immigration—and create an international crisis where one did not earlier exist (Richardson 2006)

WHAT TO DO

I contend that migrant workers embody the fear many middle- and working-class American people feel: fear of terrorists, fear of crime, fear for their jobs, but most especially fear that their very way of life is imperiled; that all the aspects of U.S. middle/working class life that they believe America is founded on are at risk. Those who might have once aspired to the middle class see that possibility increasingly curtailed. Migrants seem to be a proximate cause and citizens want to combat their presence in tangible ways, compared to the more nebulous and un-addressable fears they have about job security and rising health costs. I am sympathetic to those who are frustrated by the large numbers of irregular migrants in the United States. However, I also think that those in positions of power who have little interest in laws that are uniformly applied to employers and migrants or little concern with fundamental human rights have distorted the issues quite deliberately and pitted ordinary relatively poor people against other ordinary poor people.

The governments of the world, U.S. and Mexican included, use a hammer to address human rights perhaps because it has served their purpose in the past and they do not know how to use more subtle tools; or perhaps because the problems are so immense. Or perhaps, it is good for global business to maintain a hierarchical society with a few at the top fully protected and many at the bottom without any protection at all.

I read in the newspapers that former Mexican President Vicente Fox talked often with President George W. Bush, and so too did Felipe Calderón, who took office in late 2006. Together, the two leaders continued to address "illegal immigration" to the United States. Notice how they frame the issues. They talk more about "illegal immigration" than they do about why so many people migrate in the first place. The neoliberal model of development is their unmarked category and therefore it is not subject to discussion. They do not talk of the problems of people who migrate to the United States, with or without papers; they do not talk of the problems of North Americans who work full-time, yet are unable to afford health care for their families, or save for their retirement years. They certainly do not discuss at any length the problems of communities such as San Juan Mixtepec and hundreds of others much like it that migrants leave behind in Mexico. Having only hammers, they see only nails. It is unclear as of this writing whether the new U.S. president will be able to address immigration any differently in the face of a global economic crisis and renewed attention to military action in Afghanistan.

Moisés Cruz, the Mixtec activist whose story opened this essay, in seeking human rights and development for the people of San Juan Mixtepec, challenged the hammer by asking how indigenous communities can promote development such that their sons and daughters do not have to leave in droves, many of them never to return. We all need to find ways of influencing local, state and national policy in our own communities, states, and countries such that it examines the very roots of the problems migrants face, rather than blaming migrants for policy decisions made at the highest levels.

As we seek answers to higher-level questions, we also need to discover what we can do as citizens to insure that migrant workers are better able to protect themselves from human rights abuses. I offer ten suggestions. These practical steps to promote citizen activism and legislation that protects migrant workers are based on documents from the Platform for International Cooperation on Irregular Migrants (PICUM 2005).

TEN WAYS TO PROTECT MIGRANT WORKERS

1. Acknowledge the social and economic presence of undocumented migrants and engage public support through events and consumer campaigns.   Migrants, especially those without legal papers, are too often thought of as taking advantage of welfare and causing native workers to become unemployed. Changing the unfavorable image of migrants and gaining public support is vital in protecting their rights. Activists can insure that policy makers acknowledge the actual presence of undocumented migrants, as well as the structural implications of their presence—their buying power, the taxes they pay, their social and cultural contributions to the community, their contributions to the social security system, and the necessary work they do. Denying the structural importance of undocumented migrants leads to ineffective social, employment and migration policies.

2. Prioritize the collection of data. Migration, employment, social welfare and of course border policies are often developed in the absence of concrete qualitative and quantitative data. To develop genuine policies in the fields of migration, integration, and employment, it is important that policy makers and the general public understand who undocumented migrants are, what they do, why they leave their country, why they return and how they survive on both sides of the border. It is also important that policy makers understand the social impact of policies they enact on both sending and receiving countries.

3. Involve local organizations in conducting research and making policies. The collection of information on undocumented people is difficult because they are often reluctant to talk about their situation. Local organizations that provide assistance to irregular migrants on a daily basis are important partners for researchers. Based on their expertise, local organizations should be asked for input about research priorities and the dissemination of research results. Local organizations' expertise is also critical to policy makers but is rarely sought. Collected data need to be located centrally, electronically if possible. They also need to be presented in venues and in forms completely accessible to policy makers, the general citizenry, and migrants themselves.

4. Inform migrants about their rights and safeguard their right to equality before the law. Migrants often are unaware that even if they do not have legal documentation to be in a country, they have certain rights, most essentially the right to equality before the law. Unaware of their rights, they often do not challenge abusive or exploitative employers. Informing workers of their rights and ways in which they can be protected from arbitrary repatriation is a step towards ending the silent suffering. The right to equality before the law is a universal human right. To deny people the right to defend themselves renders claims to any other right problematic. If irregular migrants were informed of their rights and had the means to enforce those rights legally, employer incentives to exploit migrants would be reduced. There should be no risk of deportation if an undocumented worker files an official complaint against his or her employer and the immigration status of a complainant should not affect any decision taken by a judge or jury. Undocumented migrants are understandably reluctant to turn to government agencies for help. Nevertheless, most agencies are not legally entitled to ask about workers' status when they try to uphold fair working conditions. An accompanying advocate can insure that agencies do not ask inappropriate questions

5. *Mediation and migrants' rights in the legal system.* Collective actions and mediation launched by immigrant rights groups may be sometimes useful in upholding migrants' rights. When other means of protecting irregular workers' rights are unsuccessful, workers can file official collective claims through legal channels. This is difficult, time consuming and challenging, and therefore not the first choice of action, but there have been some legal rulings in Europe and the United States in favor of irregular migrants.

6. *Build capacities through empowerment.* In order to prevent and stop exploitation and abuse, workers must be able to exercise their rights effectively. Working with migrant groups and helping leaders enhance their capacities counteracts a system of dependency. Workers need to be able to defend themselves and engage in and influence the policy-making that affects their lives. Asserting one's rights is a major challenge for a person working alone. Unionizing migrants, especially irregular workers, is important in countries where it is possible. This is difficult in the United States, where unions have in recent decades been under attack and in decline, but a few unions have managed to enhance protection of irregular migrants. Generally speaking, unions are stronger in Europe and other countries in the Americas.

7. *Work with employers to prevent exploitation and advocate laws that hold them accountable to fair labor standards. Institute regular workplace inspection.* One way to prevent violations of migrants' rights in the workplace is to approach employers. There are several successful examples of organizations that invite—and sometimes pressure—employers to respect minimum standards of employment. But legal measures that hold employers accountable if they exploit or abuse employees are also needed. This brings us to workplace inspection. The overwhelming focus in policy debates and enforcement is the supply side, as if there was no demand for undocumented labor. Authorities need to shift the focus from border control and to invest more on workplace inspection. Irregular workers are attractive to some employers because they are not protected and find it difficult to complain against exploitative conditions. The chance that an employer will be caught and penalized for exploiting irregular workers is small compared to the potential profits they gain by hiring them. Governments must implement laws penalizing employers who exploit and abuse workers and evade their responsibilities towards them.

8. *Regularize undocumented migrants.* Society as a whole benefits

from reducing the number of people living outside of the system. By regularizing migrants, the government can incorporate people into society rather than leaving them subject to exploitation and illegal practices that violate their human rights. Regularizing workers also regularizes jobs, thus more contributions are brought into the social welfare system. Finally, regularizing undocumented workers combats the informal economy and stops the deterioration of general working conditions, which in the end affects *all* workers.

9. Open the debate on the future of the low-wage sector. Regularizing migrants is not the only solution. Experience suggests that when one group of irregular workers is legalized, new ones replace them. This is because a number of industries depend on a cheap and vulnerable workforce. This cannot be addressed only by regularizing some workers. Policy makers need to think about *why* the low-wage sector relies heavily on irregular migrants and what can be done about *that*.

10. Ratify the International Migrant Workers Convention. The United States needs to ratify the 1990 International Convention for the Protection of the Rights of All Migrant Workers and the Members of Their Families (ICMW), which guarantees various social rights to undocumented migrant workers. So does Mexico. So do all countries. And after they have ratified this Convention, each country needs to put into place the enabling legislation to protect the rights contained in it.

These are just some of the things that those of us who are citizens or legal residents can do to work with migrants and migrant communities in our own and other countries.

Notes

MARTÍNEZ, INTRODUCTION

1. http://www.migrantwatch.org/.

2. To name just a few outstanding studies and edited volumes on migration policy, see Cornelius, Martin, and Hollifield 1994; Freeman 1994; Joppke 1998a and 1998b; Massey et al. 1998; and Meyers 2004

3. Intensified efforts to prohibit unauthorized immigration at particularly heavily transited points of the U.S.-Mexico border began in 1993, in the El Paso Border Patrol section through Operation Hold the Line, followed the next year by Operation Gatekeeper in San Diego (Eschbach, Hagan, and Rodríguez 2003). These initiatives had the intended purpose of raising the cost of crossing the border by sealing off the most accessible channels. Surveillance by Border Patrol agents intensified, aided by night vision cameras, ground sensors, and other advanced technology, along with the construction of new fences along the border (Nagengast 1998).

4. Even as the intention of the border buildup was obvious—to dissuade unauthorized immigration by driving up the monetary and human costs of crossing the border—its aggregate effects have been counterintuitive. In addition to the negative effects on migrant mortality and debt already mentioned, Jorge Durand and Douglas Massey (2003, see also Massey, Durand, and Malone 2002) find that unauthorized immigrants are much sooner frightened away from *returning* to their home countries than dissuaded from entering the United States in the first place. One unintended effect of heightened border policing, then, has been to convert what was a circulating group, among whom even the undocumented made frequent return trips home, into a largely stationary population, thus increasing rather than diminishing the number of unauthorized workers in the United States. As more unauthorized workers enter and fewer return home, the immigrant population has also spread geographically in search of new economic niches, generating another unintended effect, the nationalization of an unauthorized immigrant population that previously was found mainly in three states, California, Texas, and Illinois.

5. In their introduction to the second edition of this book, Wayne Cornelius and Takeyuki Tsuda (2004: 13) sustain much the same argument.

6. Gary Freeman (1994) concludes that liberal democracies choose not to use their unprecedented technical capacity and bureaucratic resources to control immigration, largely because political leaders find it expedient to bow to the pressure against harsh control measures exerted by businesses and immigrant communities and their advocates. Christian Joppke (1998b) takes issue with Freeman's conclusion mainly by asserting that going easy on immigration is not a political decision so much as a judicial imposition: any legislative concession to anti-immigrant sentiment is rapidly knocked down by courts upholding the rights of immigrants to government services and due process. While placing primary emphasis on pressures emanating from global economic integration, even the leftist world-systems analyst Saskia Sassen (1996: ch.3) argues that international human rights standards impose an external constraint on the discretion of states to exclude noncitizens from their territories.

7. A similar employment eligibility verification system, E-Verify, was inaugurated for voluntary employer use in 2008. That system is like the Social Security Administration (SSA) "no-match" letter system, which was placed on indefinite hold in 2007, in that E-Verify involves checking employee-provided identification information against SSA records. E-Verify differs in having been rolled out initially as a voluntary program and in its being intended for use only to verify new hires' employment eligibility rather than as a regulation that obligated employers to rid themselves of existing employees whose work eligibility could not be confirmed. Court challenges are pending as this book goes to press.

8. http://www.dhs.gov/xnews/releases/press_release_0890.shtml; http://www.ice.gov/partners/287g/Section287_g.htm.

2. HEYMAN, PORTS OF ENTRY

1. Speech to the Central Business Association of El Paso, 10 March 2004. I should note, however, that I did this research and wrote this passage prior to the intensification of the national moral panic over "illegal immigration" in 2005–6. It may well be that immigration has risen within the balance of securitized issues since that time.

2. I thank my research collaborator, Patrick Gurian, for drawing this to my attention.

3. While we cannot explore this at length in this chapter, there is a history of the U.S. government's making policy to this effect (for example, in 1989 the Secretary of Defense declared drug interdiction to be a "high priority national security mission" [Dunn 1996: 124]).

3. SALYER, THE TREATMENT OF NONCITIZENS AFTER 9/11

1. For instance, in ruling that Bush administration's policy of holding immigration hearings in secret was unconstitutional, the United States Court

of Appeals for the Sixth Circuit stated, "The Executive Branch seeks to uproot people's lives, outside the public eye, and behind a closed door. . . . Democracies die behind closed doors. The First Amendment, through a free press, protects the people's right to know that their government acts fairly, lawfully, and accurately in deportation proceedings." *Detroit Free Press v Ashcroft*, 303 F.d 681, 683 (6th Cir. 2002), but see *North Jersey Media Group, Inc. v Ashcroft*, 308 F.d 198 (3rd Cir. 2002).

2. To be sure, numerous immigration restrictions had previously been implemented. For instance the Chinese Exclusion Act of 1882 discriminated based on race and the Act of 3 March 1903 prohibited anarchists. The quota laws were, however, the first to set absolute numerical limits on the number of immigrants who would be admitted to the United States and created a systematic framework that established which aliens would be considered undesirable because of their nation of origin that essentially remained in effect until the passage of the Immigration Act of 1965.

3. This cartoon was also reprinted in the 5 July 1919 issue of *The Literary Digest* accompanying an article entitled, "To Clap the Lid on the Melting Pot."

4. *Ex Parte Jackson*, 263 Fed. 110, 113 (1920).

5. *Colyer v Skeffington*, 265 Fed. at 40–41, 43, 45, & 48.

4. CHAVEZ, MEXICANS OF MASS DESTRUCTION

I would like to thank Francis Hasso and Samuel Martínez for their generous editorial suggestions.

1. Other such instances of discursive prefiguration of anti-immigrant backlash by politicians and the media are examined by J. C. Salyer and Susan Akram and Kevin Johnson, in their chapters in this volume, on the Red Scare, the Japanese internment during the Second World War, and the pre-9/11 "demonization" of Arabs and Muslims.

2. In 1993, for complicated political reasons, Bustamante voted as a member of the California State Assembly in favor of a bill that would prevent undocumented immigrants from getting driver's licenses.

3. Josiah Heyman's chapter in this volume explores the contradictions and challenges involved in attempting to interdict the entry of unauthorized immigrants and contraband while permitting expanding flows of licit goods and authorized migrants to cross at ports of entry on the U.S.-Mexico border.

4. It is no surprise, then, to find echoes of these fears coming from the mouths of U.S. citizens, as Nancy Naples reports in her chapter in this volume, based on her lengthy ethnographic research in one small Iowa city that has in recent years received large numbers of Mexican immigrants.

5. AKRAM AND JOHNSON, THE DEMONIZATION OF ARABS AND MUSLIMS

1. Armour 1995: 733; Delgado and Stefancic 1992: 1258; Lawrence 1987: 317, 322–23; Lee 1996: 402–52; Russell 1991: 243.

2. *St. Francis College v Al-Khazraji*, 481 U.S. 604, 610 n.4 (1987), held that a U.S. citizen born in Iraq could bring a civil-rights action for discrimination based on Arab ancestry. Michael Omi and Howard Winant (1986: 68) have labeled the process of socially constructing race identities as "racialization."

3. U.S. Federal Bureau of Investigation 1987: 13.

4. The historian Tony Judt has experienced a similar fate (see, e.g., Wieseltier 2006; *Chronicle Review* 2006; Hansen 2006).

5. A class action was brought by the American-Arab Anti-Discrimination Committee, numerous civil rights organizations, and several individuals (Second Amended Complaint for Injunctive and Declaratory Relief and Damages, *Am.-Arab Anti-Discrim. Comm. v Anti-Defamation League of B'nai B'rith*, No. Cv 93–6358-RAP [C.D. Cal. 20 Oct. 1993]; Final Settlement, *Am.-Arab Anti-Discrim. Comm. v Anti-Defamation League*, Civ Action No. 93–6358 RAP [C.D. Cal. 1999]). See also King and Berlet 1993: 31; Opratny and Winokur 1993a, 1993b; Berg 1999; Gillespie 1999: 43; Egelko 2002: A23.

6. http://www.israeloncampuscoalition.org.

7. http://www.Campus-Watch.org.

8. McNeil (2002) gives a good description of Campus Watch in the context of threats to academic freedom.

9. For some of the extensive coverage of the Columbia and other campus campaigns, see Arenson and Kleinfield 2005; Gaines 2005; Rohrs 2004.

10. http://www.adc.org/index.php?id=2386&no_cache=1&sword_list%5 B%5D=cafferty.

11. Hing 2002; Goodstein and Lewin 2001; Lewin and Niebuhr 2001. See also 147 Cong. Rec. E2150 (daily ed. 28 November 2001) statement of Rep. Conyers, Jr., indicating that between 11 September and 28 November 2001, the American-Arab Anti-Discrimination Committee had investigated over 450 hate crimes; 147 Cong. Rec. H8174, 8174 (14 November 2001) statement of Rep. Woolsey, recounting statistical data showing a precipitous rise in hate crimes against Muslims and Arabs immediately after September 11. Between September 11 and 8 February 2002, over 1700 anti-Muslim incidents were reported to the Council on American Islamic Relations (http://www.cair-net. org/nr/statements.asp). By April 2002, the Department of Justice was investigating over 250 post-9/11 hate crimes against Arabs and Muslims nationwide (interview by Susan M. Akram with Casey Stavropoulos and Dan Nelson, U.S. Department of Justice, Civil Rights Section, Public Information Division (Oct. 2001). See also U.S. Department of Justice, *Enforcement and Outreach Following the September 11 Attacks* (http://www.usdoj.gov/crt/legalinfo/discrim update.htm).

12. http://www.gc.cuny.edu/faculty/research_briefs/aris/aris_part_two.htm.

13. The Arab American Institute (AAI) claims there are 3.5 million Americans of Arab heritage, the majority of whom are Lebanese. AAI concludes that 75% of the Arab population in America is Christian, with 25% Muslim, or around 850,000 Arab Americans(http://www.aaiusa.org/demographics.htm).

14. Editorial, "Don't Judge Islam by Verdicts," *Orlando Sentinel*, 8 March 1994, A10.

15. Abraham 1994: 162; also, *Ethnically Motivated Violence Against Arab-Americans: Hearing Before the Subcommittee on Criminal Justice of the House Committee on the Judiciary*, 99th Congress 57, 64 (1988).

16. At the time of this murder, the *New York Times* quoted the head of the JDL, Irv Rubin, as stating, "No Jew or American should shed one tear for the destruction of a P.L.O. front in Santa Ana or anywhere else in the world" ("Bomb Kills Leader of U.S. Arab Group," *New York Times*, 12 October 1985, A5). In 2002, Rubin was indicted for conspiring to bomb a Los Angeles mosque, the Muslim Public Affairs Council, and the office of U.S. Congress member Darrell Issa (Rosenzweig 2002; Hanley 2002b: 16), and later died in custody.

17. Jabara later filed a civil rights suit against the federal government. See *Jabara v Webster*, 691 F.2d 272 (6th Cir. 1982), *cert. denied*, 464 U.S. 863 (1983).

18. A faction of the Palestine Liberation Organization (PLO) that had broken with Yasser Arafat was ultimately found to be responsible for the attacks on the Rome and Vienna airports (Chomsky 1987: 118).

19. Akram 1999: 52–53; Belkin 1991; LaFraniere 1991; Sachar 1991.

20. In 1987, Congress enacted a law mandating the closure of the Palestine Information Office (PIO) in Washington, which represents the PLO in the United States, and the PLO Observer Mission at the United Nations. Constitutional challenges to the law failed (*Palestine Info. Office v Schultz*, 853 F.2d 932, 934 [D.C. Cir. 1988]; *Mendelsohn v Meese*, 695 F. Supp. 1474, 1490 [S.D.N.Y. 1988]; *United States v Palestine Liberation Org.*, 695 F. Supp. 1456 [S.D.N.Y. 1988].

21. National Security Decision Directive no. 207, *The National Program for Combatting Terrorism*, at http://www.gwu.edu/nsarchiv/NSAEDD/NSA EBB55/nsdd207.pdf (20 January 1986).

22. *Legislation to Implement the Recommendations of the Commission on Wartime Relocation and Internment of Civilians: Hearing on H.R. 442 before the Subcommittee on Admin. Law and Gov't Relations of the House Comm. on the Judiciary*, 100th Cong. 67 (1987) (submission of Investigations Division of the Immigration and Naturalization Service).

23. Memorandum from Investigations Division, Immigration and Naturalization Service, Alien Border Control (ABC) Group IV-Contingency Plans 16 (18 November 1986) (with attachments including INS, *Alien Terrorists and Undesirables: A Contingency Plan* [1986]).

24. For consideration of this case from different vantage points, see Banks 2000; Hernandez-Truyol 2000; Motomura 2000; Neuman 2000.

25. For a description of the arrests, charges, and proceedings against the LA Eight, see Akram 1989, 1999: 73; Overend and Soble 1987; Dempsey and Cole 1999: 33–34.

26. *Nomination of William H. Webster: Hearings before the Select Committee on Intelligence of the United States Senate*, 100th Cong., 1st Sess. 95 (1987) (testimony of FBI Director William Webster).

27. *American-Arab Anti-Discrimination Committee v Meese*, 714 F. Supp. 1060 (C.D. Cal. 1989).

28. *American-Arab Anti-Discrimination Committee v Reno*, 70 F.3d 1045, 1053 (9th Cir. 1995).

29. INA 212(a)(3)(B)(iii), 8 U.S.C. 1182(a)(3)(B)(iii). After 9/11, Congress further expanded the definition of "terrorist activity." In addition to the many new post-9/11 policies, a number of provisions of the USA PATRIOT Act and other lesser-known laws give the government new and expanded authority to remove, exclude, and detain Arab and Muslim noncitizens, and to criminalize various activities based on their political and family associations. For example, the terrorist activity and terrorist organization provisions of Section 411 of the USA PATRIOT Act expand the class of immigrants who are subject to removal on terrorism grounds. Section 411 expands the definition of "terrorist activity" to include any crime that involves the use of a "weapon or dangerous device." The government can find that an organization engages in terrorist activity under this definition if it seeks to fund the lawful ends of an organization—such as political or humanitarian activities. The definition of "terrorism" was greatly expanded under the USA PATRIOT Act to include "acts dangerous to human life that are a violation of the criminal laws" if they "appear to be intended to influence the policy of a government by intimidation or coercion," and if they "occur primarily within the territorial jurisdiction of the United States." Section 411 appears to impose restrictions solely based on political associations protected by the U.S. Constitution's First Amendment.

30. *Reno v American-Arab Anti-Discrimination Committee*, 525 U.S. 471, 471–72 (1999).

31. P.L. 109-13, Division B (2005). After twenty years of trying, the U.S. government in 2007 agreed to dismiss removal proceedings against the remaining two LA Eight defendants (Weinstein 2007).

32. *Rafeedie v INS*, 688 F. Supp. (D.D.C. 1988), *aff'd in part, rev'd in part, remanded*, 880 F.2d 506 (D.C. Cir. 1989).

33. *Rafeedie*, 688 F. Supp. at 734–35; *Rafeedie*, 880 F.2d at 516 & 524.

34. Antiterrorism and Effective Death Penalty Act of 1996 (AEDPA), Pub. L. No. 104–132, 110 Stat. 1214 (1996); Whidden (2001: 2841–83) summarizes the genesis of AEDPA and analyzes its impact on Arabs and Muslims. See also Illegal Immigration Reform and Immigrant Responsibility Act of 1996, Pub. L. No. 104–208, 110 Stat. 3009 (1996). For discussion of the U.S. government's use of these provisions against Arabs and Muslims, see Ross 2001: 146; Scanlan 2000.

35. Immigration courts, which generally do not publish decisions, made many of the important decisions in the secret evidence cases. Citations to many of the following cases are from immigration court decisions and related materials. Court documents in the cases discussed below are on file with Kit Gage, national coordinator of the National Coalition to Protect Political Freedom, 3321 12th Street, N.E., Washington, DC 20017.

36. *The National Security Considerations Involved in Asylum Applica-*

tions: Hearings before the Senate Judiciary Committee on Technology, Terrorism and Government Information, 105th Congress 5-14 (1998) (testimony of INS General Counsel Paul Virtue) (FDCH Political Transcripts). The one non-Arab/Muslim case is *Cheema v Ashcroft,* 372 F.3d 1147 (9th Cir. 2004) (involving an individual of Sikh faith).

37. Section 401 creates a special removal court for "alien terrorists" that gives the special court the power to "examine, ex parte and in camera, any evidence for which the Attorney General determines that public disclosure would pose a risk to the national security of the United States or to the security of any individual because it would disclose classified information" (AEDPA 401 [codified at 8 U.S.C. 1534(e)(3)(A)]); see also Scaperlanda 1996: 23.

38. 8 C.F.R. 240.33(c)(4) (2001); see also *107th Congress Continues to Wrap Up Assignments; House Immigration Oversight Proposed,* 78 Interpreter Releases 361, 363 (2001).

39. AEDPA 504(e)(3)(B) and (C), 303(f)(2)(B), & 504(e)(3)(C).

40. None of the decisions in these cases was published. However, there were press reports and some published articles by the lawyers involved in the cases.

41. In August 2000, one respondent who did not accept the settlement agreement, Ali Yasim Mohammed Karim, was found not to be a security threat, and was granted political asylum ("Dissident Released After Four Years," The Associated Press, 19 August 2000, http://www.washingtonpost.com/wp-srv/aponline/20000819/aponline203106_002.htm).

42. *United States v Rahman,* 189 F.3d 88, 103 (2d Cir. 1999); Binny Miller (1994: 561) acknowledges that stereotypes about "terrorist Arabs out to destroy American democracy" posed difficult challenges to the defense in this case.

43. 60 Minutes, "How Did He Get Here?" CBS television broadcast, 14 March 1993.

44. INA 235, 8 U.S.C. 1225; Aleinikoff et al. 1998: 863–71, 1028–29.

45. Davis 1997: 425, 442–43; Harris 1999: 265, 298–300; Maclin 1998: 333, 342–62.

46. *United States v Brignoni-Ponce,* 422 U.S. 873, 886–87 (1975).

47. *United States v Montero-Camargo,* 208 F.3d 1122 (9th Cir. 2000) (en banc), *cert. denied,* 531 U.S. 889 (2000).

48. Law enforcement measures based on alleged group propensities for criminal conduct run afoul of the U.S. Constitution, which is generally premised on the view that individualized suspicion is necessary for police action (*United States v Sokolow,* 490 U.S. 1, 7 [1989]; *Terry v Ohio,* 392 U.S. 1, 27 [1968]).

6. DOLE, SECURITY AND INSECURITY

1. The conceptualization of "Muslim space in North America" draws on Barbara Metcalf's edited volume *Making Muslim Space in North America and Europe* (1996). In this chapter, however, I am developing a connection between the spatialization of security and its implications for *remaking* Muslim space in America.

2. For alternative conceptualizations of security within anthropology, see Weldes, Laffey, Gusterson, and Duvall 1999.

3. Unless otherwise noted, I will use the term "national security" to refer to these institutional, bureaucratic, and ideological structures and practices being mobilized to defend the state against "terrorist" threat.

4. That these measures are being taken through immigration law is significant, for it takes one into a juridical system significantly more flexible and less rigorous than the standards of criminal law, a realm into which many rights afforded citizens are not extended. See Cole 2003a for a legal analysis of this issue in relation to post-9/11 detentions.

5. See Human Rights Watch 2002 for documentation of detainee abuses (2002).

6. According to the U.S. Bureau of Citizenship and Immigration Enforcement (formerly the INS), 83,519 individuals were interviewed, fingerprinted, and photographed under this program as of September 2003. An additional 93,741 underwent registration at ports of entry and exit. Of the domestic registrations, 13,799 have had deportation proceedings initiated against them and 2,870 have been detained.

7. As compared to cities such as Detroit, New York, or Chicago, Boston's Arab and Muslim populations are neither large nor residentially concentrated. With an estimated 6,000 Arab and 70,000 Muslim residents (including immigrants, American-born Muslims, and converts), the Arab-Muslim presence in the Boston metropolitan area is nonetheless sizable. These figures, however, are based on census data (U.S. Census Bureau 2003) and are the subject of intense debate. They likely underrepresent the actual number of Arab residents of Boston. For a consideration of the early history of Arab immigrants in Boston and Worcester, Massachusetts, see Shakir 1997 and Boosahda 2003, respectively. For a sampling of research considering contemporary Arab-American and/or Muslim-American communities, see Abraham and Shryock 2000, Suleiman 1999, Naber 2000, Fischer and Abedi 1990, Haddad and Smith 1994 and 2002, Haddad 2002, and Metcalf 1996. For a review of the scholarly literature on Muslims in the United States, see Leonard 2003. For discussions of the impact of 9/11 on Arab and South Asian Muslim communities, see Cainkar 2004 and 2009, and Ewing 2008.

8. On 13 January 2004, for instance, the *Boston Globe* reported that eight suspected supporters of Al-Qaeda were arrested in Switzerland based upon phone numbers found in the cell phones of terrorist suspects in Saudi Arabia (Higgins 2004). While at first glance such an article merely reveals the high-tech front across which "war" is being waged, its implications are far-reaching and reflect the ways in which seemingly benign objects have taken on new significance.

9. The threat and consequences of being associated with "terrorism" also articulates within existing social and familial conflicts, as seen in cases where false accusations of membership in "terrorist" organizations are used to settle personal or social acrimony (Reuters 2004).

10. For comparison, see Aswad and Bilgé 1996, Hermansen 1991.

7. NAPLES, POLICING THE BORDERS IN THE HEARTLAND

1. I use the term *citizenship* in a broader sense than is typical in studies of immigration and migration to examine ways in which citizens and others with legal standing in the United States achieve legitimate status as full members of specific geographic communities (also Coutin 2000). I view citizenship claims beyond T. H. Marshall's (1965) conceptualization of civil, political, and social rights to include exploring how newcomers make claims on the social, civic, and physical spaces and other features of particular locales.

2. I also use the terms *Latino* and *Anglo* interchangeably with *Mexican/ Mexican American* and *white European American,* respectively, although both terms have very specific racial-ethnic meaning that may not capture accurately the specificity of the identities as defined by the Mexican and Mexican American residents as well as the diversity within the white population in Midtown.

3. Some of the Mexican workers are recent immigrants from several towns in Mexico and others are long-term residents of the United States. Consequently, I will refer to these workers as Mexican and Mexican American. None of the white residents referred to the new residents as "Chicanos," including the Mexican-American community worker and missionary working with the "Hispanic population" [sic] in Midtown. The only terms heard throughout the fieldwork were "Mexican" and "Hispanic." In fact, white European-American residents did not differentiate between Mexicans and Mexican-American residents, referring to all individuals of Mexican descent as Mexicans or Hispanic.

4. This embedded intersectional approach sharpens the view of the multiple sites through which state agents and nonstate or extended agents of the state contribute to the *social regulation of citizenship.* As a result, my approach reveals the complex processes that influence the social regulation of citizenship, processes that are invisible in other modes of analysis. Recent work by feminist social geographers are offering new ways to conceptualize the relationship between gender and place (Massey 1994; Momson and Townsend 1987; Rocheleau, Thomas-Slayter, and Wangari 1996; Rose 1993).

5. The climate for nonwhite and non-English-speaking migrants to the rural Midwest reflects the xenophobic political and social climate in the United States more generally. Captured in California's Proposition 187 and embedded in the 1996 federal welfare legislation that initially denied legal immigrants and their children access to public assistance, this climate intensifies the resistance faced by those who address the problems of non-white or non-English-speaking migrants and immigrants in any U.S. community (Park 1998). Such efforts should not be viewed as only recent phenomena. In many small white European-American communities throughout the Midwest, white supremacist groups have long been active, although their presence remains firmly denied by town officials and long-term residents (Fink 1998).

6. In Midtown, Iowa, the Economic Development Corporation decided to build a new medical facility as well as a new home for the physician who accepted their offer to set up his office in town.

7. In 2003, the Immigration and Naturalization Service (INS) was merged

into the Department of Homeland Security (DHS) and renamed the U.S. Citizenship and Immigration Services (USCIS). However, since the research for this chapter was conducted prior to this change, I will continue to refer to the U.S. immigration authority as the INS.

8. The links between residents in Midtown and other parts of the United States as well as Mexico illustrates the maintenance of a transnational community. Residents of Midtown draw on their national and transnational community for information on other job possibilities, immigration law, and other forms of less tangible support. They, in turn, provide financial assistance among other resources to family and former neighbors living in other parts of the United States and Mexico (Espiritu 1992; *Ethnic and Racial Studies* 1999).

9. In keeping with the stereotypical construction of "*machismo/marianismo*," many white residents constructed Mexican women as "submissive, maternal, and virginal" (Cantú 1999).

10. In Naples 1997, I discuss what I term the "outsider phenomenon," concluding that most people interviewed in Midtown over the course of the ethnographic investigation expressed feeling like outsiders to the perceived community of insiders. The term, "outsider phenomenon" was generated to highlight the way in which different "community members are created as 'others'—a process through which all members participate to varying degrees—and by which feelings of 'otherness' are incorporated into self-perceptions and social interactions" (Naples 2003: 50).

8. GABANY-GUERRERO, AN ANATOMY OF MEXICAN REPATRIATION

Acknowledgments: This paper would not have been possible without the dedicated work of Padre Francisco P. and Casa del Migrante volunteers, as well as student researchers at the University of Texas at El Paso (UTEP): Maria Eugenia Hernández-Sánchez, M.A. (now at UACJ), Guillermo Rodríguez (UTEP), Victoria Vásquez (UTEP), and Dr. Francisco Martínez González (Universidad de Guanajuato). Special thanks also to Fr. Pellizari and Lic. Irigoyen, both of whom facilitated the work at the Casa del Migrante and engaged my participation in the issues that confront migrants in Ciudad Juárez, and to Dr. Kathy Staudt and Carla Cardosa of Community Partnerships at UTEP for the small grant funded by the Kellogg Foundation.

1. For the purposes of this article, the term *deportee* refers to people who have signed voluntary departure agreements, have received deportation orders, or have been caught crossing the border and forcibly repatriated. Even though lumping together these categories obscures U.S. policy distinctions, this chapter attempts to view the process from the perspective of Mexican deportees. For the deportee the distinctions among various legal categories were essentially moot; they were not permitted to re-enter the United States on threat of imprisonment for up to ten years. The salient difference was criminal versus noncriminal charges. Under voluntary departure, deportees agree to make

no claim to reunite with family members and must leave the country within thirty days. Their departure is facilitated at ICE-authorized detention centers, where detainees are moved as rapidly as possible to their eventual release at U.S.-Mexico border crossings.

2. The research was conducted with support from the Center for Interamerican & Border Studies at the University of Texas at El Paso (specifically, a Kellogg Community Partnerships Grant) in collaboration with an NGO, Casa del Migrante (CDM). CDM was founded by the Scalabrini Order of Catholic missionaries to provide shelter, food, and basic medical care to migrants of any national origin on the U.S.-Mexico border in Ciudad Juárez. CDM was selected as a research partner because it holds records regarding migrants of unparalleled time-depth in Ciudad Juárez. The data collected by volunteers, though subject to some divergence in methods of collection, provided consistent records regarding services provided for migrants over the period from 1991 to 2001. Despite the existence of many NGOs on the U.S.-Mexico border, few have served as a basis for social science research in the El Paso–Ciudad Juárez metro area. For exceptions, see Marquez 1995 and Staudt 1998; on *maquilas*, see the classic work by Fernández-Kelly and Sassen (1995), as well as Hertel's (2006) study of activists, which includes and extends beyond the border zone.

3. The Legal Arizona Workers Act, passed in 2007, gives the state authority to suspend or revoke the business license of any employer found to have knowingly or intentionally hired an illegal immigrant.

4. California Senate Bill 670.

5. Entry beyond the ten-kilometer zone requires an application for what is normally up to a ninety-day visa for U.S. travelers. Here one's auto is the Mexican government's primary concern. While U.S. agencies are primarily concerned with undocumented Mexicans, illegally imported autos and trucks are the biggest concern of Mexican agencies concerned with protecting the national auto industry.

6. High-level government officials and entrepreneurs may purchase a bridge pass that, for a large fee and an extensive security check, provides virtually "no waiting" access to both the United States and Mexico. This illustrates the advantage of class at the border. The classed dimension of border crossing is also evidenced by the malls on the U.S. side, which cater to upscale shoppers from Mexico. With the imposition of long crossing delays, Ciudad Juárez has created its own upscale malls, theaters, and eateries, which now successfully compete with the U.S. malls.

7. After U.S. Congressional passage of the Illegal Immigration Reform and Immigrant Responsibility Act (IIRIRA) in 1996, all undocumented workers became subject to criminal detention and prosecution.

8. A separate shelter for women is operated by another NGO.

9. A phone card worth US$10 was provided for each participant in an interview.

10. Obtaining documents from Mexico was particularly difficult for low-income people. It appeared that many people had never obtained birth cer-

tificates from their respective county *(municipio)* offices, or their births had never been registered. Although rather uncommon now in rural Mexico, this problem was more frequent thirty or more years ago due to the cost of registering a child with a birth certificate. Birth certificates and proof of citizenship also would have been more difficult to obtain for the children of single head-of-household women who had not been married, had been abandoned, or had been separated from their husbands. Obtaining an original birth certificate under these conditions would have required securing witnesses to the birth and a whole series of legal procedures in Mexico that would have required the person's presence in the *municipio*. The cost and complication of these legal requirements were so overwhelming to most of the men interviewed that they simply could not process their papers, even if they would have qualified under previous U.S. amnesty provisions. Although *municipio* records in some parts of Mexico are computerized, in other (particularly rural) areas they are frequently difficult to locate, and most *municipios* do not have the resources to maintain historical records.

11. For more information on this subject see the DIF and UNICEF 2004, and the news report by *Frontera Norte Sur* in the October–December 2005 issue, "UN Official Speaks Out on Child Deportations" (http://www.nmsu.edu/~frontera/Oct-Dec05/Mexicalinews.html).

9. BLOCH, U.S. POSITIONS ON "TRAFFICKING"

1. This relatively permeable border policy beginning in the 1990s is linked to Turkey's status as one of the signatories of the Black Sea Economic Cooperation agreement; Albania, Armenia, Azerbaijan, Bulgaria, Georgia, Greece, Moldova, Romania, Russia, and Ukraine are also signatories (Aktar and Ögelman 1994: 348). Of the eleven signatories, in 1992 only Greece and Turkey had a positive rate of real GDP growth: Greece, 1.3 percent, and Turkey, 5.9 percent. In 1992, the others had significantly worse rates of growth, ranging from Russia's -15 percent real Net Material Product (NMP) growth rate to Armenia's -40 percent real NMP growth rate. "Real NMP growth" is a concept used by the late communist governments of Eastern and Central Europe and the Soviet Union to evaluate economic accounts; it is roughly equivalent to GDP (Aktar and Ögelman 1994: 352).

2. In 2002 the Federal Migration Service of Russia counted 50,000 people leaving the country for work, while 359,000 entered to work. One scholar estimates that taking into account those working illegally in Russia would raise the number of foreign labor migrants to nearly 3 million people (2005 est., Tiurukanova 2003: 179).

3. Jack Schafer (2004b) wrote, "It's an outrage if just one [person] spends a night enslaved. But 'The Girls Next Door' fails miserably to establish that widespread and abundant sex slavery exists here. In a nutshell, Landesman and the *Times Magazine* are guilty of inflating a compelling story to the bursting point." http://slate.msn.com/id/2094580/.

4. A growing number of films have recently been made dedicated to the subject of "trafficking." One documentary film entitled *Trafficking Cinderella* was made in Canada with funds from the Open Society Institute (2001; director, Mira Niaglova). The Canadian documentary *Trafficking in Women* was aired in October 2005 by the Canadian Broadcasting Corporation. A widely distributed feature film, *Lilya 4-Ever*, was made in Sweden (2002; director, Lukas Moodysson [Memfis Folm AB/Nordisk Film and TV Fond]).

5. http://www.osce.org/activities/13029.html.

6. A three year grant (2002–5) from the Canadian government's Social Science and Humanities Research Council funded this research.

7. Hansen Chou provided invaluable research assistance on the section of this chapter drawing on USAID websites.

8. Moşneaga and Echim base their analysis on a critical assessment of a survey of return migrants to Moldova. The survey, conducted by the IOM in 2003, conflates sex work with labor migration.

9. http://www.usaid.gov/our_work/cross-cutting_programs/wid/pubs/trafficking_2005.pdf.

10. http://www.state.gov/g/tip/rls/tiprpt/2005/.

11. In 1994, the OSCE's total budget was EUR 21 million, while in 2005 it increased to EUR 168.6 million (http://www.osce.org). In 2005, nearly EUR 123 million were budgeted for "field operations," where "antitrafficking" was just one of the 18 activities undertaken by OSCE offices. The other areas of concentration are arms control, border management, combating terrorism, conflict prevention, democratization, elections, environmental activities, gender equality, human rights, media, military reform, minority rights, policing, rule of law, and tolerance and nondiscrimination.

12. Several scholars have explored the ways in which the fall of former socialist governments in Eastern Europe was a boon for local and international NGOs and development organizations (see Hemment 2004; Sundstrom 2003), and one scholar examines the growth of extensive corruption in these new NGO spheres (Wedel 1998). Based on her research in seven regions of Russia, including in the Russian Far East, Lisa Sundstrom (2003: 146) has argued, "Assistance to NGOs in democratizing states is a rapidly growing phenomenon, which fundamentally affects the kinds of activities in which NGOs engage, as well as the nature of their transnational interactions."

13. All translations are my own. Pseudonyms are used for individuals named in the text.

14. The newspaper *Dal'Press* is published weekly in Vladivostok and distributed throughout the Russian Far East. In contrast to newspapers with an emphasis on news coverage, this one is more of a tabloid with a heavy emphasis on classified advertisements.

15. There is little social science research on the transnational sex trade from the Russian Far East into Korea, Japan, and China. One of the few scholars working in this area (Erokhina 2000) based her research on police reports about women trafficked across the border to China. Erokhina does not mention labor

migration of men or women, thus implying that all those discussed by border police were trafficked.

16. With the fall of the Soviet Union in late 1991, borders with neighboring countries such as China were relaxed, and the sheer number of people moving across the Chinese-Russian border grew radically in a short time. For instance, in 1988 in the Amur oblast, a Russian Far East area bordering China, there were 6,233 border crossings, while in 1992 there were 287,215 border crossings (Wishnick 2002: 156). While the largely male labor migration from China and North Korea into Russia is beginning to be recognized, it is the female migration out of Russia that catches the attention of the press and NGOs seeking to prevent trafficking.

17. In the case of the United Arab Emirates, for more than a decade tourist visas for women under age thirty have been limited to those traveling with their husbands. One Web site indicates that unless the married couple has the same last name, the woman very likely will be denied entry (Russian Emirates Advertising Company, http://www.emirat.ru/visa/).

18. Information on "entertainment" visas or "working holiday" visas is not available for China, and apparently these types of visas do not exist. Apparently in response to being targeted in 2001 as "one of 23 countries" that were not meeting the USAID minimum standards for eliminating trafficking, South Korea restricted the options for immigration (http://www.anyworkany where.com/visas_kr.html): "If granted a working holiday visa one may not be employed as a receptionist, dancer, singer, musician, acrobat etc. all places of entertainment which might endanger good morals and manners." In the case of Japan, the "working holiday" visa holders are permitted to "engage in any kind of job as long as their stay is deemed to be primarily a holiday in Japan. They may not, however, work in places where business is being regulated by the Law on Control and Improvement of Amusement and Entertainment Business, such as nightclubs and dance halls" (Ministry of Foreign Affairs of Japan, http://mofa.go.jp/j_info/visit/w_holiday/programme.html). This new visa restriction was also discussed in interviews by NGO representatives in Vladivostok and Khabarovsk in 2003.

19. One scholar studying labor migration in the Russian Federation, and particularly in Moscow, reports that approximately 250 such tour agencies were operating in Russia in 2003 (personal communication with Elena Tiuriukanova, July 2003).

20. http://www.winrock.org. I am indebted to Elena Tuirukanova for her assistance in making contacts with scholars and NGOs for this research.

21. Ironically, one of the Tsiunami organizers told me that she hoped to expand her nanny agency to arrange temporary work arrangements for clients abroad. She was exploring how to have her clients qualify for the Canadian Live-In Caregiver program, which until recently was primarily used by Filipinas (http://www.cic.gc.ca/english/pub/caregiver/index.html).

22. See Sundstrom (2002: 214) on how women's NGOs in Russia are detached from public opinion due to ideological differences.

10. HESS, "WE ARE NOT TERRORISTS!"

1. "Uighur" is spelled a variety of ways in English: Uygur, Uyghur, Uighur and Weigur. Although I use "Uighur," other spellings will be found in the names of groups, Web sites, and in quotations cited throughout this chapter.

2. From the poem "Secrets of Tibet," published by the Tibet Information Network (www.tibetinfo.net/news-updates/2005/0902.htm).

3. Amnesty International (2004) reports that although few Uighurs have fled to Nepal, at least sixteen have sought asylum in Nepal since 2000, with several cases of refoulement. At least seven Uighurs have been forcibly returned from Pakistan since 2002.

4. See the Tibet Information Network (www.tibetinfo.net), World Tibet Network News (www.tibet.ca), and Voice of Tibet (www.vot.org).

5. See www.phayul.com; www.worldbridges.com; and www.tibetlink.com.

6. See International Campaign for Tibet, Tibetan Center for Human Rights and Democracy, Tibet Justice Center, Friends of Tibet, Amnesty International, Human Rights Watch, and Friends of Tibet.

7. See www.uyghuramerican.org, uygurletter.blogspot.com, and www.uhrp.com.

8. See www.etnfc.com; www.uygur.org.

9. The message board is located on the Uyghur American Association's Web site, www.uyghuramerican.org.

10. www.uyguramerican.org, 24 June 2005.

11. RESTREPO-RUIZ AND MARTÍNEZ, PLAN COLOMBIA AND FORCED DISPLACEMENT

1. Former Humanitarian Assistance and Protection program coordinator for Care-Colombia. Personal interview with first author, February 2005.

2. All translations from Spanish-language sources are by the authors.

3. BBC, "Bush Pledges More Aid to Colombia." 22 November 2004. http://news.bbc.co.uk/1/hi/world/americas/4033069.stm.

4. Definition of displaced person given at the *Meeting on Permanent Consultancy about Forced Displacement in the Americas* (Reunión Técnica de la Consulta Permanente sobre Desplazamiento en las Américas), www.desplazados.org.co. This definition closely resembles that established by the Congress of Colombia, in Law 387 of 1997.

5. http://www.ohchr.org/english/issues/idp/issues.htm#1.

6. Our overview draws from several critical analyses of Plan Colombia, particularly the essays in Estrada Alvarez 2001 and 2002.

7. Piedad Córdoba Ruiz, "El Plan Colombia: El escalamiento del conflicto social y armado." http://Nizkor.org.

8. http://ciponline.org/colombia.

9. We base our analysis in this section on reports by Colombian NGOs, most prominently the Consultoría para los Derechos Humanos y el Desplaza-

miento (CODHES) and on studies by María Clemencia Ramírez (2004) and Elsa Nivia (2002) concerning Plan Colombia's effects on the inhabitants of the regions where it has been implemented most intensively.

10. BBC News. http://www.bbc.co.uk/spanish/especiales/colombia_baig/desplazados/8.stm.

11. See statements by Ivette Perfecto, Anna Cerderstav, Tedd Schettler, Janet Chernela, and Rachel Massey at http://amazonalliance.org/aerialeradicationinformation.html.

12. LIBAL AND HARDING, INGOS AND THE IRAQI REFUGEE CRISIS

Part of this article is reprinted with permission from *Middle East Report* 244 (fall 2007). The first epigraph is from Frelick 2007 (p. 4); the second is cited in Allam 2007.

1. An important distinction exists between refugees and forced migrants. The UN Special Rapporteur on the Human Rights of Migrants has proposed that "forced migrants" may include those who are typically thought of as refugees in international law, as well as others who may or may not seek asylum or permanent resettlement but have fled their country in the wake of conflict (Gzesh 2008). In international law refugees are defined more narrowly than forced migrants, namely those impelled to cross national boundaries due to well-founded fear of harm or persecution based on one's race, religion, nationality, political opinion, or membership in a particular social group. We use the term "refugee" to identify those Iraqis who have fled across Iraqi borders since 2003. Most of these Iraqis have not applied for resettlement in "third countries" and live for some time in "limbo" in Jordan, Syria, and other neighboring countries.

2. Harding (2007: 296) defines human-made disaster as a condition resulting from a range of policies and "deliberate state actions" which "produce adverse impacts on the economy and infrastructure of a country and facilitate the breakdown of social networks and community." These include war, actions of repressive regimes, failure to stem the spread of preventable disease and epidemics, economic sanctions, and neoliberal economic strategies.

3. We solicited participants for this study from organizations that have had direct contact with Iraqi refugees in Jordan, Syria, or Turkey since 2003 and/or were involved in advocacy on behalf of refugees in the United States. Some have also been involved in advocacy efforts in Europe, the Middle East, and at the United Nations. Subjects were identified through direct outreach to targeted national and international nongovernmental organizations, and via a snowball technique. In the United States, we interviewed NGO representatives from organizations engaged in advocacy and direct service to Iraqi refugees, as well as congressional staff. In Jordan we interviewed key informants from international and local NGOs, specifically those who are or have been providing assistance to Iraqi refugees in Jordan, and the United Nations. We utilized

semistructured interviews, with an emphasis on understanding the politics of NGO advocacy and the provision of humanitarian assistance. We asked informants about the specific needs of Iraqi refugees, barriers to service provision, the capacity of local and international NGOs to provide services, the role of key global actors like the United States and UN, and the various strategy and tactics of advocacy on this issue by NGOs.

4. Economic sanctions as a foreign policy tool have become increasingly controversial. As Mertus and Hallward put it, "sanctions themselves were a form of violence that led to even greater violence" (2006: 320). Harding (2004) underscores the pernicious effects of this international policy. He notes that scant public attention has been paid to the use of such policies to force political change, highlighting the "silence" of professional circles like social work, which ostensibly are driven by social justice and human rights mandates.

5. The Public Distribution System (PDS) provides monthly food rations to most Iraqis.

6. The official poverty rate in Jordan is 30 percent; the unemployment rate is officially 12.5 percent (2004) and unofficially 30 percent (2004) (*CIA Factbook* 2006).

7. Following the 2003 invasion of Iraq, the Unites States has significantly increased financial and material aid to Jordan (Alissa 2007).

8. Fagen (2007) focuses on the implications of the Iraqi refugees for Syria and Jordan. While refugees have stimulated the economies, it is clear that "the burdens of the Iraqi presence are falling most heavily on poorer segments of the population and on people with fixed incomes, who constitute the majority" (26).

9. The authors participated in this meeting. The quotes cited in this paragraph are drawn from our notes.

10. Conference notes, obtained through NGO contacts.

11. Throughout the Bush administration, 70,000 slots have been set aside annually. In FY 2002 the numbers of actual admissions plummeted, in part due to new Homeland Security processing requirements, and only 27,110 refugees were actually admitted. This reduction is striking given the extent of displacement that has occurred since 2000 (e.g., Sudan, Colombia, Iraq). For a full listing of actual admissions from 1998 to 2006, see Bruno 2006 (3).

MARTÍNEZ, CONCLUSION

1. According to Peter Andreas (2001: 107–8), "the interaction between law enforcement and clandestine labor migration across the U.S.-Mexican border has perversely generated a more organized and sophisticated migrant smuggling business." Contrary to common wisdom, trafficking is not a product of porous borders: where borders are truly permeable, people will just walk across on their own and not bother with procuring a guide (ibid.: 110). The need to rely on a smuggler, who may stand revealed as an abusive trafficker if he seeks to restrict the entrants' freedom on the other side, has increased in

response to the U.S. government's border buildup. The increased difficulty of clandestine passage in turn raises smuggling fees, deepens the immigrant's debt, and lengthens the period of time for which she or he is saddled with debt payments and threats of reprisal from the smuggler (or any third person to whom he sells the immigrant's debt). These conditions are virtually a recipe for debt bondage, involuntary servitude, or other forms of labor control verging on slavery. As Phil Marshall and Susu Thatun (2005: 53–54) conclude, on the basis of their extensive antitrafficking experience in the six-nation greater Mekong region, "bringing migration policies more closely into line with labor market realities would be the single greatest step a country could take against trafficking." "Added to evidence that tighter border controls exacerbate trafficking," they write, "there is also evidence that the converse holds true, that liberalized border controls have the opposite effect."

2. There appears to be a mismatch between how little attention has been given to gender-specific assumptions and dynamics at the macro-level of immigration policy and the international political economy of migration, on the one hand, and the extensive study devoted to the gender dynamics of international migration's microstructures of family and community, on the other.

3. I take the term "securitization" from John Tirman (2004). See also Josiah Heyman's discussion of the term's meaning in his chapter in this book.

4. According to McCarthy (2003), the replacement of in-person hearings with video teleconferencing, for example, can and does frequently make it more difficult for the applicant to establish credibility and overcome barriers of translation, and prevents her or him from being accompanied by her or his attorney. Forensic examination of all documents can and does frequently undermine petitions for asylum: the revelation that some of an applicant's documents are false can be judged to diminish her or his credibility, even if those documents are not directly related to the claim.

5. Email communication with author, 12 March 2007.

6. See Julia Hess's discussion of the case of the Uighur asylum seeker Sonam Chodon in chapter 11 of in this volume.

7. The parallels with the treatment accorded to the Haitian boat people include (1) the projection of U.S. military power, on the U.S. president's executive authority, beyond this country's borders; (2) applying search criteria that presume the guilt of persons of certain nationalities; (3) to hold detainees found in places outside their own nations' space (in international waters or in third countries); (4) under the pretense that, because detention takes place not on U.S. territory but on U.S. military bases abroad, the detainees stand outside the jurisdiction of the courts of the U.S. Department of Justice, (5) these circumstances having been interpreted to permit circumvention of due process regulations and restrictions on mistreatment, stipulated by instruments of international law, to which the U.S. government is signatory. To these must be added (1) the use of U.S. military personnel as jailers and (2) containment of the legal proceedings relating to the detainments within secret, parallel tribunals (immigration courts, for the Haitians, and military courts, for the "enemy

aliens"), further distancing the treatment of the detainees from the scrutiny of the press and attorneys, and permitting their indefinite confinement in U.S. custody, (3) U.S. administrations having justified these extraordinary measures at least partially in terms of the overriding interest of protecting national security (i.e., averting an "immigration emergency," in the case of the Haitians, and gathering information on Al-Qaeda, in the case of the enemy aliens).

8. *The Economist*, 20 September 2007 (www.economist.com/world/display story.cfm?story_id=9832877#top).

9. Coalición de Derechos Humanos/Alianza Indígena sin Fronteras (www .derechoshumanosaz.net/deaths.php4).

10. For more information on the topics of U.S.-Mexico border enforcement, human rights abuses on the border, and U.S. economic dependence on cheap, nonunion immigrant labor, consult the companion Web site to this book (http:// www.imhr.uconn.edu).

11. I thank Ellen Messer (personal communication, 3 March 2006) for drawing my attention to the large numbers of recent immigrants employed in poultry production in the United States.

12. Nor does the work environment in the packing plants seem to encourage the cooperation of poultry workers with public health authorities. According to a Human Rights Watch (2005c) investigation of conditions among immigrant meat processing workers, "The real-life consequences of workers' immigration status spilled into every area investigated by Human Rights Watch—health and safety, workers' compensation, and workers' organizing rights. One Smithfield Foods worker told Human Rights Watch, 'In the packing department everything is fast, fast *(rapido, rapido)*. I was sick a lot from the cold and the damp. I never wanted to make a claim against the company because they fire people and they might call Immigration.'"

NAGENGAST, AFTERWORD

1. See the United Nation Declaration on the Right to Development at http:// www.ohchr.org/english/law/rtd.htm. Ibid., Article 2(1). The notion that the human person is the central subject of development is reiterated in the Vienna Declaration and Programme of Action, World Conference on Human Rights, Vienna, 25 June 1993, UN Doc. A/CONF. 157/24, para. 10. See also http://www .ohchr.org/english/law/vienna.htm.

2. UN G.A. Res. 59/241 of 22 December 2004.

3. UN G.A. Res. 45/158 of 18 December 1990. http://www.ohchr.org/english/ law/cmw.htm. To date, thirty-four countries have ratified the Convention: Algeria, Azerbaijan, Belize, Bolivia, Bosnia-Herzegovina, Burkina Faso, Cape Verde, Chile, Colombia, Ecuador, Egypt, El Salvador, Ghana, Guatemala, Guinea, Guyana, Honduras, Kyrgyzstan, Libya, Mali, Mexico, Morocco, Nicaragua, Peru, Philippines, Senegal, Seychelles, Sri Lanka, Syria, Tajikistan, Timor-Leste, Turkey, Uganda, and Uruguay. A further fifteen countries have signed the Convention: Argentina, Bangladesh, Benin, Cambodia, Comoros, Gabon,

Guinea-Bissau, Indonesia, Lesotho, Liberia, Paraguay, Sao Tome and Principe, Serbia and Montenegro, Sierra Leone, and Togo. The Convention entered into force on 1 July 2003.

4. International Covenant on Civil and Political Rights (ICCPR) (UN G.A. Res. 2200A [XXI] of 16 December 1966), International Covenant on Economic, Social and Cultural Rights (ICESCR) (UN G.A. Res. 2200A [XXI] of 16 December 1966), International Convention on the Elimination of All Forms of Racial Discrimination (ICERD) (UN G.A. 2106 [XX] of 21 December 1965), Convention on the Elimination of All Forms of Discrimination against Women (CEDAW) (UN G.A. 34/180 of 18 December 1979), Convention against Torture and Other Cruel, Inhuman or Degrading Treatment or Punishment (CAT) (G.A. Res. 39/46 of 10 December 1984). See http://www.ohchr.org/english/law/index.htm.

5. UN, ESCOR, CHR, Sub-Commission on the Promotion and Protection of Human Rights, 55th Session, Item 5 of the Provisional Agenda, The Rights of Non-Citizens, Final Report of the Special Rapporteur, Mr. David Weissbrodt, submitted in accordance with Sub-Commission decision 2000/103, Commission Resolution 2000/104 and Economic and Social Council Decision 2000/283, Doc. E/CN.4/Sub.2/2003/23 (26 May 2003) at p. 2 (Executive Summary). See also Committee on the Elimination of Racial Discrimination (CERD), General Recommendation No. 30: Discrimination against Non-Citizens: 1/10/2004 (http://www.unhchr.ch/tbs/doc.nsf/(Symbol)/e3980a673769e229c1256f8d00 57cd3d?Opendocument), paras. 2 and 3.

6. Center for Economic Policy and Research, http://www.cepr.net/index.php.

7. Parenthetically, because of endemic racism directed towards indigenous people in Mexico, they rarely seek or find jobs in the maquilas.

8. Teachers in Oaxaca went on strike in May 2006, demanding more material resources for the schools and a living wage. The governor refused to negotiate and classes were not resumed until October. The strike morphed into a political movement called the Peoples Popular Assembly of Oaxaca (APPO is its Spanish acronym). Among other things, APPO is calling for the resignation of the state's governor—who is widely perceived as corrupt—and the dramatic improvement of the state's education system. The federal government sent in troops to end the strike and disperse the peaceful demonstrations in November 2006, which it did with significant use of violence. As of spring 2007, there were still many people in prison, Amnesty International charged that officials were torturing and mistreating many prisoners, and the demonstrations continued, though the troops reclaimed the central plaza. The education system in Oaxaca remains one of the poorest in all of Mexico.

9. Pamela Starr, quoted in Dickerson (2006).

10. American Immigration Law Foundation, http://www.ailf.org/ipc/ipc _index.asp.

11. http://www.forbes.com/2006/09/21/americas-400-richest-biz_cx_mm _06rich400_0921richintro.html

12. While many of these children are eligible for State Children's Health Insurance Program or SCHIP, which is a federal and state government-sponsored

plan to aid families who earn too much to qualify for Medicare, some states have frozen their SCHIP plans, thus preventing eligible children from receiving benefits.

13. American Immigration Law Foundation, http://www.ailf.org/ipc/ipc _index.asp.

14. The Supreme Court decided in *Hamdan v Rumsfeld* on 29 June 2006 that political prisoners are entitled to the protections of Common Article 3 of the Geneva Convention. On September 28–29 the House and the Senate passed the Military Commissions Act, which establishes procedures to try detainees and adopts standards for their treatment. President Bush signed the bill into law. The McCain amendment to the 2006 Appropriations Bill reaffirmed the ban on torture and the inhumane treatment of detainees wherever they are held. On September 6, the Department of Defense released an updated policy manual and field directive that claims to prohibit torture and require adherence to the standards spelled out in Common Article 3. However human rights organizations, including Amnesty International and Human Rights Watch remained highly critical of the Bush administration's definition of torture and cruel, inhuman, and degrading treatment as contained in the Military Commissions Act and in the McCain amendment, arguing that what U.S. policy now allows for does in fact rise to the level of cruel, inhuman, and degrading treatment and in some cases torture. See Amnesty International's Web site at http://amnesty.org.

References

Abraham, Nabeel. 1994. "Anti-Arab Racism and Violence in the United States." In *The Development of Arab-American Identity*. Ernest McCarus, editor. Pp.155–214. Ann Arbor: University of Michigan Press.

Abraham, Nabeel, and Andrew Shryock, eds. 2000. *Arab Detroit: From Margin to Mainstream*. Detroit: Wayne State University Press.

Abu-Lughod, Lila, 1993. *Writing Women's Worlds: Bedouin Stories*. Berkeley and Los Angeles: University of California Press.

Acevedo, Juan Camilo. 2000. "¿Desplazamiento o despojo?" In *Exodo, patrimonio e identidad*. Memorias V Cátedra Anual de Historia, Ernesto Restrepo Tirado. Pp.62–66. Bogotá: Museo Nacional de Colombia.

Ackleson, Jason. 2003a. "Securing through Technology? 'Smart Borders' after September 11th." *Knowledge, Technology, & Policy* 16: 56–74.

———. 2003b. "Directions in Border Security Research." *The Social Science Journal* 40: 573–581.

Acuna, Rodolfo. 1981. *Occupied America: A History of Chicanos*. New York: Harper & Row.

Adam, I. 2006. "Plan Colombia—Six Years Later." International Policy Report. http://www.ciponline.org/colombia/0611ipr.pdf.

Agamben, Giorgio. 2002. "Security and Terror." Translated by Carolin Emcke. *Theory & Event* 5(4).

Aho, Paul. 2006. "The U.S. Poultry Industry and Hispanic Immigration." *Broiler Economics Bulletin* 14(2). http:// www.aviagen.com/docs/April% 202006%20Broiler%20Economics_email.pdf.

Akram, Susan M. 1989. "Historic Court Decision Protects First Amendment Rights of Dissident Aliens." *Immigration Newsletter* 18: 1, 7–9.

———. 1999. "Scheherezade Meets Kafka: Two Dozen Sordid Tales of Ideological Exclusion." *Georgetown Immigration Law Journal* 14: 51–113.

Akram, Susan M., and Kevin R. Johnson, 2002. "Race, Civil Rights, and Immigration Law after September 11, 2001: The Targeting of Arabs and Muslims." *N.Y.U. Annual Survey of American Law* 58(3): 295–355.

Akram, Susan M., and Terry Rempel. 2004. "Temporary Protection as an Instrument for Implementing the Right of Return for Palestinian Refugees." *Boston University International Law Journal* 22(1): 1–162.

Aktar, Cingiz, and Nedim Ögelman. 1994. "Recent Developments in East-West Migration: Turkey and the Petty Traders." *International Migration* 32(2): 343–354.

Aleinikoff, T. Alexander, et al. 1998. *Immigration and Citizenship: Process and Policy.* 4th ed. St. Paul, MN: West Group.

Alissa, Sufyan. 2007. *Rethinking Economic Reform in Jordan: Confronting Socioeconomic Realities.* Washington, DC: Carnegie Endowment for International Peace.

Allam, Hannah. 2007. "U.S. Accused of Ignoring Crisis for 4.5 Million Displaced Iraqis." McClatchy Newspapers, 13 November. http://www.mcclatchy dc.com/100/story/21470.html.

Allen, Garland E. 1986. "The Eugenics Records Office at Cold Spring Harbor, 1910–1940: An Essay in Institutional History." OSIRIS, 2nd Series, 2: 225–264.

Alvarez, Robert R. 2001. "Beyond the Border: Nation-State Encroachment, NAFTA, and Offshore Control in the U.S.-Mexican Mango Industry." *Human Organization* 60: 121–127.

Ambrus, Steven. 2007. "Dominion of Evil." *Amnesty International: The Magazine of Amnesty International USA* 33(1): 16–20.

American-Arab Anti-Discrimination Committee. 2003. *Report on Hate Crimes and Discrimination against Arab-Americans: The Post-September 11 Backlash (September 11, 2001—October 11, 2002).* Hussein Ibish, editor. Pp.123–130. Washington, DC: American-Arab Anti-Discrimination Committee Research Institute.

Amnesty International. 1998. "From San Diego to Brownsville: Human Rights Violations on the USA-Mexico Border." http://web.amnesty.org/library/Index/ENGAMR510331998?open&of=ENG-2M2.

———. 2002. *Amnesty International's Concerns Regarding Post September 11 Detentions in the USA.* New York: Amnesty International.

———. 2004. "People's Republic of China: Uighurs Fleeing Persecution as China Wages Its 'War on Terror.'" *AI Index,* 7 July. http://web.amnesty.org/library/index/engasa170212004.

———. 2005. *Iraq: Decades of Suffering, Now Women Deserve Better.* New York: Amnesty International. 22 February.

———. 2007. *Millions in Flight: The Iraqi Refugee Crisis.* New York: Amnesty International. 24 September.

Anderson, Benedict. 1983. *Imagined Communities.* London: Verso.

Andreas, Peter. 1998a. The U.S. Immigration Control Offensive: Constructing an Image of Order on the Southwest Border." In *Crossings: Mexican Immigration in Interdisciplinary Perspectives.* Marcelo Suárez-Orozco, editor. Pp.343–356. Cambridge, MA: Harvard University Press for the David Rockefeller Center for Latin American Studies.

———. 1998b. "The Escalation of U.S. Immigration Control in the Post-NAFTA Era." *Political Science Quarterly* 113: 591–601.

———. 2000. *Border Games: Policing the U.S.-Mexico Divide.* Ithaca, NY: Cornell University Press.

———. 2001. "The Transformation of Migrant Smuggling across the U.S.-Mexico Border." In *Global Human Smuggling: Comparative Perspectives.* David Kyle and Rey Koslowski, editors. Pp.107–125. Baltimore: Johns Hopkins University Press.

———. 2003. "A Tale of Two Borders: The U.S.-Canada and U.S.-Mexico Lines after 9–11." In *The Rebordering of North America: Integration and Exclusion in a New Security Context.* Peter Andreas and Thomas J. Biersteker, editors. Pp.1–23. New York: Routledge.

Andreas, Peter, and Thomas J. Biersteker, eds. 2003. *The Rebordering of North America: Integration and Exclusion in a New Security Context.* New York: Routledge.

Anti-Defamation League of B'nai B'rith. 1983. *Pro-Arab Propaganda in America: Vehicles and Voices. A Handbook.* Boston: Anti-Defamation League.

Appadurai, Arjun. 1996. *Modernity at Large: Cultural Dimensions of Globalization.* Minneapolis: University of Minnesota Press.

Arellano, Gustavo. 2003. "Fear of a Brown Planet." *OC Weekly,* 5 September: 16–21.

Arenson, Karen, and N.R. Kleinfield. 2005. "President, an Expert on Free Speech, Gets an Earful." *New York Times,* 25 May: A1.

Armas, Genero C. 2003. "U.S. Foreign Born Population Hits High." The Associated Press, 10 March.

Armour, Jody. 1995. "Stereotypes and Prejudice: Helping Legal Decisionmakers Break the Prejudice Habit." *California Law Review* 83: 733–772.

Aswad, Barbara, and Barbara Bilgé, eds. 1996. *Family and Gender among American Muslims: Issues Facing Middle Eastern Immigrants and Their Descendants.* Philadelphia: Temple University Press.

Bakalar, Nicholas. 2007. "The Line between Torture and Cruelty. *New York Times,* 6 March: D6.

Baker, Bob. 1986. "Anti-Arab Violence Represents 17% of Racial, Religious Attacks in 1985." *Los Angeles Times,* 1 March, part 1: 29.

Baker, Dean. 2006. "Increasing Inequality in the United States." Center for Economic and Policy Research. http://www.cepr.net/cepr_news/faf_2006_11.pdf.

Balderrama, Francisco, and Raymond Rodriguez. 1995. *Decade of Betrayal: Mexican Repatriation in the 1930s.* Albuquerque: University of New Mexico Press.

Balz, Dan. 2006. "Political Splits on Immigration Reflect Voters' Ambivalence." *The Washington Post,* 3 January: A7.

Banks, William C. 2000. "The 'LA Eight' and Investigation of Terrorist Threats in the United States." *Columbia Human Rights Law Review* 31: 479–519.

Bard, Mitchell G. 2004. "Tenured or Tenuous: Defining the Role of Faculty in

Supporting Israel on Campus." http://www.jewishvirtuallibrary.org/pub/tenure.html.

Barr, Nicholas. 1994. "Income Transfers: Social Insurance." In *Labour Markets and Social Policy in Central and Eastern Europe: A World Bank Book.* Nicholas Barr, editor. Pp. 192–225. New York: Oxford University Press.

Barrett, James R. 1992. "Americanization from the Bottom Up: Immigration and the Remaking of the Working Class in the United States, 1880–1930." *Journal of American History* 79(3): 996–1020.

Barry, Tom. 2005. "Anti-Immigrant Backlash on the 'Home Front.'" *NACLA Report on the Americas* 38(6): 28–32.

Bassiouni, M. Cherif. 1974. "Introduction." In *The Civil Rights of Arab-Americans: "The Special Measures."* M. Cherif Bassiouni, editor. Pp.v–viii. North Dartmouth, MA: Association of Arab-American University Graduates, Inc.

BBC News. 2006. "Coca-Growing Spreads in Colombia." 15 April. http://news.bbc.co.uk/2/hi/americas/4912582.stm.

———. 2009. "Row Erupts over Guantanamo Deal." BBC World News, 12 June. http://news.bbc.co.uk/2/hi/americas/8096335.stm.

Beard, Charles A., and Mary R. Beard. 1927. *The Rise of American Civilization, Volume II.* New York: MacMillan.

Becker, Arielle Levin, and Daniela Altimari. 2006. "Fear Delays Call for Help: Worker's Fall Now an Immigration Case." *Hartford Courant*, 24 May: A1.

Becquelin, Nicholas. 2004. "Criminalizing Ethnicity: Political Repression in Xinjiang." *China Rights Forum* 1: 39–46.

Belkin, Lisa. 1991. "For Many Arab-Americans, FBI Scrutiny Renews Fears." *New York Times*, 12 January: A4.

Béller-Hann, Ildikó. 1995. "Prostitution and Its Effects in Northeast Turkey." *European Journal of Women's Studies* 2: 219–235.

Berg, Martin. 1999. "ADL Agrees to Stop Spying on Civil Rights Groups." *LA Daily*, 28 September: 1.

Berke, Richard L. 2000. "Gore and Bradley Duel, Briefly, on Racial Issue." *New York Times*, 18 January: A20.

Bernal, Victoria. 2004. "Eritrea Goes Global: Reflections on Nationalism in a Transnational Era." *Cultural Anthropology* 19(1): 3–25.

Besserer, Federico. 1999. *Moisés Cruz: Historia de un transmigrante.* Culiacán Rosales, Sinaloa: Universidad Autónoma de Sinaloa; México, D.F.; Universidad Autónoma Metropolitana, Iztapalapa.

———. 2004. *Topografías transnacionales: Hacia una geografía de la vida transnacional.* México, D.F.: Plaza y Valdés: Universidad Autónoma Metropolitana, Unidad Iztapalapa.

Bhagwati, Jagdish N. 1984. "Incentives and Disincentives: International Migration." *Weltwirtschaftliches Archiv* 120(4): 678–704.

Biersteker, Thomas J. 2003. "The Rebordering of North America: Implications for Conceptualizing Borders after September 11." In *The Rebordering of North America: Integration and Exclusion in a New Security Context.*

Peter Andreas and Thomas J. Biersteker, editors. Pp.153–165. New York: Routledge.

Blanchard, Olivier Jean, Kenneth A. Froot, and Jeffrey D. Sachs. 1994. *The Transition in Eastern Europe.* Chicago: University of Chicago Press.

Bloch, Alexia. 2003a. *Red Ties and Residential Schools: Indigenous Siberians in a Post-Soviet State.* Philadelphia: University of Pennsylvania Press.

———. 2003b. "Victims of Trafficking or Entrepreneurial Women?: Narratives of Post-Soviet Entertainers in Turkey." *Canadian Woman Studies/les cahiers de la femme* 22 (3/4): 152–158.

Bloch, Alexia, and Laurel Kendall. 2004. *Museum at the End of the World: Encounters in the Russian Far East.* Philadelphia: University of Pennsylvania Press.

Blumberg, Rae Lesser, and Olha Shved. 2002. *Curbing Sex Slavery Abroad by Helping Women Earn a Living in Ukraine: Assessment of the Economic-Empowerment Aspects of the Anti-Trafficking Project, USAID/Kiev.* Washington, DC: U.S. Agency for International Development, Office of Women in Development.

Boosahda, Elizabeth. 2003. *Arab-American Faces and Values: The Origins of an Immigrant Community.* Austin: University of Texas Press.

Bornstein, Erica. 1994. "Mapping Change." Unpublished paper. University of California, Irvine.

Boswell, Terry, and David Jorjani. 1988. "Uneven Development and the Origins of Split Labor Market Discrimination: A Comparison of Black, Chinese, and Mexican Immigrant Minorities in the United States." In *Racism, Sexism, and the World System.* Joan Smith, Jane Collins, Terence K. Hopkins and Akbar Muhammed, editors. Pp. 169–186. New York: Greenwood Press.

Bosworth, Allan R. 1967. *America's Concentration Camps.* New York: W. W. Norton.

Brennan, Denise, 2004. *What's Love Got to Do With It?: Transnational Desires and Sex Tourism in the Dominican Republic.* Durham: Duke University Press.

Brock, Deborah. 1998. *Making Work, Making Trouble: Prostitution as a Social Problem.* Toronto: University of Toronto Press.

Brookings Institution. 2009. *Iraq Index: Tracking Variables of Reconstruction & Security in Post-Saddam Iraq.* http://www.brookings.edu/iraqindex.

Brooks, Rosa. 2006. "Do You Feel Safer?" *Los Angeles Times,* 8 September. http://www.latimes.com/news/columnists/la-oe-brooks8sep08,1,796343 63.column?coll=la-news-columns.

Brotherton, David. 2003. "The Deportees." *NACLA Report on the Americas* 37(2): 8–11.

Brown, Wendy. 1995. *States of Injury: Power and Freedom in Later Modernity.* Princeton, NJ: Princeton University Press.

Bruno, Andorra. 2006. *Refugee Admissions and Resettlement Policy.* Congressional Research Service publication. Washington, DC: Library of Congress.

Buckley, Cara, and Michael R. Gordon. 2007. "U.S. Says Attacks in Iraq Fell to the Level of February 2006." *New York Times*, 19 November: A1, A6.

Buck-Morss, Susan. 2003. *Thinking Past Terror: Islamism and Critical Theory on the Left*. London: Verso.

Burnham, Gilbert, Riyadh Lafta, Shannon Doocy, and Les Roberts. 2006. "Mortality after the 2003 Invasion of Iraq: A Cross-Sectional Cluster Sample Survey." *The Lancet* 368(9545): 1421–1428.

Bush, George W. 2002. *The National Security Strategy of the United States of America*. The White House, Washington, DC. http://www.whitehouse .gov/ncs.html.

Busza, Joanna, Sarah Castle, and Aisse Diarra. 2004. "Trafficking and Health." *British Medical Journal* 328: 1369–1371.

Buzan, Barry, Ole Wæver, and Jaap de Wilde. 1998. *Security: A New Framework for Analysis*. Boulder: Lynne Rienner.

Byman, Daniel L. 2007. "The Next Phase of the Iraq War." Brookings Institution. http://www.bookings .edu/opinions/2007/1115_iraq_byman.aspx?p=1.

Cainkar, Louise. 2004. "The Impact of the September 11 Attacks on Arab and Muslim Communities in the United States." In *The Maze of Fear: Security and Migration after 9/11*. John Tirman, editor. Pp.215–239. New York: The New Press.

———. 2009. *Homeland Insecurity: The Arab American and Muslim American Experience After 9/11*. New York: Russell Sage Foundation.

Calavita, Kitty. 1984. *U.S. Immigration Law and the Control of Labor: 1820–1924*. London: Academic Press.

———. 1992. *Inside the State: The Bracero Program, Immigration, and the I.N.S.* New York: Routledge.

Canada Newswire. 2006. "New GM Models Post Strong February Sales, Retail Sales Up 1 Percent; Overall Sales Decline 2.5 Percent Compared to Year-Ago Level." March 1, 2006.

Canadian Broadcasting Corporation (CBC). 2005. "Sex Slaves." Aired 15 October.

Cantú, Lionel. 2009. *Border Crossings: Mexican Men and the Sexuality of Migration*. Nancy A. Naples and Salvador Vidal-Ortiz, editors. New York: New York University Press.

Caplan, Jane, and John C. Torpey, eds. 2001. *Documenting Individual Identity: The Development of State Practices in the Modern World*. Princeton, NJ: Princeton University Press.

Capps, Randy, and Michael Fix. 2004. "Undocumented Immigrants: Facts and Figures." http://www.urban.org/UploadedPDF/1000587_undoc_immi grants_facts.pdf.

Cave, Damien. 2007. "Nonstop Theft and Bribery Stagger Iraq." *New York Times*, 2 December: A1, A26.

Ceballos, Marcela. 2003. *Plan Colombia: Contraproductos y crisis humanitaria—Fumigaciones y desplazamiento forzado en la frontera con Ecuador*. Bogotá: Consultoría para los Derechos Humanos y el Desplazamiento.

Center for Preventing Women in Trafficking. 2001. *Trafficking in Women in the Republic of Moldova*. Chisinau, Moldova: Association of Women Law Professionals.

Chavez, Leo. 1991. "Outside the Imagined Community: Undocumented Settlers and Experiences of Incorporation." *American Ethnologist* 18: 257–278.

———. 1992. *Shadowed Lives: Undocumented Immigrants in American Society*. Fort Worth, TX: Harcourt, Brace, Jovanovich.

———. 2001. *Covering Immigration: Popular Images and the Politics of the Nation*. Berkeley and Los Angeles: University of California Press.

———. 2007. "The Spectacle in the Desert: The Minuteman Project on the U.S-Mexico Border." In *Global Vigilantes: Anthropological Perspectives on Justice and Violence*. David Pratten and Atreyee Sen, editors. Pp. 25–46. New York: Columbia University Press.

Chin, Gabriel J. 1998. "Segregation's Last Stronghold: Race Discrimination and the Constitutional Law of Immigration." *UCLA Law Review* 46: 1–74.

Chisti, Muzaffar A., Doris Meissner, Demetrios G Papademetriou, Jay Peterzell, Michael J. Wishnie, and Stephen W. Yale-Loehr. 2003. *America's Challenge: Domestic Security, Civil Liberties, and National Unity after September 11: Appendix*. Washington, DC: Migration Policy Institute.

Chomsky, Noam. 1987. *Pirates & Emperors: International Terrorism in the Real World*. Montreal: Black Rose Books.

Christoffersen, Gaye. 2002. "Constituting the Uyghur in U.S.-China Relations: The Geopolitics of Identity Formation in the War on Terrorism. *Strategic Insights* 1(7). Available at Columbia International Affairs Online, http://ciaonet.org.

Chronicle Review. 2006. "Tony Judt, Israel, and Free Speech." *The Chronicle of Higher Education*'s *Chronicle Review* 53(11): 4.

CIA Factbook. 2006. https://www.cia.gov/library/publications/the-world-factbook.

Clark, Lesley. 2009. "GOP Ratchets Up Debate over Releasing Guantanamo Detainees." McClatchy Newspapers, 8 May.

Clarkson, Stephen. 2003. "The View from the Attic: Toward a Gated Continental Community." In *The Rebordering of North America: Integration and Exclusion in a New Security Context*. Peter Andreas and Thomas J. Biersteker, editors. Pp.68–89. New York and London: Routledge.

Clary, Mike, and Patrick McDonnell. 1998. "Sentenced to a Life in Limbo." *Los Angeles Times*, 9 September: 1.

Coben, Stanley. 1964. "A Study in Nativism: The American Red Scare of 1919–1920." *Political Science Quarterly* 79(1): 52–75.

CODHES (Consultoría para los Derechos Humanos y el Desplazamiento). 2004. "Ni seguridad, ni democracia." *CODHES Informa*, No 47. http://www.codhes.org.co.

Colburn, David R. 1973. "Governor Alfred E. Smith and the Red Scare, 1919–1920." *Political Science Quarterly* 88(3): 423–444.

Cole, David. 1993. "Guilt by Association: It's Alive and Well at INS." *The Nation* 256: 198–199.

———. 2002. "Their Liberties, Our Security: Democracy and Double Standards." *Boston Review* 27(6). http://bostonreview.net/BR27.6/cole.html.

———. 2003a. *Enemy Aliens: Double Standards and Constitutional Freedoms in the War on Terrorism.* New York: The New Press.

———. 2003b. "The New McCarthyism: Repeating History in the War on Terrorism." *Harvard Civil Rights–Civil Liberties Law Review* 38: 1–30.

Colhoun, Jack. 1991. "Trading with the Enemy." In *Covert Action: The Roots of Terrorism.* Ellen Ray and William H. Schaap, editors. Pp.212–219. New York: Ocean Press.

Congressional-Executive Commission on China. 2005. *Annual Report 2005.* http://www.cecc.gov/pages/annualRpt/annualRpt05/2005_6_tibet.php.

Constable, Nicole. 2003. *Romance on a Global Stage: Penpals, Virtual Ethnography, and Correspondence Marriage.* Berkeley and Los Angeles: University of California Press.

Cornelius, Wayne. 2002. "Ambivalent Reception: Mass Public Responses to the 'New' Latino Immigration to the United States." In *Latinos: Remaking America.* Marcelo M. Suárez-Orozco and Mariela M. Páez, editors. Pp.165–189. Berkeley and Los Angeles: University of California Press.

Cornelius, Wayne, Philip L. Martin, and James F. Hollifield. 1994. "Introduction: The Ambivalent Quest for Immigration Control." In *Controlling Immigration: A Global Perspective.* Wayne A. Cornelius, Philip L. Martin, and James F. Hollifield, editors. Pp. 3–41. Stanford, CA: Stanford University Press.

Cornelius, Wayne, and Takeyuki Tsuda. 2004. "Controlling Immigration: The Limits of Government Intervention." In *Controlling Immigration: A Global Perspective.* 2nd edition. Wayne A. Cornelius, Takeyuki Tsuda, Philip L. Martin, and James F. Hollifield, editors. Pp. 3–48. Stanford: Stanford University Press.

Couldrey, Marion, and Tim Morris. 2007. "From the Editors." *Forced Migration Review* (June, special issue): 3.

Coulter, Ann. 2001. "This Is War." *National Review Online,* 13 September. http://www.nationalreview.com/coulter/coulterprint091301.html.

Coutin, Susan Bibler. 2000. *Legalizing Moves: Salvadoran Immigrants' Struggle for U.S. Residency.* Ann Arbor, MI: University of Michigan Press.

Cox, Coriline. 1995. "Glyphosate: Human Exposure and Ecological Effects." *Journal of Pesticide Reform* 15(4): 14–20.

Cunningham, Hilary. 1999. "The Ethnography of Transnational Social Activism: Understanding the Global as Local Practice." *American Ethnologist* 26(3): 583–604.

Dagher, Sam. 2007. "Baghdad Safer, But It's a Life Behind Walls." *Christian Science Monitor,* 10 December. http://www.csmonitor.com/2007/1210/p01s04-wome.html.

Daniels, Roger. 2004. *Guarding the Golden Door: American Immigration Policy and Immigrants Since 1882.* New York: Hill and Wang.

Davis, Angela J. 1997. "Race, Cops, and Traffic Stops." *University of Miami Law Review* 51: 425–443.

DeCesare, Donna. 1998a. "The Children of War: Street Gangs in El Salvador." *NACLA Report on the Americas* 32(1): 21–29.

———. 1998b. "Deported 'Home' to Haiti." *NACLA Report on the Americas* 32(3): 6–10.

De Genova, Nicholas. 2002. "Migrant 'Illegality' and Deportability in Everyday Life." *Annual Review of Anthropology* 31: 419–447.

Delgado, Richard, and Jean Stefancic. 1992. "Images of the Outsider in American Law and Culture: Can Free Expression Remedy Systemic Social Ills?" *Cornell Law Review* 77: 1258–1297.

Dempsey, James X., and David Cole. 1999. *Terrorism and the Constitution: Sacrificing Civil Liberties in the Name of National Security*. Los Angeles: First Amendment Foundation.

Dib, George. 1988. "Laws Governing Migration in Some Arab Countries." In *International Migration Today, Volume I: Trends and Prospects*. Reginald T. Appleyard, editor. Pp.168–179. Perth: University of Western Australia for the United Nations Educational, Scientific, and Cultural Organization.

Dickerson, Marla. 2006. "Placing Blame for Mexico's Ills." *Los Angeles Times*, 1 July: C1–C10.

DIF and UNICEF. 2004 *Niñez migrante en la frontera norte: Legislación y procesos*. Desarrollo Integral de la Familia, Mexico and UNICEF.

Doezema, Jo. 2000. "Loose Women or Lost Women? The Re-Emergence of the Myth of White Slavery in Contemporary Discourses of Trafficking in Women." *Gender Issues* 18(1): 23–50.

Douglas, Mary. 1966. *Purity and Danger: An Analysis of the Concepts of Pollution and Taboo*. London: Routledge and Kegan Paul.

Downey, Dennis J. 1999. "From American to Multiculturalism: Political Symbols and Struggles for Cultural Diversity in Twentieth-Century American Race Relations." *Sociological Perspectives* 42(2): 249–278.

Doyle, Charles. 1996. "Antiterrorism and Effective Death Penalty Act of 1996: A Summary." American Law Division, Federation of American Scientists. http://www.fas.org/irp/crs/96-499.htm.

Duke, Lynne. 1991. "Islam Is Growing in U.S. Despite an Uneasy Image." *Washington Post*, 24 October: A1.

Dunn, Timothy J. 1996. *The Militarization of the U.S.-Mexico Border, 1978–1992: Low-Intensity Conflict Doctrine Comes Home*. Austin: Center for Mexican American Studies, University of Texas at Austin.

———. 1999. "Military Collaboration with the Border Patrol in the U.S.-Mexico Border Region: Inter-Organizational Relations and Human Rights Implications." *Journal of Political and Military Sociology* 27: 257–277.

Duong, Thu Huong. 1995. *Novel without a Name*. Translated by Phan Huy Duong and Nina McPherson. New York: W. Morrow.

Durand, Jorge, and Douglas S. Massey. 2003. "The Costs of Contradiction: U.S. Border Policy, 1986–2000." *Latino Studies* 1(2): 233–252.

Egelko, Bob. 2002. "Jewish Defense Group Settles S.F. Spying Suit." *San Francisco Chronicle*, 23 February: A23.

Eggen, Dan. 2002. "Alleged Remarks on Islam Prompt an Ashcroft Reply." *Washington Post*, 14 February: A31.

Ehrenreich, Barbara, and Arlie Russell Hochschild. 2002. "Introduction." In *Global Woman: Nannies, Maids, and Sex Workers in the New Economy.* Barbara Ehrenreich and Arlie R. Hochschild, editors. Pp.1–14. New York: Metropolitan Books.

———, eds. 2002. *Global Woman: Nannies, Maids, and Sex Workers in the New Global Economy.* New York: Metropolitan Books.

Elliott, Andrea. 2006. "After 9/11, Arab Americans Fear Police Acts, Study Finds." *New York Times*, 12 June: A15.

Engdahl, William. 2004. *A Century of War: Anglo-American Oil Politics and the New World Order.* Revised edition. London: Pluto Press.

Erokhina, L. 2000. "Mashtaby vyvoza zhenshchin v strany aziatsko-tikhookeanskogo regiona" [The scale of the export of women to countries of the Asia-Pacific region]. In *2nd International Conference on Trafficking in Women.* Moscow, Russia. October 23-November 3. Volume II. Koalitsia Angel, editor. Pp.122–129.

Eschbach, Karl, Jacqueline Hagan, and Nestor Rodríguez. 2003. "Deaths during Undocumented Migration: Trends and Implications in the New Era of Homeland Security." http://www.uh.edu/cir/death.htm.

Espenshade, Thomas J., and Charles A. Calhoun. 1993. "An Analysis of Public Opinion toward Undocumented Immigration." *Population Research and Policy Review* 12: 189–224.

Espenshade, Thomas J., and Katherine Hempstead. 1996. "Contemporary American Attitudes toward U.S. Immigration." *International Migration Review* 30: 535–570.

Espiritu, Yen Le. 1992. *Asian American Panethnicity: Bridging Identities and Institutions.* Philadelphia: Temple University Press.

Estrada Alvarez, Jairo, ed. 2001. *Plan Colombia: Ensayos críticos.* Bogotá: Universidad Nacional de Colombia.

———. 2002. *El Plan Colombia y la intensificación de la guerra: Aspectos globales y locales.* Bogotá: Universidad Nacional de Colombia.

Ethnic and Racial Studies. 1999. "Special Issue: Transnational Communities." 22(2).

Evans, Sara. 1979. *Personal Politics: The Roots of Women's Liberation in the Civil Rights Movement and the New Left.* New York: Vintage Books.

Ewing, Katherine, ed. 2008. *Being and Belonging: Muslims in the United States since 9/11.* New York: Russell Sage Foundation.

Fafo Institute for Applied International Studies. 2007. *Iraqis in Jordan 2007: Their Number and Characteristics.* Oslo: Fafo.

Fagen, Patricia Weiss. 2007. "Iraqi Refugees: Seeking Stability in Syria and Jordan." Report published by the Institute for the Study for International Migration, Georgetown University, and the Center for International and

Regional Studies, Georgetown University School of Foreign Service in Qatar.

Fajardo, Darío. 2000. *Bases para una política de asentamientos humanos, prevención de los desplazamientos forzados y acceso a la tierra para los desplazados*. Bogotá: Unidad Técnica Conjunta (ACNUR-RSS).

Federal Bureau of Investigation (FBI). 1987. "Domestic Terrorism in the 1980s." *FBI Law Enforcement Bulletin*, October: 13.

Fernández-Kelly, María Patricia. 1983. *For We Are Sold, I and My People: Women and Industry in Mexico's Frontier*. Albany: State University of New York Press.

Fernández-Kelly, María Patricia, and Saskia Sassen. 1995. "Recasting Women in the Global Economy: Internationalization and Changing Definitions of Gender." In *Women in the Latin American Development Process*. Christine Bose and Edna Acosta-Belén, editors. Pp.99–124 Philadelphia: Temple University Press.

Fink, Deborah. 1992. *Agrarian Women: Wives and Mothers in Rural Nebraska 1880–1940*. Chapel Hill: University of North Carolina Press.

———. 1998. *Cutting into the Meatpacking Line: Workers and Change in the Rural Midwest*. Chapel Hill: University of North Carolina Press.

Fischer, Michael M.J. 2007. "To Live With What Would Otherwise Be Unendurable: Return(s) to Subjectivities." In *Subjectivity*. Joao Biehl, Byron Good, and Arthur Kleinman, editors. Pp. 423-446. Berkeley and Los Angeles: University of California Press.

Fischer, Michael M.J., and Mehdi Abedi. 1990. *Debating Muslims: Cultural Dialogues in Postmodernity and Tradition*. Madison: University of Wisconsin Press.

Flynn, Stephen. 2000. "Beyond Border Control." *Foreign Affairs* 79(6): 57–68.

———. 2002. "America the Vulnerable." *Foreign Affairs* 80(1): 60–74.

———. 2003. "The False Conundrum: Continental Integration versus Homeland Security." In *The Rebordering of North America: Integration and Exclusion in a New Security Context*. Peter Andreas and Thomas J. Biersteker, editors. Pp. 110–127. New York: Routledge.

Foreman-Peck, James. 1992. "A Political Economy Model of International Migration, 1815–1914." *The Manchester School* 60: 359–376.

Freeman, Gary P. 1992, "Migration Policy and Politics in the Receiving States." *International Migration Review* 26: 1144–1167.

———. 1994. "Can Liberal States Control Unwanted Immigration?" *Annals of the American Academy of Political and Social Science* 534: 17–30.

———. 1995. "Modes of Immigration Politics in Liberal Democratic States." *International Migration Review* 29: 881–902.

———. 1998. "The Decline of Sovereignty? Politics and Immigration Restriction in Liberal States." In *Challenge to the Nation-State: Immigration in Western Europe and the United States*. Christian Joppke, editor. Pp.86–108. Oxford: Oxford University Press.

Frelick, William. 2007. "The Human Cost of War: The Iraqi Refugee Crisis."

Testimony before the Congressional Human Rights Caucus, 15 November. http://hrw.org/english/docs/2007/11/15/iraq17340.htm.

Frenzen, Niels W. 1999. "National Security and Procedural Fairness: Secret Evidence and the Immigration Laws." *Interpreter Releases* 76: 1677–1685.

Fry, Rick. 2005. *The Higher Dropout Rate of Foreign-Born Teens: The Role of Schooling Abroad.* Pew Hispanic Center Reports and Fact Sheet. http://pewhispanic.org/files/reports/55.pdf.

Fund for Peace and *Foreign Policy* Magazine. 2007. *The Failed States Index 2007.* http://www.foreignpolicy.com/story/cms.php?story_id=3865.

Gabany-Guerrero, Tricia. 2001. "The Implications of Border Deportation Policies: Mexican Deportees in Ciudad Juárez, Chihuahua, México." Paper presented at the Anthropology and Sociology Departments, The University of Texas at El Paso.

———. 2002. *Partnering on the Border: La Casa del Migrante.* Unpublished report for Community Partnerships, Kellogg Foundation Grant, The University of Texas at El Paso.

Gaines, Robert. 2005. "Amid Other Attacks on Academic Freedom, Columbia Crisis Continues." *Washington Report on Middle East Affairs*, May/June: 40, 45, 49.

Gandelman, Joe. 1986. "Wilson Would Back Marines on Border if Reform Move Fails." *San Diego Union*, 6 April: A3.

Gerrull, Sally-Anne, and Boronia Halstead. 1992. *Sex Industry and Public Policy.* Canberra: Australian Institute of Criminology.

Gesser, Charles R. 1974. "A Non-Arab Looks at an Anti-Arab American Policy." In *The Civil Rights of Arab-Americans: "The Special Measures."* M. Cherif Bassiouni, editor. Pp.16–27. North Dartmouth, MA: Association of Arab-American University Graduates, Inc.

Ghencea, Boris, and Igor Gudumac. 2004. *Labor Migration and Remittances in the Republic of Moldova.* Chisinau: Moldova Microfinance Alliance and Soros Moldova.

Gil, Rocío. 2006. *Fronteras de pertenencia: Hacia la construcción del bienestar y el desarrollo comunitario transnacional de Santa María Tindú, Oaxaca.* México, D.F.: Casa Juan Pablos, Fundación Rockefeller, Universidad Autónoma Metropolitana, Unidad Iztapalapa.

Gilboy, Janet. 1992. "Penetrability of Administrative Systems: Political 'Casework' and Immigration Inspectors." *Law and Society Review* 26: 273–314.

Gillespie, Michael. 1999. "Los Angeles Court Hands Down Final Judgment in Anti-Defamation League Illegal Surveillance Case." *Washington Report on Middle Eastern Affairs*, December: 43, 137.

Gladney, Dru C. 1997. *Ethnic Identity in China: The Making of a Muslim Minority Nationality.* Wadsworth Publishing.

———. 2004a. *Dislocating China: Muslims, Minorities, and other Subaltern Subjects.* Chicago: University of Chicago Press.

———. 2004b. "Xinjiang: Assessing Stability or Instability." Unpublished paper.

Glava Administratsii khabarovskogo kraia. 2000. *O protivodeistvii vovlech-eniiu v zaniatie prostitutsiei grazhdan, vyezhaiushchix za rubezh s ter-ritorii khabarovskogo kraia* [Concerning efforts to combat drawing women from the Khabarovsk region into foreign prostitution]. Postanovlenie ot 16 oktiabria, n. 354.

Glick Schiller, Nina. 1999. "Citizens in Transnational Nation-States: The Asian Experience." In *Globalization and the Asia-Pacific: Contested Territories.* Kris Olds, Peter Dicken, Philip Kelly, and Henry Wai-chung Yeung, editors. Pp.202–212. New York: Routledge.

Global IDP Project. 2004. *La política de "seguridad democrática" fracasa en mejorar la protección a los desplazados internos.* http://www.idpproject.org.

Golden, Deborah. 2003. "A National Cautionary Tale: Russian Women New-comers to Israel Portrayed." *Nations and Nationalism* 9(1): 83–104.

Goldstein, Melvyn C. 1989. *A History of Modern Tibet, 1913–1951: The Demise of the Lamaist State.* Berkeley and Los Angeles: University of California Press.

———. 1999. *The Snow Lion and the Dragon: China, Tibet, and the Dalai Lama.* Berkeley and Los Angeles: University of California Press.

González Bustelo, Mabel. 2001. *Desterrados: El desplazamiento forzado en Colombia.* Doctors without Borders, Spain. http://www.disaster-info.net/desplazados/informes/msf/informedesplazados.htm.

Goodstein, Laurie, and Tamar Lewin. 2001. "Victims of Mistaken Identity, Sikhs Pay a Price for Turbans." *New York Times,* 19 September: A1.

Goott, Amy Kaufman, and Steven J. Rosen. 1983. *The Campaign to Discredit Israel.* Washington, DC: American Israel Public Affairs Committee.

Gordon, Michael R., and Stephen Farrell. 2007. "Iraq Unprepared as War Refu-gees Return, U.S. Says." *New York Times,* 30 November: A1, A12.

Green, Linda. 2003. "The Creation of Fear on the U.S.-Mexico Border." Paper presented at the 102nd Annual Meeting of the American Anthropological Association, Chicago, IL, 22 November.

Greene, Richard A. 2005. "War Takes Toll on Iraqi Mental Health." *BBC News,* 12 August. http://news.bbc.co.uk/1/hi/world/middle_east/4620279.stm.

Guerin-Gonzales, Camilla. 1994. *Mexican Workers and American Dreams: Immigration, Repatriation, and California Farm Labor, 1900–1939.* New Brunswick, NJ: Rutgers University Press.

Guterres, António. 2007. "Statement by Mr. António Guterres, United Nations High Commissioner for Refugees, Conference on Addressing the Humani-tarian Needs of Refugees and Internally Displaced Persons inside Iraq and in Neighboring Countries," 17 April. http://www.unhcr.org/admin/ADMIN/46249041.html.

Guy, Donna J. 1990. *Sex and Danger in Buenos Aires: Prostitution, Family, and Nation in Argentina.* Lincoln: University of Nebraska Press.

Gzesh, Susan. 2008. "Redefining Forced Migration Using Human Rights." *Migración y Desarrollo* 10: 87–113.

Haddad, Yvonne, ed. 2002. *Muslims in the West: From Sojourners to Citizens.* New York: Oxford University Press.

Haddad, Yvonne, and Jane Smith, eds. 1994. *Muslim Communities in North America.* Albany: State University of New York Press.

———. 2002. *Muslim Minorities in the West: Visible and Invisible.* Walnut Creek, CA: Altamira Press.

Hagan, John, and Alberto Palloni. 1999. "Sociological Criminology and the Mythology of Hispanic Immigration and Crime." *Social Problems* 46(4): 617–632.

Hagopian, Elaine. 1975–76. "Minority Rights in a Nation-State: The Nixon Administration's Campaign against Arab-Americans." *Journal of Palestine Studies,* Autumn-Winter: 97–114.

———, ed. 2004. *Civil Rights in Peril: The Targeting of Arabs and Muslims.* Chicago: Haymarket Books.

Hall, Kermit L. 1989. *The Magic Mirror: Law in American History.* New York: Oxford University Press.

Hamilton, Walter. 2006. "Middle Class May Lose a Home in NYC." *Los Angeles Times,* 24 October: A-10.

Hanley, Delinda C. 2002a. "Muslim-American Activism: ADL and AJC Demand Muslim Panelists Be Excluded." *Washington Report on Middle East Affairs,* January-February: 82–84.

———. 2002b. "Freeze on Jewish Defense League Assets Called for after JDL Bomb Plot Foiled." *Washington Report on Middle East Affairs,* January-February: 16.

Hann, C.M., and I. Béller-Hann. 1992. "Samovars and Sex on Turkey's Russian Markets." *Anthropology Today* 8(4): 3–6.

Hansen, Suzy. 2006. "Judt at War." *New York Observer,* 16 October: 1.

Harding, Scott. 2004. "The Sound of Silence: Social Work, the Academy, and Iraq." *Journal of Sociology and Social Welfare* 31(2): 179–197.

———. 2007. "Man-made Disaster and Development: The Case of Iraq." *International Social Work* 50: 295–306.

Hardt, Michael, and Antonio Negri, 2001. *Empire.* Cambridge: Harvard University Press.

Harris, David A. 1999. "The Stories, the Statistics, and the Law: Why 'Driving while Black' Matters." *Minnesota Law Review* 84: 265–326.

Hatton, Timothy J., and Jeffrey G. Williamson. 1998. *The Age of Mass Migration: Causes and Impact.* New York: Oxford University Press.

Hayes, Linda B. 1994. "California's Prop 187." Letter to the Editor, *New York Times,* 15 October.

Hemment, Julie. 2004. "The Riddle of the Third Sector: Civil Society, Western Aid, and NGOs in Russia." *Anthropological Quarterly* 77(2): 215–241.

Hermansen, Marcia. 1991. "Two-Way Acculturation: Muslim Women in America between Individual Choice (Liminality) and Community Affiliation (Communitas)." In *The Muslims of America.* Edited by Yvonne Yazbeck Haddad. Pp.288–204. New York: Oxford University Press.

Hernandez, David M. 2005. "Undue Process: Immigrant Detention, Due Process, and Lesser Citizenship." Institute for the Study of Social Change. ISSC Fellows Working Papers. Paper ISSC_WP_06. http://repositories.cdlib.org/issc/fwp/ISSC_WP_06.

Hernández Sánchez, María Eugenia. 2007. *Niños migrantes en Ciudad Juárez, dos momentos: Años veinte y presente.* Master's thesis, anthropology. Escuela Nacional de Antropologia e Historia-Unidad Chihuahua (ENAH-Chihuahua) and Centro de Investigaciones y Estudios Superiores en Antropología Social (CIESAS), Mexico.

Hernandez-Truyol, Berta Esperanza. 2000. "Nativism, Terrorism, and Human Rights: The Global Wrongs of Reno v. American-Arab Anti-Discrimination Committee." *Columbia Human Rights Law Review* 31: 521–559.

Hertel, Shareen. 2006. *Unexpected Power: Conflict and Change among Transnational Activists.* Ithaca, NY: Cornell University Press.

Hess, Julia Meredith. 2006. "Statelessness and the State: Tibetans, Citizenship, and Nationalist Activism in a Transnational World." *International Migration* 44(1): 79–103.

———. 2009. *Immigrant Ambassadors: Citizenship and Belonging in the Tibetan Diaspora.* Stanford, CA: Stanford University Press.

Heyman, Josiah McC. 1995. "Putting Power in the Anthropology of Bureaucracy: The Immigration and Naturalization Service at the Mexico-United States Border." *Current Anthropology* 36: 261–287.

———. 1998. *Finding a Moral Heart for U.S. Immigration Policy: An Anthropological Perspective.* Washington, DC: American Anthropological Association.

———. 1999a. "Why Interdiction? Immigration Law Enforcement at the United States-Mexico Border." *Regional Studies* 33: 619–630.

———. 1999b. "State Escalation of Force: A Vietnam/U.S.-Mexico Border Analogy." In *States and Illegal Practices.* Josiah McC. Heyman, editor. Pp.285–314. Oxford: Berg.

———. 1999c. "United States Surveillance over Mexican Lives at the Border: Snapshots of an Emerging Regime." *Human Organization* 58: 430–438.

———. 2000. "Respect for Outsiders? Respect for the Law? The Moral Evaluation of High-Scale Issues by U.S. Immigration Officers." (Curl Prize Essay.) *Journal of the Royal Anthropological Institute* (N.S.) 6: 635–652.

———. 2001. "Class and Classification on the U.S.-Mexico Border." *Human Organization* 60: 128–140.

———. 2002. "U.S. Immigration Officers of Mexican Ancestry as Mexican Americans, Citizens, and Immigration Police." *Current Anthropology* 43: 479–507.

———. 2004. "Ports of Entry as Nodes in the World System." *Identities* 11: 303–327.

Higgins, Alexander. 2004. "Phone Numbers Cited in Swiss Terror Probe." *Boston Globe,* 13 January: A11.

Higham, John. 1988. *Strangers in the Land: Patterns of American Nativism, 1860–1925*. New Brunswick: Rutgers University Press.

Hiltermann, Joost. 2007. *A Poisonous Affair: America, Iraq, and the Gassing of Halabja*. New York: Cambridge University Press.

Hing, Bill Ong. 2002. "Vigilante Racism: The De-Americanization and Subordination of Immigrant America." *Michigan Journal of Race and Law* 7: 441–456.

Hoffman, Bruce. 1986. *Terrorism in the United States and the Potential Threat to Nuclear Facilities*. Santa Monica, CA: Rand Corporation.

Hollifield, James F. 1992. "Migration and International Relations: Cooperation and Control in the European Community." *International Migration Review* 26: 569–595.

Hondagneu-Sotelo, Pierrette, and Michael Messner. 1994. "Gender Displays and Men's Power: 'The New Man' and the Mexican Immigrant Man." In *Theorizing Masculinities*. Harry Brod and Michael Kaufman, editors. Pp. 200–218. Thousand Oaks, CA: Sage Publications.

hooks, bell. 1990. *Yearning: Race, Gender, and Cultural Politics*. Boston: South End Press.

Howard, Lawrence. 1992. *Terrorism: Roots, Impact, Responses*. New York: Praeger.

Howell, Sally, and Andrew Shryock. 2003. "Cracking Down on Diaspora: Arab Detroit and America's 'War on Terror.'" *Anthropological Quarterly* 73: 443–462.

Hufbauer, Gary Clyde, and Gustavo Vega-Cánovas. 2003. "Wither NAFTA: A Common Frontier?" In *The Rebordering of North America: Integration and Exclusion in a New Security Context*. Peter Andreas and Thomas J. Biersteker, editors. Pp. 128–152. New York: Routledge.

Hughes, Donna M. 2000. "Trafficking in 'Natashas'—The Transnational Black Market in Women." In Proceedings of Koalitsia Angel, 2nd International Conference on Trafficking in Women. Moscow, Russia. October 23–November 3. Pp. 67–84.

Human Rights Watch. 1992. *Brutality Unchecked: Human Rights Abuses along the U.S. Border with Mexico*. New York: Human Rights Watch.

———. 1995. *Crossing the Line: Human Rights Abuses along the U.S. Border with Mexico Persist amid Climate of Impunity*. http://www.hrw.org/reports/1995/Us1.htm.

———. 1998. *Detained and Deprived of Rights: Children in the Custody of the U.S. Immigration and Naturalization Service*. http://www.hrw.org/reports98/ins2/index.htm#TopOfPage.

———. 2000a. *Fingers to the Bone: United States Failure to Protect Child Farmworkers*. http://www.hrw.org/reports/2000/frmwrkr.

———. 2000b. *Unfair Advantage: Workers' Freedom of Association in the United States under International Human Rights Standards*. http://www.hrw.org/reports/2000/uslabor.

———. 2001. "Bush-Fox Summit: Human Rights Watch Backgrounder on

U.S.-Mexico Ties." http://www.hrw.org/backgrounder/americas/mexo212. htm.

————. 2002. *Presumption of Guilt: Human Rights Abuses Post-September 11 Detainees.* http://hrw.org/reports/2002/us911.

————. 2005a. *Devastating Blows: Religious Repression of Uighurs in Xinjiang.* http://www.hrw.org/reports/2005/china0405.

————. 2005b. "Human Rights Watch Recommendations with Respect to the Regulatory Decree for Law 975 of 2005." http://hrw.org/english/docs/2006/05/31/colomb13487.htm.

————. 2005c. "Immigrant Workers in the United States Meat and Poultry Industry." Submission by Human Rights Watch to the Office of the United Nations High Commissioner for Human Rights, Committee on Migrant Workers. Day of General Discussion: Protecting the Rights of All Migrant Workers as a Tool to Enhance Development. Geneva, Switzerland, 15 December 2005.

————. 2007. "Colombia: Events of 2006." http://hrw.org/englishwr2k7/docs/2007/01/11/colomb14884.htm.

Hunaiti, Doukhi, and Soud M. Al-Tayeb. 2005. "The Estimation of Absolute and Abject Poverty Lines in Some of the Remote Areas in the Southern Region of Jordan and Comparing Them with the Official Poverty Line." *Dirasat: Human and Social Sciences* 32(1): 25–44.

Huntington, Samuel P. 2000. "The Special Case of Mexican Immigration: Why Mexico Is a Problem." *The American Enterprise*, December: 20–22.

————. 2004. "The Hispanic Challenge." *Foreign Policy*, March/April 2004: 30–45.

Huysmans, Jef. 1995. "Migrants as a Security Problem: Dangers of 'Securitizing' Societal Issues." In *Migration and European Integration: The Dynamics of Inclusion and Exclusion.* Robert Miles and Dietrich Thränhardt, editors. Pp.53–72. London: Pinter.

ICE (U.S. Immigration and Customs Enforcement). 2006. *Fiscal Year 2006 Annual Report. Protecting National Security and Upholding Public Safety.* http://www.ice.gov.

ICRC (International Committee of the Red Cross). 2007. *Iraq: Civilians without Protection. The Ever-Worsening Humanitarian Crisis in Iraq.* Geneva: ICRC.

ILO. 2004. *Report VI: Towards a Fair Deal for Migrant Workers in the Global Economy.* International Labour Conference, 92nd Session. Geneva: International Labour Office.

Immigration and Naturalization Service. 2000. *1998 Statistical Yearbook of the Immigration and Naturalization Service.* Washington, DC: Government Printing Office.

Inda, Jonathan Xavier. 2006. *Targeting Immigrants: Government, Technology, and Ethics.* Oxford: Blackwell.

Instituto Nacional de Migración (Mexico). 2009. *Estadísticas migratorias.* http://www.inami.gob.mx/index.php?page/Estadistcas_Migratorias.

International Organization for Migration (IOM). 2005. "IOM Helpline Helps Rescue Trafficked Victims." Press briefing notes, 5 August. http://www.iom.int/en/news/PBN050805.shtml.

Iraq Ministry of Planning and Development Cooperation. 2008. *Iraq National Report on the Status of Human Development 2008.* Baghdad.

Isaacson, Adam. 2003. "Washington's 'New War' in Colombia: The War on Drugs Meets the War on Terror." *NACLA Report on the Americas* 36(5): 13–18.

Isikoff, Michael. 2003. "Investigators: The FBI Says, Count the Mosques." *Newsweek* 3 February: 4.

Jabara, Abdeen. 1993. "The Anti-Defamation League: Civil Rights and Wrongs." *Covert Action* 45 (summer): 28–37.

Jacobson, David. 1997. *Rights across Borders: Immigration and the Decline of Citizenship.* Baltimore: Johns Hopkins University Press.

Jahic, Galma, and James O. Finckenauer. 2005. "Representations and Misrepresentations of Human Trafficking." *Trends in Organized Crime* 8(3): 24–40.

Jamous, Mukhaimer Abu. 2007. "The World Must Shoulder Iraq Burden." *Forced Migration Review* (June, special issue): 17–18.

Johnson, Chalmers. 2004. *The Sorrows of Empire: Militarism, Secrecy, and the End of the Republic.* New York: Metropolitan/Owl Books.

Johnson, Kevin R. 1996. "'Aliens' and the U.S. Immigration Laws: The Social and Legal Construction of Nonpersons." *University of Miami Inter-American Law Review* 28: 263–292.

———.1997. "The Antiterrorism Act, the Immigration Reform Act, and Ideological Regulation in the Immigration Laws: Important Lessons for Citizens and Noncitizens." *St. Mary's Law Journal* 28: 833–882.

———. 2000. "The Case against Racial Profiling in Immigration Enforcement." *Washington University Law Quarterly* 78: 675–736.

Jonakait, Randolph N. 2003–2004. "A Double Due Process Denial: The Crime of Providing Material Support or Resources to Designated Foreign Terrorist Organizations." *New York Law School Law Review* 48: 125–172.

Joppke, Christian, ed. 1998a. *Challenge to the Nation-State: Immigration in Western Europe and the United States.* Oxford: Oxford University Press.

———. 1998b. "Why Liberal States Accept Unwanted Immigration." *World Politics* 50(2): 266–293.

Joseph, Suad. 1999. "Against the Grain of the Nation—The Arab." In *Arabs in America: Building a New Future.* Michael W. Suleiman editor. Pp.257–271. Philadelphia: Temple University Press.

Kateel, Subhash. 2007. Comments presented at the panel "Human Rights Considerations in Reform Processes." at the conference "Hacia políticas migratorias integrales" [Toward comprehensive migration policies], Santo Domingo, 28–30 March.

Kearney, Michael. 1996. *Reconceptualizing the Peasantry.* Boulder: Westview Press.

Kelly, John. 2003. "U.S. Power, after 9/11 and before It: If Not an Empire, Then What? *Public Culture* 15(2): 347–369.

Kempadoo, Kamala. 2003. "Globalizing Sex Workers' Rights." *Canadian Woman Studies/les cahiers de la femme* 22(3/4): 143–151.

Kennedy, Edward. 2007. "Making an Example of New Bedford Workers Doesn't Solve the Problem." *The New Bedford Standard Times*, Tuesday, March 13, 2007.

Kessler, Jonathan S., and Jeff Schwaber. 1984. *The AIPAC College Guide: Exposing the Anti-Israel Campaign on Campus.* Washington, DC: American Israel Public Affairs Committee.

Khalidi, Rashid. 2004. *Resurrecting Empire: Western Footprints and America's Perilous Path in the Middle East.* Boston: Beacon Press.

King, Dennis, and Chip Berlet. 1993. "ADLgate." *Tikkun* 8(4): 31.

King, Desmond. 2000. *Making Americans: Immigration, Race, and the Origins of the Diverse Democracy.* Cambridge: Harvard University Press.

King, Peter. 2005. "Lives of Worry, Sadness, 'Why?'" *Los Angeles Times*, 30 June. http://www.latimes.com/news/printedition/la-fg-laeight30jun30,1,74 3032.story.

Klare, Michael T. 2002. *Resource Wars: The New Landscape of Global Conflict.* New York: Metropolitan/Owl Books.

Krikorian, Mark. 2003. "Dealing with Illegal Immigrants Should Be a Top Priority of the War on Terror." *National Review Online*, 12 February. http://www.nationalreview.com/scrpt/printpage.asp?ref=debates/debates0212 03.asp.

Kuo, Lenore. 2002. *Prostitution Policy: Revolutionizing Practice through a Gendered Perspective.* New York: New York University Press.

Desmond Lachman. 2009. "Welcome to America, the World's Scariest Emerging Market." *Washington Post*, March 29. http://www.washingtonpost .com/wp-dyn/content/article/2009/03/25/AR2009032502226.html.

LaFraniere, Sharon. 1991. "FBI Starts Interviewing Arab-American Leaders." *Washington Post*, 9 January: A14.

Lamphere, Louise, ed. 1992. *Structuring Diversity: Ethnographic Perspectives on the New Immigration.* Chicago: University of Chicago Press.

Landesman, Peter. 2004. "The Girls Next Door." *New York Times Magazine*, 25 January: 30–39, 66–69, 72, 74.

Laski, Harold J. 1948. *The American Democracy: A Commentary and Interpretation.* New York: Viking Press.

Lawrence, Charles R. III. 1987. "The Id, the Ego, and Equal Protection: Reckoning with Unconscious Racism." *Stanford Law Review* 39: 317–388.

Lawrence, Susan V. 2004. "Why China Fears This Uyghur Exile." *Far Eastern Economic Review.* 15 July: 30–32.

Lee, Cynthia Kwei Yung. 1996. "Race and Self-Defense: Toward a Normative Conception of Reasonableness." *Minnesota Law Review* 81: 367–428.

Legomsky, Stephen H. 2002. *Immigration and Refugee Law and Policy.* 3d ed. Westbury, NY: Foundation Press.

Leonard, Karen. 2003. *Muslims in the United States: The State of Research.* New York: Russell Sage Foundation.

Levchenko, E. A. 2000. "Torgovlia zhenshchinami: Narushenie prav cheloveka ili dobrovol'noe rabstvo?" [Trade in women: Human rights abuse or voluntary slavery?]. *Obshestvennye nauki i sovremennost'* 4: 58–67.

Levine, Phillippa. 1994. "Venereal Disease, Prostitution, and the Politics of Empire: The Case of British India." *Journal of the History of Sexuality* 4(4): 579–602.

Lewin, Tamar, and Gustav Niebuhr. 2001. "Attacks and Harassment Continue on Middle Eastern People and Mosques." *New York Times*, 18 September: B5.

Lilienthal, Alfred M. 1993. "The Changing Role of B'nai B'rith's Anti-Defamation League." *Washington Report on Middle East Affairs*, June: 18.

Loescher, Gil. 2002. "War in Iraq: An Impending Refugee Crisis? Uncertain Risks, Inadequate Preparation and Coordination." Working Paper 67. Center for Comparative Immigration Studies, University of California, San Diego. http://www.ccis-ucsd.org/PUBLICATIONS/wrkg67.pdf.

Lopez, Ian F. Haney. 1994. "The Social Construction of Race: Some Observations on Illusion, Fabrication, and Choice." *Harvard Civil Rights–Civil Liberties Law Review* 29: 1–62.

———. 2000. "Institutional Racism: Judicial Conduct and a New Theory of Racial Discrimination." *Yale Law Journal* 109: 1717–1884.

Lutz, Chris. 1987. *They Don't All Wear Sheets: A Chronology of Racist and Far Right Violence 1980–1986*. Atlanta, GA: Center for Democratic Renewal.

Maclin, Tracey. 1998. "Race and the Fourth Amendment." *Vanderbilt Law Review* 51: 333–393.

Maher, Kristen Hill. 2002. "Who Has a Right to Rights? Citizenship's Exclusions in an Age of Migration." In Alison Brysk (ed.), *Globalization and Human Rights*. Pp.19–43. Berkeley and Los Angeles: University of California Press.

Malarek, Victor. 2003. *The Natashas: The New Global Sex Trade*. Toronto: Viking.

Malone, David M. 2006. *The International Struggle over Iraq: Politics in the UN Security Council 1980–2005*. New York: Oxford University Press.

Malysheva, M. M., and E. V. Tiuriukanova. 2000. "Zhenshchiny v mezhdunarodnoi trudovoi migratsii" [Women in international labor migration]. *Narodonaselenie* 2: 91–101.

Marfleet, Philip. 2007. "Iraq's Refugees: 'Exit' from the State." *International Journal of Contemporary Iraqi Studies* 1(3): 397–419.

Markon, Jerry. 2005. "Woman Seeking Asylum Accused of Lying About Being a Nun." *Washington Post*, 25 March: B7.

Marquez, Benjamin. 1995. "Organizing Mexican-American Women in the Garment Industry: *La Mujer Obrera*." *Women & Politics* 15(1): 65.

Marshall, Phil, and Susu Thatun. 2005. "Miles Away: The Trouble with Prevention in the Greater Mekong Sub-Region." In *Trafficking and Prostitution Reconsidered: New Perspectives on Migration, Sex Work, and Human Rights*. Kamala Kempadoo, editor. Pp.43–63. Boulder: Paradigm Publishers.

Marshall, T. H. 1965. *Class Citizenship and Social Development: Essays by T. H. Marshall.* New York: Doubleday & Company.

Martínez, Samuel. 2003. "The Haitian Prologue." Paper presented at the 102nd Annual Meeting of the American Anthropological Association, Chicago, IL, 22 November.

Masis, Julie. 2007. "Guatemalan Workers Sue U.S. Firm over Exploitation." *Reuters,* 8 February. http://today.reuters.com/news/articleinvesting.aspx ?storyID=2007–02–09T003651Z_01_N08345386_RTRIDST_0_USA-GUA TEMALA-LAWSUIT.XML.

Massey, Doreen. 1994. *Space, Place, and Gender.* Minneapolis: University of Minnesota Press.

Massey, Douglas S. 1987. "Understanding Mexican Migration to the United States." *American Journal of Sociology* 92(6): 1372–1403.

———. 1988. "International Migration and Economic Development in Comparative Perspective." *Population and Development Review* 14: 383–414.

———. 1990. "Social Structure, Household Strategies, and the Cumulative Causation of Migration." *Population Index* 56: 3–26.

———. 1998. "March of Folly: U.S. Immigration Policy under NAFTA." *The American Prospect* 37: 22–33.

———. 1999. "International Migration at the Dawn of the Twenty-First Century: The Role of the State." *Population and Development Review* 25: 303–323.

Massey, Douglas S., Joaquín Arango, Graeme Hugo, Ali Kouaouci, Adela Pellegrino, and J. Edward Taylor. 1998. *Worlds in Motion: Understanding International Migration at the End of the Millennium.* Oxford: Clarendon Press.

Massey, Douglas S., Jorge Durand, and Nolan J. Malone. 2002. *Beyond Smoke and Mirrors: Mexican Immigration in an Era of Economic Integration.* New York: Russell Sage Foundation.

Massey, Douglas S., Luin P. Goldring, and Jorge Durand. 1994. "Continuities in Transnational Migration: An Analysis of 19 Mexican Communities." *American Journal of Sociology* 99: 1492–1533.

Matloff, Judith. 1998. "Bye Bye Babushka, More Russian Women are Boss." *Christian Science Monitor* 90(58), 19 February: 10, section c.

Mattawa, Khaled. 2002. "Assimilation and Resistance in Arab Detroit." *Michigan Quarterly Review* 41(1): 155–161.

McCaffrey, Barry. 2000. "Remarks to the Atlantic Council of the United States." Washington DC, 28 November. http://www.acus.org/docs/001128 -Barry_McCaffrey_Regional_Implications_Plan_Colombia.pdf.

McCarthy, Mary Meg. 2003. "The Color of Law: Asylum and Human Rights in the Post 9/11 Era." Paper presented at the 102nd Annual Meeting of the American Anthropological Association, Chicago, IL, 22 November.

McDonald, Lynn, Brooke Moore, and Natalya Timoshkina. 2000. *Migrant Sex Workers from Eastern Europe and the Former Soviet Union: The Canadian Case.* University of Toronto: Centre for Applied Social Research.

McDonnell, Patrick J. 1986. "Hunter Asks for National Guardsmen along Border." *Los Angeles Times*, 24 June: B3.

McGee, Kim. 1993. "Jewish Group's Tactics Investigated." *Washington Post*, 19 October: A1.

McLagan, Meg. 1996. "Computing for Tibet: Virtual Politics in the Post-Cold War Era." In *Connected: Engagements with Media*. George E. Marcus, editor. Pp.159–194. Chicago: University of Chicago Press.

———. 2003. "Human Rights, Testimony, and Transnational Publicity." *The Scholar and Feminist Online* 2(1). http://www.barnard.edu/sfonline.

McNeil, Kristine. 2002. "The War on Academic Freedom." *The Nation*, 11 November. http://www.thenation.com/doc.mhtml?i=20021125&s=mcneil.

MedAct. 2004. *Enduring Effects of War: Health in Iraq 2004*. London: MedAct.

Meertens, Donny. 2001. "Facing Destruction, Rebuilding Life: Gender and the Internally Displaced in Colombia." *Latin American Perspectives* 28(1): 132–148.

Meissner, Doris. 1999. "Statement of Doris Meissner, Commissioner, Immigration and Naturalization Service." Hearing on Criminal Aliens and Border Patrol Funding, House Judiciary Committee, Subcommittee on Immigration and Claims, 25 February. http://uscis.gov/graphics/aboutus/congress/testimonies/1999/990225.pdf.

Mendoza, Moises. 2006. "Most Uninsured Children Have a Parent Who Works." *Los Angeles Times*, 29 September: A-20.

Mera Naam Joker. 1970. Film. Raj Kapoor, director.

Mertus, Julie A., and Maia Carter Hallward. 2006. "The Human Rights Dimensions of War in Iraq: A Framework for Peace Studies." In *Human Rights and Conflict: Exploring the Links between Rights, Law, and Peacebuilding*. Julie Mertus and Jeffrey W. Helsing, editors. Pp. 309–341. Washington, DC: United States Institute of Peace Press.

Mesa de Trabajo Mujer y Conflicto Armado. 2002. *III Informe sobre violencia sociopolítica contra las mujeres, jóvenes y niñas en Colombia*. Bogotá: Ediciones Antropos.

Metcalf, Barbara Daly, ed. 1996. *Making Muslim Space in North America and Europe*. Berkeley and Los Angeles: University of California Press.

Meyer, J. Stryker. 1986. "Sheriff Urges Posting Marines along Border." *San Diego Union*, 6 April: A3.

Meyers, Deborah Waller. 2003. "Does 'Smarter' Lead To Safer? An Assessment of the Border Accords with Canada and Mexico." *MPI (Migration Policy Institute) Insight* 2: 1–22.

Meyers, Eytan. 2004. *International Immigration Policy: A Theoretical and Comparative Analysis*. New York: Palgrave Macmillan.

Midtown News. 1992. "Immigration Officials Visit Midtown; Police Report Threat." *Midtown News*, 19 February: 1.

Millard, Ann V., and Jorge Chapa. 2001. *Apple Pie and Enchiladas: Latino Newcomers in the Rural Midwest*. Austin: University of Texas Press.

Miller, Binny. 1994. "Give Them Back Their Lives: Recognizing Client Narrative in Case Theory." *Michigan Law Review* 93: 485–576.

Miller, Greg, and Nick Anderson. 2001. "Mood Swiftly Changes on Immigration." *Los Angeles Times*, September 18: A12.

Miyoshi, Masao. 1993. "A Borderless World?: From Colonialism to Transnationalism and the Decline of the Nation-State." *Critical Inquiry* 19: 726–751.

Mohanty, Chandra Talpade. 1991. "Under Western Eyes: Feminist Scholarship and Colonial Discourses." In *Third World Women and the Politics of Feminism*. Chandra Talpade Mohanty, Ann Russo, and Lourdes Torres, editors. Pp.51–80. Bloomington: Indiana University Press.

Molano Bravo, Alfredo. 2000. "Desterrados." In *Exodo, patrimonio e identidad. V Cátedra Anual de Historia Ernesto Restrepo Tirado. Memorias 2000*. Bogotá: Museo Nacional de Colombia.

Mondragón, Héctor. 2007. "Democracy and Plan Colombia." *NACLA Report on the Americas* 40(1): 42–44.

Montejano, David. 1987. *Anglos and Mexicans in the Making of Texas, 1836–1986*. Austin: University of Texas Press.

Moodysson, Lukas. 2002. *Lilya 4-ever*. Videorecording. Stockholm: Memfis Film.

Morris, Roger. 2003. "A Tyrant 40 Years in the Making." *New York Times*, 14 March: A29.

Moşneaga, Valeriu, and Tatiana Echim. 2003. "Counteraction towards the Trafficking of "Human Beings": The Experience of the Republic of Moldova." *Migracijske i etničke teme* 19(2–3): 223–238.

Mother Jones. 2004. "Crossing a Line." 2 February. http://www.motherjones.com/news/dailymojo/2004/02/01_589.html.

Motomura, Hiroshi. 2000. "Judicial Review in Immigration Cases after AADC: Lessons from Civil Procedure." *Georgetown Immigration Law Journal* 14: 385–452.

Murakami, Haruki. 1999. *The Wind-Up Bird Chronicle*. Translated by Jay Rubin. London: The Harvill Press.

Naber, Nadine. 2000. "Ambiguous Insiders: An Investigation of Arab American Invisibility." *Ethnic and Racial Studies* 23(1): 37–61.

Naff, Alixa. 1985. *Becoming American: The Early Arab Immigrant Experience*. Carbondale: Southern Illinois University Press.

Nagengast, Carole. 1998. "Militarizing the Border Patrol." *NACLA Report on the Americas* 32(3): 37–41.

———. 2002. "Inoculations of Evil: Symbolic Violence and Ordinary People: An Anthropological Perspective on Genocide." In *Annihilating Differences: The Anthropology of Genocide*. Alex Hinton, editor. Berkeley and Los Angeles: University of California Press.

Nagengast, Carole, Rodolfo Stavenhagen, and Michael Kearney. 1992. *Human Rights and Indigenous Workers: The Mixtecs in Mexico and the United States*. Pp. 325–347. La Jolla: Center for U.S.-Mexican Studies, University of California, San Diego.

Naples, Nancy A. 1994. "Contradictions in Agrarian Ideology: Restructuring Gender, Race-Ethnicity, and Class in Rural Iowa." *Rural Sociology* 59(1): 110–135.

———. 1996. "A Feminist Revisiting of the 'Insider/Outsider' Debate: The 'Outsider Phenomenon' in Rural Iowa." *Qualitative Sociology* 19(1996): 83–106.

———. 1997. "Contested Needs: Shifting the Standpoint on Rural Economic Development." *Feminist Economics* 3(2): 63–98.

National Commission on Terrorist Attacks upon the United States. 2004a. "Statement of Jose E. Melendez-Perez to the National Commission on Terrorist Attacks upon The United States." Seventh Public Hearing, 26 January. http://www.9–11commission.gov/hearings/hearing7/witness_melendez.htm.

———. 2004b. "Entry of the 9/11 Hijackers into the United States." Staff Statement no. 1. Seventh Public Hearing, 26 January. http://www.9–11commission.gov/hearings/hearing7/staff_statement_1.pdf.

———. 2004c. "Three 9/11 Hijackers: Identification, Watchlisting, and Tracking." Staff Statement no. 2. Seventh Public Hearing, 26 January. http://www.9–11commission.gov/hearings/hearing7/staff_statement_2.pdf.

Neuman, Gerald L. 2000. "Terrorism, Selective Deportation, and the First Amendment after Reno v. AADC." *Georgetown Immigration Law Journal* 1: 313–346.

Nevins, Joseph. 2001. *Operation Gatekeeper: The Rise of the 'Illegal Alien' and the Remaking of the U.S.-Mexico Boundary.* New York: Routledge.

Niaglova, Mira. 2001. *Trafficking Cinderella.* Videorecording. Essex Junction, VT: Miran Productions.

Nivia, Elsa. 2002. "Las fumigaciones aéreas sobre cultivos ilícitos sí son peligrosas." In *El Plan Colombia y la intensificación de la guerra: Aspectos locales y globales.* Jairo Estrada, editor. Pp. 383–404. Bogotá: Universidad Nacional de Colombia.

Notimex. 2006. "Repatriados de EU casi medio millón de mexicanos durante 2006: INM." *Notimex,* 31 December.

Oboler, Suzanne, ed. 2006. *Latinos and Citizenship: The Dilemma of Belonging.* New York: Palgrave Macmillan.

Obregón, Liliana, and Maria Stavropoulou. 1998. "In Search of Hope: The Plight of Displaced Colombians." In *The Forsaken People: Case Studies of the Internally Displaced.* Roberta Cohen and Francis M. Deng, editors. Pp.399–453. Washington, DC: Brookings Institution Press.

Office of the Inspector General (United States). 2003. *The September 11 Detainees: A Review of the Treatment of Aliens Held on Immigration Charges in Connection with the Investigation of the September 11 Attacks.* Washington, DC: U.S. Department of Justice.

Oliver, Mark. 2007. "Migration Body Urges More Aid for Displaced Iraqis," *The Guardian,* 17 July. http://www.guardian.co.uk/Iraq/Story/0,,2128422,00.html.

Omi, Michael, and Howard Winant. 1986. *Racial Formation in the United States: From the 1960s to the 1980s.* New York: Routledge and Kegan Paul.

Ong, Aihwa. 1999. *Flexible Citizenship: The Cultural Logics of Transnationality.* Durham: Duke University Press.

———. 2006. *Neoliberalism as Exception: Mutations in Citizenship and Sovereignty.* Durham: Duke University Press.

Oppel, Richard A., Jr. 2006. "Qaeda Official Is Said to Taunt U.S. on Tape." *New York Times,* 11 November: A8.

Opratny, Dennis, and Scott Winokur. 1993a. "Israeli Man Held by Israel Linked to Spy Case." *San Francisco Examiner,* 12 February: A1.

———. 1993b. "Police Said to Help Spy on Political Groups." *San Francisco Examiner,* 9 March: A1.

Orozco, Manuel. 2004. *The Remittance Marketplace: Prices, Policies, and Financial Institutions.* Reports and Fact Sheets, Pew Hispanic Center. http://pewhispanic.org/reports/report.php?ReportID=28.

Osorio, Flor Edilma. 2000. *Territorios, identidades y acción colectiva: Pistas para la comprensión del desplazamiento.* Bogotá: Consultoría para los Derechos Humanos y el Desplazamiento, CODHES.

Outshoorn, Joyce, ed. 2004. *The Politics of Prostitution: Women's Movements, Democratic States, and the Globalization of Sex Commerce.* Cambridge: Cambridge University Press.

Overend, William, and Ronald L. Soble. 1987. "7 Tied to PLO Terrorist Wing Seized by INS." *Los Angeles Times,* 27 January: A1.

Paddock, Rick. 1993. "A Spy for the Anti-Defamation League: Did a Liberal Civil Rights Group Get Caught with Its Binoculars Up?" *California Journal,* 1 June: 2–5.

Palafox, José. 2001. "Gatekeeper's State: Immigration and Boundary Policing in an Era of Globalization." *Social Justice* 28(2): 1.

Park, Lisa Sun-Hee. 1998. "Navigating the Anti-Immigrant Wave: The Korean Women's Hotline and the Politics of Community." In *Community Activism and Feminist Politics: Organizing across Race, Class, and Gender.* Nancy A. Naples, editor. Pp.175–195. New York: Routledge.

Passel, Jeffrey S. 2006. "The Size and Characteristics of the Unauthorized Migrant Population in the U.S.: Estimates Based on the March 2005 Current Population Survey." Pew Hispanic Center. http://pewhispanic.org/files/reports/61.pdf.

Passel, Jeffrey S., Randy Capps, and Michael Fix. 2004. "Undocumented Immigrants: Facts and Figures." Urban Institute Immigration Studies Program. http://www.urbaninstitute.org/UploadedPDF/1000587_undoc_immigrants_facts.pdf.

Pécaut, Daniel. 2000. "The Loss of Rights, the Meaning of Experience, and Social Connection: A Consideration of the Internally Displaced in Colombia." *International Journal of Politics, Culture and Society* 14(1): 89–105.

Pérez, S.B. 2001. "Hoja de hechos: Efectos de las fumigaciones aéreas en los municipios del Valle del Guamés y San Miguel, Putumayo. December

2000-February 2001." http://www.mamacoca.org/junio2001/hoja_de_hech os.htm.

Peteet, Julie. 2007. "Unsettling the Categories of Displacement." *Middle East Report* 244: 2–9.

Phillips, Scott, Jacqueline Maria Hagan, and Nestor Rodriguez. 2006. "Brutal Borders? Examining the Treatment of Deportees during Arrest and Detention." *Social Forces* 85(1): 93–109.

PICUM (Platform for International Cooperation on Irregular Migrants). 2005. *Ten Ways to Protect Undocumented Migrant Workers and Ten Recommendations for Policy Makers.* Brussels: PICUM. http://www.picum.org.

Piore, Michael J. 1980. *Birds of Passage: Migrant Labor and Industrial Society.* Cambridge: Cambridge University Press.

Prensa Latinoamerica. 2007. "México: El número de niños migrantes deportados por la frontera Sonora aumentó de 6 mil en 2005 a casi 9 mil en 2006." 10 January. http://www.aulaintercultural.org/printbrev.php3?id_breve=957.

Preston, Julia. 2007. "Judge Suspends Key Bush Effort in Immigration." *New York Times*, 11 October: A1.

Preston, William, Jr. 1963. *Aliens and Dissenters: Federal Suppression of Radicals, 1903–1933.* New York: Harper and Row.

Pritchard, Justin. 2004. "A Mexican Worker Dies Every Day, AP Finds." *Newsday*, 14 March.

Prodis, Julia. 1997. "Texas Town Outraged at Marines over Shooting of Goat Herder." *The Orange County Register*, 29 June: News 10.

Ramírez, María Clemencia. 2004. "El Plan Colombia después de tres años de su ejecución: Entre la guerra contra las drogas y la guerra contra el terrorismo." *MAMACOCA*, October. http://www.mamacoca.org/Octubre2004/doc/EL_PLAN_COLOMBIA_DESPUES_DE_TRES_ANOS_DE_EJECU CION.htm.

Ramos Pérez, Jorge. 2006. "Se reduce el número de Mexicanos deportados por EU." *El Universal*, 31 December.

Red de Solidaridad Social. 2001. "Desplazamiento forzado en Colombia: Magnitud, extensión territorial y grupos poblacionales afectados." Mimeographed document.

Refugees International. 2007a. *Iraqi Refugees: Donor Governments Must Provide Bilateral Assistance to Host Countries.* Washington, DC: Refugees International.

———. 2007b. *The World's Fastest Growing Displacement Crisis: Displaced People Inside Iraq Receiving Inadequate Assistance.* Washington, DC: Refugees International.

———. 2007c. "Iraqi Refugees: A Lot of Talk, Little Action." Washington, DC: Refugees International. http://www.refugeesinternational.org/content/article/detail/10294.

Reimers, David M. 1998. *Unwelcome Strangers: American Identity and the Turn against Immigration.* New York: Columbia University Press.

Renshaw, Patrick. 1968. "The IWW and the Red Scare 1917–1924." *Journal of Contemporary History* 3(4): 63–72.

Restrepo-Ruiz, Maytte. 2005. "Colombian Internally Forced Displacement Crisis and the State Response: Between Pure Social Assistance and Restitution of Rights." M.A. thesis, Program in Latin American and Caribbean Studies, University of Connecticut.

Reuters. 2004. "U.S. Man's Vendetta Led to Terror Hoax Calls." 13 January.

Reyes, Belinda, Hans Johnson, and Richard Van Swearingen. 2002. "Has Increased Border Enforcement Reduced Unauthorized Immigration?" Research brief, Public Policy Institute of California, issue 61. http://www.ppic.org/main/publication.asp?i=158.

Reza, H.G. 1997. "Patrols Border on Danger." *Los Angeles Times* 29 June: A1.

Richardson, Louise. 2006. *What Terrorists Want: Understanding the Enemy, Containing the Threat*. New York: Random House.

Robinson, William I. 1993. "The Global Economy and the Latino Populations in the United States: A World Systems Approach." *Critical Sociology* 19(2): 29–59.

Rocco, Raymond. 2006. "Transforming Citizenship: Membership, Strategies of Containment, and the Public Sphere in Latino Communities." In *Latinos and Citizenship: The Dilemma of Belonging*. Suzanne Oboler, editor. Pp.301–327. New York: Palgrave Macmillan.

Rocheleau, Dianne, Barbara Thomas-Slayter, and Esther Wangari, eds., *Feminist Political Ecology: Global Issues and Local Experiences*. New York: Routledge.

Rodriguez, Clara E. 1997. *Latin Looks: Images of Latinas and Latinos in the U.S. Media*. Boulder: Westview Press.

Rodriguez, Nestor, and Jacqueline Maria Hagan. 2004. "Fractured Families and Communities: Effects of Immigration Reform in Texas, Mexico, and El Salvador, *Latino Studies* 2: 328–351.

Rohrs, Kelly. 2004. "PSM Draws Continued Criticism, Jewish Schools Withdraw Support from Duke." *The Chronicle*, 29 September. http://www.chronicle.duke.edu/vnews/display.v/ART/2004/09/29/415aa16425330.

Rojas, Jorge. 2000. "Desplazados: Lógicas de la guerra, incertidumbres de paz." Paper presented at Seminario Internacional: Desplazamiento, Conflicto, Paz y Desarrollo, Bogotá. http://www.codhes.org.co.

Rojas, Jorge, and Marco Romero. 2000. "Conflicto armado y desplazamiento forzado interno en Colombia." In *Esta guerra no es nuestra: Niños y desplazamiento forzado en Colombia*. Pp.4–34. Bogotá: Codhes-UNICEF. http://www.unicef.org/colombia/pdf/esta-guerra.pdf.

Romero, Victor C. 2000. "Racial Profiling: 'Driving While Mexican' and Affirmative Action." *Michigan Journal of Race and Law* 6: 195–207.

Rosaldo, Renato. 1997. "Cultural Citizenship, Inequality, and Multiculturalism." In *Latino Cultural Citizenship*. William V. Flores and Rina Benmayor, editors. Pp.27–38. Boston: Beacon Press.

Rose, Gillian. 1993. *Feminism and Geography: The Limits of Geographical Knowledge.* Minneapolis: University of Minnesota Press.

Rosenzweig, David. 2002. "2 JDL Leaders Are Indicted by U.S. Grand Jury." *LA Times,* 11 January: B3.

Ross, Susan Dente. 2001. "In the Shadow of Terror: The Illusive First Amendment Rights of Aliens." *Communication Law and Policy* 6: 75–122.

Russell, Margaret M. 1991. "Race and the Dominant Gaze: Narratives of Law and Inequality in Popular Film." *Legal Studies Forum* 15(3): 243–254.

Russian Emirates Advertisement Company. 2006. Web site. http://www.emirat.ru/visa/.

Sachar, Emily. 1991. "FBI Grills NY Arab-Americans." *Newsday,* 29 January: 6.

Said, Edward W. 1996. "A Devil Theory of Islam." *The Nation,* 12 August.

Saito, Natsu Taylor. 2001. "Symbolism under Siege: Japanese American Redress and the 'Racing' of Arab Americans as 'Terrorists'." *Asian Law Journal* 8: 1–29.

Salyer, J. C. 2002. "Abuse of Immigration Detainees: Before and after September 11." *Criminal Justice Ethics* 21(1): 61–63.

Sanders, Ben, and Merrill Smith. 2007. "The Iraqi Refugee Disaster." *World Policy Journal* 24(3): 23–28.

Sassen, Saskia. 1988. *The Mobility of Labor and Capital: A Study in International Investment and Labor Flow.* Cambridge: Cambridge University Press.

———. 1996. *Losing Control? Sovereignty in an Age of Globalization.* New York: Columbia University Press.

———. 1998. "The de Facto Transnationalizing of Immigration Policy." In *Challenge to the Nation State: Immigration in Western Europe and the United States.* Christian Joppke, editor. Pp.49–85. Oxford: Oxford University Press.

Sassoon, Joseph. 2009. *The Iraqi Refugees: The New Crisis in the Middle East.* New York: I. B. Tauris.

Savage, Charlie. 2005. "Judge Nears Decision on Fate of 15 Guantanamo Detainees." *Boston Globe.* 13 December: A28.

Save the Children. 2007. *State of the World's Mothers 2007. Saving the Lives of Children Under 5.* Westport, CT.

Saywell, John T. 1978. *The Rise of the Party Quebecois 1967–1976.* Toronto: University of Toronto Press.

Scanlan, John A. 2000. "American-Arab—Getting the Balance Wrong—Again!" *Administrative Law Review* 52: 347–422.

Scaperlanda, Michael. 1996. "Are We That Far Gone?: Due Process and Secret Deportation Proceedings." *Stanford Law and Policy Review* 7: 23–30.

Schafer, Jack. 2004a. "Doubting Landesman: I'm Not the Only One Questioning the *Times Magazine*'s Sex Slave Story." *Slate,* 27 January 27. http://slate.msn.com/id/2094502.

———. 2004b. "The *Times Magazine* Strikes Back." *Slate,* 28 January. http://slate.msn.com/id/2094580/.

Schrag, Philip G. 2000. *A Well-Founded Fear: The Congressional Battle to Save Political Asylum in America.* New York: Routledge.

Schwartz, Martin, Niels Frenzen, and Mayra L. Calo. 2001. "Recent Developments on the INS' Use of Secret Evidence Against Aliens." *Immigration & Nationality Law Handbook,* 2001–2: 300–311.

Schwartz, Ronald. 1996. *Circle of Protest: Political Ritual in the Tibetan Uprising.* Delhi: Motilal Banarsidass Publishers.

Schweickart, David. 2002. *After Capitalism: New Critical Theory.* Lanham, MD: Rowman & Littlefield Publishers.

Sell, Ralph R. 1988. "Egyptian International Labor Migration and Social Processes: Toward Regional Integration." *International Migration Review* 22: 87–108.

Shaheen, Jack G. 2001. *Reel Bad Arabs: How Hollywood Vilifies a People.* New York: Olive Branch Press.

Shakir, Evelyn. 1997. *Bint Arab: Arab and Arab American Women in the United States.* Westport, CT: Praeger.

Shakya, Tsering. 1999. *The Dragon in the Land of Snows: A History of Modern Tibet Since 1947.* New York: Penguin Compass.

Shipman, Pat. 1994. *The Evolution of Racism: Human Differences and the Use and Abuse of Science.* New York: Simon & Schuster.

Shughart, William, Robert Tollison, and Mwangi Kimenyi. 1986. "The Political Economy of Immigration Restrictions." *Yale Journal on Regulation* 51: 79–97.

Smith, Dorothy E. 1987. *The Everyday World as Problematic: A Feminist Sociology.* Toronto: University of Toronto Press.

Smith, James F., and Edwin Chen. 2001. "Bush to Weigh Residency for Illegal Mexican Immigrants." *Los Angeles Times* September 7: A-1.

Smith, James P., and Barry Edmonston. 1997. *The New Americans: Economic, Demographic, and Fiscal Effects of Immigration.* Washington, DC: National Academy Press.

Smith, Jeffrey R., and Josh White. 2004. "General's Speeches Broke Rules; Report Says Boykin Failed to Obtain Clearance." *Washington Post,* 19 August: A23.

Smith, Warren W., Jr. 1996. *Tibetan Nation: A History of Tibetan Nationalism and Sino-Tibetan Relations.* Boulder: Westview Press.

Soderlund, Gretchen. 2005. "Running from the Rescuers: New U.S. Crusades against Sex Trafficking and the Rhetoric of Abolition." *NWSA Journal* 17(3): 64–87.

Specter, Michael. 1998. "Contraband Women, a Special Report: Traffickers' New Cargo: Naïve Slavic Women." *New York Times,* 11 January: A1,A6.

Sperl, Markus. 2007. "Fortress Europe and the Iraqi 'Intruders': Iraqi Asylum-Aeekers and the EU, 2003–2007." New Issues in Refugee Research Paper no. 144. New York: UNHCR.

Stanley, Kathleen. 1994. "Industrial and Labor Market Transformation in the U.S. Meatpacking Industry." In *The Global Restructuring of Agro-Food*

Systems. Philip McMichael, editor. Pp.129–144. Ithaca, NY: Cornell University Press.

Stark, Oded. 1991. *The Migration of Labor.* Cambridge: Basil Blackwell.

Starn, Orin. 1986. "Engineering Internment: Anthropologists and the War Relocation Authority." *American Ethnologist* 13(4): 700–720.

States News Service. 2007. "U.S.-Colombian Counternarcotics Effort a Model for Afghanistan." 25 January.

Staudt, Kathleen. 1998. *Free Trade? Informal Economies at the U.S.-Mexico Border.* Philadelphia: Temple University Press.

Streitfield, David. 2006. "Illegal—but Essential." *Los Angeles Times,* 1 October: A1, A28–29.

Strossen, Nadine. 1997. "Criticisms of Federal Counter-Terrorism Laws." *Harvard Journal of Law and Public Policy* 20: 531–541.

Suleiman, Michael W. 1999. "Introduction: The Arab Immigrant Experience." In *Arabs in America: Building a New Future.* Michael W. Suleiman editor. Pp.1–21 Philadelphia, PA: Temple University Press.

———, ed. 1999. *Arabs in America: Building a New Future.* Philadelphia: Temple University Press.

Sullivan, Stephen. 2004. "The Uyghur Acrobats Who Did the Flip on China." *Media Monitors Network,* 8 February. http://usa.mediamonitors.net/head lines/the_uygur_acrobats_who_did_the_flip_on_china.

Sundstrom, Lisa. 2002. "Women's NGOs in Russia: Struggling from the Margins." *Demokratizatsiya* 10(2): 207–229.

———. 2003. "Limits to Global Civil Society: Gaps between Western Donors and Russian NGOs." In *Global Civil Society and Its Limits.* Gordon Laxer and Sandra Halperin, editors. Pp.146–165. New York: Palgrave.

Susman, Tina. 2007. "U.N. Report and Times Data Paint Grim Iraq Picture." *Los Angeles Times,* 25 April. http://www.latimes.com/news/nationworld/world/la-fg-iraq26apr26,1,2865510.story.

Susskind, Yifat. 2007. *Promising Democracy, Imposing Theocracy: Gender-Based Violence and the U.S. War on Iraq.* New York: MADRE.

Taussig, Michael. 1992. *The Nervous System.* New York: Routledge.

———. 1997. *The Magic of the State.* New York: Routledge.

Thomas, Robert J. 1985. *Citizenship, Gender, and Work: Social Organization of Industrial Agriculture.* Berkeley and Los Angeles: University of California Press.

Tibet Justice Center. 2002. *Tibet's Stateless Nationals: Tibetan Refugees in Nepal.* Berkeley: Tibet Justice Center.

Timmer, Ashley S., and Jeffrey G. Williamson. 1998. "Immigration Policy Prior to the 1930s: Labor Markets, Policy Interactions, and Globalization Backlash." *Population and Development Review* 24: 739–772.

Tirman, John, ed. 2004. *The Maze of Fear: Security and Migration after 9/11.* New York: The New Press.

Tiuriukanova, E. V. 2002. "Zhenskaia trudovaia migratsiia iz Rossii v kontekste migratsionnogo rezhima" [Women's labor migration from Russia in the context of a migration regime]. In *Rossiia v XXI veke: Ekonomika, politika, kul'tura.* Vladivostok: 1: 123–139.

———. 2003. "Zashchita prav trudiashchikhsia-migrantov v rossii i perspektivy prisoedineniia k konventsii oon 1990g" [Defending the rights of labor migrants in Russia and perspectives on adopting the 1990 UN Convention]. In *Trudovaia migratsiia i zashchita prav gastarbaiterov: Praktika postkommunisticheskikh stran.* Pp.177–189. Kishinev: Moldavskii gosudarstvennyi universitet.

Todaro, Michael P. 1976. *Internal Migration in Developing Countries.* Geneva: International Labor Office.

Torpey, John C. 2000. *The Invention of the Passport: Surveillance, Citizenship, and the State.* Cambridge: Cambridge University Press.

Transparency International. 2007. *Global Corruption Report 2007. Corruption in Judicial Systems.* Cambridge: Cambridge University Press.

Tsing, Anna. 2000. "The Global Situation." *Cultural Anthropology* 15(3): 327–360.

Tsiunami. 2003. *Oproverzhenie mifov.* Vladivostok.

Tyner, James A. 1999. "The Geopolitics of Eugenics and the Exclusion of Philippine Immigrants from the United States." *Geographical Review* 89(1): 54–73.

UN Office on Drugs and Crime. 2004. *Colombia: Censo de cultivos de coca en diciembre de 2003.* http://www.unodc.org/pdf/colombia/Informe%20coca %20colombia%202003%20final%20espanol.pdf.

———. 2006. "Definitions of Terrorism." http://www.unodc.org/unodc/terror ism_definitions.html.

UN World Food Programme. 2006. *Baseline Food Security Analysis in Iraq.* New York: UNDP.

Ünal, Rahime Arzu. 2006. "Transformations in Transit: Reconstitution of Gender Identity among Moldovan Domestic Workers in Istanbul Households." Unpublished M.A. thesis, Boğaziçi University.

UNAMI (United Nations Assistance Mission for Iraq). 2006. *Human Rights Report 1 May–30 June 2006.* New York: UNAMI.

———. 2007a. *Human Rights Report 1 November–31 December 2006.* New York: UNAMI, 16 January.

———. 2007b. *Humanitarian Briefing on the Crisis in Iraq.* New York: UNAMI, 2 May.

———. 2007c. *Humanitarian Crisis in Iraq: Facts and Figures.* New York: UNAMI, 13 November.

UNDP (United Nations Development Program). 2004. *Jordan Human Development Report 2004.* New York: UNDP.

———. 2005. *Iraq Living Conditions Survey 2004.* New York: UNDP, 12 May.

UNHCR (United Nations High Commissioner for Refugees). 2004. "Desplazamiento y políticas públicas de restablecimiento en Colombia." Conference proceedings, Seminario Internacional, Análisis de Experiencias en Restablecimiento de la Población en Situación de Desplazamiento, Bogotá, Colombia: Presidencia de la República, Red de Solidaridad Social, Naciones Unides, Oficina del Alto Comisionado para los Refugiados, Agencia de los Estados Unidos para el Desarrollo Internacional, 3–5 December.

———. 2007a. *UNHCR's Eligibility Guidelines for Assessing the International Protection Needs of Iraqi Asylum-Seekers.* New York: UNHCR.

———. 2007b. *UNHCR Says Time not Right for Large-Scale Iraq Repatriation.* New York: UNHCR.

———. 2007c. *Humanitarian Needs of Persons Displaced Within Iraq and across the Country's Borders: An International Response. HCR/ICI/2007/ 2.* New York: UNHCR.

———. 2009. *Iraq Situation, UNHCR Global Appeal 2009 Update.* Geneva: UNCHR. http://www.unhcr.org/publ/PUBL/4922d4230.pdf.

UNICEF (United Nations Children's Education Fund). 2007. *Immediate Needs for Iraqi Children in Iraq and Neighbouring Countries.* Geneva: UNICEF. 23 May.

United Nations. 2002. *International Migration Report 2002.* New York: United Nations, Department of Economic and Social Affairs. ST/ESA/SER.A/220. http://www.un.org/esa/population/publications/ittmig2002/2002ITTMIG TEXT22–11.pdf.

———. 2007. *Strategic Framework for Humanitarian Action in Iraq.* New York: United Nations. April.

Urban Institute. 2003. "Brief No. 4: A Profile of the Low-Wage Immigrant Workforce." http://www.urban.org/310880_lowwageimmigwkfc.pdf.

U.S. Agency for International Development (USAID). 2001. "Trafficking in Persons: USAID's Response 2001." http://www.usaid.gov/wid/pubs/traffick inginpersons.pdf.

———. 2004. "Trafficking in Persons: USAID's Response 2003." http://www .usaid.gov/our_work/cross-cutting_programs/wid/pubs/trafficking_in_per son_usaids_response_march2004.pdf.

———. 2005. "Trafficking in Persons: USAID's Response 2004." http://www .usaid.gov/our_work/cross-cutting_programs/wid/pubs/trafficking_2005 .pdf.

U.S. Census Bureau. 2003. *The Arab Population: 2000.* U.S. Census Bureau http://www.census.gov/prod/2003pubs/c2kbr-23.pdf.

U.S. Citizenship and Immigration Services. 2005. "History of the United States Asylum Officer Corps." http://uscis.gov/graphics/services/asylum/ history.htm#C.

U.S. Committee for Refugees and Immigrants. 2006. *World Refugee Survey 2006.* Washington, DC: U.S. Committee for Refugees and Immigrants.

———. 2008. *World Refugee Survey 2008.* Washington, DC: U.S. Committee for Refugees and Immigrants.

U.S. Department of Justice. 2004. "Report to Congress from Attorney General John Ashcroft on U.S. Government Efforts to Combat Trafficking in Persons in Fiscal Year 2003." http://www.usdoj.gov.

U.S. Department of State. 2001. "State Department Fact Sheet on U.S. Policy toward the Andean Region." 17 May. http://ciponline.org/colombia/051703 .htm.

———. 2003. *China (Includes Tibet, Hong Kong, Macau). Country Reports on Human Rights Practices—2002.* U.S. Department of State, Bureau of Democracy, Human Rights, and Labor. http://www.state.gov/g/drl/rls/hrrpt/ 2002/18239.htm.

———. 2006. *Guidelines for NGO Projects for Assistance to Iraqi Refugees and Returnees.* Washington, DC.

———. 2007. *Proposed Refugee Admissions for Fiscal Year 2008 Report to the Congress.* Washington DC.

———. 2009. "Iraq Status Report." April 15. http://www.state.gov/documents/ organization/122032.pdf.

U.S. Departments of State, Homeland Security, and Health and Human Services. 2006. *Proposed Refugee Admissions for Fiscal Year 2007 Report to the Congress.* Washington DC.

U.S. Federal Bureau of Investigation (FBI). 2002. *Hate Crime Statistics 2001.* Washington, DC: Government Printing Office. http://www.fbi.gov/ucr/01 hate.pdf.

U.S. Government Accountability Office (GAO). 2007. *Border Security: Despite Progress, Weaknesses in Traveler Inspections Exist at Our Nation's Ports of Entry.* GAO Report 08-219. Washington DC. http://www.gao.gov/prod ucts/GAO-08-219.

U.S. Immigration and Naturalization Service. 1997. *1996 Statistical Yearbook of the Immigration and Naturalization Service.* Washington, DC: U.S. Government Printing Office.

U.S. Mission to the United Nations in Geneva. 2007. "Statement by the United States Delegation at the UNHCR International Conference on the Humanitarian Needs of Iraqi Refugees and IDPs." Geneva, Switzerland. 17 April. http://geneva.usmission.gov/Press2007/0417dOBRIANSKYunhcr.html.

U.S. Senate. 2007. "The Plight of Iraqi Refugees." Hearing before the Committee on the Judiciary, serial no. J-110–2, 16 January.

Uygun, Nilgun. 2000. "'Natashas': Gender, Transnationalism, and the Sex Trade in Turkey." Presented at the 99th Annual Meeting of the American Anthropological Association, San Francisco, CA, 4 December.

Volpp, Leti. 2002. "The Citizen and the Terrorist." *UCLA Law Review* 49: 1575–1600.

Wæver, Ole. 1995. "Securitization and Desecuritization." In *On Security.* Ronnie Lipschutz, editor. Pp.46–86. New York: Columbia University Press.

Wallerstein, Immanuel. 2006. "Walls and the World." Commentary no. 185 (May 15). Fernand Braudel Center, Binghamton University.

Watenabe, Satoko. 1998. "From Thailand to Japan: Migrant Sex Workers as Autonomous Subjects." In *Global Sex Workers: Rights, Resistance, and Redefinition.* Kamala Kempadoo and Jo Doezema, editors. Pp. 114–123. New York: Routledge.

Wedel, Janine. 1998. *Collision and Collusion: The Strange Case of Western Aid to Eastern Europe., 1989–1998.* New York: St. Martin's Press.

Weiner, Myron. 1982. "International Migration and Development: Indians in the Persian Gulf." *Population and Development Review* 8: 1–36.

Weinstein, Henry. 2007. "Final Two L.A. Defendants Cleared." *Los Angeles Times*, 1 November: B1.

Weldes, Jutta, Mark Laffey, Hugh Gusterson, and Raymond Duvall, eds. 1999. *Cultures of Insecurity: States, Communities, and the Production of Danger.* Minneapolis: University of Minnesota Press.

Whidden, Michael J. 2001. "Unequal Justice: Arabs in America and United States Antiterrorism Legislation." *Fordham Law Review* 69: 2825–2888.

White, Luise. 1990. *The Comforts of Home: Prostitution in Colonial Nairobi.* Chicago: University of Chicago Press.

Wieseltier, Leon. 2006. "The Shahid." *New Republic* 235(17): 38.

Williams, David. 1981. "The Bureau of Investigation and Its Critics, 1919–1921: The Origins of Federal Political Surveillance." *Journal of American History* 68(3): 560–579.

Wines, Michael. 1999. "Rava-Ruska Journal: The Border Is so Near, the Smuggling so Easy." *New York Times* 1 March: A4.

Wishnick, Elizabeth. 2002. "Sino-Russian Relations in a Changed International Landscape." *China Perspectives* (Hong Kong), September–October.

———. 2004. "Chinese Migration to the Russian Far East: A Human Security Dilemma." http://gsti.miis.edu/CEAS-PUB/200209Wishnick.pdf.

Witness/American Friends Service Committee. 2005. "Rights on the Line: Vigilantes on the Border." http://www.witness.org/option,com_rightsalert/Itemid,178/task,story/alert_id,43.

Wonders, Nancy A., and Raymond Michalowski. 2001. "Bodies, Borders, and Sex Tourism in a Globalized World: A Tale of Two Cities—Amsterdam and Havana." *Social Problems* 48(4): 545–571.

World Tibet Network (WTN). 1995. "Three Tibetan Monks Granted Asylum by U.S." *World Tibet Network News*, 19 October. http://www.tibet.ca/en/newsroom/wtn/archive/old?y=1995&m=10&p=19_3.

———. 2005a. "Official Report Justifies Proceedings in Tenzin Deleg Rinpoche Case." Reprinted from *Tibet Information Network*, 27 January, 2005. http://www.tibet.ca/en/newsroom/wtn/archive/old?y=2005&m=1&p=27_5.

———. 2005b. "Tibet Resolutions Passed at PEN International." Press release, Tibet Justice Center, 20 June. http://www.tibet.ca//en/newsroom/wtn/archive/old?y=2005&m=6&p=20_1.

Yousef, Ahmen, and Caroline F. Keeble. 1999. *The Agent: The Truth behind the Anti-Muslim Campaign in America.* Springfield, VA: United Association for Studies and Research.

Zhurzhenko, Tat'iana. 1999. "Gender and Identity Formation in Post-Socialist Ukraine: The Case of Women in the Shuttle Business." In *Feminist Fields: Ethnographic Insights.* Rae Bridgeman, Sally Cole, and Heather Howard-Bobiwash, editors. Pp.243–263. Peterborough, Ontario: Broadview Press.

Zlotnik, Hania. 1987. "The Concept of International Migration as Reflected in Data Collection Systems." *International Migration Review* 21: 925–946.

Zúñiga, Víctor, and Rubén Hernández-León, eds. 2005. *New Destinations: Mexican Immigration in the United States.* New York: Russell Sage Foundation.

Zwerdling, Daniel. 2005. "The Death of Richard Rust." National Public Radio, *All Things Considered,* 5 December. http://www.npr.org/templates/story/story.php?storyId=5022866.

Contributors

SUSAN M. AKRAM is a clinical professor at the Boston University School of Law, teaching immigration law, comparative refugee law, and international human rights law, and supervising students in BU's asylum and human rights program. She speaks and publishes in the fields of immigration law, refugee law, and human rights.

ALEXIA BLOCH is associate professor of anthropology at the University of British Columbia. Her research has focused on indigenous peoples and the nation-state, the politics of memory, and most recently labor migration into and out of the former Soviet Union.

LEO R. CHAVEZ (Ph.D., Stanford University) is a professor of anthropology at the University of California, Irvine. His research examines the integration of immigrants into society, medical anthropology, media spectacles, and issues of citizenship.

CHRISTOPHER DOLE is assistant professor of anthropology at Amherst College, where he teaches courses on medical anthropology, psychiatry and politics, global health, healing, and the Middle East. He is completing a book on the politics of healing and secular aesthetics in Turkey and is currently conducting research on global and humanitarian psychiatry in Turkey.

TRICIA GABANY-GUERRERO is assistant professor of anthropology at California State University, Fullerton. Her research focuses on migration, ethnohistory, and archaeological research relating to Mexico, with a particular emphasis on the U.S.-Mexico borderlands at Ciudad Juarez–El Paso and the Purhepecha region of Central-West Mexico in Michoacan.

SCOTT HARDING is assistant professor of community organization in the School of Social Work at the University of Connecticut. He is associate editor of the *Journal of Community Practice*. He has written on community organizing and labor unions, and on social development and the war in Iraq.

JULIA MEREDITH HESS is a postdoctoral fellow at the University of New Mexico's Prevention Research Center. She is the author of *Immigrant Ambassadors: Citizenship and Belonging in the Tibetan Diaspora* (2009).

JOSIAH MCC. HEYMAN (Ph.D., CUNY) is professor of anthropology and chair of the department of sociology and anthropology at the University of Texas at El Paso. He is the author or editor of three books and more than fifty articles, book chapters, and essays on borders, state bureaucracies, migration, power, and anthropological theory.

KEVIN R. JOHNSON is dean of the University of California Davis School of Law. A *magna cum laude* graduate of Harvard Law School, he has written extensively on issues of immigration and civil rights and is one of the editors of the ImmigrationProf blog, http://lawprofessors.typepad.com/immigration/.

KATHRYN LIBAL is assistant professor at the School of Social Work at the University of Connecticut. She has written on women's and children's rights movements and social welfare, especially in Turkey, and on social development and the war in Iraq.

SAMUEL MARTÍNEZ is associate professor of anthropology and Caribbean and Latin American studies at the University of Connecticut, Storrs. He is the author of two ethnographic monographs and several peer-reviewed articles on the migration and labor and minority rights of Haitian nationals and people of Haitian ancestry in the Dominican Republic.

DOUGLAS S. MASSEY is Henry G. Bryant Professor of Sociology and Public Affairs at Princeton University. The current president of the American Academy of Political and Social Science and a past president of the American Sociological Association, he is the author or editor of many books on migration, urban sociology, and education, including *New Faces in New Places: The New Geography of American Immigration*.

CAROLE NAGENGAST is a professor of anthropology at the University of New Mexico. A former chair of the board of directors for Amnesty International-USA, she is the co-editor (with Carlos G. Vélez-Ibáñez) of *Human Rights: The Scholar as Activist* (2004).

NANCY A. NAPLES is a professor of sociology and women's studies at the University of Connecticut. She is the author of many books, including *Grassroots Warriors: Activist Mothering, Community Work, and the War on Poverty* (1998) and *Feminism and Method: Ethnography, Discourse Analysis, and Activist Scholarship* (2003). Most recently, she is the co-editor (with Salvador Vidal-Ortiz) of Lionel Cantú's *The Sexuality of Migration: Border Crossing and Mexican Immigrant Men* (2009).

MARÍA TERESA RESTREPO-RUIZ is an independent scholar who currently works at the Connecticut Coalition against Domestic Violence as its cultural diversity outreach program coordinator. She holds a master's degree in international studies with an emphasis in Latin America from the University of Connecticut. She worked for several years in Colombia with a leading women's human rights organizations and was the project coordinator for the Bogotá chapter of Ruta Pacífica de las Mujeres.

J. C. SALYER   is the staff attorney for the Arab-American Family Support Center in Brooklyn, New York, and is a Ph.D. candidate in anthropology at the Graduate Center of City University of New York.

Index